The Hidden Chapter

To the Memory of
Thomas of Bononia,
Physician to Charles VIII,
King of France
1483–1498

The Hidden Chapter

An investigation into the custody of lost knowledge

Joy Hancox

BYROM PROJECTS

First published in the United Kingdom in 2011 by
Byrom Projects
Andrew Mann Ltd.
1 Old Compton Street,
London W1D 5JA
Email: info@andrewmann.co.uk

Copyright © Joy Hancox 2011

All rights reserved. No part of this publication may be reproduced or transmitted in any form or by any means, electronic or mechanical including photocopying, recording or any information storage or retrieval system, without prior permission in writing from the publishers.

The right of Joy Hancox to be identified as the author of this work has been asserted by her in accordance with the Copyright, Designs and Patents Act 1988

ISBN 978–0–9566394–0–0

Produced by The Choir Press
Printed and bound in Great Britain

Contents

Prelude		page xii
Chapter One	The Church by the River	1
Chapter Two	Medieval Revelations	20
Chapter Three	The Legendary Tewdric	31
Chapter Four	Merovingian Visitors	40
Chapter Five	Royal Relics	61
Chapter Six	Tintern Wireworks Charter, 1568	71
Chapter Seven	Herbert and his College	79
Chapter Eight	Francis Bacon	97
Chapter Nine	Intellectual Brotherhood	116
Chapter Ten	Chains of Command	132
Chapter Eleven	Beneath the Surface	139
Chapter Twelve	Masonic Maze	152
Chapter Thirteen	Truth Lies Buried	161
Chapter Fourteen	Stranger than Fiction	175
Chapter Fifteen	The Charade	190
Chapter Sixteen	Where There's a Will	199
Chapter Seventeen	Pedigree and Power	211
Chapter Eighteen	Eternal Triangles	231
Chapter Nineteen	A Twist in the Tale	238
Coda One	An Allegorical Painting	257
Coda Two	The Funerals of Lady Russell and J.L. Baldwin	266
Coda Three	Some Reflections	276
Notes		287
Bibliography		293
Index		299

List of illustrations

1a.	The Monad, Byrom Collection-Drawing	xiv
1b.	Map of England and Wales, showing the area being studied	xv
1c.	A nineteenth-century view of Tintern, Monmouthshire	xvi
2.	Church of St. Michael, Tintern Parva	4
3.	Tomb of interest	6
4.	Rectors' List, St. Michael's Church	21
5.	Merovingian genealogy	36
6.	Dated geometric triangle	41
7.	Church of St. Dennis, Llanishen	43
8.	Westminster Abbey (geometric features)	56
9.	Ground plan of Westminster Abbey	58
10.	Layout of Westminster Abbey with triangle superimposed	60
11.	Edward I genealogy	63

colour plates 12a and 12b between pages 80 and 81

12a.	Sir Thomas Herbert 1606–1681	colour plate
12b.	Nurtons	colour plate
13.	Schweighardt, 'The Tabernacle'	91
14.	Schweighardt illustration (note detail of Noah's Ark)	95
15.	Francis Bacon	98
16.	Alice Barnham	102
17.	John Byrom	119
18.	Edmonds family genealogy	127
19.	Three trenches (Cambrian Archaeological Projects Ltd.)	144

colour plates 20–28 between pages 160 and 161

20.	Tomb X and pudding stone wall with measuring rod	colour plate
21.	Grave cut photo and drawing (Cambrian Archaeological Projects Ltd.)	colour plate
22.	Slipway on English side of riverbank	colour plate
23.	Slipway wall, keystone and ashlar (Stratascan Ltd.)	colour plate
24.	Detail of slipway, slipway wall and adjacent churchyard	colour plate
25.	Keystone and flat-topped feature	colour plate

26.	Chancel pit	colour plate
27.	Chancel and altar	colour plate
28.	Tomb and 72 cubits	colour plate
29.	Jacob Cats: *Lampada Trado*, 1655, Dee and Bacon	166
30.	Jacob Cats: *Lampada Trado*, 1658, Dee and Bacon (mirror image and changes)	168
31.	Jacob Cats: *Verita*, Chancel Tomb, 1655	172
32.	John Byrom, Geometric Drawing	173
33.	John Loraine Baldwin	178
34.	The double grave of John Loraine Baldwin and Lady Francis Russell	195
35.	Two burials	196
36.	Marriage certificate	212
37.	Sir Lambton Loraine	214
38.	Sir Percy Loraine	215

colour plates 39–40 and 43–48 between pages 256 and 257

39.	Jean Cocteau mural, French Church, London	colour plate
40.	Jean Cocteau grave and mural, Milly-la-Forêt	colour plate
41.	Gateway dimensions, St. Michael's	235
42.	Gateways	241
43.	Rose drawing with significant features highlighted	colour plate
44.	*An Allegory*, full length	colour plate
45.	*An Allegory*, top section	colour plate
46.	*An Allegory*, middle section	colour plate
47.	*An Allegory*, bottom section	colour plate
48.	*An Allegory*, German script	colour plate
49.	Jacob Cats: *Lampada Trado*, 1655, Dee and Bacon from Manly P. Hall's *Orders Of Universal Reformation*	282

General Acknowledgements

I would like to thank the staff of The Choir Press, in particular Miles Bailey for his courtesy and care during the preparation of this book, Fiona Thornton for her editing, as well as Rachel Woodman and Adrian Sysum for their technical skills. I am also grateful for the marketing acumen of Duncan Beale and Cathi Poole at York Publishing Services. I must also acknowledge the support of my agent, Anne Dewe of Andrew Mann Ltd., and the Trustees of the Byrom Collection.

I am greatly indebted to Stratascan Ltd., Geophysics for Archaeology and Engineering, for the meticulous professionalism of the managing director, Peter Barker, the initiatives of Richard Smalley and the expertise of others on his staff. My thanks are also due to Kevin Blockley and his team at Cambrian Archaeological Projects Ltd. for their efficient attention to detail, and to Euroscan Ltd.

I am grateful for the legal advice of Michael Darlington and for the cooperation and support early in my work of the Rev. Phil Rees and, later, of the Revs. John Dearnley and Nora Hill. I have also had the benefit of help from Major and Mrs. David Cowell in many matters relating to St. Michael's Church, Tintern Parva.

Public libraries at Bristol, Chepstow, Manchester and Newport have provided invaluable information. I am similarly indebted to Record Offices in Bristol, Cwmbran, Manchester and the Nelson Museum in Monmouth.

I have valued greatly the hospitality and active help of Elsa and Adrian Wood of Nurtons, in particular their readiness to place their collection of estate papers at my service, and also the willingness of Jim and Mary Simpson to share their local knowledge. I am especially indebted to Sue and Barry Cooke of the Wye Valley Hotel, Tintern Parva, for their endless generosity and cooperation over many years.

My personal assistant, Elaine Ogden, has been a loyal and constant help, most recently in preparing the index with the Byrom Projects technical consultant, David Almond. The Rev. Neville Barker Cryer has been a sensitive guide with numerous Masonic matters. I am grateful to John Davies for many acts of practical kindness, to Anne Rainsbury at Chepstow Museum and to Leon Crickmore, Sylvia Francke, Suzie Hardie,

Marke Pawson, Keith Prince, the staff at Cartridge World (Manchester Central), Peter Welsford and Angela Wood.

Finally, my grateful thanks go to those too numerous to mention individually who, with my husband Allan, have provided endless help and support and often the necessary inspiration to move forward.

Illustration Acknowledgements

I would also like to thank the following individuals and institutions for permission to reproduce illustrations.

Michael Baigent (No. 40), The British Library (Nos. 13 & 14), The Trustees, The Byrom Collection (Nos. 1a, 6, 32 & 43), Cambrian Archaeology (Nos. 19, 20 & 21), Chetham's Library, Manchester (No. 17), Family Record Centre (No. 36), Glasgow University Library (Nos. 29 & 31), Manchester Central Library (Nos. 12a, 16, 30, 33, 37, & 38), Notre Dame de France, London (No. 39), The Philosophical Research Society, Los Angeles (No. 49), Mr & Mrs J. Simpson (No 7), Stratascan Ltd. (Nos. 3, 23–28, 34, 35, 41 & 43), Ian Taylor (No. 15), and Elsa & Adrian Wood (No. 12b). The owners of the painting *An Allegory* have provided all the reproductions for Coda One. All other illustrations are taken from the author's own collection.

Prelude

THIS IS THE story of a hunt that began when a parcel of immaculately drawn diagrams arrived at my home through the post some twenty-five years ago and that has continued right up to the publication of this book.

In 1992 I became the licensee of the Collection and published my first book, *The Byrom Collection* in 1992. My work with the drawings had really begun.

A reconstruction of Shakespeare's Globe was about to be built in Southwark, London. It was my wish that the theatre drawings in the Collection should be in the public domain to help with that project, if possible. An understandable aspiration, I thought, but I had not anticipated the challenges which that wish brought. Establishing the provenance of the drawings, and the absence of experts who understood the geometry and numerology inherent in them, were only two of the major difficulties I had to face. But I found an important clue in my hunt when I was able to identify certain brass plates connected with some of the drawings and decided to search for the place where those plates could have been made. This led me to Tintern in Monmouthshire, where the first brassworks in England and Wales was set up in 1568. A detailed account of this part of my adventure is given in *Kingdom for a Stage*, published in 2001.

A further ten years on and I have learned totally unexpected facts about the history of Tintern, its medieval origins, the great landowners of the area – particularly the various families of the Herbert dynasty including the Elizabethan Earls of Pembroke and their forebears – and the role of Sir Francis Bacon, his involvement with the brassworks and his association with individuals connected with the playhouses and players. The church and churchyard of St. Michael at Tintern Parva in particular have produced a succession of surprises.

'History' is the perceived view of past events recorded for posterity. But that perceived view is always subject to change. New facts, once proven, have to be accommodated. Our universities have hitherto been the traditional channels for original research, and been responsible for the adjustment of past perceptions. However today, with such rapid technological changes in the dissemination of information, they no longer have control of all new data.

Moreover, in the UK at present, socioeconomic and commercial pressures seem to influence more and more the academic areas that merit particular attention. In this context the private researcher becomes an even rarer figure whose views receive comparatively little consideration. I am not complaining when I say I have enjoyed neither public bursary nor private patronage to carry out my research. I merely wish to disabuse others of that mistaken assumption. I have financed my work myself, believing in the importance of the Collection and its value to scholarship at large.

My hope is that, in sharing the fruits of my personal odyssey with others, some of the connections made along the way may be of use to them and perhaps throw light on related subjects that they themselves pursue.

Some mysteries still remain to tantalise us, but this hidden chapter in our country's cultural history is now ready to be revealed.

Bon voyage.

THE MONAD
Byrom Collection-Drawing

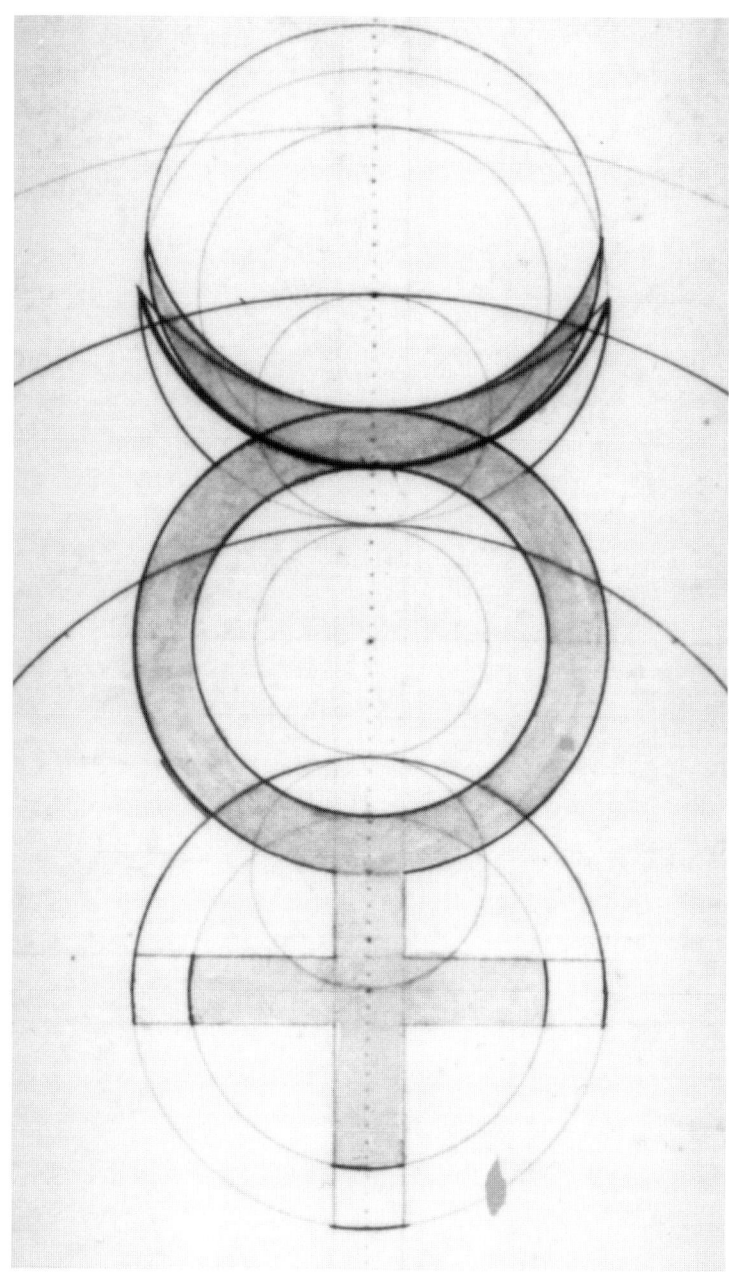

1a. This symbol formed the frontispiece of Dee's 'Monas Hieroglyphica' (1564). An entry in his diary for 1 May 1577 records 'I received from Mr. William Herbert of St. Gillian (St. Julians) his notes upon my Monas.'

1b. Map of England and Wales, showing the area being studied

1c. A nineteenth-century view of Tintern, Monmouthshire

CHAPTER ONE

The Church by the River

In OCTOBER 1999 I arranged to visit the charming little village of Tintern in Monmouthshire, Wales. I had one specific objective in mind: to find out whether a particular house dating from the reign of Elizabeth I, and central to my latest historical research, still existed. I would have been satisfied to set eyes on the house I was hunting. However, Fate or Chance decreed otherwise and I found more than I bargained for. Along this stretch of the Wye Valley where the tree-covered hills were beginning to turn gold and bronze, a discovery lay waiting at my unsuspecting feet – one that altered the direction of my work.

The house I was searching for had once been the property of a member of the far-flung Herbert dynasty. To distinguish him from the many other William Herberts in history, this one is known as Sir William Herbert of St. Julian's, that being the name of his chief estate just outside Newport. Sir William was an important figure in the political life of Monmouthshire and more so of Ireland where Queen Elizabeth sent him to found a Protestant colony as part of her attempt to pacify that country.

Sir William's London home was at Mortlake and this made him a neighbour of John Dee, the great mathematician and astrologer, much favoured by the queen herself. It was Dee who had decided on the most propitious day for Elizabeth's coronation. Dee and Herbert worked together on material for the secret network of spies that had been created for the queen by Sir Francis Walsingham. This relationship was one reason why I wanted to hunt down Herbert's property in Tintern. But there were other reasons too.

In 1992 I had introduced a remarkable collection of geometrical drawings to the world in my first book *The Byrom Collection*. They took their name from their one-time owner or custodian John Byrom (1691–1763). The collection included a series of drawings that I had identified with the design concept of the Elizabethan playhouses. Later I traced the brass plates from which the theatre drawings had been printed. They were part of a collection of scientific materials housed in the Science Museum in Kensington, London. When I learned that the first attempts to make brass in England were at a wireworks set up in Tintern at the time the earliest theatres were being built, it was obvious that I would have to visit Tintern to see what I could learn there about the history of the brass plates, their provenance and their creators.

During the initial stages of my preparations I came across an entry in the Calendar of State Papers Domestic for 7 May 1611. It concerned the wireworks at Tintern and states:

> Robert, Lord Lisle, Sir Francis Bacon and others of the Company of Wireworks (to Salisbury). Ask for preference as purchasers of the King's wood to be sold in the Forest of Dean for the use of their works at Tintern and Whitebrook.

This matter-of-fact record was an important find. Francis Bacon was and remains one of the great figures of his age. His legal career started during the reign of Elizabeth I and by 1611 he was already Solicitor General. Two years later he became Attorney General and eventually, in 1618, Lord High Chancellor, Baron Verulam of Verulam. Finally in one momentous year, 1621, he was created Viscount St. Alban for his services, charged with accepting bribes, sentenced and then pardoned by James I.

Apart from a career in law, he wrote *The Advancement of Learning* (1605) in which he laid down the principle of experimentation in science and is generally recognised as the father of the modern scientific method. The standard biographies deal at length with these twin aspects of his career, but do not mention that Bacon was at one time a part owner in the wireworks at Tintern. It may appear a small detail but it is one with serious implications for a true picture of him. It provided me with an even more pressing reason to visit Tintern. Suddenly the combination of Sir William Herbert's base in Tintern and Bacon's interest in the wireworks transformed this rural retreat on the border of England and Wales into a centre of compelling historical interest.

Despite being granted preferential treatment in the purchase of wood, within two years Bacon and his partners were experiencing problems over the supply of wood for the wireworks. They complained of 'much abuse and disorder in the felling and cutting down of wood and tymber trees'. Because of this and the 'contracte lately made on his Majestie's behalf with the Earle of Pembroke touching the delivery of certain cordes of wood, at a rate, for his Lordship's iron works', the Privy Council took action and in November 1613 issued a warrant to the Constable of the Forest of Dean to sort out the complaint.[1]

I noted with interest the addition of a third name to the list of owners. Another William Herbert, this time the third Earl of Pembroke, was apparently involved with Robert, Lord Lisle (the brother of Sir Philip Sidney) and Sir Francis Bacon in running the wireworks at Tintern. They made a truly formidable trio. Pembroke was the grandson of the William Herbert who had married the sister of Catherine Parr, Henry VIII's sixth wife. He had been made Earl of Pembroke by Edward VI, and the Herberts were one of the leading families in the realm. It was to the third Earl, William, and his brother, Philip, that the First Folio of Shakespeare's plays was dedicated. The wireworks was evidently a major enterprise and this added to the importance of Tintern in my eyes.

The report about the abuse of the tree-felling appeared curious, especially since the date of the entry was quite close to the time when the Globe playhouse in London had been burned down. It seemed as though a considerable amount of wood was being felled and that this was causing problems at the wireworks. Moreover, because each of these three men was connected with the world of the Elizabethan playhouses, it seemed possible that some of the timber might be being used to rebuild the Globe. Were the 'needs' of the wireworks being used as a convenient cover for excessive tree-felling?

In mulling this over it seemed fair to assume that there were matters connected with the history of Tintern that have, perhaps, escaped scrutiny. In addition, Sir William Herbert of St. Julian's, too, had shares in the wireworks. More intriguingly, he was known to have expressed a wish to establish a college. For all these reasons I travelled to Chepstow planning to look a little more closely at the area and hoping to find the site chosen by Sir William Herbert for his College at Tintern.

It was now that the unexpected intervened – but so stealthily that for some months I did not realise what had happened. Before returning from Tintern to Chepstow, I found myself standing on a sunny autumn afternoon looking at the church of St. Michael at the opposite end of the village, in Tintern Parva. The church is hidden from the main road down a little track: a small, sandstone building, plain and simple, but with a quiet charm of its own. The churchyard itself leads down to the river Wye, which forms its southern boundary. What was left of the afternoon passed quickly as I busied myself making notes from the papers and magazines on the church table, and assessing the interior of the church. There was little time to investigate the churchyard apart from registering some ancient tombstones that I thought I ought to look at when I had more time.

Closing the lych gate I studied the silent fields around. The sleepy isolation was suddenly broken by the sight of a young woman trekking down the long hillside opposite, walking in my direction. I had a sketch of a house in my hands as I watched her approach, and thought she might be curious as to why I seemed so interested in her progress through the field. So, when she finally crossed the road, I engaged her in conversation, asking whether there was a house over in the direction from which she had come.

The Hidden Chapter

2. Church of St. Michael, Tintern Parva

The Church by the River

She said there was and that she lived in a flat there. I explained that my interest was simply in the history of the area, and gave her my card for the owners. She assured me that they would be interested in any historical information I could give them. With that she went on her way.

Some three weeks later, a telephone call from the owners enquiring about my interest in their property was the beginning of a dialogue about the history of their small estate called 'Nurtons'. This, they told me, was once part of a much larger estate. As a result I returned to Tintern the following January. Staying again in Chepstow, I had arranged to spend a day at the home of Mr. and Mrs. Wood who had promised to show me some unusual features in the architecture of their house. I spent a most interesting time there, for Nurtons indeed proved to be an architectural curiosity, raising all sorts of questions.

On the way to the house in the morning I stopped to take photographs of some of the tombs in the churchyard at St. Michael's that I had noticed on my earlier visit. They might be useful, I thought, in my study of the history of the church. When these were developed, my attention was caught by one photograph in particular. It showed a tomb with a sword carved along the full length of its top. I had not had time to study the gravestones on the day, but the detail now visible close-up helped me later. A similar sword could be seen on a slab in the floor of the aisle inside the church, and that was clearly a very ancient stone. The original medieval church had been mainly rebuilt in 1846 and stones from the churchyard had been used in laying a new floor in the aisle. The photograph revealed some distinctive iconography around the handle of the majestic-looking sword in the churchyard. Unfortunately the tip of the blade was not visible in the photograph.

I took a piece of paper and tried to follow the line of the curves of this design. The iconography seemed to consist of four letter 'C's: two facing and two reversed on either side of the handle. For a moment one might have thought that they were broken circles; but they were not. Where the circle broke, as it were, and left a gap, one could distinctly see two blobs either side of the break, showing it to be intentional. Each broken circle was the same. Each had a blob, showing carefully that it was part of the design. So, the sword displayed four letter 'C's.

I was absorbed by the possible implications of this unusual feature and arranged for more photographs to be taken so that I could examine the carving in more detail with the help of close-up shots of the stone from every conceivable angle, including the foot. The results showed that the iconography at the top of the sword's handle was repeated at the base. There are two lots of four 'C's positioned in exactly the same way. I looked carefully on the stone for any dedication that might have been inscribed to

The Hidden Chapter

3. Tomb of interest

help identify the person buried in the grave but none of the photographs showed any such inscription.

The design on the tomb brought several things to my mind in rapid succession. Firstly, the watermark on the last page of the First Folio of Shakespeare contains two letter 'C's, one of which is reversed. Secondly, 'C' is the Roman numeral for 100 or 'centum'. Thirdly, the Elizabethan alphabet consisted of twenty-four letters only (I and J, and U and V being interchangeable) and if you replace each letter in Bacon's name with its numerical equivalent and add up all the numbers, they come to a total of 100, viz:

$$\begin{array}{cc} \text{F R A N C I S} & \text{B A C O N} \\ \text{6 17 1 13 3 9 18 (67)} & \text{2 1 3 14 13 (33)} \end{array}$$

If readers find this bizarre, they should know that a contemporary writer, John Marston (1575–1634), published a series of satires in his *Scourge of Villanie* in 1598. In the fourth satire he refers to an unnamed poet 'Whose silent name one letter bounds'. It is not always easy to identify the figures he mocks but Edward Johnson suggests that Marston is referring to Francis Bacon since the letters in his name can be replaced by the single letter 'C'. In other words the name is 'bound up' in C or 100.[2] Every Elizabethan grammar school boy received a grounding in Latin and so Marston's riddle would be more easily recognised then. Fourthly, Bacon's surname adds up to 33. In a handwritten catalogue of items at the Science Museum, dating from 1770 but *not listed in numerical order*, the brass plates connected with Byrom's Collection appear as item 33, coming after item 39 and before 36. One Baconian editor known to Byrom was aware of Bacon's use of codes. Reviewing all these facts together, I felt there was sufficient reason to consider a possible connection between the carving on the tomb and Bacon himself.

Furthermore, in establishing Bacon's part ownership of the wireworks I had found that he was said to have owned a house in the area called Mount St. Alban's, close to Herbert's house at St. Julian's. I also remembered something which has troubled people for a long time – an instruction left by Bacon in his will:

> For my burial I desire it may be in St. Michael's Church near St. Albans. For my name and memory I leave it to men's charitable speeches and to foreign nations and the next ages.

The tomb I was interested in is positioned in the churchyard of St. Michael's Church, Tintern Parva. That, too, can be described as 'near St. Albans' – not in Hertfordshire, however, but in Monmouthshire, near

Newport. This Welsh St. Michael's Church stands near the border of England and Wales, just on the other side of the border in fact, *in* Wales.

In her biography, *Sir Francis Bacon* (1981), Jean Overton Fuller deals with the mystery that has long surrounded Bacon's death: 'Rawley [Francis Bacon's chaplain] tells us he died in the early morning of April 9th 1626 of a fever and defluction of rheum so plentiful he suffocated.' That year, April 9th was Easter Day. Jean Overton Fuller continues:

> Did Rawley see this or take it from the steward? The question is asked because it has not been possible to ascertain the place of Bacon's burial. It used to be thought it was under the statue erected to him by Meautis in St. Michael's, Gorhambury, but recent excavations revealed there was no coffin. The inscription reads not 'hic jacet' but 'sic sedebat' and the present Verulam family are adamant he was never interred there. The relevant page from the burial register is missing and it has not been possible to discover any reference to his funeral.
>
> There is a legend that at Highgate he simply gave the world the slip and sailed via Holland for America. The end, like the beginning, is mystery.[3]

The burial place of Francis Bacon is still questioned by some today. So, I began to wonder whether there was any possible connection between Bacon's involvement with Tintern wireworks and the church of St. Michael in Tintern Parva. Accordingly, I asked my solicitor, Michael Darlington, to write to the church on my behalf for any information available on the identity of the person buried in the tomb.

The reply stated that the records of the church were incomplete and did not indicate who was buried in that grave. This made it even more necessary to obtain a clear understanding of the history of the area.

Tintern was part of the ancient Lordship of Usk. The third and fourth Earls of Pembroke owned that Lordship and so had direct links with Tintern. The third Earl of Pembroke became Governor of the Society for Mineral and Battery Works and in so doing obtained government protection for the waterworks close by at Trellech in 1607. The same year he became Warden of the neighbouring Forest of Dean. Thus, as well as being major shareholders of the wireworks at the same time as Francis Bacon, the Pembrokes held a strong power base in the vicinity. Nearby, Mount St. Albans, said to have been owned by Bacon, was also in the Lordship of Usk.

In *Kingdom for a Stage* I discussed at some length a remarkable volume known as the 'Schweighardt MS'.[4] I have no doubt that its authors were presenting a case for Elizabeth I and Robert Dudley being the natural parents of Francis Bacon. If that were so then the third and fourth Earls of Pembroke, through their maternal grandmother, Mary Dudley, Robert Dudley's sister, would have been second cousins to Francis Bacon. This kinship might be relevant to a possible connection between a tomb at St. Michael's and Francis Bacon.

Originally it was the Byrom drawings and the search into the history of the brass plates that had brought me to St. Michael's churchyard. Now I was faced with a fresh mystery. The area surrounding St. Michael's seemed central to the enquiry, raising unexpected questions that had to be addressed.

Perhaps the most important source book for the area is the monumental *History of Monmouthshire* by Sir Joseph Bradney, published in 1911. In Volume 2 Part 2 we are told that the immediate area around St. Michael's was bought in 1640 by another member of the Herbert dynasty who had come originally from York, one Thomas Herbert. At that time he was 34. However, when he was a young man of 21, his father died, and, needing to make his way in the world, Thomas sought and gained the patronage of his kinsman, the third Earl of Pembroke. At that time the estate in the manor of Tintern Parva once owned by Dee's friend, Sir William Herbert, was owned by his daughter, Mary Herbert. Mary was succeeded by her son, Richard, who married Mary Egerton, the granddaughter of Sir Thomas Egerton, a former Keeper of the Great Seal. Was it on this estate that Herbert's College had secretly flourished and had St. Michael's Church in some way been part of it?

This background made further research essential before discussing the iconography of the tomb with anyone. First of all I needed to be sure that there *was* a genuine mystery in this half-hidden spot. Perhaps recent developments in geophysics could help – with some form of non-invasive investigation. Accordingly I approached Euroscan Sub-surface Imaging Ltd. to ask whether they could carry out such a survey around the tomb and my solicitor wrote to the church authorities for permission.

It was time for the unexpected to intervene once more. On 27 September 2000, I received the letter granting permission for the survey. My delight, however, was tempered by some surprising information passed on by my solicitor from the churchwarden, Major Cowell:

> Major Cowell has also indicated that following the receipt of the photograph of the memorial, he has carried out a thorough inspection after a careful cleaning of the tomb and has identified the following inscription: 'In memory of Christopher Heath, late of Chippenham, Wiltshire, who died at Brockweir on 12 July 1864 in the 77th year of his life. I am the resurrection and the life.' Major Cowell also indicates that the register of burials records that Christopher Heath was buried on 18th July 1864 and his abode is given as Woollaston.

I could not believe what I had read. There *was* a name on the tomb – Christopher Heath, and a date – 1864! It was now practically twelve months since I had first noticed the tomb. No inscription was visible then. Nine months had elapsed since I had photographed it in January. During all that time I had been researching the historical background of the area. Because of what those researches revealed I had tentatively commissioned a geophysical survey and, just when the church had given permission, a name had been revealed. What should I do?

By eleven o'clock the same day I was on the train to Chepstow. It was too late to visit St. Michael's but the following morning I hurried on to Tintern. By ten thirty, I was standing by the side of a freshly scrubbed tomb photographing the newly revealed inscription.

The lettering immediately seemed to be much too amateur for the style and stature of the tomb itself. The name 'Christopher Heath' and the date '1864' were clear but the words of the dedication were not in a straight line. They looked as if they had been added to a monument already in position, close to the ground. If that were so, the mason would have had to kneel to work and would have experienced some difficulty in chiselling the words artistically in relation to the rest of the top of the tomb. They looked too clumsy compared with the careful carving of the sword and I admit to feeling a certain relief at this. In the light of all the research I had done, the inscription did not seem to me to match aesthetically the rest of the overall design of the tomb. So, I went ahead with the first geophysical survey.

Accordingly on Saturday, 14 October, exactly one year to the day after my first visit, I found myself once again at St. Michael's Church. The survey proved to be a surprisingly uncomplicated procedure. With measuring tapes and stakes a grid was mapped out on the part of the churchyard immediately in front of the west door of the church. Readings were taken on a small, compact radar machine, and the data recorded in a notebook. It all looked deceptively simple. Once the survey was completed it was a question of waiting for the data to be analysed.

The following Monday I visited Monmouth's local history museum to study local records. Part of Tuesday was spent at Cwmbran Record Office. Going through some very interesting documents on Tintern, I found one that had been prepared on St. Michael's Church, Tintern Parva, for the Gwent Family History Society by David Woolven. On 2 January 1989, he had visited the churchyard to record the gravestones. He had allotted each a number and copied their inscriptions. On the front of his document he states, 'No stones more modern than the early 19 hundreds have been recorded.' Interestingly, although 'more modern' stones hadn't been recorded, there was no reference either to the tomb of interest or any of the graves in its vicinity. Mr. Woolven seemed to have concentrated on the other side of the path leading to the west door of the church. Some time later I managed to track him down and asked how he came to record the stones in the first place. I had understood that there were no official plot records and Mr. Woolven told me that he had spent some years documenting local churchyards because there seemed to be few records available to show who was buried where. Gwent Family History Society had deposited this document, along, presumably, with others, in the Cwmbran Record Office.

I knew I would have to account for the inscription on the tomb and investigate further how Heath's name came to be on it. For the time being I felt reasonably satisfied that it was a later addition.

By the end of November I had received a draft copy of the radar survey report. This contained another surprise. I had been warned that the geo-radar technique was not yet advanced enough to be able to distinguish between different types of archaeological material such as masonry and timber. Nevertheless, I still hoped that some evidence would emerge in or around the tomb that might give some indication of the burial. Did it, for instance, contain a lead coffin? Accordingly I was intrigued to read that a radar scan running along the tombstone from the head to the foot showed up as an area almost devoid of signals reflecting changes in the soil underground. Indeed there were very few reflections below the surface down to a depth of about 2 metres. At that apparent depth signals did begin to appear toward the foot of the tomb of such a magnitude that they were not considered the kind of images one would expect from a burial. One interpretation of this could be that there was *not* a normal burial within the customary depth of 6 feet 6 inches for a grave.

This was not all. Another scan running south to north within one metre of the foot of the tomb produced data quite different from anything else in the churchyard. A wealth of certain reflections at depths of *below* 2 metres could represent a combination of structural features and cavities. The position of the tomb appeared to tally with this possibility. All these findings were disturbing since they seemed to imply that the tomb itself might not be a grave in the normal sense, but possibly some sort of marker.

Because of this I felt that I had to go back to the church to get some clarification from its records on Christopher Heath. On 9 December 2000 I wrote to Major Cowell to ask how it was possible for Christopher Heath, who had not lived in the parish, to be buried in St. Michael's churchyard.

Major Cowell was unable to explain that, but he furnished me with some useful facts:

> The Burial Register shows the following details about Mr. Heath. Name: Christopher Heath. Abode: Woolaston (no actual address). When buried: 18 July 1864. Aged 76 years. By whom ceremony was performed: John Mais, Rector.
> I cannot explain why Heath was buried in a different parish from that in

which he died. The inscription on the tomb indicates he was 'late of Chippenham, Wiltshire', and he apparently died in Brockweir. Brockweir is the parish on the opposite bank of the river Wye from Tintern.

With the help of documents from the Public Record Office and Census Lists from the nineteenth century I was able to put together a profile of Christopher Heath and those immediately connected with him.

On his death certificate his occupation is described as 'formerly a solicitor' and the cause of death is given as 'epilepsy for years, debility'. The informant of the death is named as 'E.S. Marsh in attendance, Brockweir, Woolaston'. This, of course is the same address as that given for Christopher Heath himself. Brockweir, Woolaston is not the name of a house. Brockweir is a small village which in 1830 had some 350 inhabitants. In the Letters of Administration attached to Christopher Heath's will dated 12 July 1864, his address is given again as 'Brockweir, in the parish of Woolaston in the county of Gloucester'. The local paper, *The Monmouthshire Beacon*, for 16 July 1864, announces his death as 'Heath, July 11th at Brockweir. Mr. Christopher Heath aged 76.'

Despite the fact that he had lived in the parish of Woolaston in Gloucestershire there is an entry for him in the church burial register of the neighbouring parish of St. Michael's, Tintern Parva, Monmouthshire for 18 July 1864. As mentioned earlier, the entry was made by the rector, the Rev. John Mais. In that register Heath's abode is given simply as 'Woolaston'. The failure of those registering his death to be more specific about Heath's address raises questions when one looks at more detailed entries on other certificates attached to this enquiry.

Nowhere, apart from the two censuses for 1851 and 1861, is a more precise address given. In 1851 he is described as a 'visitor', and in 1861 as a 'lodger' in the manse at Brockweir, as part of the household of the Moravian minister, Lewis West. It is clear this was Heath's address for thirteen years. Nonetheless he was not buried in the Moravian churchyard at Brockweir nor in the churchyard of the parish church of Woolaston. Furthermore, although Heath's name appears on the tombstone at St Michael's, the data from the geophysical investigation of October 2000, when analysed, seemed to indicate that the tomb had not been used for a burial at the customary level of interment. This was very puzzling.

I had established that Christopher Heath was an epileptic living with the Moravian minister at Brockweir for thirteen years. The sole executor of his will, Broome Pinniger, was also a solicitor and the offices of the family firm were at Chippenham where Christopher came from. Broome Pinniger died on 5 July 1864, seven days before Heath himself! He was therefore unable to carry out his duties as Heath's executor. It appears that Pinniger died without making a will. Letters of Administration published for 1865 state:

> Pinniger Broome, 21 January 1865. Effects under £800. Letters of Administration of the personal estate and effects of Broome Pinniger, late of Newbury in the county of Berks, gentleman, a solicitor, deceased who died 5th July 1864, at Newbury aforesaid, were granted at Oxford to Broome Pinniger of Newbury aforesaid, gentleman, a solicitor, the son of the said deceased, he having been first sworn.

Since Broome Pinniger senior had a son with the same name who was also a solicitor, no doubt in his father's firm, it would appear to have fallen to him to act as the executor to Heath's will.

The surviving data suggest that Heath had been a sick man for some years and was a solitary figure. Checking the extensive genealogical records of the Mormons, I learned that Christopher Heath married Mary Heath on 5 August 1811. He was the son of John and Anne Heath and made his will in 1819. This will remained unaltered right up to the time of his death in 1864. I have not been able to find any more records about his wife or details of any descendant(s).

I visited the Moravian church at Brockweir. The church guide contained some useful facts. Improvements were made to the manse, called the 'labourers' house', in 1839 by the addition of a cellar and two more rooms. The gallery was erected in the church. In 1840, the infant school, held in the hall, was developed by Sister Ellen Sims into a more general village school. She also started educational classes for adults. The Rev. Lewis West continued to minister at Brockweir for thirty-eight years, retiring to Bristol in 1870. His one concern had been that Brockweir, its chapel, its children, and the whole population might be abandoned for the want of sufficient maintenance of a minister.

Curious about this establishment and why, when the manse had a name, it was never given as the proper address for Christopher Heath, I decided to get a copy of the death certificate of the informant, E.S. Marsh. This was Edward Sidney Marsh and at the time of Christopher Heath's death he, too, was living in the Moravian establishment. At the time of his own death, however, he was living in Bristol at 40, Cornwallis Crescent, Clifton. He is described as a gentleman, of 61 years, and he died from an attack of asthma from which he had suffered for thirteen years. This last fact had interesting implications. It meant that Marsh was already ill with asthma when he first took up residence with Lewis West. Two gentlemen of independent means, Heath and Marsh, suffering from two debilitating conditions, were living at the manse at the same time. Was West running some sort of hospice? This could well have been so, since West had been criticised by a Moravian elder for having pretensions to medical skills which, it was implied, interfered with his religious duties. Now it turned out that the informant of Marsh's death was none other than Lewis West. The address in Clifton at which Marsh died was West's home. West eventually retired to Clifton and died on his own doorstep in Cornwallis Crescent some years later.

As I pondered further over the documentation of Heath's death, it seemed that Lewis West and Sidney Marsh (and perhaps others), for some reason that was still not clear, did not want to acknowledge that Christopher Heath had been living at the manse. I found it curious that Heath was recorded as having been buried in the neighbouring parish, which was in fact over the border from Gloucestershire, in Monmouthshire in Wales. This appeared strange in the light of the findings of the radar scan of the tomb: so much so that I found it necessary to look closer into the career of the Rev. John Mais.

In the 1844 edition of *The Clergy Lists*, the entry for John Mais reads as follows:

> Tintern, Little, R.: Monmouth, post town: Chepstow, Diocese: Llandaff, John Mais, B.D. 1827, Incumbent and year of Admission.

He remained the incumbent until 1871, a period of 44 years. He died the same year. The value of the living was £162 a year and the population in 1844 was 375. According to *The Clergy Lists*, in addition to this living Mais was the chaplain at the Infirmary at Bristol until 1864. *Crockford's Clerical Directory* for 1865 described him as 'Formerly Chaplain of the Infirmary at Bristol', so from this it would appear that he left the chaplaincy the year Christopher Heath died, 1864. He it was who recorded Heath's burial in the register at St. Michael's. I wondered how, in the middle of the nineteenth century, the Rev. Mais was able to hold two positions, one in Bristol and the other some distance away in Tintern. The River Severn separated them, with no bridge to shorten the distance. How did he manage the travelling to carry out both sets of responsibilities properly? And what were his responsibilities at the Infirmary? I also pondered on the coincidence of the timing of his departure from the chaplaincy and the date of Heath's death in 1864. Yet he remained rector at Tintern until 1871, seven years later, the year of his own demise.

Bristol Reference Library provided an invaluable source of information in *A History of Bristol Royal Infirmary* by G. Munro Smith. I needed to know the administrative arrangements of the Infirmary when Mais was chaplain, what duties were expected of the chaplain, how much time Mais would need to fulfil those duties, and how he managed to combine them with being rector at Tintern Parva.

Turning eagerly to the index, I found the following entry under his name: 'Mais, Mr. and body snatching, p. 213'; 'the Rev. John, p. 300 and p. 482.' A hurried check confirmed these entries referred to the right man. The entry on p. 213 was part of a longer section on body snatching:

> The newspaper accounts of these affairs were frequently jocular. On this occasion body snatchers are referred to as death-dealing rogues. And when Yates, one of the constables, hit one of the robbers in the face with the butt-end of a pistol it is remarked he did this to 'dissect his nose'. The gravediggers made money out of both parties. They received bribes, helped sometimes in removing the body and occasionally sided with the authorities. In the Committee Minute Book we find an entry under November 27th 1822: 'The grave diggers attended and held a complaint against Mr. Mais, a pupil of Mr. Hetling's for trespass in the burial ground', and on December 11th 1822 'Mr Mais was called in and reprimanded for his misconduct in offering money to a grave digger for filling up a grave in the burial ground. (For example filling it up after the coffin had been opened up and the body taken.)' Imagination can fill in the details of this picture, the Committee sitting on benches in a room lit by only one burner of oil gas. They met in the evening then, interviewing the clay-soiled grave diggers and young Mais receiving a stately reprimand.'

It appears that the Rev. John Mais took over in 1825 from the Rev. John Sweet who had been chaplain since 1817, for at the top of p. 300, I read:

> On his [Sweet's] resignation in 1825, the Reverend John Mais who had for some months undertaken most of the chaplain's duties was appointed on May 15th. Mr. Mais was admitted to Holy Orders in 1814; he was a Bachelor of Divinity and for nine years curate of St. Mary Redcliffe.

St. Mary Redcliffe was one of the great civic churches in England. Mais ministered there for nine years prior to moving to Tintern Parva. Munro Smith's account continues:

> Like Goldsmith's village parson 'passing rich on £40 a year', he received £20 from the Corporation and the same sum from the Merchant Venturers per annum for his work at the Infirmary. The Corporation was precluded by the Reform Act of 1835 from using any portion of their money for ecclesiastical purposes and consequently from 1835 to 1856 the only certain income Mr. Mais received for his services to the charity was £20 from the Merchants.[5]

There seems to have been some confusion in recording the dates of Mais's time at the Infirmary and at St. Michael's, Tintern Parva. In *A History of the Bristol Royal Infirmary* John Mais is said to have resigned from the chaplaincy in 1856. According to *Crockford's Clerical Directory* (which depends for its information on returns from incumbents) the year is given as 1864. Why this discrepancy of eight years? Nevertheless his appointment as chaplain was an extraordinary find. To be absolutely sure of the facts, I checked the manuscript of the original minutes of the Infirmary Committee which Munro Smith had used, now deposited at Bristol Record Office.

The minute book recorded all the House Committee meetings and is a source of fascinating sociological information concerned with the development of the Infirmary. The temptation to digress was great but I had to concentrate on the entry for 11 December, 1822. The careful copperplate script of the Minute Book clearly states:

> Resolving that Mr. Mais be called in and reprimanded for his mis-conduct in offering money to the grave digger for filling up a grave in the burial ground and improper behaviour towards the Committee. And that he be informed the Committee are determined to punish the pupils belonging to this House or any other person that shall be brought before them, for disturbing any dead bodies that shall be deposited in the Infirmary burying ground.

The minutes are signed by 'Thomas Richardson'.

Some three years later, we find the following minute entered for 1 June 1825. It is a letter sent to the Committee by the Rev. John Sweet, the chaplain immediately prior to Mais.

> Gentlemen,
> The distance of my present residence from Bristol and my other engagements occasion me so many interruptions to my discharging the important duties which devolve upon the Chaplain to the Infirmary that I feel myself called upon to resign that office from the 24th of this month. I have, however, during the last two years availed myself of the zealous and persevering labours of the Rev. Mr. Mais, who has by your kind permission assisted me in attending to the spiritual wants of the afflicted inmates of the House. Permit me in retiring from the office to offer you my sincere thanks for this favour and for the uniformly kind attention which I have experienced from the Committee during the eight years that I have filled the office.

The letter is signed 'Redland, June 1, 1825'.

The minutes contain another letter for the same day written by the Rev. John Mais.

> Gentlemen,
> Having been informed by Dr. Sweet that he intended to resign this evening the office of Chaplain to Bristol Infirmary, I take this early opportunity of offering myself as a candidate to succeed him. Opportunities of judging of my suitableness for the chaplainship have been offered during two years for

which period I have, by your sanctions, assisted Dr. Sweet. I will, therefore, appeal for your information to what has passed rather than make promises for the future beyond this general pledge that, should your choice place me in the responsible office, I will endeavour to perform conscientiously its duties. I am, gentlemen, your obedient servant, John Mais.

Some two years later, on 26 September, 1827, Mais wrote again to the Infirmary Committee.

Gentlemen,
I have been presented to a small benefice in Monmouthshire on which it is my intention to reside during three months in the year. I, therefore, request permission to obtain assistance at the Infirmary for that period annually. I shall not be absent altogether for the time, but attend personally to the duties of the chaplainship a few days in each of the three months. I am, gentlemen, your obedient servant, John Mais.

The following week, on 3 October, he wrote again to name his stand-in at the chaplaincy.

Gentlemen,
In reply to the communication of your Secretary, I beg to inform you that the gentleman whom I propose to officiate for me at the Infirmary during my absence is the Reverend J.A. La Trobe, curate of Temple Church. He is acquainted with the nature of the Chaplain's services and has expressed his readiness to pursue the same methods of visiting and instruction. I am, Gentlemen, your obedient servant, John Mais, Chaplain.

Thereupon the Committee granted his request, 'So long as no inconvenience arises therefrom.'

A picture of the Rev. John Mais was beginning to emerge. He had been curate for nine years at St. Mary Redcliffe, the church reputedly praised by Elizabeth I as 'the fairest, goodliest and most famous parish church in England'. According to his letter of 26 September, Mais intended to be in Tintern for only three months of the year. Who was to officiate during the rest of the year? One cannot anticipate every birth, death and marriage in advance. Granted Tintern was a small village, but burials certainly could not be confined to the three months Mais was going to be resident in the parish. It was unlikely, too, that baptisms and marriages could all be planned around his presence. On reflection there seemed more to be said about this appointment.

Let us look for a moment at the marriages he performed. Mais was rector at St. Michael's from 1827 to 1871. During that time 73 marriages were solemnised of which he performed only 10; of these he performed one in the first thirty years between 1827 and 1858, and the other nine between 1858 and 1868. If we look at the baptisms, the low rate continues, for out of a total of 363 baptisms he performed only 58, just under a sixth. Most of these took place after he had resigned from the chaplaincy in 1856. Before that no regular pattern can be seen except for one period when from 1851 to 1855 he conducted one a year, always in October.

There is something about the time spent by Mais at Tintern Parva, particularly in his early years, that is puzzling. First of all there is the way he announces to the Infirmary Committee that he had been 'presented to a small benefice in Monmouthshire'. The use of the word 'small' is factual but almost self-deprecating. Then comes the statement that 'it is my intention to reside' there for three months of the year. He very quickly suggests a stand-in at the Infirmary, the Rev. J.A. La Trobe, from another Bristol church, the Temple.

Unlike St. Michael's, the Temple Church, Bristol, was not a 'small benefice'. Its very name summons up immediately its Templar origins. Its past history may account in part for why Mais chose La Trobe to assist in the chaplaincy. The two men served at two of the most prominent city churches in Bristol and may have shared similar interests. Perhaps his sterling qualities were obvious at the start. John Antes La Trobe was the son of a bishop of the Moravian Church. His father insisted that he break off his engagement to a Moravian girl because he had not asked for permission. This led him to join the Church of England which he served devotedly, dying unmarried as an honorary Canon of Carlisle. During his early years in Bristol he and Mais lived for a time at the same address, 13 Somerset Square, a residence for unmarried clergy. La Trobe was a man of character, but it was too soon to draw any further conclusions. At this stage I confined myself to those facts that had a bearing on Christopher Heath.

It was while checking on the duties performed by Mais at Tintern that I found that La Trobe stood in for him there as well. In the first year, 1828, the baptismal register shows that La Trobe performed three baptisms between February and June; the rest, apart from one, were performed by Mais. In 1829 La Trobe conducted four between May and July and Mais performed the rest. In 1830 La Trobe conducted six between February and July. After that his name does not appear in the register. A similar pattern occurs with the marriages, with La Trobe officiating at the time of Mais's absence. So there was clearly an arrangement between the two men whereby La Trobe officiated in the absence of Mais both at St. Michael's, Tintern Parva and at Bristol Infirmary. What emerges from an analysis of the registers for both marriages and baptisms is that, broadly speaking, Mais chose to be resident in Tintern Parva for the last quarter of the year. That remained the pattern of his Rectorship until, according to the

Infirmary records, he resigned from his duties as chaplain in 1856. According to *Crockford's Directory* he resigned in 1864.

1864 was the year Christopher Heath died. One particular question should be asked in connection with Heath's death. Is it possible that his body was used for some sort of medical research? Given that he had suffered from epilepsy and considering the poor state of medical knowledge about the condition at the time, this is not an unreasonable hypothesis. The Rev. John Mais had been the incumbent at St. Michael's for 44 years, and Lewis West, the Moravian minister, had served in neighbouring Brockweir for 38 years. Their ministries overlapped and it would be most surprising if they did not come to know each other well.

There may have been some agreement between the two ministers over the supposed interment of Heath in St. Michael's churchyard, Tintern Parva (not, as we know, his own parish). Heath himself may have given permission for his body, in particular his brain, to be used for research. This would account for the apparently empty tomb and be consistent with some of the earlier recorded behaviour of the Rev. John Mais in his younger years. Mais no doubt had some empathy with the doctors and surgeons at the Infirmary. We have seen that, while one of the curates at St. Mary Redcliffe Church in Bristol, he was described as a 'pupil' in the Minute Book. So there is some evidence of an interest in and study of medical matters before he was appointed chaplain to the Infirmary. The rebuke he received for removing a body should perhaps be viewed in the light of that interest. No doubt it was a practice not unknown to the authorities. How were doctors expected to improve their knowledge of pathology? On the other hand, had the Rev. John Mais some other allegiance?

The question of Heath's burial had not been a digression. It had been vital to discover the reason for the memorial inscription on the tomb and its likely date. The facts I had uncovered confirmed my belief that the inscription was deliberately misleading. It does not state that Heath is *buried* in the tomb. It is very carefully worded. The inscription is 'in memory' of Christopher Heath, regardless of the fact that he had not lived in the parish. It was, in other words, to honour his memory, record his passing and, possibly, the disposal of his remains. Alive, he no doubt preferred to be nursed quietly in the care of Lewis West rather than be subjected to the very primitive treatments then in fashion. With apparently no kin to mourn him, he may well have been content to leave his body for medical research. The documentation I had discovered about him and John Mais permits such a conclusion. But why was this particular tomb chosen to be his memorial? Questions remained. I needed to look at the history of Tintern Parva in a much wider context. I now proceeded to do just that.

CHAPTER TWO

Medieval Revelations

I̶N LOOKING FURTHER into the history of Tintern Parva the mystery only increased. Documentation for the early history of St. Michael's Church was scarce. Bradney includes a list of incumbents in his *History of Monmouthshire*. It begins in 1348 but unfortunately contains gaps. Even so, I could see that the patron of the church from 1348 to at least 1402 was always the king. During that time the church was much smaller than it is today, minuscule compared to the magnificent Abbey dominating the landscape just round a bend in the river.

I discovered, too, that King Edward VI was the patron in 1553 when he decided to settle its future care differently: my attention had been drawn to a document in ecclesiastical Latin written at the express wish of King Edward VI and dated 27 April 1553, a little over two months before the young king's death. The document consists of letters patent granting certain rights and privileges to none other than his loyal subject William Herbert, Earl of Pembroke, in recognition of his services.

Part of the document is concerned with Tintern and has a direct bearing on our story. William Herbert had already received a number of generous royal grants from both Henry VIII and Edward VI. What, I wondered, was so special about this one and its timing? To answer this question we have to leave Tintern Parva and turn our attention to London and events surrounding the king and the question of his successor.

Edward VI was the son of Jane Seymour, the third wife of King Henry VIII. At the time of his birth he had two older half-sisters: Princess Mary, already a grown woman of twenty, the Catholic daughter of Catherine of Aragon, and Princess Elizabeth, aged four, the Protestant daughter of Anne Boleyn. As Henry's only legitimate son, the prince succeeded to the throne when Henry died in 1547. Edward was nine years old at the time but showed a quick intelligence and King Henry ensured that he received a thorough education from the finest scholars in the land. As he developed, King Edward VI looked as if he would be a worthy successor to his father. Henry had also decreed that during his minority the country should be governed by a council of regency. Among the members of the council of

TINTERN PARVA.

PATRON.	DATE OF INSTITUTION.	INCUMBENT.
The king, by reason of the priory of Chepstow being in his hands on account of the war with France.	22 Dec. 1348.	Adam de Couton.[1]
The king, for the same reasons.	26 Feb. 1350.	William Baker, chaplain.[2]
Do.	22 May 1389.	Hugh ap David,[3] resigned 1391 on appointment to Lee in the diocese of Rochester, in exchange with William Glastynbury.[4]
Do.	10 May 1391.	William Glastynbury, previously parson of Lee in the diocese of Rochester, in exchange with Hugh ap David; resigned 1395[4] on appointment to Thundurle.
Do.	8 July 1394.	John Golmonchestre, vicar of Thundurle in the diocese of London,[5] in exchange with Wm. Glastynbury.[5]
Do.	21 Sept. 1394.	David Carlion, chaplain of a charity in the collegiate church of Leicester, in exchange with Wm. Glastynbury.[6] (These two could not have taken effect.)
Do.	26 Jan. 1395.	Adam Payne, on the resignation of Wm. Glastynbury.[7]
Do.	14 June 1396.	John ap David,[8] resigned 1399 on appointment to the chantry of Marnhull in the diocese of Salisbury, in exchange with Adam Russheburye.
	26 July 1399.	Adam Russheburye, chaplain of the chantry of Marnhull, in exchange with John ap David.[8]
		Walter de Bury, resigned 1402 on presentation to the chantry at Lytlyngton in the diocese of London, in exchange with Peter Warde.[9]
The king	20 Nov. 1402.	Peter Warde, previously chaplain of the chantry at the altar of St. Mary in the church of Lytlyngton.[9]
		Walter Loring in 1412.[10]
	.... 1632.	William Prichard, M.A. Jesus College, Oxford, son of Francis Prichard of Abergavenny.
		Hugh Evans, died about 1697.
The bishop	19 July 1697.	John Quick, M.A. New Inn Hall, Oxford, son of John Quick of Burringham, co. Somerset; resigned 1702.
Wm. ffielding, esq.	15 Sept. 1702.	Amos Boyland.
John Curre, esq., guardian of Elizabeth ffielding, a minor.	9 Aug. 1713.	Anthony Barrow, B.A. Jesus College, Oxford, son of Edward Barrow of St. Briavels, gent.
George I.	31 July 1719.	Thomas Hill, M.A. Magdalen Hall, Oxford, son of Thomas Hill of Hereford; also in 1723 vicar of Llanarth.
		George Harris; resigned 1734.
John Curre, esq.	20 Sept. 1734.	Mallet Bateman, Pembroke and Jesus College, Oxford, son of Richard Bateman of Prendergast, co. Pembroke.
John Curre of Itton, esq.	18 Jan. 1752.	Edward Lewis.
Do.	8 Dec. 1756.	John Williams.
	.... 1768.	Thomas Edmunds; died 1804-5.
Thomas Fielding Manning and Sarah his wife; Wm. Shopp Osborne; Isaac Freeme; and Wm. Osborne.	24 June 1805.	Daniel Drape.
	25 Sept. 1827.	John Mais, B.D. Queen's College, Cambridge. (William Richard Ferguson, curate in 1851, afterwards rector of Llandogo.)
	.... 1871.	Henry John Williams; resigned 1878.
	.... 1878.	Joseph Frederick Jones.
	.... 1882.	Edward Richard Godley; resigned 1887; also held Chapel Hill; resigned 1886.
	.... 1887.	William Elitto Rosedale, M.A. New College, Oxford; resigned 1889.
	.... 1889.	Alfred Trask Pullin, B.A. Trinity College, Dublin.
	.... 1892.	Harold Barclay Hennell; also held Chapel Hill.
	.... 1901.	William Donald Istance Mackintosh; also held Chapel Hill.[11]
The crown.	8 Oct. 1903.	Alfred Wm. Washington Palmer, son of Alfred Vaughan Palmer; also holds Chapel Hill.

1 *Cal. Rot. Pat.*, Edw. III., 1348—50, p. 216.   2 *Ibid.*, p. 471.   3 *Cal. Rot. Pat.*, Ric. II., 1388—92, p. 40.
4 *Ibid.*, p. 464.   5 *Ibid*, p. 466.   6 *Ibid.*, p. 480.   7 *Ibid.*, p. 527.   8 *Ibid.*, p. 714.
9 *Cal. Rot. Pat.*, Hen. IV., 1401—5, p. 173.   10 *Ibid.*, 1408—13, p. 448.
11 I have been unable to obtain the names of the patrons who presented the above clergymen. The *Directories* give them—in 1851 (Lascelles') William Gale; in 1861 (Webster's) Robert Vaughan Hughes, clk.; in 1884 (Kelly's) Robert Hamilton Williams and Henry Edward Burney.

4. Rectors' List, St. Michael's Church

regency was Sir William Herbert. His marriage to the younger sister of Catherine Parr, King Henry's sixth wife, assured his rise in importance and wealth. Henry gave him the rich lands of the former Abbey at Wilton in Wiltshire, which Herbert demolished to replace with a splendid mansion. Later, in 1551, King Edward made him Earl of Pembroke. Falling seriously ill in April the following year, the young king was taken on a 'progress' around the southern counties as part of his convalescence. The new earl entertained him at Wilton, serving his sovereign from plates of pure gold and his courtiers from silver gilt. When Edward left, Pembroke presented him with the entire service.

Edward's reign marks the real foundation of Protestantism as the religion of the country. Under the watchful eye of Archbishop Cranmer, the king was brought up a strong Protestant. William Herbert shared the same strict beliefs. In 1549 Cranmer introduced the first version of the Book of Common Prayer in English to standardise the form of church services throughout the country. This sparked off violent opposition and Herbert, with a force of two thousand Welshman, helped to put down the revolt in Devon and Cornwall, making a good profit financially from it. In addition, in the following year, 1550, King Edward made further grants of land to him.

In January 1553, however, Edward showed the first symptoms of consumption. By May it was clear that the illness was terminal, and on 6 July the same year, he died at the age of sixteen.

As it became obvious that the king was going to die, John Dudley, the Duke of Northumberland and head of the government, played on the king's dislike of Princess Mary's stubborn adherence to her Catholic faith. If she became queen, and she was next in line, the Protestant cause would be lost. So a plot, or 'Devise' as it became known, was hatched to exclude Princess Mary and endow the succession on Lady Jane Grey. Ambitious for his family, Northumberland had married his son, Guildford, to Lady Jane Grey on 21 May 1553. Equally ambitious, Herbert, now Earl of Pembroke, arranged for his eldest son, Henry, to marry Jane's sister, Catherine, the same day in a joint ceremony at Durham House, Northumberland's London home. In this way two leading families joined together to maintain, if not increase, their power.

Pembroke was ready to act with Northumberland to have the succession of Lady Jane accepted by the council. She reigned for nine days. When Pembroke saw the support growing for Princess Mary he abandoned Northumberland and went over to Mary's side. Northumberland was executed. So too, later, were Lady Jane and her husband. Pembroke avoided the same fate, served Mary well and won the favour of her Catholic husband, Philip of Spain. Not surprisingly, on Queen Mary's death he hurried to

Hatfield to swear allegiance to her Protestant successor, Queen Elizabeth I. The Earl of Pembroke was a born survivor.

The date of the letters patent, 21 April 1553, places it securely in the middle of the 'Devise' approved by the dying Edward to change the succession, a change supported by Herbert. The document reads like a generous reward. But it seems to be more than that. It is not simply a gift of lands and financial privileges. It lists certain ecclesiastical rights also. There is nothing unusual about that. What is different is the care taken to spell out in far more detail the rights and privileges in respect to one church than is the case with other ecclesiastical rights which Pembroke was given in this document. The church was at Tintern Parva and had to be St. Michael's. There was no other. The wording seems to give Pembroke and someone by the name of William Clarke the right not only to appoint the clergy but to have complete control of the church building and its fabric. Translated, the relevant passage reads as follows:

> Moreover, the advowson, the right to innovate, the right of presentation, the free patronage and the right of priority at the Rectory and Church of Tynterne Parva in our said County of Monmouth.'[1]

Coupled with the unusually specific rights at Tintern Parva is another ecclesiastical grant again made jointly to the Earl and William Clarke.

> Furthermore all that Manor of Usk and Rectory of Trostrey and the Chapel and Rectory of Llandeny in our said county of Monmouth together with the rights, portions and all pertaining to the former Priory of Usk in the same County, now recently dissolved.

A closer look at these two grants is enlightening. Those connected with the 'Rectory and Church of Tynterne Parva' are particularly intriguing. The 'right to innovate', for example, is not a privilege mentioned elsewhere in the grant, and one is compelled to ask in what way the Earl could or would 'innovate' at this church. It stood in a remote and sparsely populated area not very far from the abandoned Abbey. What was so special about it that made the dying king anxious to ensure its future control at this time? Moreover these ecclesiastical rights were to be shared equally by the Earl and one 'William Clarke, gentleman, of Pondesborne in the County of Hertfordshire'. But there was a difference: Clarke's rights were to end with his death; Pembroke's were to remain with his heirs and assigns in perpetuity.

Who Clarke was, and why the king linked him in this way with the Earl, must be significant. More important for the moment, however, is the clear intention expressed in these words to ensure the permanent and continued control of this church by the Herbert dynasty. The church itself was vastly altered in 1846 but a clue to its earlier history survives in the vaulted ceiling of the south porch. Here visitors can still see Tudor roses carved in the red sandstone. These must date from the time of Pembroke and Clarke and may have been part of a rebuilding programme in the mid-sixteenth century commemorating their custody.[2]

As we have seen, William, Earl of Pembroke, was linked closely at this time with the Duke of Northumberland in the 'Devise', but they had other links in common in their pursuit of power. One was John Dee. In December 1551, fresh from the triumph of his lectures on Euclid in Paris, Dee was introduced at court to King Edward VI. He presented the king with two treatises on astronomy and was later awarded a royal pension. Then, in February 1552, Dee joined the Earl of Pembroke's household. It was probably Pembroke who in 1553 recommended him to the Duke of Northumberland as a tutor to his sons.

Dee had a marked impact on the Northumberland family. Long after the death of the Duke's eldest son, John, Dee recalled his pupil's love of the sciences and mathematics. Another, more famous, son, Robert Dudley, who was to become Earl of Leicester and the great favourite of Queen Elizabeth, was an outstanding patron of learning and the sciences in his time. Intriguingly, the boys' mother, the Duchess of Northumberland, asked Dee to write two treatises in 1553. One of these concerned *The true cause and account of Floods and Ebbs*. The church of St. Michael stands on the bank of a stretch of the river Wye where it is still strongly tidal.

The wireworks at Tintern had been set up in 1568 during the reign of Elizabeth I. By then the great Cistercian Abbey stood in ruins after its dissolution by Henry VIII. Small as it was, St. Michael's survived the ravages of the Reformation. It was in fact older than the Abbey and a Celtic church had stood on the same site as far back as AD 765.

The first Earl of Pembroke died in 1570. It was around this time that Dee formed his close association with Pembroke's kinsman Sir William Herbert of St. Julian's, whose Tintern house I had been looking for. It may be that Dee's interest in Tintern began some years earlier when he first joined the Earl of Pembroke's household. There were, too, other connections. The brass plates of the theatre drawings containing the design concept of the Elizabethan playhouses owed much to Dee's advocacy of geometry in his *Mathematical Preface* to Euclid. I believe those plates were made at Tintern.

The deed of 1553 seemed to push the importance of St. Michael's Church and the surrounding area further back. I looked again at the list of incumbents to see if the church's earlier history could yield any clues to its importance. In 1348, when that list begins, this part of the Wye Valley would have been even more thinly populated than in 1553. The Abbey had been founded in 1131 and had already grown in size. It had been deliberately placed in a secluded spot away from the distractions of the world. Its extensive lands were now being leased out for others to farm in return for fixed rents. So the church of St. Michael, standing as it did just outside the boundaries of the Abbey itself, did not serve a large or thriving parish.

Even so, it seems to have been important enough for the appointment of a priest associated with the great Abbey of Glastonbury, the largest monastery in the country and itself dedicated to St. Michael. 'William Glastynbury', i.e. William *of* Glastonbury, exchanged a living in the London diocese of Rochester for this rural retreat in May 1391. What makes this move even more interesting is that twice in 1394 successors were nominated, but William remained in office until a third choice was found the following year. Neither his predecessor nor successor stayed as long.

Like any other church, the Rectory of St. Michael did not exist in isolation. Its immediate setting is the manor of Tintern Parva and while the *church* remains consistently under the patronage of the king, the *manor* or estate passes by the will or permission of the king to a succession of aristocratic supporters. For example, in the reign of Edward II, the king's niece Eleanor gave her sister Elizabeth de Burgh various estates in exchange for 'Parva Tintern' and other manors. This transaction was not completed until the reign of Edward's successor and we shall look at it more closely in Chapter Five. For the moment we should note that the change of ownership concerned simply the *manor*, and not the church. Detailed evidence can be seen in the extracts from royal grants quoted by Bradney.[3] The manorial lands changed hands but the church remained firmly with the king and within the administrative diocese of Llandaff.

From the evidence of the letters patent of 1553 it is clear that there was a deliberate break with precedent. Royal patronage came to an end just before Edward VI died and one must ask why. It then remained with the Pembrokes until the sudden and unexpected death of the third Earl in 1630 when it reverted back to the Crown in the person of King Charles I. It would have stayed with Charles until the Civil War and his execution in 1649. The interruption of the Commonwealth accounts for the patronage passing eventually to the Bishop of Llandaff in 1697.

The strong Protestant beliefs of King Edward VI and of the first Earl of Pembroke, culminating in the plot to deprive Princess Mary of her right of succession, may be one reason for granting the earl control over St. Michael's. The shadowy figure of William Clarke of Pondesbourne may provide others.

Pondesbourne was part of the manor of Hatfield in Hertfordshire. Hatfield is the site of the historic mansion originally built for the Bishops of Ely that became a favourite haunt of Henry VIII. From 1514 he visited it frequently and in 1538 he finally got possession of it from the bishop. The same year he took over Pondesbourne as well. At Hatfield House the young Prince Edward and Princess Elizabeth spent much of their childhood together. It remained a favourite palace for Elizabeth, who received here the news of Queen Mary's death and her own succession to the throne.

The parish church at Hatfield contained a chapel connected with the lords of the manor of Pondesbourne. This was evidence of their religious devotion. Here services were held annually for their souls and the souls of their ancestors. This was important in an age when people still believed in hellfire and damnation. Up and down the country the rich and the powerful would leave money for masses to be said for them when they were dead to atone for their past misdeeds and ensure their passage to heaven. Because Henry VIII quarrelled with the Pope over his divorce, he is sometimes mistakenly thought to have ceased to be a Roman Catholic. But it was the Pope's authority that he objected to. As his will shows, when Henry died he did not ask the Virgin Mary to pray for his soul: he practically ordered her to do so.

In 1553 William Clarke is still referred to as of 'Pondesbourne' although the manor was sold to Henry in 1538. The *Victoria History Of Hertfordshire* mentions that in Hatfield church

> There are references in the 16th century to a Gild or Fraternity of St. John the Baptist. In 1510 a bequest was made to it by John Lowen and others, in 1514 by Nicholas Lanam, and in 1520 by William Clarke. In 1538 a tenement in Woodside yielding a yearly rent of 4s. belonged to a 'brotherhood', and in 1545 a Fraternity is entered as paying 6d towards a subsidy. After this it disappears.[4]

From this we know that a William Clarke was resident at Pondesbourne in 1520 and was connected with a Guild or Fraternity dedicated to St. John the Baptist established in the chapel. He is either the man mentioned in the letters patent of 1553 or his son.

The letters patent describe him as 'generosus' or a gentleman. This indicates a person of some substance and position, who, although not a member of the aristocracy, was worthy of the notice of his sovereign. The lord of the manor was not necessarily a titled nobleman. Clarke's commitment to the Fraternity at Pondesbourne in 1520 is indicative of his standing. At that time Henry VIII was making frequent hunting trips to Hatfield. He was still married to Catherine of Aragon and his quarrel with the Pope was a long way off. Clarke's endowment to the Pondesbourne chapel in Hatfield church would have been known locally and bring him naturally into the orbit of the king's circle there.

The first reference we have to Pondesbourne chapel is dated 1510. That takes the chapel back with certainty to the beginning of the reign of King Henry VIII. The chapel and the Fraternity of St. John would have existed much earlier. Hatfield Church was originally built in the thirteenth century. It was continually altered and extended. Small chapels maintained by important benefactors were a common feature in pre-Reformation England. The Pondesbourne chapel would have been a typical example. But Pondesbourne had an historical significance beyond Hatfield. Part of the manor of Pondesbourne had once been owned by William de Valence and his son Aymer, Earl of Pembroke.

These two men were powerful figures, both as soldiers and diplomats. William was half-brother to King Henry III, who invited him over to England from France. Appointed commander of the army in West Wales in 1294 he helped to suppress a revolt in South Wales. More importantly, in 1270, he went to the Holy Land with the young Prince Edward, the future Edward I. Aymer was repeatedly employed as an ambassador to France, fought against the Scots at Bannockburn and acted as a mediator between Edward II and his turbulent barons. After the decision in 1307 to suppress the Knights Templar, the Pope ordered Edward II to hand over their vast headquarters in London to the Knights Hospitaller of St. John. At first the king gave them to Aymer de Valence, now Earl of Pembroke, before deciding to comply. Ironically, the 'whirligig of time' saw the headquarters of the Knights Hospitaller at Clerkenwell given to another Earl of Pembroke, William Herbert, by King Edward VI in 1550.

The association of Pondesbourne with important figures such as the de Valences should not be overlooked. Their presence there resonates down the years to the reign of Henry VIII. It colours the prolonged Tudor love of nearby Hatfield shown so strongly first by Henry VIII, then by Edward VI and later by Elizabeth. That love had a variety of reasons. For Henry, apart from his own personal pleasure in the estate at Hatfield, the house itself had special associations as the birthplace of Jasper Tudor, the man who had brought up his father Henry VII. For Edward and Elizabeth it held memories of a shared childhood. Similarly down the centuries the constant devotion of a brotherhood to St. John the Baptist in Pondesbourne Chapel was due to more than simple piety. The Hospitallers of St. John had been chosen by the Pope as the successors to the Knights Templar; they were the inheritors of their power and learning. So when William Clarke made a bequest to the Fraternity of St. John in Pondesbourne, he was displaying more than a charitably pious instinct, he was signalling allegiance to a long-established and far-flung organisation, custodians of a priceless inheritance.

William Clarke made his bequest in 1520 when Henry VIII had been king for nine years. Thirty-three years later King Edward VI decided to invest William Clarke with certain specified rights in the Rectory at Tintern Parva. That is a substantial interval and it would appear that the William Clarke of the 1553 document is the son of the earlier William Clarke. The proof for this reveals some facts worth pondering.

In 1553 the MP for Monmouth was one John Morgan. His daughter Jane married three times, and her third husband was one 'Clark of Barrow in Somerset'. That marriage produced a son who was christened William. Jane's husband is, I believe, the William Clarke of the 1553 document. But Jane's brother, William Morgan of Pentre-bach, had a daughter Florence, sometimes referred to as Florencia. (This is the family which produced the 'Welsh Jacobite' David Morgan, whom we shall meet in Chapter Nine.) Florence married Sir William Herbert of St. Julian's. This marriage made William Clarke an uncle to Sir William. It also drew Clarke closer into the circle of luminaries centred on Tintern Parva. Such dynastic ties were very important in the close-knit, hierarchical society of the time. In today's more fluid society we may not appreciate that importance.

Moreover, William Morgan, Clarke's brother-in-law, was a man of wealth and importance, linked with the leading families of the county. He succeeded his father as the local MP in 1555 and in 1560 was buying large tracts of land from the Earl of Pembroke. Morgan's political status, wealth and land deals would bring him into the earl's circle. At the same time William Clarke's place in the Morgan family was a very good recommendation to Pembroke and goes part of the way to explaining why he was coupled with the earl when Edward VI wished to decide the future control of Tintern Parva church.

But it is only part of the explanation. According to the Morgan family pedigree Jane's husband came from Barrow in Somerset. That was Barrow Gurney near Bedminster, not far from Bristol and Glastonbury. Close by stood the Hospital of St. Katharine, a small hospice founded in the thirteenth century to tend the sick, the infirm and the needy traveller. This was not a religious foundation so it escaped closure at the time of the Dissolution. It was run by a warden with the help of a number of brethren who wore 'the garment of secular priests with the badge of a St. Catherine wheel on the left breast'.[5] From the rents of this foundation a pension was paid to the rector of Bedminster, together with two wax candles to be offered yearly on the Feast of St. John the Baptist. A tribute paid on that particular feast day links this brotherhood to the Fraternity of St. John the Baptist we saw functioning at the Pondesbourne chapel in Hatfield church.

In 1543, one 'William Clerke' was listed as the Master at Bedminster. (Despite the advent of printing, spelling was still fluid.) Henry VIII was still king. By that time the purpose of the hospital was not to maintain or relieve the poor with money, but to assign them cottages belonging to the hospital to dwell in. That was Clarke's responsibility. 'Other relief they have none but as God sendeth.'[6]

Ten years later, by 1553, Clarke had proved himself a safe pair of hands at Bedminster. Thus this shadowy figure emerges briefly into the sunlight as someone judged by the king and his counsellors as capable through family connections and proven worth of being entrusted jointly with the highest in the land to carry out an important commission. He comes across as unassuming but reliable. Confident of his own dignity but not flawed by the overweening ambition that destroyed so many able men, William Clarke stood out like a beacon – and is just what is needed to light us through the miles between Pondesbourne in Hertfordshire, Bedminster in Somerset and Tintern in Monmouthshire. What was it that linked these seemingly disparate places into a meaningful whole? Could it be the mysterious Fraternity of St. John the Baptist?

It might help us to answer that question, if we look briefly at the history of the Knights Hospitaller of St. John in England.

The Knights Hospitaller owe their title and origin to an ancient hospice founded in Jerusalem about 600. After the First Crusade (*c.* 1099) many crusaders were nursed here and the hospital became famous throughout Europe for its life-saving treatment and care. Not surprisingly the hospital became a favourite object for charitable donations. A new Order of Hospitallers was set up and moved into an old monastery in Jerusalem dedicated to St. John the Baptist. As a result he was adopted as the patron saint of the Order. Hospitallers took vows of chastity, poverty and obedience, before Dagobert, the Patriarch of Jerusalem, and dedicated themselves to the care of the sick and the poor in the Holy Land. Eventually, increasing pressure of threats and violence from the surrounding Arab population forced the Hospitallers to become in part a military order, like the Knights Templar, to protect themselves.

During the course of their history the Hospitallers enjoyed especially close support from two English kings: Henry VII and his son Henry VIII. In recognition of this both sovereigns were awarded the title 'Protector of the Order'.

Unfortunately, it was inevitable that Henry VIII saw the wealth of the Hospitallers as a ready source of income. Since there were no longer any crusaders requiring their attention and care, he planned to make the English branch of the Order responsible for the defence of the English fortress at Calais and pay for it themselves. The idea was eventually dropped but it typified the growing uncertainty of Henry's affections. Then came the problem of the king's divorce and it was only a matter of time before the Knights Hospitaller in England went the way of the great monastic foundations in the realm. In May 1540 they were dissolved and the Knights forbidden to wear the long black habit and white cross of their insignia. All their lands went to the Crown.

It is instructive to view the activities of the two William Clarkes against this background. Henry VIII's attitude to the Knights Hospitaller of St. John veered violently from benevolent support in 1520 to ruthless destruction in 1540. In 1520 one William Clarke is making bequests to a Fraternity dedicated to John the Baptist in Pondesbourne. In 1543 another William Clarke is installed as Master of a Hospice that singles out John the Baptist for annual commemoration. Their consistency in honouring St. John is in stark contrast to the behaviour of Henry VIII.

Today St. John is known to many simply as the patron of a band of first-aid workers seen on duty at large public gatherings such as football matches and similar outdoor events. But he is far more than that. To the Christian believer he was a reincarnation of the Jewish prophet Elijah sent to prepare people for the coming of Jesus. He thus has an important place in Christianity for both Roman Catholics and Protestants and is something of a mystery himself.

The brotherhood at Pondesbourne and the Hospice at Bedminster are examples of embryonic units from which greater organisms grow and develop. Oak trees may be felled but the continued existence of acorns ensures that trees survive. Similarly, the two William Clarkes, one supporting the brotherhood at Pondesbourne, the other managing the Hospice at Bedminster, provide a constant – the constant of a father and son with shared loyalties. They represent reliability and continuity in a century that displayed great religious and political turbulence. I pondererd over this and it looked as if it were the qualities of dependability and trust that dictated the choice of William Clarke – not necessarily the figure of St. John himself. He was, if you like, the means by which that trust was demonstrated. Looking at the letters patent of 1553 in this light, it seemed it was necessary to ensure some form of continuity at the little church of St. Michael through its administration and ministry.

CHAPTER THREE

The Legendary Tewdric

WHAT WAS IT that required such careful and continuous supervision? The question remained. Was the answer to be found much further back in time, earlier even than the foundation of the Abbey?

Tintern is mentioned in the pages of a medieval text, the *Liber Landavensis* or *Book of Llandaff* written circa 1200 and concerned mainly with the life of a little-known Welsh saint, St. Teilo. The book contains a brief account of another saint, Tewdric, who also happened to have been a king.

He was descended from one of the princely families that rose to power in Wales with the decline and departure of the Romans. Indeed the name Tewdric appears to be a Celtic version of the Roman name Theodoric. Tewdric ap Teithfallt (or son of Teithfallt) ruled as King of Morgannwg in the south-eastern border country in the late sixth century. Valiant and victorious in battle, Tewdric established a period of peace and just rule for his people before turning his back on the world to devote himself to spiritual concerns. He handed over the kingdom to his son, Meurig, and retired to live the life of a hermit 'in rupibus Dyndim', among the rocks of Tintern.

When Saxon pagans invaded the kingdom, Meurig appealed to his father for help. At this point legend mingles with fact. Tewdric was told by an angel to help his people against the enemies of the Church. Victory would be certain but so, too, would be his death – three days after receiving a single blow to the head 'in the district of Rhyd Tintern' or near the ford at Tintern – in other words on the bank of the Wye. The date was probably around AD 595 for eight years later, when St. Augustine travelled from Canterbury to meet the Welsh bishops in AD 603, he went no further than St. Aust. Historians have concluded that this was the boundary between land conquered by the Saxons and that saved for the Welsh by Tewdric in his last battle.

The account of his death is embedded in myth. After receiving a mortal wound at Tintern, Tewdric was carried on a cart drawn by two stags that appeared, as if by a miracle, yoked and ready at the house where he lay dying. He wished to be buried at Ynis Echni (thought to be the island of Flat Holm) but got no further than Mathern where he died in a meadow. A fountain of clear water flowed nearby and can still be seen a few yards from the present parish church. When Meurig heard the news of his father's death he built an oratory there dedicated to St. Oudoceus in honour of his father.

It is impossible at this distance to sort out the facts from the fictions surrounding Tewdric but historians have concluded on balance that the main outline is true. There *was* a King Tewdric and a battle; he died and was buried at Mathern. Interestingly, that was not the original name of the parish. Early ecclesiastical documents call it 'Merthyr Tewdric', or 'the burial place of Tewdric'. The name was changed to Mathern sometime between 1128 and 1200 and comes from two words meaning 'the place of the king'. That in itself is some confirmation of the special nature of this place.

And special it has been: situated near to Chepstow and five miles from Tintern, Mathern, as a royal foundation, was one of the most important Welsh parishes in the Middle Ages. According to the *Liber Landavensis* Tewdric's son and grandson made three successive grants of land at Mathern to Bishops of Llandaff and for nearly four hundred years Mathern contained the official house of those bishops. One of these, Miles Salley, who is buried in the church, left instructions that his heart should be buried before the high altar near the grave of 'King Theodorick'.

On 27 May 1608 Bishop Godwin of Landaff wrote a letter to his friend the great antiquarian William Camden in which he mentions Tewdric's tomb:

> This name of Theodoricus putteth me in mind of Theodoricus rex and martyr, that lieth entombed here in our church of Mathern, and gave unto this place the name of Merthyr Tewdric … His tomb, partly ruinated, I have repaired, and added a memorial or epitaph, the copy whereof I send you enclosed.[1]

In addition to the warrior saint's coffin, an urn was found which almost certainly contained the heart of Bishop Salley. The north wall of the chancel bears an inscription erected by Bishop Godwin:

> Here lyeth entombed the body of Theodorick, King of Morganrick or Glamorgan, commonly called St. Thewdrick and accounted a martyr because he was slain in a battle against the Saxons, being then pagans, and in defence of the Christian religion. The battle was fought at Tintern, where he obtained a great victory. He died there being on his way homeward, three days after the battle, having taken order with Maurice, his son who succeeded him in his kingdom, that in the same place he should happen to

decease, a Church should be built and his body buried in ye same: which was accordingly performed in the year 600.²

Clearly in his letter to Camden Godwin had been writing about another Theodorick whose name reminded him of the royal St. Tewdric. Was that the Frankish king 'Theodoric', son of Clovis? Another writer has suggested that St. Tewdric and Theodoric were related. In that event Tewdric would be of Merovingian descent.

The tomb was opened again in 1881. Naturally I wondered why. The vicar at Mathern had embarked on a programme of restoration in 1879 which was not completed until 1893, and that might have been the reason for this second examination of the tomb. When it was opened the bones and skull were still there and near the stone coffin was an urn that contained a heart, no doubt that of Bishop Salley. A tablet recording this event was placed beneath the earlier one erected by Bishop Godwin. A local historian, Fred J. Hando, writes that a parishioner recalled seeing as a young girl Tewdric's stone coffin in the chancel in 1881 and the hole made by the spear point in his skull.³

When I looked a little closer into the restoration programme it proved not quite as straightforward as it first appeared. The vicar, the Rev. Watkin Davies, was happy to use his own money for the renovations but, as one might expect, he had financial support from his wealthier parishioners. One was particularly generous. That was the Rev. Robert Vaughan Hughes and he has a special place in our story. For he was also, for some years, patron of St. Michael's in Tintern and the owner of Nurtons, the house I had been looking for on my very first visit.

Vaughan Hughes had studied for the ministry, but never became an actual incumbent of a church. He was spared the necessity of earning a living by marrying a woman of considerable means. Her wealth automatically became his and enabled him to purchase Wyelands, an impressive house in extensive grounds close to Mathern Church. It is interesting to note that he became patron of St. Michael's in Tintern Parva in 1858. At the time Mais was the rector, had recently resigned from the chaplaincy at Bristol and was concentrating on his responsibilities at St. Michael's.

Although Mathern and Wyelands are some distance away, Vaughan Hughes remained patron at St. Michael's for at least fifteen years. What struck me was that he was happy to dispense his charity on his local parish church. Apart from a new font and pulpit to match, he provided the altar table, a splendid east window, a new Bible and service books for the congregation. But his generosity did not seem to extend towards St. Michael's in any obvious way. The church had been practically rebuilt in 1846 and its larger proportions were ideal for decoration. Despite his long tenure as patron he is not recorded as one of its benefactors. Improving its interior was evidently not part of his agenda.

I found myself wondering why he took over the patronage. Even allowing for the fact that Mathern was his parish church, there is a distinction in his attitude to the two churches. For example, at Mathern the ancient baptismal font was replaced the year Tewdric's tomb was opened in 1881. It seems there was no need for a new one. The medieval, stone baptismal font had been in constant use for centuries. Suddenly it was removed and its fate remained unknown for sixty years. In 1943 it was discovered and excavated from under the church porch where it had been buried, apparently at the instigation of Vaughan Hughes. This treatment of the old font was disapproved of by many, including Hughes's own descendants. It was cleaned, rebuilt and now stands in the north-east corner of the nave. This may seem a relatively small matter – a minor storm in a baptismal teacup, but the incident reveals a high-handed trait in Vaughan Hughes in getting his own way. One is left pondering his interest in being patron of St. Michael's Church. He was happy to incur quite unnecessary expense to improve Mathern Church yet leave St. Michael's quite unadorned. Was that deliberate? Was it, perhaps, to avoid drawing attention to it?

The questions persist when one learns that the Rev. Vaughan Hughes took steps to buy up land that was once part of the Manor of Tintern Parva which abutted directly onto the church. His steady acquisition of land so close to the church is not easily explained by the desire to extend his existing boundaries at Nurtons.

Around this time the railway line to Tintern was being planned. It was to run close by his land. Vaughan Hughes may have been simply displaying the opportunism of an entrepreneur. But his interest in Tintern Parva seemed to me to centre entirely on the small unassuming church. An obvious link between the two churches at Mathern and Tintern Parva is St. Tewdric. This royal saint retired from his kingdom to a cave among the rocks of Tintern. Perhaps this was the site. Later he died of wounds at Mathern. Did Vaughan Hughes see himself as having a responsibility to the memory of the saint? Tewdric died protecting his fellow Christians from the pagan invaders. This public role was publicly honoured in his burial and tomb. This, as we saw, was opened again in 1881. Was that at Vaughan Hughes's instigation? Did he pay for it? Tewdric's life as a hermit was not recorded for posterity. His retirement was a private act and treated as such. Was Vaughan Hughes concerned with a different agenda at Tintern Parva, one that required discretion, even secrecy? Was the site of 'the rocks of Tintern' special in a different way?

I looked again at what little we know of Tewdric, his possible lineage from the Frankish King Theodoric and, through him, with the Merovingian monarchs of France. Theodoric was the eldest son of Clovis I. As a result of his success in battle against the Visigoths, Clovis converted to Christianity and was baptised at Reims. Clovis is seen today as the Founder of France and his baptism is regarded as a major turning point in the religious destiny of the French nation.

When we think of Merovingian France we must remember that we are dealing with territory that extended into what is now Belgium in the north and Germany in the east. The dynasty takes its name from Merovech, a shadowy figure about whom few facts are known, and those facts are embroidered again with legend and myth. The Merovingians ruled from *c.* AD 476 to 750 and are regarded as the first line of French kings. Repeatedly the former Roman province of Gaul was united under a particularly strong member of the family and then divided up among his sons who fought and squabbled with each other. Eventually three distinct kingdoms emerged: Austrasia in the east, Neustria in the West and Burgundy in the south.

Legends abound concerning the origin and supernatural powers of the Merovingians, just as they did around our own King Arthur. However, a picture of them that is generally considered reliable can be found in the writings of Gregory of Tours (*c.* 538–594), who served as bishop under four successive Merovingian kings. In his *Histories* Gregory tells us that Theodoric captured the treasure of the Visigoths from their capital, Toulouse. In 1961 the Merovingian scholar, J.M. Wallace-Hadrill, made the dramatic suggestion that Clovis may have added more to it from Carcassonne including the 'treasure of Solomon' taken by Alaric I when he plundered Rome in 410.[4] A pedigree derived from such a powerful and wealthy dynasty would have enhanced the figure of Tewdric at the time in the eyes of those who knew. Accordingly, we need to note that the Merovingians had connections with a church and a priory in Monmouthshire surprisingly close to each other.

Apart from the gift of the church and Rectory at Tintern Parva, in the letters patent of 1553, Edward VI made another grant jointly to the Earl of Pembroke and William Clarke that aroused my particular interest. It concerned 'the rights, portions and all pertaining to the former Priory of Usk in the same County now recently dissolved'. The Priory of Usk lies some nine miles west of Tintern Parva and had been 'recently dissolved' during the religious upheavals of Henry VIII. It was originally a Benedictine foundation for five nuns and a prioress. All the nuns were to be girls of noble birth. Well endowed at its foundation, by the late fourteenth century constant warfare had reduced the Priory to poverty. From

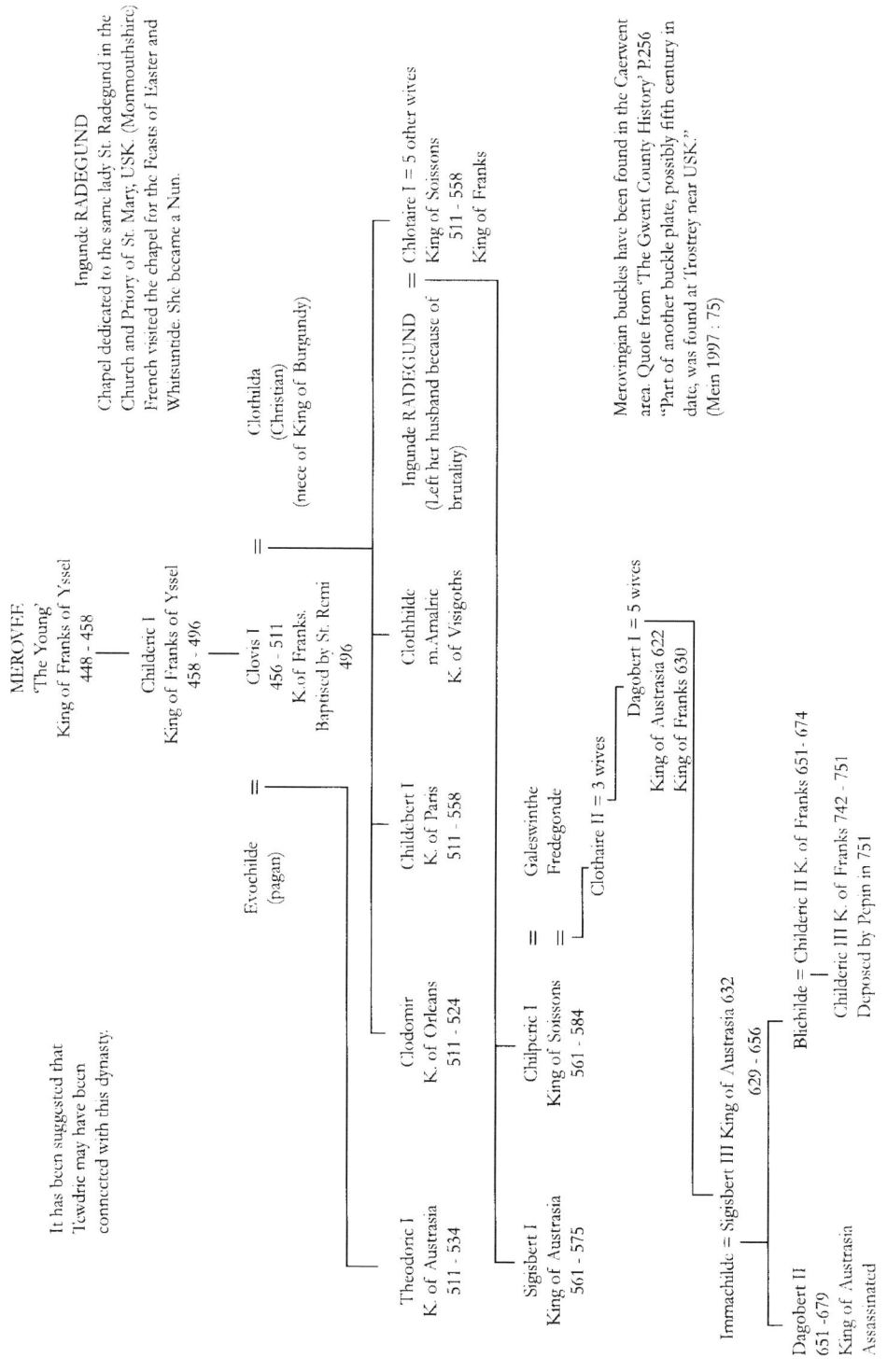

5. Christian Merovingian monarchs were buried in the Abbey of St. Denis, Paris

a petition sent in 1404 by a lawyer, 'Adam of Usk', to the Pope requesting his support we learn an intriguing fact:

> within the walls of the said monastery is a certain chapel built in honour of St. Radegund, a virgin nun, formerly queen of France, to which men of that country pay great devotion and which they often and especially at the feasts of Easter and Pentecost are wont to visit.[5]

Who was this saint who inspired pilgrimages by members of the French aristocracy each year at Easter and Whitsuntide to her chapel in Usk?

Radegunda was the wife of a Merovingian king, Chlotar I, Theodoric's youngest brother. A Thuringian princess by birth, she was captured by Chlotar in his war against her country when he allegedly killed her brother. She found such brutal behaviour barbaric. Despite her rank as queen, she lived piously and frugally, tending the sick and the poor and eventually was permitted to leave her husband to become a nun. She later founded a convent at Poitiers, where she died in 587. The bishop and historian St. Gregory of Tours attended her funeral. Her exemplary life led to her canonisation, thus making Radegunda one of the first Merovingian saints.

Tewdric and Radegunda linked Tintern Parva and Usk together and, however extraordinary it appeared, the link was the Merovingian dynasty of France. The two saints were contemporaries, dying within eight years of each other. The cult of St. Radegunda had spread across the Channel to Wales. The petition to the Pope on behalf of the Convent of Usk was sent in 1404. Her name may mean nothing to the majority of people today but it is clear from the date of the letter that she was the object of veneration at Usk for over 800 years. Frenchmen visited this country regularly to worship at her shrine. Why, I wondered, did they take the trouble to do that instead of visiting the convent where she was buried at Poitiers in France? Was it her Merovingian status?

Tewdric's grave at Mathern was turned into a shrine. One bishop had his heart interred there. At the bottom of a small hill nearby an ancient well can still be seen. Around its waters legends concerning Tewdric accrued. Today people still talk of Tewdric's cave at Tintern. If, as some think, that cave was situated near the site of St. Michael's Church, then it, too, would have been a special place, venerated because of its association with a royal saint centuries before Edward VI.

Although she lived much earlier, Radegunda is a reminder of the strong French influence in England from the time of the Norman Conquest. The annual pilgrimages from France to Usk indicate how strong her cult was in Wales. If, as seems likely, her importance arose from her perceived status as a Merovingian queen as well as her reputed sanctity, then we should note that sanctity and royalty are linked together in Tewdric as well. In addition he has also been credited with possible Merovingian antecedents. Was that common lineage a factor to be taken into account in any consideration of the mystery emerging around St. Michael's?

Is there any more evidence of a Merovingian presence in the area? New research, archival and archaeological, constantly enables us to revise our knowledge and enrich our understanding of a particular period. So it was exciting for me to read at this juncture of certain finds documented in the first volume of *The Gwent County History*, published in 2004.

Just eight miles south of Usk lies Caerleon. Here the Romans garrisoned the Second Augusta legion during their occupation. In discussing the fate of the fortress after their departure, a contributor to *The Gwent County History* describes the discovery of belt buckles in the area. He continues:

> Interestingly, similar artefacts have been recovered from Caerwent. A group of late belt buckles or buckle fragments with unrecorded contexts has been known for some time (Hawkes and Dunning 1961). Particularly important are three distinctive triangular buckles, one recovered from House VIII in Insula 4 in 1909. Such cast-in-one buckles appeared in the fourth century and became widespread in post-Roman Europe, giving rise to large seventh-century Merovingian buckles. One of the Caerwent examples was very well made, with a ridged tongue piece ending in a stylised animal head … Part of another buckle plate, possibly fifth century in date, was found at Trostrey.[6]

These buckles were found at different locations in the area during excavations in the twentieth century. They ranged in date from the fourth to the seventh centuries. Since their design is recognisably Merovingian they are indicators of a related Merovingian presence in the area.

Buckles are an item of dress that allows a society to express itself in art. These examples display such decorative flourishes as outward facing horses and dolphins confronting each other. Their discovery so many hundreds of years after the events leading to their being lost or abandoned provides a further clue in our enquiry. They tell us something of the interests of the society as well as its wealth. Such skills lead one to ask what else we know of Merovingian art. We can get some idea of this from the discovery of the tomb of one Merovingian monarch, Childeric I, who died in AD 481. He was buried at Tournai in France. The treasures interred with him are described by J.M. Wallace-Hadrill:

> His grave, discovered in 1653, yielded treasure, the small remaining part of which proves that he was laid to rest with magnificent war-gear, a cloak embroidered with some three hundred gold 'cicadas', a fine gold bracelet and buckles, a crystal globe and a miniature bull's head in gold, the severed

head of his warhorse caparisoned in precious materials, a signet-ring bearing his name and showing him wearing his hair over his shoulders, a purse of one hundred gold coins and a box of two hundred ornamental, silver coins.[7]

Evidently they had both the skilled craftsmen and precious materials necessary to create priceless works of art. We can only regret that so few of them seem to have survived. Time and again throughout history we read of great artistic creations of one era disappearing in another.

Childeric was buried in splendour in 481; Tewdric died *c.* 595. One hundred years separate them but Merovingian art doubtless continued to flourish during that time. If Tewdric was the son of Theodoric, then he was also the grandson of Clovis I. His grandmother would have been the first wife of Clovis: Evochilde, a pagan. The conversion and baptism of Clovis inevitably entailed the baptism of his other four sons by Clothilde, his second wife, for she was already a Christian. The decision of Clotaire, Clovis's youngest son, to release Radegunda from their marriage to become a nun is more the act of a fellow-Christian than a pagan. A pagan would hardly have been so accomodating. Unexpected though it may be, it looks as if Tewdric might have been Radegunda's nephew by marriage and that would be another link in the chain between Tewdric's kingdom in Wales and Merovingian France.

CHAPTER FOUR

Merovingian Visitors

I HAD ALREADY BEEn alerted to a Merovingian connection with one group of drawings, in John Byrom's extraordinary collection. Only a few of the 516 drawings held direct clues to their meaning, but one card did so in a striking way.

It is a triangle in shape and, like so many of the drawings, contains a highly organised pattern of geometry. Unlike the other drawings, however, this one had a series of dates written down the left-hand side. Each date was associated in the margin with a straight line in the overall geometric plan. Enigmatic but deliberate, the dates pointed the way to somewhere or something like stepping stones through time. After prolonged study of this drawing and others in the group to which it seemed to belong, I came to the conclusion that the geometry in them was related to the ground plans of certain churches in this country. To verify the correlation of a drawing to a building, I had acetates made of the appropriate geometrical drawing which I then superimposed on a ground plan of the relevant building to decide if the 'match' was consistent and appeared meaningful. In this way I was able to conclude that the dated drawing was concerned with Westminster Abbey. The match revealed a most interesting feature – intersections in the geometry coincided with a number of important positions in the ground plan of the Abbey.

That was in 1992. In December 2005, a spokesman for the Abbey announced that the site of the original tomb of its founder, Edward the Confessor, had been rediscovered in October that year. The plan they produced showing its position coincided with intersections visible on the Byrom drawing. Here was clear confirmation that I had identified the drawing correctly as connected with the Abbey and that the geometry on it was used to convey information in a hidden form. Moreover, it also meant that whoever was responsible for the drawing knew those facts at the time it was drawn.

The earliest date however – 713 – was not identifiable with a physical spot in the Abbey. Its importance seems to lie in it being the first of the dates and in being a commemoration of an event in Merovingian France. It was recorded by James Anderson in his *Royal Genealogies* (1732).

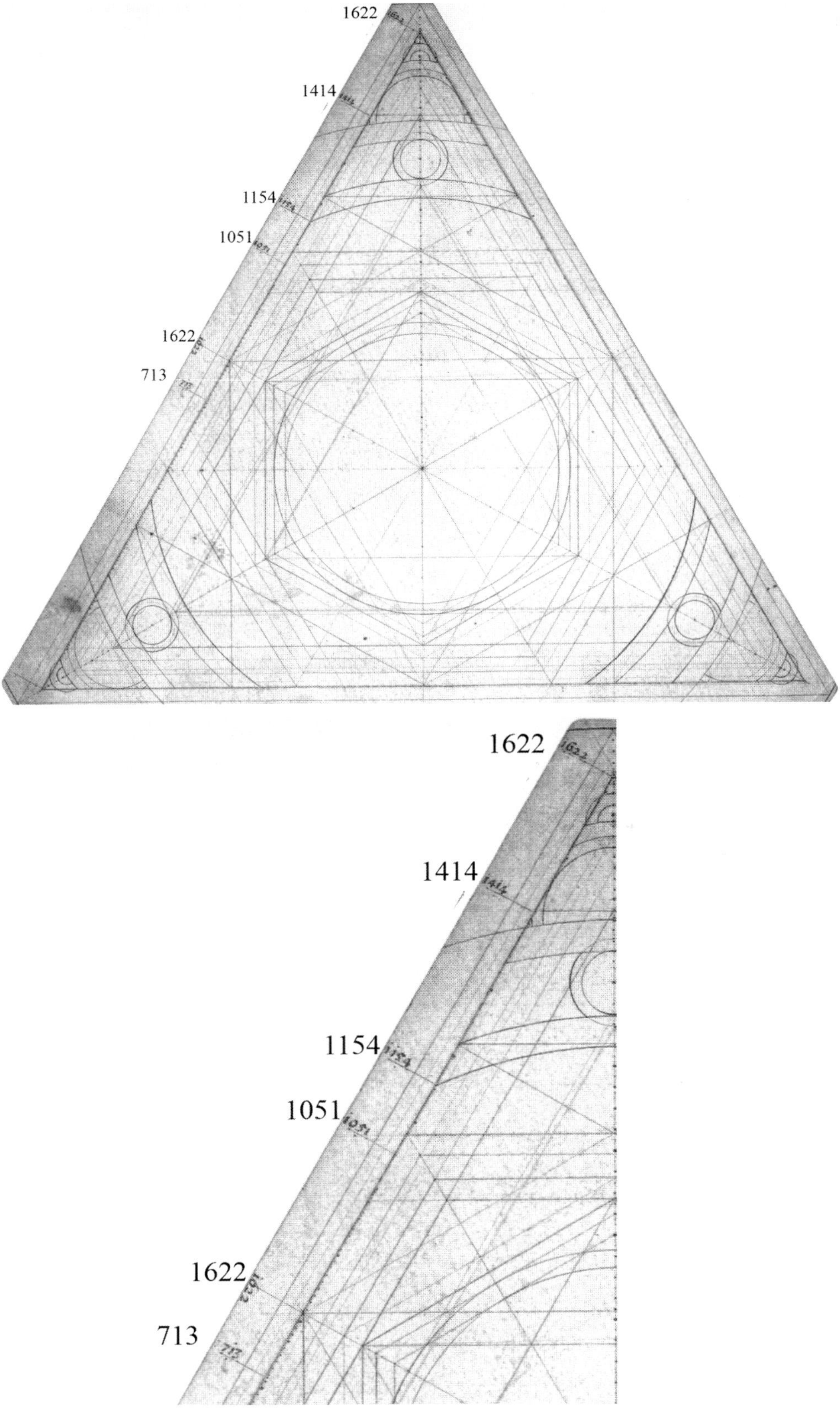

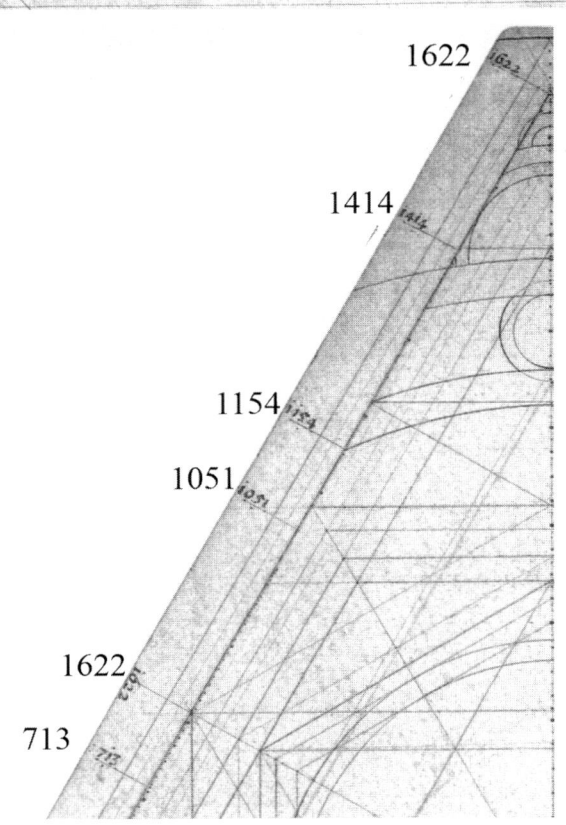

6. Dated geometric triangle

Anderson was a Scottish Presbyterian minister and prominent Freemason who produced his *Constitutions* in 1723, laying down what he considered were the fundamental regulations of Freemasonry after the foundation of Grand Lodge.

When Tewdric fell in battle defending his small Welsh kingdom in AD 595, the Merovingians had been ruling part of France and Germany for almost 120 years. These men seem to have combined the roles of king and chief priest and remained above and outside the day-to-day running of the country. That was the function of another figure, called the 'Major Domus' or 'mayor of the palace'. He held the reins of government. This division of authority between the monarch and his first minister was bound to be a cause of tension. By the beginning of the eighth century an internal power struggle between the two was under way and in 713 the current 'Major Domus', Grimoald, was assassinated in Liège.

The assassination was intended to facilitate a major shift in power in the Frankish kingdom. This was eventually achieved by Charles Martel. He started out as the 'mayor of the palace' in Austrasia, the eastern part of the Frankish kingdom. By the time he died in 741 he had reunited once more the divided kingdom of the Franks. What is important for us to remember is that Martel was not a member of the Merovingian dynasty and ruled without aspiring to make himself king.

The Merovingians did extraordinarily well to maintain their power, even nominally, from the fourth to the eighth century AD. The Dark Ages was not a period when genealogy was reliable nor could it guarantee succession by right. On the contrary, power belonged to the strongest and changed hands frequently. Myth frequently endowed the origins of kings with glamour. Individual monarchs with great ability like Clovis I gave substance to that glamour and that substance was the immense wealth acquired in both land and material riches. The Roman Church saw in Clovis's united kingdom a structure which could help it grow and spread in western Europe.

So, when Martel set out to take over the Frankish kingdom, he did not do so by right of birth. He was the illegitimate son of a 'mayor of the palace' and succeeded in his ambition by sheer strength and determination. Eventually Martel was succeeded by his son, Pippin III, who was eager to ally himself and his kingdom with the papacy. In 750 he wrote to Pope Zacharias asking, 'Is it wise to have kings who hold no power of control?' The Pope replied, 'It is better to have a king able to govern. By apostolic authority I bid that you be crowned king of the Franks.'[1] In November 751 Pippin was duly anointed king at Soissons by Archbishop Boniface and thus established the Carolingian dynasty, named after his father, Charles Martel. Pippin's own son Charlemagne became the greatest

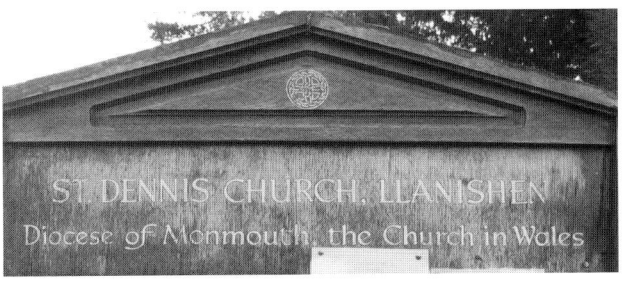

7. Church of St. Dennis, Llanishen

ruler in Europe and was crowned Holy Roman Emperor in 800. By this time some kind of genealogical continuity began to be desirable. To strengthen their claims to the throne both Pippin III and Charlemagne married princesses of the Merovingian bloodline.

Among the many legends and myths surrounding the Merovingians is one concerned with their hair. Like Samson in the Old Testament they let their hair grow long for it was believed that the source of their strength and miraculous powers lay in their hair. A signet ring of Childeric I shows him with hair down to his shoulders. As a symbol of virility a tuft of hair has been found concealed in an eighth-century belt buckle. Over the years long hair may also have become an indication of social standing for an exclusive group of nobles. Be that as it may, it is significant that when Pippin III assumed the kingship, Pope Stephen ordered that the head of Childeric III should be shorn of its locks. To be tonsured in this way 'was meant as a humiliation that no ruler could survive'. In this connection, Wallace-Hadrill makes the interesting suggestion that the anointing of the Carolingian monarchs with oil may have been to compensate for the breaking of an oath of loyalty to the Merovingians first made at the baptism of Clovis in Rheims rather than to compensate for the loss of magical properties believed to reside in the hair of the deposed dynasty.

At this point we need to return from speculation to the tangible reality of the drawing in John Byrom's collection that is inscribed with dates. The first three dates in chronological order are 713, 1051 and 1154. We have already noted that 713 points to an attempt to change the fortunes of the Merovingian dynasty. 1051 was the date when Edward the Confessor sought to effect another dynastic change by promising the throne of England to William the Conqueror. We should not, perhaps, be surprised that 1154, the year Henry II succeeded to the throne, marks another change of dynasty, for Henry II was the first of fourteen Plantagenet kings of England.

The coronation of Henry II and his consort Eleanor, Duchess of Aquitaine, took place in Westminster Abbey on 19 December 1154. The ceremony was conducted with great splendour. The crown was one originally commissioned by William the Conqueror in imitation of the imperial crown worn by the Holy Roman Emperor Charlemagne. Henry was determined to proclaim the importance of the event. The deliberate allusion to Charlemagne in the coronation crown was intended by both William the Conqueror and Henry II to equate their accession with his imperial status, a status strengthened in Charlemagne's case by his marriage to a Merovingian.

The kingdom of Henry II stretched from the north of England across the western part of France to the Pyrenees. The son of the Count of Anjou, he was very much at home on the Continent. Eleanor of Aquitaine was an intelligent and formidable woman. Her first marriage to Louis VII had been annulled on the grounds of consanguinity. The reality was that she produced only two daughters and not the male heir required by French law. Within months she married Henry and bore him five sons and three daughters. I was intrigued to learn that she, like the pilgrims to Usk, was a devotee of the cult of the Merovingian saint, Radegunda.

Henry II and Eleanor spent much of their time in France. At Chinon above the river Vienne in Anjou Henry built one of his favourite residences, the Chateau of St. George. It was here he received news in 1166 of Thomas Becket's attempt to excommunicate him in their bitter quarrel over the king's authority over the church. Here, too, Henry died in 1189.

Chinon was also the site of a cave inhabited by a sixth-century hermit known simply as John of Chinon. Born in Brittany, he moved to Chinon where he lived in poverty just outside the town. Here he was visited regularly by Queen Radegunda and became her spiritual father, reassuring her when she decided to leave her Merovingian husband Chlotaire to become a nun. After his death John was sealed up in the cell, which became a place of veneration. What was it about this man and Radegunda that made such an impression on Eleanor of Aquitaine some 500 years later? Her devotion went deep enough to inspire Eleanor to build a church enclosing the hermit's cell within it. Here she could come just as Radegunda had done herself years earlier. What caused such passion in her? In 1964 a mural was discovered on the wall of the church dating from the last decade of the twelfth century. It depicts a procession on horseback of five figures, two of them crowned. It is generally accepted that the female wearing a crown is Eleanor of Aquitaine. The other figures in the group are members of her family. The implications of this tableau were to be long-lasting.

The marriage of Eleanor and Henry II in 1152 was riven with conflict because of his persistent infidelities. Although she bore him eight children, he sought unsuccessfully to have their marriage annulled and was determined to limit Eleanor's ambitions. Henry, eleven years her junior, even tried to persuade her to become a nun. However, by the time this mural was painted she was a widow, for Henry died at Chinon in 1189.

Eleanor lived for another fifteen years, dying at the age of eighty-two. It can be no coincidence that, centuries later, another determined and ambitious French Queen, Anne of Austria, at odds with her husband (in this instance Louis XIII) renovated the same Chapel of St. Radegunda in honour of the saint who had resisted her husband's will. The difficult relationships with their husbands was the common denominator between the three queens. To Eleanor and Anne she was a patron saint to whom they looked in their distress and frustration for guidance and support.

Long before Henry II succeeded to the throne, Geoffrey of Monmouth had produced his *History of the Kings of Britain*. In it he deals with the figure of Arthur and the legends surrounding him. These stories captivated the attention of people as much then as now and spread throughout England and France. Eleanor, of course, was regarded as a champion of the idea of courtly love, a literary movement in France in which troubadours and poets celebrated the chivalric devotion of the knight for his lady. People began to flock to sites associated with the legendary king. One of these was at Caerleon in Monmouthshire and another at Glastonbury. When Glastonbury Abbey was devastated by fire in 1184, Henry granted a Charter for its restoration. The monastery was described as 'founded by the disciples of our Lord themselves'.[2] From this it would appear that Henry believed that Joseph of Arimathea was its founder.

His reason for thinking that takes us back to the beginnings of Christianity and the later years of Joseph of Arimathea. From the New Testament we learn that Joseph was the owner of the sepulchre in which the body of Jesus Christ was laid after the Crucifixion. He is described in the Gospel of Mark (Chapter 15, Verse 43) as 'an honourable counsellor, which also waited for the kingdom of God' and by St. John (Chapter 19, Verse 38) as 'a disciple of Jesus' who 'secretly, for fear of the Jews' asked Pilate for the body of Jesus so that he could bury it. After the Crucifixion, according to several early accounts, Joseph was imprisoned, but on his release sailed to Marseille in AD 35. There is also a tradition that he came to Britain at about the same time to preach the gospel. Landing in the West Country, he built a church at Glastonbury dedicated to St. Mary. Later a monastery was added to the site. Documents that miraculously survived the destruction of Glastonbury Abbey at the time of the Dissolution of the Monasteries describe him as a 'decurio', or overseer of tin mines. Tin was regularly transported by Jewish tin traders from Britain to Marseille and Narbonne in Gaul. This commerce, therefore, provides an historical structure and explanation for Joseph's presence in France and Britain. How that commercial role is reconciled with his mission of conversion is another matter.

Years before the devastating fire of 1184, Henry and Eleanor visited Glastonbury. The king even ordered a search for Arthur's grave and, after the king's death, in 1190 bones thought to be those of Arthur and Queen Guinevere were discovered, together with a leaden cross inscribed, 'Here lies Arthur, the famous king in the island of Avalon'. The bones were reburied in the Abbey and ever since Glastonbury has been associated with Avalon where Arthur was said to have been taken before he died.[3] It is hardly surprising that Glastonbury grew into the largest monastery in Britain. It provided the twelve Benedictine monks who formed the first community at the Monastery of Westminster, later Westminster Abbey. Until its destruction Glastonbury remained second in importance in the country to Westminster.

The triangular drawing and the three dates had given me further clues to the relevance of the Merovingians to my quest in Tintern. In addition there was the local folklore about Tewdric, his possible Merovingian pedigree and the indisputable presence of a chapel to St. Radegunda at Usk nearby. Such clues could not be ignored.

Further tangible evidence was to be found in the letters patent of Edward VI drawn up in 1553. The way this document was set out, associating Tintern Parva and Usk together in a special way, must have been deliberate. There could be no doubt of that. The young king and his Council would not want any ambiguity over his wishes. But behind the grant to Pembroke and Clarke, there are implications – of something known about these two sites but not openly stated, probably because it was not for general consumption.

Reviewing what I had learned to date, it seemed to me that the title and office of Earl of Pembroke was repeatedly bound up with the Tintern site. Down the centuries, no matter which dynasty of Pembrokes was in power – Marshall, de Valence or Herbert – certain holders of that title appeared to be given special responsibilities. Name followed name stirring strong but hidden undercurrents.

The first Earl of Pembroke was Gilbert FitzGilbert, created in 1138 by King Stephen, the successor of Henry I. It was his uncle Walter Fitz Richard de Clare who had founded Tintern Abbey in 1131. It is not surprising therefore that Gilbert was also a benefactor of the Abbey and was buried there in 1148. In addition he was, I noticed, a benefactor of the Templars. He was succeeded by his son, Richard. It was Richard who founded the church of St. Mary and the Priory at Usk with its chapel dedicated to St. Radegunda. He continued his family's tradition as a benefactor of Tintern Abbey as well.

Twenty-two years later, around 1170, the same Richard was seeking his fortune in Ireland. The most likely reason was a promise he had made to Dermot, the exiled King of Leinster, to help him regain his kingdom in exchange for the hand of Eva, his daughter, and the right of succession to his throne.

Richard married Eva the following year. A series of successful battles in Ireland aroused the jealousy of King Henry II who brought him to heel but allowed him to retain some of his Irish conquests. In 1173 he was campaigning at Henry's side in France and Henry made him Constable of Gisors. He died in Dublin in 1176 and was buried in Holy Trinity Church.

Later, in the reign of Elizabeth I, when Sir Henry Sidney was Lord Deputy of Ireland, his daughter, Mary, married the current Earl of Pembroke and her father restored Richard's effigy in honour of the family's alliance with the Pembrokes. Richard's only son, Gilbert, was still a young boy when his father died and was never invested with the title of Earl before dying himself around 1185.

However in 1185 the earldom passed to Gilbert's sister, Isabel. She was referred to as the Countess of Pembroke, daughter of Richard and Eva. When she married William Marshall the Pembroke family name changed accordingly to Marshall.

William Marshall started life as the fourth son of an obscure Wiltshire baron and at the age of twenty-two laid the foundations of his future greatness in a characteristic display of bravery. In March 1168 he was in France serving with his uncle, Earl Patrick of Salisbury, and accompanying Queen Eleanor out riding. The royal party was ambushed but the queen managed to escape while the earl was fatally wounded. It was the young William Marshall who held off the attackers before being wounded and captured. Tall, well-built and handsome, he had already attracted the notice of the queen by his performance in tournaments and she paid the ransom for his release. He was for ever after devoted to Eleanor and her children. Stephen Langton, the Archbishop of Canterbury, described him as 'the best knight who ever lived'. He served four kings in succession: Henry II, Richard the Lion Heart, John and Henry III.

Marshall was present at the deathbed of Henry II in Chinon and escorted the dead king's body to its last resting place in Fontevrault Abbey. King Richard the Lion Heart gave him Isabel, Countess of Pembroke, in marriage. By then Marshall was forty-two years old. Queen Eleanor was in charge of the arrangements for Richard's coronation and as a mark of special favour to Marshall he was appointed to carry the gold sceptre and cross during the service.

He supported King John's claim to succeed Richard and worked tirelessly for him during his reign. On the succession of Henry III at the age of nine, William Marshall was the unanimous choice for Regent and successfully fought off the French invaders hoping to take over the kingdom. He founded several religious communities and carried on the Pembroke tradition as a benefactor of Tintern Abbey and the Templars.

Marshall died in May 1219 after a long illness during which he was received into the Order of the Templars by the Master of the Temple Church, London, and was buried there. One year later his wife, Isabel, died and was interred at Tintern Abbey.

Between 1219 and 1245 the earldom passed to each of his five sons in turn, each of them dying without issue, almost as if they had become the victims of some fatal curse. Two of them were buried with their father at the Temple Church and two at Tintern Abbey, demonstrating the twin loyalties of the dynasty.

With the death of the five Marshall brothers the right to the title passed to one of William Marshall's five daughters, Joan. Her daughter, Joan de Munchensy, married William de Valence. We noted his connections with the Manor of Pondesbourne and William Clarke in Chapter Two. William de Valence was the half-brother and close companion of Henry III. In addition to his considerable estates in the south of England, he was closely linked with the area around Tintern. Two weeks before his marriage in 1247, Henry III had given him Goodrich Castle just north of Monmouth. He developed the fortifications there extensively as a bastion from which he could control the countryside around. The castle remained in the family for generations.

By 1247 the chapel dedicated to St. Radegunda at Usk Priory had been built. It was, therefore, with great interest that I noted that the marriage took place, soon after de Valence arrived in England, on 13 August, the anniversary of that saint's death. Her feast day was his wedding day. Although we have seen and can understand the devotion of Eleanor of Aquitaine to Radegunda, it still comes as a surprise that the same day was chosen for this particular wedding. What was the reason? The last five earls of Pembroke, all uncles of the bride, had died without issue and it is possible that Radegunda's feast day might have seemed an auspicious occasion, one that might make the union fruitful. Did William and Joan hope to gain a special blessing from the royal saint whose sanctity stemmed from a refusal to submit to a meaningless, enforced marriage? The date chosen would seem to have lent an extra weight to the solemnity of the vows exchanged that day.

We have already seen the importance to Queen Eleanor of St. Radegunda's Chapel at Chinon. That was understandable since the Merovingians were an important part of French history. But that pockets of the Merovingian legacy were to be found in Wales was altogether unexpected. Radegunda's chapel at Usk lay within the new domain of William de Valence. The marriage might even have been solemnised there. Members of the de Clare dynasty, powerful and supportive, were still in evidence in the area. We have also seen signs of an earlier, Merovingian presence – in the belt buckles dating from the fourth to the seventh centuries. Whatever the reason for the choice of date, some 660 years had elapsed between Radegunda's death in France and the wedding of William and Joan in Britain. One is led to conclude that there was something very special about this marriage arranged for his brother by the king and celebrated on this of all days. There is also something very special about this area.

Henry III heaped honours on his young half-brother. William de Valence was still only twenty-two when Henry knighted him some eight weeks after his marraige on 13 October, and he was naturally anxious to distinguish himself in tournaments before the king. Although never formally invested with the title of Earl of Pembroke he was regarded and styled as such because his wife had inherited the earldom from her grandfather, William Marshall. The date Henry chose to knight William de Valence was carefully chosen, as we shall see. The marking of anniversaries was just as important to the Crown as it was to the Church. It was part of the ritual and panoply of government.

In return for all his honours William de Valence served the king well not only in battle but also on several diplomatic missions to the King of France. He fought alongside Henry III against rebels in England, and from 1270 to 1272 saw service in the Holy Land where he accompanied the king's son, the future Edward I, bringing back a cross with a base wrought in gold and emeralds. Two of his children were buried in the Sanctuary at Westminster Abbey near the famous cosmati pavement. William was made commander of the army in West Wales and defeated uprisings in Snowdonia and South Wales. After his death in 1296 he, too, was buried in the Abbey in a splendid tomb covered in Limoges enamel work. Much of the decoration of his effigy has since been lost, but originally its exquisite workmanship proclaimed his importance in the realm.

13 October was an appropriate date for Henry III to bestow a knighthood on William de Valence. It was a date of great importance for the new line of Norman kings of England. Edward the Confessor, as we have seen, promised the English throne to William the Conqueror. The Saxon Council chose instead Harold who was defeated at the battle of Hastings by his rival on 14 October 1066. Before Edward died, he had started to rebuild Westminster Abbey in the new Norman style. The work was not completed until after his death and he was buried in the new Abbey before the High Altar. Later, after his canonisation in 1161, Henry II decided to build a new shrine in his honour and on 13 October 1163 Edward's remains were reburied with great pomp and ceremony in the presence of the king and Thomas Becket, by then Archbishop of Canterbury.

There Edward's body remained for over a hundred years until 1269, when on the same date, 13 October, it was transferred to yet another, more magnificent, shrine built this time by Henry III who was in the process of rebuilding the Abbey completely. Edward the Confessor, after all, was not just an ordinary saint. He was the last Saxon king of England. His choice of a French successor was ultimately the reason why Henry III himself was king. Thereafter 13 October was celebrated with great solemnity by the Abbey every year until the monasteries were dissolved by Henry VIII. Today Edward the Confessor's Feast Day is still celebrated on 13 October, and remains an important date in the Abbey's year. In 1272 Henry III himself was buried in the empty tomb of Edward the Confessor, to be moved eventually to another part of the Abbey.

13 October was also chosen by a later king as the date for the creation of another Earl of Pembroke. In 1339 Edward III ennobled Laurence de Hastings as Earl of Pembroke on the grounds that he was descended from the eldest sister of Aymer de Valence, Earl of Pembroke and son of William de Valence. Evidently the date still mattered in royal ceremonial, although in the intervening years it had gathered another, less pleasant, association.

Today, Friday 13 October 1307 is remembered chiefly as the date when all the Knights Templar in France were arrested prior to their trial and destruction. The end of the Order was achieved with such ruthlessness that, ever since, Friday the thirteenth has been regarded as the most inauspicious date in the calendar.

However, what had caught my attention was the importance these two dates had for William de Valence. He was married on 13 August and knighted on 13 October. No doubt the significance of both dates was clear to him. After a long and eventful life he died fighting at Bayonne in 1296. His widow, Joan, died one month before the destruction of the Templars in 1307.

The recurrence of dates and years seemed to link a number of people connected with our story. 1291 was such a year, proving to be significant in several ways. It was the year that Acres, the last of the crusaders' fortresses in Palestine, was captured by the Saracens. Its loss marked the end of the European dream of a Christian Holy Land that had begun two hundred years earlier with the First Crusade. It was also the year that the heart of Henry III was taken from England to France.

Henry III's ambition in rebuilding Westminster Abbey was to provide a worthy monument for Edward the Confessor. When he died in November 1272 before the work was completed his body had been placed temporarily before the High Altar and laid in the grave that had once held the Confessor's remains. There it stayed for nineteen years. Then in 1291 Henry's body, without his heart, was interred in the tomb specially built for him by his son Edward I. That same year, in accordance with Henry's wishes, his heart was taken by the Abbot of Westminster, Walter de Wenlocke, and given to the Abbess of Fontevrault to be buried in the last resting place of Henry III's mother, Isabella of Angouleme, and his grandparents, Henry II and Eleanor of Aquitaine. His body remained in

The Hidden Chapter

the country he had ruled but his heart went back to the family he had loved. This act of family devotion is illustrated in the canopy above a window in the Abbey's nave. There it is witnessed by Edmund Crouchback, Edward I's brother and William de Valence, Edward's uncle, both of them slain at Bayonne in 1296. Below this tableau the two main figures in the window are King Edward I, the son of Henry III, and Abbot Walter de Wenlocke.

But in 1307 Edward I, Abbot Walter de Wenlocke, and Edward's daughter Joan d'Acres all died. So, too, did the widow of William de Valence.

Joan had been born in Acres while her father was there on crusade in 1270. In 1290 she married Gilbert de Clare, the seventh in line of the powerful Earls of Gloucester and Hertford. But Edward insisted that the Earl handed over his lands to him and only returned them when Gilbert disinherited the children of his first marriage in favour of any offspring from Joan. This manipulation of inheritance laws was used several times by the king to suit his own interests. In this instance it meant that, after Gilbert's death in 1295, Joan became the sole owner of the estate of Tintern Parva, holding it for life – or as long as her father saw fit.

Two years later Edward I decided to marry her to Amadeus V of Savoy only to discover that she had secretly married a young squire, Sir Ralph de Montherimer, a member of her first husband's household whom she had previously persuaded her father to knight. Edward I had a notoriously violent temper but in later life he learned to keep it in check. Joan must have pleaded well for her husband, for although de Montherimer was imprisoned in Bristol Castle, a few months later he was released and all the Clare estates were restored to him and Joan. However her death in April 1307 was followed shortly after by the death of Edward I in July. Her only son (Edward's grandson) Gilbert de Clare, inherited the earldom and lands, including Tintern Parva. Seven years later, in 1314, he was cut down in savage, hand-to-hand combat at the battle of Bannockburn and the fate of Tintern Parva came under review again, as we shall see in the next chapter. For the moment it is sufficient to note that Edward I had taken deliberate steps to ensure that Tintern Parva was in royal hands.

In pursuing the changes of ownership of Tintern Parva at this time, I encountered another in the growing number of surprises that seemed to be accompanying my investigations.

I learned from Bradney that the customary inventory of land and property made after Joan's death included the church of St. Dennis at Llanishen, four miles from Tintern Parva. Here in a remote part of the Welsh countryside was a church dedicated to a saint inextricably linked with the Merovingian monarchy, whose fame and importance was due in the first place to the prominence given to him by the long-haired kings.

Originally, St. Denis (or Denys in old French spelling) was one of seven bishops sent from Rome to promote Christianity in Gaul in the third century. He became the first Bishop of Paris, but was persecuted by local pagans, imprisoned and beheaded. As with so many early saints extraordinary legends grew up around his death – one was that he managed to walk some distance from where he had been attacked carrying his severed head. A small church was built on the site which over the years became a place of pilgrimage. This was later replaced by a Benedictine abbey built by the Merovingian King Dagobert in 630, who embellished it with gold and precious stones, none of which survives today. There is, however, some evidence of an earlier Merovingian interest in the site by Clovis after his conversion to Christianity in 496. Clovis's first wife, Evochilde was a pagan but his second, Clothilde, was the Christian daughter of the King of Burgundy.

The small chapel at Llanishen was another reminder of the French dominance in this part of Wales. The distinguished genealogist Sir William Dugdale notes the existence of the church of St. Dionysius or Dennis alongside taxation returns for Tintern Abbey drawn up in 1291. That, as we know, was the year Acres fell and the year King Henry III's heart was transferred from Westminster Abbey to Fontevrault.

Many Merovingian priest-kings were educated and buried at the Abbey of St. Denis in Paris. Even Charles Martel, who replaced the Merovingian monarchy, had his tomb there and the new dynasty of Charlemagne was keen to be associated with the monastery. The future of the Abbey became intricately bound up with the fate of the long-haired monarchs and by 750 it had changed from a Merovingian to Carolingian community. A stabilising influence for the new dynasty, it became one of the richest and most famous abbeys in France. The present church, commenced in 1140, is one of the finest Gothic buildings in France. Its lasting grandeur is the work of the twelfth-century abbot Suger, the adviser to two French kings, Louis VI and VII.

Suger, a brilliant son of peasant stock, was educated at the Abbey of St. Denis. The saint's shrine had by now become an object of great veneration. Suger saw that the future of the French monarchy and the Abbey were closely intertwined. He set out deliberately to develop a symbolic relationship between the king and the saint. Louis VI had sent his son, the future Louis VII, to be educated under Suger at the Abbey, but insisted rightly that his religious studies should be balanced with lessons in statecraft and the skills of the medieval knight. On 25 July 1137 the young Louis, still only a youth of sixteen, married the fifteen-year-old Eleanor, Duchess of

Aquitaine. In this way his father hoped to strengthen the possessions and power of France. No one would have dreamed that eleven years later this marriage would be annulled and within months Eleanor would be the wife of Henry II and Queen of England.

The young prince was accompanied south to Aquitaine to meet his bride by a retinue of 500 knights. Abbot Suger went with him as one of his three advisers. One of the gifts Eleanor gave her young husband was a beautiful vase made of rock crystal, decorated with gold and pearls and the sign of the fleur de lys, the royal emblem of France. On 1 August on their journey home to Paris after their wedding the young couple learned of the death of Louis VI. They were now the King and Queen of France.

By 1144 Suger had completed the rebuilding of the Abbey of St. Denis. It was dedicated to the saint in the presence of Louis VII, his mother the Dowager Queen Adelaide and his wife Eleanor. Among the hundreds of guests filling the Abbey was Bernard of Clairvaux. He had been preaching the cause of the Second Crusade throughout France. The Abbey is an acknowledged masterpiece in stone, illumined by magnificent stained-glass windows. Its splendour inspired Henry III to rebuild Westminster Abbey on a similar grand scale. Among the many gold and silver ornaments was the vase Eleanor had given Louis as a wedding present. Prominently displayed, too, was the banner of St. Denis, the Oriflamme, together with the royal standard of the French kings. Suger had already persuaded Louis VI to carry the Oriflamme into battle as a rallying cry for victory. The promotion of the saint's national status through the Oriflamme now reached a new height.

On 7 June 1147 Louis VI and Eleanor lodged at the Abbey of St. Denis before setting out on the Second Crusade to the Holy Land. Next day in a ceremony deliberately filled with symbolism Louis appeared in the Abbey Church dressed as a simple pilgrim with a black tunic emblazoned with a red cross. The Pope handed to him the Oriflamme of St. Denis to take with him. The congregation cheered at the spectacle. As was intended, the ritual devised for this solemn occasion invested the enterprise with sacred overtones. After arriving in Jerusalem in May 1148, Louis laid the Oriflamme on the altar of the Church of The Holy Sepulchre, the site of Jesus's tomb. The Oriflamme was repeatedly used in this way to bind the people of France closer to their king. It continued to be carried into war by the king himself right up to the battle of Agincourt in 1415.

In this way St. Denis came to represent the spirit of France. His pre-eminence amongst French saints derives ultimately from his importance to Dagobert and the devotion and cultivation that king began to encourage with the abbey he built to house tombs of successive Merovingian monarchs. It is not surprising therefore that vestiges of the importance of St. Denis are to be found in this country when one considers how thorough was the rule of the last 'foreigners' to invade and seize control in Britain. It is only when we investigate the years of Norman French supremacy that we understand the richness and diversity of their legacy.

Again we have to remind ourselves that Edward the Confessor's choice of a French successor was a decision of immense importance. Today most people may be forgiven if they know so little about him. It is the Battle of Hastings, the arrow in the eye of Harold and his defeat that most of us remember from our school books with the help of the awe-inspiring visual heritage of Norman keep and castle. It comes as a shock to realise that 'the French connection' goes much deeper and wider.

We saw earlier how Henry II in the ceremonial of his coronation deliberately referred back to William the Conqueror by using his coronation crown. William had it designed to resemble the imperial crown of Charlemagne. That crown was something more than a statement of status or intent.

Edward the Confessor was the son of a Saxon king (Ethelred the Unready) and a French mother, Emma, daughter of Richard II, Duke of Normandy. After his father's death in 1016, Edward was driven out of England to live in exile in Normandy for twenty-five years. It is not surprising that when he returned in 1041 he brought many Normans with him or that he promised his throne to William. But that promise was not simply an act of gratitude. William, through his forebears, the Dukes of Normandy, was descended from Charlemagne. Since Charlemagne had deliberately married a Merovingian princess the bloodline of the Merovingians continued down to the Conqueror from Charlemagne's wife. In choosing the same coronation crown, Henry II was stating, amongst other things, his recognition of and link with that bloodline.

That recognition was another reason why Henry was so determined to honour Edward the Confessor by building a splendid new abbey for him at Westminster. It also helps to explain why the Abbey itself contains so many references to the 'French' origins of the English monarchs. One of the many intriguing features of the Abbey is the fate of the relics it once contained. The guide book to Westminster Abbey states that the relics were originally kept where the Chantry Chapel of Henry V now stands. However, after the Chantry was built

> they were moved to a chest placed between the tomb of Henry III and the shrine [of the confessor], and there remained until the dissolution of the Monastery. The most precious among them were: the Virgin Mary's Girdle presented by Edward the Confessor; a stone marked with the print of

8. Westminster Abbey (geometric features)

Christ's foot at the Ascension; His blood in a crystal vase and a piece of the Cross, set in jewels, brought from Wales, and given by Edward I; the head of St. Benedict brought from France and presented by Edward III ... But in 1540 came the dissolution of the Monastery; the Shrine was despoiled of its relics and the body of the saint was removed and buried in some obscure place.[4]

During the reign of Queen Mary I the body was restored to its final resting place but the alleged holy relics have never been found.

We have travelled a long way to understand the dates on the triangular drawing related to Westminster Abbey. That is because those dates are connected not just with English but French history as well. The same European dimension is evident in the last two dates on the card. It is time we looked at them: 1414 and 1622.

It will be seen that 1622 is special because it appears twice. Its first position draws the eye to a geometrical intersection in the centre of two concentric circles within a hexagon. When superimposed on the Abbey ground plan this intersection falls precisely at the entrance to the Choir. This is literally the source of the harmony to be heard during the Abbey's services and can, therefore, be taken as a symbol of harmony in a wider sense.

1622 was also the year that Count Michael Maier disappeared in Magdeburg amidst the chaos and confusion of the Thirty Years War. Maier was the court physician to the Holy Roman Emperor, Rudolf II and the promoter of philosophic ideals that he hoped would act as a means of uniting a Europe divided by bitter religious conflict between the Roman and the Protestant churches. After the Emperor's death, Maier spent some time in England between 1612 and 1616 cultivating both physicians and scholars such as Robert Fludd, and not surprisingly his name appears on other drawings in the Collection.

Maier's interest in science, alchemy and astrology puts him right at the centre of the tradition of John Dee and Francis Bacon. During his lifetime and for much of the seventeenth century he had a very high reputation for his learning. There is some evidence that he became acquainted with James I, for he sent him a famous birthday card illustrated with a rose and a cross. The two symbols are indicative of his attempt to synthesise both Christian and hermetic ideas in his work. The repetition of the date of his death at the apex of the triangle shows his importance to the creator of the drawing while at the same time suggesting an air of finality.

The last date on the drawing we have to address is 1414. It is to be found towards the top of the triangle and concerns the area of the Abbey now occupied by the Chantry Chapel of King Henry V (born at Monmouth). Commencing at the east end of the Confessor's shrine and leading

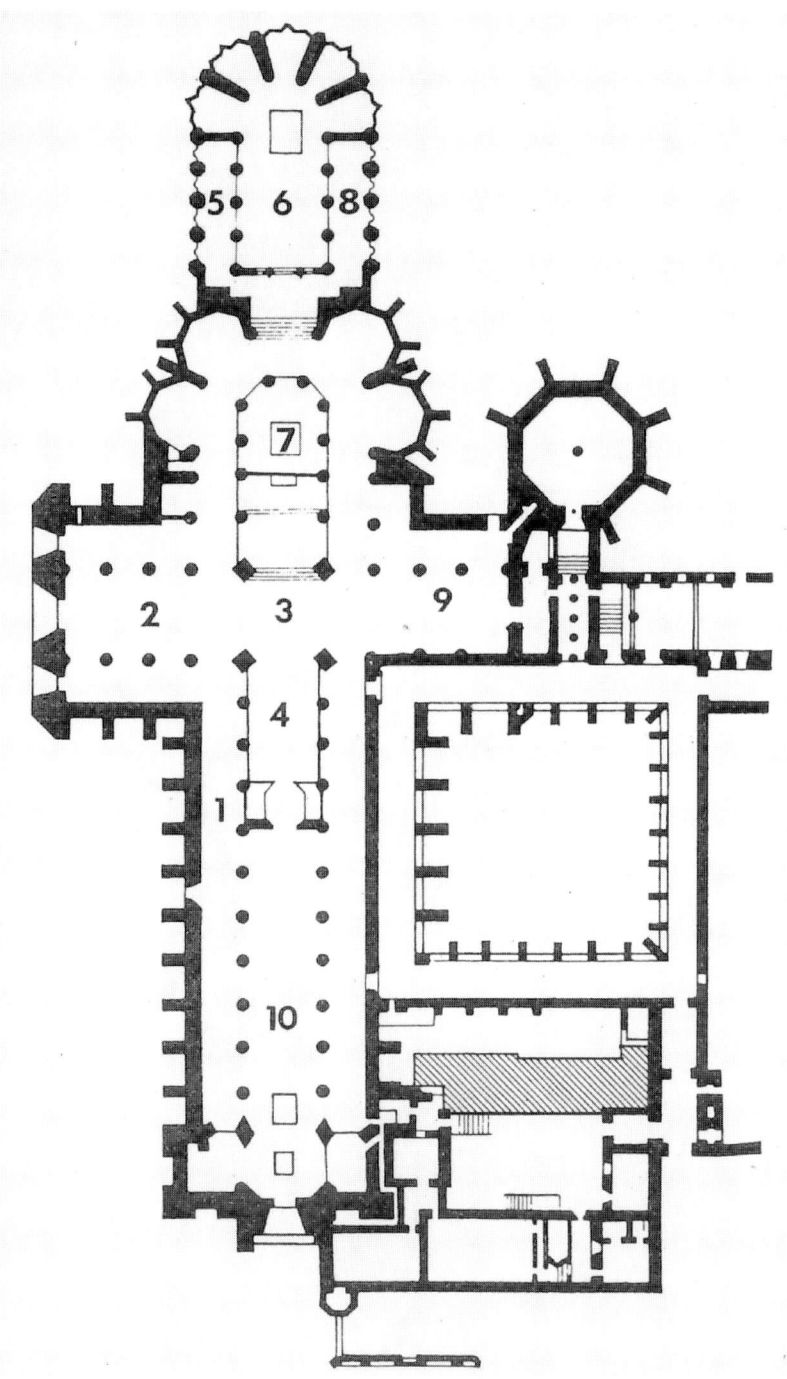

1 Musicians' Aisle
2 Statesmen's Aisle
3 The Lantern
4 The Choir
5 Tomb of Queen Elizabeth I
6 Chapel of King Henry VII
7 Chapel of St. Edward the Confessor
8 Tomb of Mary Queen of Scots
9 Poets' Corner
10 Poets' Nave

9. Ground plan of Westminster Abbey

eastward to the Chapel of Henry VII, Henry V's Chantry forms a link between the two. It was the original site of the Abbey's much-vaunted sacred relics, but when the Chantry was built these of necessity were moved to a chest placed on the north side between the tomb of Henry III and the Shrine.

Geometric lines on the triangular drawing mark the positions of all three chapels and the acetate of a ground plan of the Abbey placed on top of the drawing demonstrates how the two correlate; so much so that one line indicates the position of the Confessor's Shrine relative to the tomb of Henry III.

1414 was the year Henry V renewed England's claims to lost possessions in France, demanding the return of Normandy and Anjou. That claim led to war, and the victory of Agincourt memorably celebrated in Shakespeare's *Henry V*. The conflict with France on this occasion was ended by the marriage of Henry to Katherine, daughter of the French king. This was another attempt at political reconciliation.

Moreover the straight line in the drawing from 1414 draws the eye into the Chapel of Henry VII who, victorious at the battle of Bosworth, likewise sought the reconciliation of opposing sides in marriage. By marrying Elizabeth of York, Henry VII brought an end to the long and wasteful Wars of the Roses. At the same time he established a new dynasty with the House of Tudor. The two themes of the dated drawings are here again – dynastic change and reconciliation. However, when placed in context with others in the Collection what else does this particular drawing tell us?

The Hidden Chapter

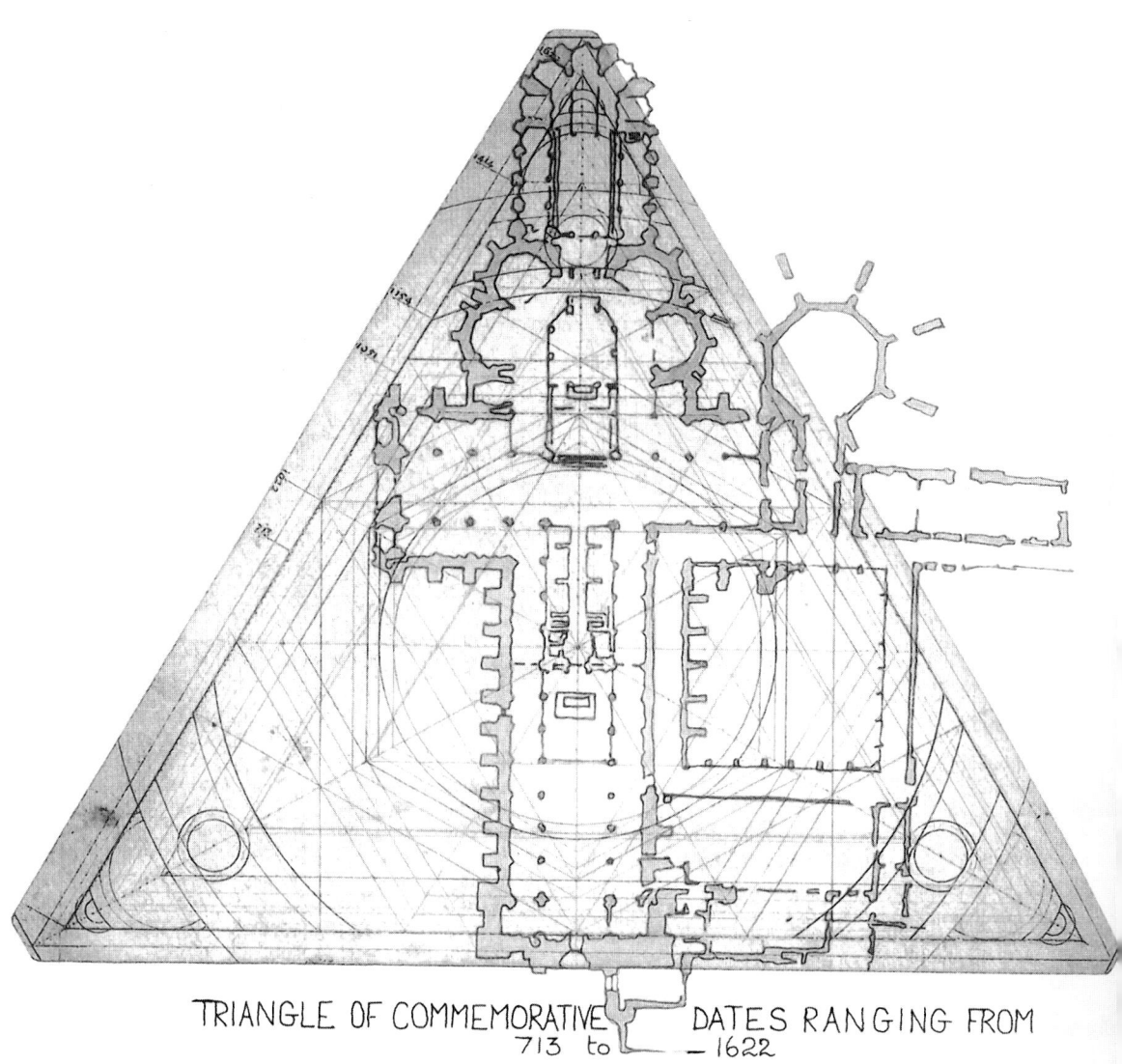

10. Layout of Westminster Abbey with triangle superimposed

CHAPTER FIVE

Royal Relics

THE TRIANGULAR CARD with dates on it was an important discovery in assessing Byrom's collection of drawings as a whole. By their very nature dates force one to think about what they are commemorating. A group of dates is even more compelling. Why those dates, and what do they have in common? Some become so well known that they are like shorthand, holding within their simple form many common associations. '1066' is one such date in England, fundamental to the country's history. Recent events in America have forever burned '9/11' into the nation's consciousness. Dates can hold surprising emotional power. The dates written down the left-hand margin of the triangular card were in effect a code of events with powerful associations for the encoder.

When I came to them centuries later, I asked myself what meaningful link there could be between a set of apparently random numbers on the card. I was helped appreciably in the first instance when I was able to place the card in the sequence concerned with churches and in particular with Westminster Abbey. I was helped further over time as my knowledge of the entire collection grew and particularly by my arrival, literally, at Tintern in pursuit of the brassworks.

Another factor must also be considered. There are in the Collection drawings from which printed copies were made. Examples of these are in existence. But there were no printed copies of the dated drawing and none has come to light. I believe this was deliberate. The information contained on the card was regarded as so important that it remained unique to its creator. He alone possessed the information *in this form*. It was for him to impart to those he chose to tell. Alternatively, of course, it could simply be a method of recording information that has been replaced and, so, lost with time.

Another drawing in the Collection is concerned with the Temple Church and is identifiable by a white Tau cross on a black background at its centre. These are the distinctive colours of the Knights Hospitaller of St. John. Historical associations with this drawing link it with the dated triangle and complement the information outlined in the previous chapter.

The Temple Church together with the rest of the Templar headquarters in London was given by Edward II to his cousin Aymer de Valence as a reward for his faithful service. In January 1308 he had been formally summoned to Edward II's coronation as Earl of Pembroke, the rank that, over the centuries, dignified many who had the king's ear. As we have seen, three of the previous Pembroke earls had been buried in the Temple Church: Aymer's great-grandfather William Marshall and his great-uncles, William and Gilbert Marshall.

Unfortunately Aymer died unexpectedly in 1324 while on an ambassadorial mission to France. He had already proved himself an able negotiator and diplomat several times to the king and his death was a blow to Edward II, whose reign was marked by emotional turbulence and political violence. Ultimately this led to the murder of Edward himself in 1327.

Trouble was caused by members of the king's own family. In addition to her son, Gilbert, Joan d'Acres, Edward II's sister, had three daughters by her first husband. These were Margaret, Eleanor and Elizabeth de Clare. It was Edward's misfortune to fall under the influence of the husbands of two of these nieces in turn. Margaret de Clare married Piers Gaveston and Eleanor married Hugh de Despenser. Gaveston's father had worked for Edward I, so no doubt this was how Piers first met Margaret de Clare and became a close friend of the young Prince Edward. Both Gaveston and Despenser were suspected of having homosexual relationships with him when he was king and both were killed. Gaveston's incompetence soon won him enemies and he was murdered in 1312. Hugh de Despenser was executed in 1326.

In the last chapter we saw that all the lands of Joan d'Acres had passed to her son, Gilbert. When he was slaughtered at Bannockburn and left no heir, those same lands were divided between his sisters Margaret, Eleanor and Elizabeth. Eleanor's portion included Tintern Parva and Usk. This was in 1314 when Edward II had been king for seven years.

Edward II was the youngest of fourteen children from Edward I's marriage to Eleanor of Castile. Seven of them died before Edward was born, others later. As a result, he was the only male heir left from the marriage. By the time of his birth in 1284, Edward I had conquered Wales and decided to consolidate that conquest by building a series of castles across the country. For political reasons he arranged that his latest child should be born in the castle at Caernarfon although it was still under construction. Rebellion broke out in Wales later in 1297 but was successfully quashed and in another political gesture, in 1301, Edward I created his seventeen-year-old son Prince of Wales, the first male royal heir to bear that title.

Edward I's eldest daughter, Eleanor, married Henri, Count de Bar. One

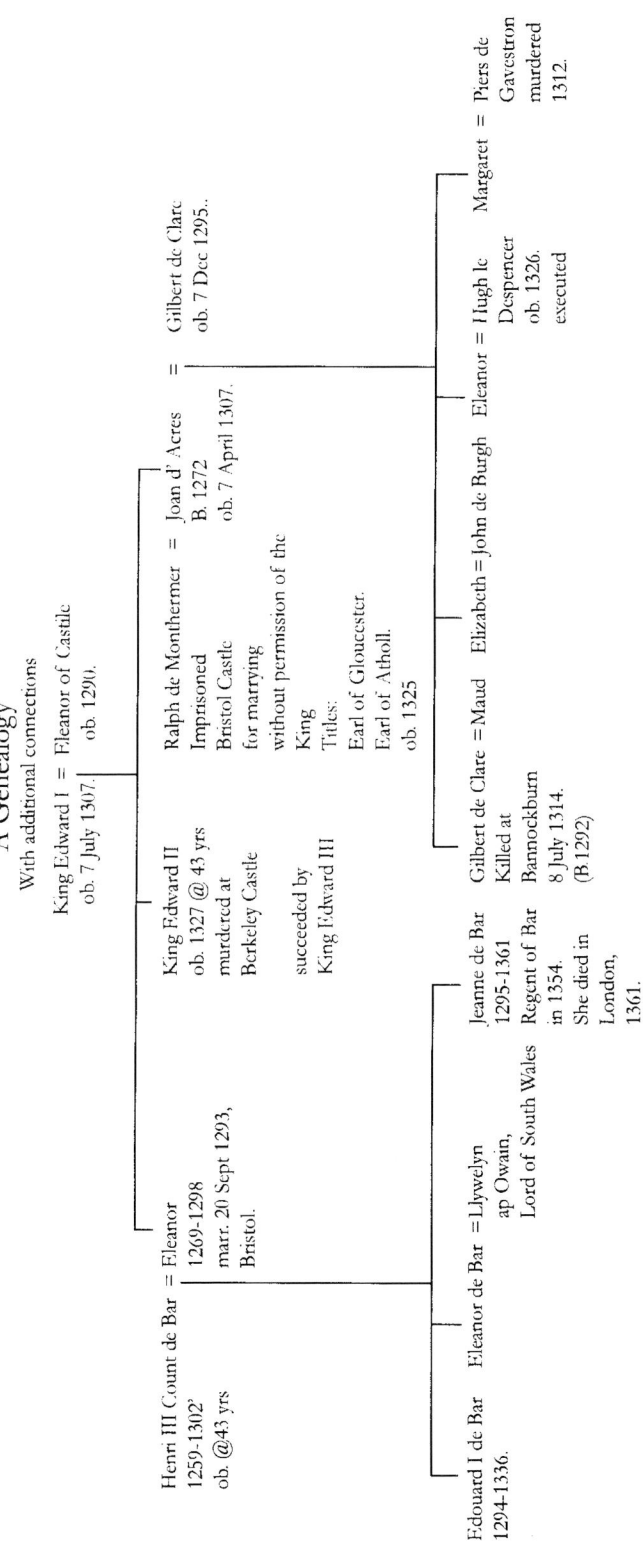

11. Edward I genealogy

of the daughters of that marriage, another Eleanor, married Llywelyn ap Owain, 'Lord of South Wales'. This seems to have been very much a political alliance and part of the king's strategy of ensuring firm control over the principality.

Wales continued to be a matter of concern during Edward ll's reign. I noticed that he, too, showed interest in the ownership of both Tintern Parva and Usk. In 1322 he began negotiations for them to be transferred from one sister, Eleanor, to another, Elizabeth. The negotiations had not been completed when Edward II was murdered in 1327, but neither were they abandoned. The transfer was finalised in law six years later on the insistence of his son and heir, Edward III. What was it, I wondered, that made the ownership of these lands so important to these kings?

For Edward III's interest did not stop here. The marriages of two of his own children helped him maintain a close eye on the area. Firstly, in 1359 his son, Lionel, Duke of Clarence, married Elizabeth de Burgh who was then the heiress of Usk. Secondly, his daughter, Margaret, married John Hastings who had been created Earl of Pembroke in 1348. Here again, I noticed, the holder of this title was close to the centre of power. It is not necessary to continue to follow the descent of the Lordships of Usk and Tintern Parva from one generation to the next. It is sufficient to say that they remained with members of the Plantagenet dynasty down to the first Tudors, Henry VII and his son Henry VIII.

Henry VIII then gave them as a gift to his second wife, Anne Boleyn, when he elevated her to the rank of Marchioness of Pembroke prior to their marriage. After her fall from grace and execution they remained within the king's gift once more, passing for a while to his last wife, Catherine Parr. The *Lordships* of Usk and Tintern Parva were then given to William Herbert, the first Herbert Earl of Pembroke, in 1550 by Edward VI.[1] Later, as we saw in Chapter Two, just weeks before his death Edward gave all the rights pertaining to the *Rectory* at Tintern Parva and the *Priory* at Usk to Earl William and William Clarke in the letters patent of 1553.

I remembered that the Rectors' List for St. Michael's at Tintern Parva begins in 1348 and refers to the patron simply as 'the king'. That meant Edward III. In the light of what I now knew I was not surprised. Here was further evidence of his interest in this seemingly unimportant spot. Edward III was followed as patron by his successor and grandson, Richard II. It was during his patronage that William Glastynbury was incumbent.

Richard II was deeply religious, devoted to the saints and the miracles claimed for them. This sentiment chimed well with his desire to enhance the mystique of kingship and reinvent the monarchy in a new guise in order to strengthen his own precarious position caused by long conflict with dissatisfied nobles. He promoted himself not as a warrior king like

Edward I, but as sovereign by divine appointment, a belief expressed by Shakespeare in *Richard II*:

> The breath of worldly men cannot depose
> The deputy elected by the Lord.

I noted with interest that one of the saints for whom Richard had a special devotion was St. John the Baptist. That reminded me of William Clarke who, two hundred years later, was faithfully serving a brotherhood dedicated to St. John in Hatfield parish, Hertfordshire, on land once owned by both William and Aymer de Valence.

The analysis of the dates on the triangular drawing seemed to be logical. But I was still left with the underlying question – what was the point of recording them in the first place? Perhaps the true significance of the card as a whole was separate from the specific events each date commemorated. They appeared to have something to do with Edward the Confessor and the development of the Abbey stage by stage.

Westminster Abbey was a Benedictine foundation and at one time boasted, through the generosity of Edward III, a relic of St. Benedict himself. The relics themselves were presented by a succession of kings or semi-royal figures. Edward the Confessor, Edward I, Edward III and Mary de Valence, Countess of Pembroke, widow of Aymer. Each of these people figured in one way or another in the questions I was trying to answer.

Whatever we may think of the very idea of sacred relics today, for centuries they had a great symbolic significance derived from the reverence of many Christians who believed they were genuine. Henry III took care to ensure the safekeeping of the Abbey's relics when he redesigned the church. They would have been guarded jealously for generations. Here, as elsewhere, their proud possessors were dedicated to their preservation.

The enigmatic figure of the 'gentleman' William Clarke rose before me once again. Although so little information about him has survived, Clarke was undoubtedly a deliberate choice, together with the contemporary Earl of Pembroke, by Edward VI to fulfil a specific role with regard to the Rectory of Tintern Parva in 1553. This, of course, was after the Dissolution of the Monasteries (1536–1540) and after the date when the chest of precious relics disappeared from Westminster Abbey. Was the reason why Clarke was chosen in the first place connected in some way with the dates on the triangular card? Putting it simply, was the concern displayed by Edward VI related to the very real interest shown in the area almost two hundred years earlier by Edward III?

When Edward became patron of St. Michael's, the Cistercian abbey less than a mile down river had undergone impressive development. The vast new abbey church rose against the skyline, clearly influenced by the Gothic magnificence of Henry III's Westminster. Up river beyond Monmouth Goodrich castle, a wedding present from King John to William Marshall in 1204, had passed into the hands of William de Valence and had likewise undergone extensive rebuilding. Goodrich represented the might of the lords temporal, Tintern Abbey the might of the lords spiritual. Between the two St. Michael's Church remained a small cell-like structure of seemingly little importance. But perhaps its apparent simplicity hid a greater truth.

Its modesty had protected it from the destruction and plundering of more splendid buildings after the Dissolution or the later assaults of bigoted Puritan reformers during the Commonwealth. We know that the gold figures and jewels decorating the shrine of the Confessor were taken for Henry VIII's coffers. The same thing happened up and down the country. At Westminster Queen Mary replaced the stolen jewels on her succession but after her reign those, too, were taken.

While the Dissolution provided Henry VIII with much-needed income, earlier monarchs could not raid the church's wealth. Time and again, the wars and personal extravagance emptied the royal purse. If the king turned to taxation to raise money that brought resentment, political unrest and hard bargaining. The Templars, as we saw with King John, were ready to advance loans to a needy sovereign and did so repeatedly. Edward I borrowed from them even before he was king. Their role as bankers was the source of their wealth and influence and in the end the cause of their downfall. Apart from King John and Prince Edward other monarchs used the Templars as bankers. Henry III pawned the English crown jewels to them. To ensure their safe delivery, his wife, Eleanor of Provence, personally took them to the Order's Preceptory in Paris.

Apart from housing the knights themselves and providing them with a sound means of defence, the Preceptories became known as places of safe storage for wealth in many forms: not just money but artefacts and important documents. The Paris Preceptory was the Order's headquarters in France and normally kept within its vaults the treasury of the French king. Its proximity to the Abbey of St. Denis was almost symbolic, for that, as we saw, was founded originally by the Merovingians to be a spiritual focus of the monarchy.

The Templars' base in Jerusalem had once been the site of Solomon's Temple. They had been founded in 1119 and took vows to live according to the rule of St. Benedict. In 1127 they gained the powerful support of St. Bernard, Abbot of Clairvaux, the champion of the newly reformed Benedictine Order of Cistercians. The closeness of the first Templars to St.

Bernard has led one writer to describe the Order as the armed fist of the Cistercians. The influence of St. Bernard played no small part in their early development. He was a man of truly European stature corresponding with popes, kings and bishops. He preached the need for the Second Crusade and was present in the Abbey of St. Denis when the Pope launched the campaign under the leadership of Louis VII.

The Knights Templar had their own role to play in that Crusade, but they had other contributions to make to the history of Europe apart from acting as bankers and warrior monks. They built their own churches and preceptories. At the same time the Cistercian Order was responsible for some of the finest buildings in Europe. The Gothic cathedrals in France were built by masons known as the Children of Solomon.[2] These were directed by Cistercian and very possibly Templar master builders.

The wealth and power of the Knights Templar together with their bravery in battle gave the Order a chivalric allure that set standards of knighthood for many a soldier of fortune. It is in this context that we should look at the final days of that outstanding knight, William Marshall, the hero who saved the life of Eleanor of Aquitaine and became her champion and her children's champion. Steadfast in his loyalty, he did not marry for over twenty years while serving her cause. During his lifetime he was called William *the Marshall*, a reference to the office of Marshall of England that he inherited in 1199 from his brother.

Interestingly, at the end of his long life he was admitted to the Knights Templar in his last illness by the Master of the Order in England and buried next to him. Surely that was a place of honour, a sign of the high regard he had won from the Master and a reward for service he had rendered. The year was 1219; Henry III was a boy of twelve and Marshall the young king's regent. Two of his own sons were also buried in the Temple Church.

On the other hand, his wife and two more sons were buried at Tintern Abbey. That made sense since, as we know, Marshall had been given Goodrich Castle by King John when he married. Clearly for the Marshalls Goodrich was a family home as well as a fortress. When all William Marshall's sons died without issue, the female line continued, allied by marriage to Henry III's half brother, William de Valence. He, too, had Goodrich as his Welsh home. Poised on the English side of the border with Wales, the castle's strategic importance mattered.

Later, two former royal servants were sent to live in the Abbey. One in 1304 had retired from Edward I's personal service, the other was placed in the monks' care by Edward II in 1314. Both were maintained by the king in the tranquillity of Tintern Abbey as a reward for their services. Such concern by the kings for their servants was impressive. But did these men have a final service to perform? Could they have been employed to keep a watching brief on the Abbey and the surrounding area for their sovereign lords?

By now I was intrigued by the growing evidence of royal connections in this area. These were physically visible in Goodrich Castle and the Priory of Usk. They were manifest in the power exercised by William and Aymer de Valence – a power that came from their closeness to the throne. In addition there was the discovery that among the properties owned by Edward I's daughter, Joan d'Acres, was a church at nearby Llanishen dedicated to St. Dennis of all people. This last was yet another reminder of the French presence here and one that might easily be overlooked. Amongst all the accumulating data, was there sufficient reason to regard St. Michael's Church as a protected site? If so, why should such a small and simple church need protection?

Certainly Edward I's importance to the Abbey itself was never more obvious than when he lay dying in Carlisle in 1307. The Abbot sent one of the monks to secure royal approval of the Abbey's lands and charters. The king confirmed twenty-two grants on his deathbed. It is evident from this how positively Edward I felt about the Abbey at Tintern.

Edward II, the younger brother of Joan, appears to have shared his father's regard. In 1326 he arrived at the Abbey on 13 October, a significant date indeed. Since this was the feast day of his namesake Edward the Confessor, the occasion would be celebrated by High Mass in the splendid new Abbey Church. No doubt Edward hoped for the saint's help in his efforts to defeat the growing opposition to his reign. He stayed there two nights before continuing to Chepstow. It was two years since Aymer de Valence had died and the loss of his loyal support would make the Abbey a welcome, if brief, refuge for the king desperate for his security. The following year Edward II was deposed and murdered.

Tintern Parva lies at the western end of the Abbey grounds and St. Michael's Church, although hidden by a bend in the river, was at this time its nearest neighbour. When I reflected on these comings and goings, Tintern Parva seemed less of a rural retreat. Beneath the surface there were evidently strong issues drawing important people to the neighbourhood. Had St. Michael's Church anything to do with this? Three reigning Edwards in succession had shown interest in the area. Edward III in particular was anxious to rearrange the ownership of significant parts including St. Michael's itself.

The reign of Edward III saw the French influence in England begin to wane. His claim on the French throne marked the beginning of The Hundred Years War with France. In addition England suffered from the

Wars of the Roses, a conflict between cousins over the succession that lasted for more than a century, until the marriage of the Lancastrian Henry VII to Elizabeth of York. It is with his son, Henry VIII, that Tintern and its Abbey return to the pages of history.

Having divorced Catherine of Aragon, Henry VIII became passionately involved with Anne Boleyn. Five months before they married in 1533 he created her Marchioness of Pembroke and with the title gave her a dowry of land that included the Lordship of Usk. Once again the Pembroke title was chosen for a close member of the royal family and the lands we have been talking about came under the jurisdiction of the mother of the future Queen Elizabeth I.

But not for long. Three years later Anne was executed in the Tower of London, on 19 May 1536, convicted of adultery and incest with her brother. Elizabeth was but a child of three. Four months later Tintern Abbey was handed over to the king's visitors on 3 September to be dissolved as a monastery, and all articles of value were sent to the royal treasury. Later the Abbey buildings were granted to the Earl of Worcester. In time Henry was to give the Lordship of Usk to his last wife, Catherine Parr.

When Henry died in January 1547 Princess Elizabeth was fourteen years old. Within months of his death, in either May or June, Catherine Parr secretly married Thomas Seymour who had courted her before the king. Catherine died in September 1548 following the birth of a daughter. The Lordship of Usk and other Monmouthshire lands reverted once more to the Crown and remained with Edward VI until he gave them to William Herbert, Earl of Pembroke.

After the reigns of her half brother, Edward VI, and half sister, Mary, Elizabeth finally succeeded to the throne in 1558 and ruled for forty-four years. Tintern Parva Estate and the Rectory of St. Michael were now in the care of the Herbert dynasty. Tintern itself was beginning to develop once more as its natural resources attracted entrepreneurs in a different way. The power of the local water was harnessed for industry and, with the award of a Charter in 1568 by Queen Elizabeth, the wireworks formally commenced.

Coincidentally, in 1568 the ascetic reformer Pope Pius V officially added the anniversary of St. Denis to the church calendar of feast days in France. The French influence had long since diminished in Monmouthshire except for echoes of St. Dennis at Llanishen and St. Radegunda at Usk. But what of St. Michael's?

I could not forget the continued interest of a succession of kings in the site. What reason was there for this? Did it concern Tewdric who had lived in his hermit's cell among the rocks? I remembered the chapel in honour of Radegunda built by Eleanor of Aquitaine over the cell of John of Chinon. Had the same happened here? Had the small church of St. Michael been built near the site of Tewdric's cell? Had that cell in consequence become a discreetly hidden repository used for different purposes, perhaps, over the years? And could it still exist?

CHAPTER SIX

Tintern Wireworks Charter, 1568

1568, THEN, WAS the year Queen Elizabeth granted a royal charter to a company operating the wireworks at Tintern. A plaque on the wall outside the Abbey commemorates the event: 'Near this place in 1568 brass was first made by alloying copper with zinc.' Among the chief shareholders of the company were William Cecil, Robert Dudley, the Earl of Leicester, and William Herbert, the first Earl of Pembroke. Less active shareholders included Sir Nicholas Bacon and Sir Henry Sidney.

Also in 1568 a goldsmith and engraver living in Nuremberg, Wenzel Jamnitzer, published a book entitled *The Perspective of Regular Bodies*, an important addition to geometrical theory. Experts brought over from Germany to help with the new company may well have brought a copy with them for it was a valuable new text book.

Wenzel Jamnitzer was one of the truly great artists in Nuremberg. Born in Vienna in 1508, he was admitted to citizenship in Nuremberg in 1534 where he worked for four Holy Roman Emperors in succession – Charles V, Ferdinand I, Maximilian II and Rudolf II – and some of the most powerful princes of his time. Three generations of Jamnitzer goldsmiths helped to establish the city's reputation as the leading centre for design and production in Europe.

Jamnitzer was very interested in perfecting the development of machinery to take over hand production and he provides a link between the wireworks at Tintern and Nuremberg. A typical Renaissance man with a wide range of skills, he also produced a variety of scientific instruments in silver and gold. His reputation and some of his work reached England long before the wireworks was established. For example he was highly skilled in designing single vessels with a dual purpose. In July 1553, when John Dudley, Duke of Northumberland (Robert Dudley's father) was arrested for his part in the 'Devise', some ten thousand ounces of plate were confiscated from his various houses. Among them were two items that combined a cup and a candlestick. Not surprisingly the same artefacts appeared later in an inventory of the jewels and plate of Elizabeth I.

A copy of Jamnitzer's book is included in a list with the brass plates in the catalogue at the Science Museum in London. The brass plates connected with the geometrical drawings of the concept of the Elizabethan theatres had been dated scientifically to the late sixteenth/early seventeenth centuries period. Looking at the plaque on the wall, I felt sure I had at last found the source of the plates of some of John Byrom's drawings. The date 1568 had an extra resonance for me since, as we have seen, the same year the Pope officially honoured St. Denis, a French saint with unmistakeable associations with the area, by adding his feast day to the Roman Catholic Calendar.

1568 was ten years into Queen Elizabeth's reign. She in fact granted two royal charters on the same day in May. One, 'The Company of the Mines Royal' was to look for minerals in the western half of the country, the other 'The Company of Mineral and Battery Works' was to manufacture wire for commercial uses and iron plate for armour and munitions.

The Company of Mineral and Battery Works was much the smaller of the two companies and was situated in Tintern, because of the easy availability of water power. Needless to say, the names of the same shareholders appear in both companies. In particular I noted the name of William Herbert, first Earl of Pembroke. This meant that he came into contact with the German appointed as managing director of the Mines Royal. This was one Daniel Hochstetter, a highly skilled engineer. It was not long before Pembroke became interested in a hydraulic process invented by Hochstetter.

That is not surprising. After all, the Earl owned the water supply to the wireworks. Moreover, he had been interested in engineering and science for many years. We know that he employed John Dee in his household and recommended him to Robert Dudley's father as a suitable tutor, and Dee was the first great advocate of the new engineering skills arising out of the Renaissance. Right up to the end of his life Pembroke was open to new ideas and willing to put them into practice. No doubt Hochstetter's skills were invaluable to him in many ways, apart from ensuring the success of the wiredrawing enterprise at Tintern. Pembroke's death in 1570, just two years after the wireworks opened, deprived the Company of a valuable member. It also meant, of course, that his guardianship of the Rectory and church at Tintern Parva passed to his son and heir.

With the arrival of the wireworks life for the inhabitants of Tintern centred around the brass and wire factory that now replaced the ruined Abbey. German workers with specialist skills were brought in to teach the local workers the art of wire-drawing and a thriving community developed.

As with so much else, Nuremberg was the centre of the mechanical revolution in wiredrawing, where scholars attribute it to someone known simply as 'Rudolf of Nuremberg' in 1350:

the greatest improvement in the art of wire-drawing was undoubtedly the invention of the large drawing machine which is driven by water.[1]

Like other technical advances the process was kept secret for years and to begin with at Tintern wire-drawing was still done by hand. There is evidence that in the immediate neighbourhood of the Forest of Dean, at Soudley, iron wire was made by 'being drawn by strength of hand' 'as early as 1565'.[2] An illustration exists of a worker in Nuremberg drawing wire by this method a century earlier, in 1425. By 1568 German expertise had developed so much it is little wonder their skills were imported. Local folklore says that cottages on the Catbrook road to Trellech were originally built for German workers imported for the wireworks. Certainly the present Rose Cottage, originally two dwellings, has features that lend support to this.

Despite one crisis or another, the wireworks remained the principal employer in the area for three hundred years. By the end of the sixteenth century there was full employment for 120 workers and temporary work for as many as 180. Apart from the production of ordnance for military purposes, Tintern was the centre for the production of good-quality wire. Dr. William Rees explains the importance of this apparently humdrum product:

> It was calculated that some five or six thousand persons in the country were dependent on the production of good-quality wire so that in addition to the supply from the works at Tintern there was a considerable trade in wire from the Low Countries. Among the array of wire goods which now appeared on the market, many of them for the first time, we find waything needles, pack needles, fish hooks, pins, corn sieves, bird cages of all kinds, spurs, bridles, bits and snaffles, girdles, buckles, stomachers and other articles of women's clothing, hooks and eyes, shuttle wire, wire chains, wire for keys, mousetraps, nails, clasps, dog chains, dog couples, gog-rings, curtain rings, etc. Most important of all were the wool-cards, humble yet essential instruments in the rapidly-spreading woollen industry, so vital in the economy of the period.[3]

Tintern profited enormously from the presence of the wireworks. The owners were good and forward-thinking employers. Long before the days of compulsory state education, the workers' children were taught at the works' school by the works' schoolmaster. It has been described as 'the earliest example of a works' school' and 'doubtless the direct forerunner of the works' school of the late XVIIIth and XIXth centuries'.[4] During lean times, periods of inflation and shortage of work the employees inevitably suffered some setbacks. In 1639 they turned to mutiny, but this was a rare occurrence, for the owners were generally very mindful of their workers' welfare as well as ensuring that the business was successful. Like the Earl of Pembroke before him, Bacon, for example, displayed very much a hands-on interest in the wireworks, intervening in 1618 to ensure the introduction of a new engine or mill for slitting iron bars into rods. His intervention on behalf of a process that initially had been rejected resulted in a better quality of iron for London nail-makers.

The third Earl of Pembroke, another William Herbert, was linked closely with Francis Bacon in their mutual interest in the wireworks at Tintern. He was appointed Governor of the Society for Mineral and Battery Works in January 1603/4, and was later given government protection for the waterworks erected nearby at Trellech to provide power for the enterprise. As Earl of Pembroke, William had, of course, inherited the Lordships of Trellech and Usk. It seemed appropriate that the brass plates for the theatre drawings were made at the wireworks, for the third Earl's involvement with the playhouses and actors was real and practical. Hence the dedication of the First Folio to William and his brother, Philip.

Not surprisingly, many people connected with Francis Bacon were also connected with Tintern. In March 1593 Sir Julius Caesar was appointed Governor of the Mineral and Battery Works throughout the country, and soon joined forces with Sir Richard Martin to write to the Lord Treasurer, Lord Burghley, concerning a debt of £1,132 owed in rent to the company at Tintern. From the beginning he was determined to see that the enterprise was properly run. Caesar and Martin also engaged in efforts to bring a long-standing conflict with one Richard Hanbury to a successful conclusion. Hanbury, who had begun as a goldsmith in London, was very much involved in the running of the wireworks and was responsible for a dispute with the shareholders, including Henry Billingsley.

Despite being a shareholder in the company Hanbury had worked to circumvent its monopoly. The charge against him involved the supply of raw materials:

> The best mines in Monmouthshire be his and almost all the woods within ten miles compass therof be his also. All of which it should seem he has gotten into his hands of purpose to bind the Company, their works and farmers, [i.e. factory workers] to his pleasure.[5]

Only imprisonment in the Fleet and the eventual confiscation of much of his property by the Privy Council forced Hanbury to mend his ways. Caesar's legal skills were put very much to use at Tintern. In addition, I noticed that he had married into Sir Richard Martin's family and that had introduced him to another family connected with the wireworks, the Catchmays. The family of William Catchmay was heavily involved in the development of industry in Monmouthshire for several generations.

1630 is a year of particular interest in the history of the wireworks. It was a year in which change occurred in the management of the wireworks. Tintern Abbey was the property of the Earls of Worcester, a gift from Henry VIII at the time of the Dissolution of the Monasteries. Accordingly residence within its grounds would be by their permission – or invitation. Although Henry, the fifth Earl, was very much alive and at the time Lord Lieutenant of the county of Monmouth, his wife Anne, Countess of Worcester, took over certain of the responsibilities concerning both the Abbey and the wireworks at Tintern.

By birth she was Anne Russell, daughter of Lord John Russell, a member of the Bedford dynasty. The situation at Tintern is worth looking at more closely. First, we should remember that Francis Bacon was a main shareholder in the Tintern works and the Earls of Worcester owned the land on which it stood. What may not be so obvious is that the Countess Anne was Francis Bacon's cousin. Her mother, Elizabeth Cooke, and Bacon's mother, Anne Cooke, were sisters. Thus both cousins, Anne Worcester and Francis Bacon, were linked by family and business interests to Tintern. Time and again one discovers the same pattern in events – family ties facilitating or implementing the career of an individual or some joint enterprise.

During the latter part of the Countess's life, Thomas Herbert was living on Worcester land in the Abbey before purchasing the nearby estate at Tintern Parva. His arrival in Tintern as a Worcester tenant coincides with the period when Countess Anne was directly concerned with the wireworks near the Abbey. By that time Thomas had earned the respect of two Earls of Pembroke, the other great landowners in the locality. He had travelled widely and, in 1632, made a good marriage to the daughter of a member of the king's household. The fifth Earl of Worcester was devoted in his service to Charles I and this marriage would be a recommendation of Thomas in itself. To both Anne Worcester and her husband, therefore, Thomas Herbert would have appeared very much the sort of man to have in position near the Tintern works at a difficult time. And times were difficult, so much so that for a while the Countess took over the management of the Tintern wireworks through her steward, John Gwyn. Accounts show him active on her behalf in 1630. The works reverted to the Worcester estate when the licence to run them was withdrawn from the leaseholder, Thomas Hackett, because

> the wire-drawers of London, both of the City and Southwark, complained, in 1626, that during Hackett's tenure of the lease, the supply of wire from Tintern was insufficient to meet the country's needs. Hackett in reply, pointed out that the shortage was only in respect of one sort of wire, viz., that used for breech hooks.[6]

Hackett, of course, used this shortage to increase his prices in contradiction to an earlier promise not to do so. Earlier complaints had been made against him by 'English clothiers, baysmakers (baise makers) and others of Colchester'.[7] Pin-makers, too, were tired of being held to ransom by Hackett. So it is not surprising that Lady Anne took over the works during this crisis. Her steward Gwyn was a local man whose family had been resident at nearby Llandogo from at least 1550.

The Tintern works were a 'monopoly' and therefore the concern about the shortage of these goods was more serious than we perhaps appreciate today. Indeed, the outcry from Southwark clothiers is a significant reminder of the connection of members of the Corporation overseeing the management of the Tintern works with the Elizabethan playhouses. (Two of these, the second Globe and second Fortune, were still very much in business.) At one time some of the costumes for the plays were made at the rehearsal rooms at St. John's Gate, London. Furthermore, three successive Earls of Worcester had been patrons of a company of players.

Lady Anne's husband, Henry, was the fifth Earl of Worcester and later the first Marquis. He was a great landowner and one of the richest men in England. Already fifty when Charles I became king, his rank and wealth gained him the friendship of his sovereign, to whom he was devoted for the rest of his life. That loyalty was tested by constant requests for money. Even before the Civil War had begun, Worcester had advanced something in the region of £100,000 to the king. His reward was to be raised to a Marquis in 1645 and have the promise of a Dukedom – a promise the king did not fulfil. It was left to Charles II to create the son of the second Marquis a Duke twenty-two years after his Restoration, in 1682.

But the wireworks could not remain a monopoly for ever. At the time of Thomas Herbert's appearance in Tintern right up to the Civil War there was a gradual increase in competition from foreign companies. Dutch and German companies were accused of flooding the English market with cheaper imports of 'brass-ware, pans and kettles'. In 1629 an illicit enterprise producing brass was uncovered in Bristol.

The Tintern wireworks survived this as well as competition from many other sources. Whatever temporary setbacks there were, for the most part the workforce was paid fairly and there was even a small fund set up to provide a limited form of pension to occasional applicants. We read in the accounts of workmen receiving a pension for years of service or in recompense for some breakdown or accident. Occasionally money was advanced to help people in debt. The paternal interest shown towards the needs of workers who fell on hard times shows a very compassionate side to the merchant adventurers of Elizabethan and Jacobean England. It was the Civil War that led to brass manufacture being diverted abroad and a temporary decline in Britain. The community at Tintern may have been small but it was productive, purposeful and prosperous.

The wireworks stood in the Chapel Hill district of Tintern village. This area is situated at the east end of the village near the Abbey. The works did not encroach on the Abbey Church but many cottages were built for the workers nearby close to the Angiddy river. It was in this area that Thomas Herbert lived when he first moved to Tintern. Today, a visitor, travelling from Chepstow to Monmouth and turning off the main road at this juncture, will soon come across an excavated site of the wireworks and some of the workmen's cottages set back in a little community of its own.

But the area was not home to just artisans. There were evidently grander houses. The Assay Master and Paymaster General, William Humfrey, one of the originators of the Tintern enterprise, was criticised for building substantial houses with accommodation for three or four servants for his leading engineers. Later managers and leaseholders such as Thomas Hackett also took up residence here. Chapel Hill was a convenient, close and tightly-knit community united in its loyalties. Some of these loyalties were evidently to the old religion for this was also the final home of Hugh Owen. He was an old and valued member of the Earl of Worcester's household at Raglan Castle. Owen, a devout Catholic, chose to retire here and translated the book of meditations *Imitation of Christ* by Thomas à Kempis into Welsh for the benefit of his fellow countrymen.

In looking into the history of the wireworks, I came across a concise gazetteer detailing evidence visible on sites today. One of the entries, 'Number 13' is of particular interest:

> Works (probable) at Tintern Parva S.O. 530008
> This is on the Cat Brook and a square stone-built chimney which seems to have been part of a furnace or kiln, stands amongst the footings of a derelict building. Much alteration has taken place in the area but remnants of a pond survive alongside, giving the appearance of a water-powered industrial site although no specific documentary evidence has been found for this.[8]

A visit to the site established that it had been part of the estate of Sir William Herbert. Readers will recall that, according to an indenture of 1640, Sir William's grandson, Richard, sold the entire estate to Thomas Herbert. A manuscript once belonging to Thomas Herbert and now lodged at Cardiff Public Library contains another indenture concerning this estate. Drawn up some time after 1640, it refers to one particular site as 'the hill Ground sometime in the occupacon [sic] of Richard Hanbury'. Consisting of some twenty acres which evidently included a 'mill or water course', this is in fact the same as the water-powered site 'on the Cat Brook' referred to in the gazetteer.

From this it would appear that there was a small industrial site *within* the boundaries of the Tintern Parva estate of Sir William Herbert. This site would have been active when Sir William was himself living in Tintern and setting up his College. He died in 1593, leaving his wife, Florencia, in charge of his affairs. At this time Richard Hanbury was still causing disruption at the main wireworks. His activities in trying to outwit the monopoly by withholding a supply of good raw material required all the legal skills of Sir Julius Caesar to put an end to them. Certainly in the early 1590s Tintern Parva was anything but a sleepy retreat.

Towards the end of the nineteenth century Tintern Parva subsided into relative obscurity. By the 1850s the wireworks were in decline and the smelting furnace fell silent. Tintern survived and remains as a picturesque tourist attraction. In July 1798 Wordsworth wrote *Lines composed a few miles above Tintern Abbey*. Although not directly descriptive of the landscape, the poem helped to inspire the return to nature that still brings people today by car, coach and on foot to view the ruins of the Abbey. Tintern Parva is a little further off with no sign of its historic past obvious from the roadside. The church of St. Michael lies in a dip below the level of the road, hidden by a row of houses. Nurtons, too, is not visible from the main road.

CHAPTER SEVEN

Herbert and his College

I HAD LONG THOUGHT that the collection of brass plates and geometrical figures now housed in the Science Museum, London, could have been part of the College Sir William Herbert had founded in Tintern. The importation of German experts to work at the wireworks, a technical German text book of the same date as the enterprise, the presence in the area of members of families connected with either the Elizabethan theatres or the site of St. Michael's Church itself, or both, had by now invested Tintern with a new and serious significance.

In addition the discovery of three triangular buckles at Caerwent and of one at Trostrey near Usk dating from the fourth century were proof of traffic between post-Roman Wales and Merovingian France. Trostrey was not far from Radegunda's chapel and provided a revealing piece in the jigsaw. Tewdric's possible Merovingian ancestry provided another. I felt compelled to look once more at the tombstone at St. Michael's that had become the centre of so much interest to me.

The name 'Christopher Heath' and the date '1864' bothered me. The incision of a name on a funeral monument has an air of finality. However, an anonymous tombstone is a different matter. Decorative swirls carved on an unnamed tomb might be intended to convey a hidden meaning. Heath's name could have been added deliberately to distract from the anonymity of the stone and prevent unwanted speculation. If that were the case, the tomb must have been known already as a marker for something or someone special.

In the light of what the radar scan seemed to have registered below ground, it was important to have the exact dimensions of what was visible above. The tombstone consists of three parts. The topmost section is a solid block measuring 6 feet in length, 12 inches wide and 8 inches down the side. One important fact I was able to establish with the help of the archaeologist, Kevin Blockley, is that it is not local stone but imported from elsewhere. In all probability the 'ornamental' carving had been done away from the site before the top stone was laid. Its transportation by river before the advent of the railway would have been no mean feat.

It rests on a plinth of about 6 feet 6 inches long by 16 inches wide. This in turn stands on a base that measures 7 feet 6 inches in length and 28 inches in width. Both these are made from local sandstone. All three sections combine to make a very solid monument, one certainly heavy enough to deter grave robbers. It looks as if it has been in situ for a long time. I had already noted the gravestones near to it and most of them were post-1900.

Even with its three layers the tomb lies modestly low. This may be why it has not attracted serious attention earlier. The workmanship of the decoration can only be seen by crossing the grass and standing at the side. Neither weekly worshippers nor occasional sightseers are likely to do that since it lies a little distance from the path to the west door of the church. Its true dignity, simple yet solemn, becomes apparent only close to. Its solidity suggests that it would be very difficult to move any of the layers without the aid of some mechanical equipment.

This led me to consider what would have been in the area at the time of the medieval church. The valley here would have been dominated by the Abbey, constantly expanding as its wealth grew. The Abbey ruins remain as a testament to its former glory and the violence of its destruction. Over the centuries other changes occurred, less evident nowadays. The few signs that remain of Tintern's former industrial importance are not visible from the main road. A casual visitor could be misled into thinking that, after the Reformation, Tintern remained untouched and obscure. Nothing I had read mentions the tomb, and I had already learned to my disappointment that the church registers only dated from 1756 for marriages and 1812 for baptisms and burials.

However, in the old churchyard there is a stone dated 1616 which predates any of those listed either in the guidebook or Mr. Woolven's inventory. From this it appeared that there might be information about the old churchyard not yet recorded. How this 1616 stone escaped notice I cannot say but it can be seen leaning against the outside of the east wall of the church. It states simply, 'Here lyeth the body of Thomas Bone'. Perhaps it has only recently come to light and been moved to this position. Although this surname does not appear in any of the volumes of Bradney's *History*, or the lists of workers connected with the wireworks, there are people of that name living in the area today.

In 1865, the year after the burial of Christopher Heath, plans were started for a local railway and on 28 October 1876 the first train of the Wye Valley Railway ran from Chepstow through Tintern to Monmouth. The line passed within a short distance of St. Michael's Church. Much earlier, in the 1820s, a major road connecting Chepstow with Monmouth had been built, forming a boundary to the north side of the church. Both these undertakings must have caused substantial alteration to the lines of the

12a. Sir Thomas Herbert 1606–1681

Artist W.E. Jones Commissioned by Clement Cruttwell 1878

12b. Nurtons

estate. Some of the land would have been absorbed into these enterprises. All this has to be borne in mind when studying the earlier records of the church.

The tomb itself lay close to the boundary wall on the west side of the churchyard, perhaps a little too close. This would have been a secluded part of the churchyard before the west door was added in 1846. From the photographs I had taken earlier it was obvious that this boundary wall marked off an old wharf. Immediately adjacent to the wall was a slipway that had been roughly filled in but still contained the remnants of an old boat. Beyond the slipway, on higher ground practically level with the churchyard, was the community car park.

The slipway had been dug out some years earlier and members of the local community remembered seeing the boundary wall that abutted on to the churchyard, parts of which were said to be about 20 feet deep. It is still in position but only the top four or five feet with the coping stones are visible today. The underground structure suggested by the radar scan would run close by. The head of the tomb is about four feet from the same wall. It would be useful to collect more evidence.

A motorist travelling today from Chepstow through Tintern towards Monmouth will soon reach the end of the village known as Tintern Parva. Indeed he may well continue driving on to Brockweir and Llandogo without registering the fact that he has passed through Parva. Before 1820 the journey to Monmouth had to be made over the ridge of the hill above Tintern Parva passing by the high wall at the rear of Nurtons before dropping down further on. A large gateway still exists in this wall, showing us where the main entrance to the estate was originally. From within the boundary of this wall the estate fell away downhill in a slope interrupted by an occasional terrace before levelling out along the banks of the Wye. Since the eighteenth century that land either as a whole or in parts has been subject to changes of ownership.

Not surprisingly, the house we still know as Nurtons underwent alterations too, and at one point was redesigned to have its front facing down towards the new road. The church of St. Michael was practically rebuilt in 1846 and is now cut off from the estate by the main road. Tintern Parva Farm likewise has undergone substantial extensions. Little else would have stood to interrupt access to the old wharf and slipway. Dwelling houses were confined to the Catbrook road to Trellech. Here can still be seen cottages said to be for the wire workers and once part of the original estate. A few others appeared down the centuries overlooked by the Hospice.

Fragmented as the estate had become, a careful study of miscellaneous documents covering a long period of time persuaded me that the focus of the estate must rest on the property now called Nurtons. The position of the house seems ideal for the site of a place for serious study – secluded but not too inaccessible for anyone seeking enlightenment. The view from one vantage point on the hillside is so unspoiled that one might be tempted to think it has been the same for centuries. The impression is almost magical. Surely a college here would not simply impart knowledge but, in the right hands, be capable of distilling wisdom? As investigations continued and data accumulated I became more convinced.

The exterior of the present house looks unmistakeably Victorian. Nurtons underwent a major reconstruction towards the end of the nineteenth century when it was purchased as a family house for the Cruttwells. However, closer observation reveals a mixture of styles caused by successive alterations and extensions. During the Second World War the house became a refuge for evacuees, so the original generous provision of space for a Victorian family must have been modified to accommodate larger numbers.

The present owners, Elsa and Adrian Wood, had looked into the history of their property before I appeared on the scene. They were hoping to be able, with time, to restore the building to something like its former glory. As they showed me round the house and grounds on my first visit, it was obvious that Nurtons had once been part of something much more substantial. The boundary wall abutting onto the original road, the pillared entrance, a succession of outbuildings, walls, and the remains of a possible stable, sets of stone steps at different places, wells and walks all spoke from the outset of an establishment designed on a very grand scale. Most telling of all was an underground chamber reminiscent of a crypt.

The Woods happily shared with me their knowledge of the house and placed at my disposal their own historical documentation. This gives us a broad outline of the history of Tintern Parva Estate down to the middle of the nineteenth century. For the moment we must focus on the period covering the reigns of Elizabeth and James I and look at the people most concerned with the property at that time and the early years of the wireworks.

The earliest information came from a collection of documents in the Cwmbran Record Office called the 'Bosanquet Papers'. Among them were two containing references to the Tintern Parva Estate. The first, dated 1591, mentions 'the lands of Sir William Herbert' in Tintern. However, we already know that the Herbert connection goes back much further to the grants made in the letters patent of April 1553 by King Edward VI to William Herbert, the first Earl of Pembroke.

Further help comes from Herbert family wills. Sir William Herbert's father died when his son was 13 years old, and the young boy appears to have been taken up by his uncle, George. George was a very colourful character, a mariner regarded as something of a buccaneer. He was certainly known to be unscrupulous in his dealings. In 1580 George left his ships to his nephew: the *James*, together with 'all manner of cabelle, anchors, ropes, tacklinge, guns and ordynance weapons' and two others – *Le Steven* with which George had traded in salt and wines from France and *Le Dragon* or *Green Dragon*. During his trading George had gained some notoriety for blatantly evading customs duties on his wares. The equipment itemised in the will tells us much about his seafaring methods and the capacity of his small fleet.

George appears to have inherited some of the bravado of his own father, Sir Walter Herbert. Walter had served in France alongside Henry VIII and a hundred of the finest English archers at the siege of Boulogne, which they captured in September 1544. His bravery in battle did not prevent him from being accused by his enemies of being the protector of thieves and murderers. The Bishop of Lichfield accused him of complicity through his servants in murders at Magor, Monmouthshire, and elsewhere. Whatever the truth of these charges was, Walter survived them and prospered. In his will, dated 30 September 1550, he left George not only his ship the *James*, but also 'lands and tenements lying at Tynterne'. The bequest of land, coupled as it is with that of the ship and a cellar filled with supplies of salt, shows the increasing wealth of this branch of the Herberts. In time, George added two more ships to his maritime enterprise and bequeathed these, together with the Tintern land, to Sir William, who added further to the family fortunes by marrying, *c.* 1577, Florencia Morgan, heiress to William Morgan, by then one of the wealthiest landowners in Monmouthshire. We saw him in Chapter Two buying large tracts of land from the Earl of Pembroke.

Sir William Herbert had, of course, also inherited his own family estate at St. Julian's. Later, Queen Elizabeth granted him more land at Liswerry. In addition he became a shareholder in the wireworks. Thus by 1589/90, on his return from service in Ireland, Sir William was a substantial landowner and his wealth was certainly sufficient to underwrite the foundation of a college. On his death in 1593 he left Tintern Parva Estate to his wife Florencia. The reason for that was a cruel quirk of fate. They had two sons, both of whom died as a result of a disastrous blunder when they ate food they did not realise had been laced with poison to kill rats who were attacking books in Sir William's precious library. With only one other child, a daughter, Mary, Sir William left the estate to his wife, a formidable woman who was empowered to bequeath it in turn to Mary, provided she married another member of the Herbert clan. Accordingly Mary, already a mature woman, married Edward Herbert while he was still a mere youth of sixteen. When Edward in turn reached maturity he left Mary to look after their three children in the Welsh countryside while he fled to London where his handsome looks and accomplished manners soon made him a great favourite with Queen Elizabeth. Mary died in 1634 before her mother, who remained the chatelaine of the Tintern Parva Estate until her death, when it passed to her eldest grandson Richard.

His father, Edward, was still living, now ennobled as first Baron Herbert of Chirbury, with his own separate estates. He is remembered today as the author of one of the first autobiographies in the English language. Richard married Mary, the daughter of Sir John Egerton who later became Earl of Bridgewater. Her grandfather was Thomas Egerton, a former Lord Chancellor, for whom Francis Bacon worked early in his career.

According to a surviving indenture, in 1640 Richard sold Tintern Parva Estate to Thomas Herbert for an undisclosed sum. By then it had been Herbert property for at least a hundred years. It is this Thomas Herbert who has left us an account of Richard's life. Thomas wrote a *History of the race of Herbert*, a manuscript copy of which survives in Cardiff City Library. In it Thomas writes glowingly of Richard's loyalty and brave service to Charles I during the Civil War. An intelligent boy, he was given a university and legal education and travelled widely in Europe to prepare him for a promising career. However, even before the outbreak of the Civil War proper, Richard took up arms in the king's service against an invasion of the Scots.

When the war did break out in 1642 he raised at his own expense a regiment of foot and a troop of cavalry numbering in total 2,800 and campaigned fearlessly in Wales until the king was driven out and he was left with barely thirty men, most of them maimed or wounded. Recognising his worth, Charles chose him to be one of the Lords to greet his wife, Queen Henrietta Maria, on her return in 1643 from raising funds in Holland and accompany her from Bridlington in Yorkshire to Oxford where Charles had set up his capital. His bravery and personal gifts won the affection of the king who, according to Thomas, 'employed him in diverse weighty affaires well knowing him to be a person able to serve his Majesty both by his sword and reason'.

Needless to say Richard suffered for his loyalty. His estates were confiscated and, after the king's execution, his castle at Montgomery was 'pull'd down having garrisoned for the King, the Deere in the Park destroyed and woods cutt down'.

I thought it curious that Thomas Herbert should buy the Tintern Parva Estate in 1640 when Richard did not die for another fifteen years, in 1655. What made him sell it in the first place? And why to Thomas? No documents have survived to tell us how much money, if any, changed hands in this transaction. Richard had 'sold' the estate two years before the war started. So the transaction was not dictated by military expediency. His generous support of Charles clearly shows he was not, in 1640 at least, short of money. He must also have been in good health to have survived the horrors of the Civil War and live on until 1655.

A loyal and brave royalist, who suffered much in the cause of Charles I, Richard Herbert was clearly a man with ideals and integrity. These virtues, as later events showed, were best seen in action, not scholarship. Thomas proved to be the more bookish of the two men. It would not require much insight for Richard to recognise that his kinsman Thomas was better suited to the responsibility of supervising the College his grandfather had started. In passing the estate to Thomas he would be placing it in suitable hands but still keeping it under the aegis of the Herberts.

Interestingly, according to the surviving indentures, a name that recurs repeatedly in the leasing (as opposed to the purchase) of land is that of the Catchmays. This continuity of interest implies the existence of a stable and trusted relationship between the two families of the Herberts and Catchmays. The humdrum detail of the day-to-day running of the estate lands, as opposed to the College, may well have been entrusted by Sir William to the Catchmays. The people entrusted with the upkeep of the land had to be not only efficient but also trustworthy. It is not surprising, therefore, to find that the Catchmays were involved with the wireworks as well.

This then is the pedigree of the owners of Tintern Parva estate during the reigns of the later Tudors, Edward VI, Mary, and Elizabeth I and the first two Stuarts, James I and his son Charles I. The tenure is marked by the stability and continuity of Sir William Herbert's dynasty. Such stability was essential to achieve Sir William's ambition to found a college.

The College

Accordingly I looked at the character and achievements of this man. At the age of fifteen he was sent to Magadelen College, Oxford and spent the next five years there, earning a reputation as both a poet and intellectual. By the time he was twenty-four he was already impressing John Dee with his observations on Dee's abstruse alchemical treatise the *Monas Hieroglyphica*. Such esoteric study did not blind him to the practical demands of day-to-day living and he made a very good marriage with Florencia Morgan. This enabled him to enter into a life in politics, first as sheriff of Glamorgan and then as deputy constable of Conway Castle, Caernarvonshire. In 1578 he was knighted by Elizabeth I and from 1580, when he was appointed MP for Monmouthshire, he became increasingly active in the public affairs of the county.

I was impressed by his apparent ability to combine a very active public career with his own intellectual pursuits. Whenever he was in London, he regularly visited John Dee, conveniently his neighbour at Mortlake. They shared the same interests in astrology, alchemy and the hermetic tradition. These two aspects of his life, the public and the private, seemed to complement each other positively. His keen intellect was responsible for the unusually sophisticated attitude he displayed in his next career move when he became involved in the queen's plans to colonise Ireland. He spent three years in that turbulent country from 1586 to 1589, producing a well argued treatise, *Croftus*, on his sojourn in Ireland, arguing the case for colonisation but with a greater understanding of the Irish than some of his compatriots.

Since 1585 he had been a shareholder in the wireworks at Tintern and his interest in the area never wavered. Inevitably his life was overshadowed by the death of his two sons. The accident occurred at the family home at St. Julian's, which may well be a reason for him choosing to live at the property he owned in Tintern. In February 1587/8 he wrote a letter to Sir Francis Walsingham in which he expressed his wish to bequeath to posterity 'a volume of poetry', 'a colony of my planting' and 'a college of my erecting'. This was not an expression of future aspirations. Each of these aims he had already achieved to varying degrees. His wish was for their survival *after* him. He returned from Ireland in the spring of 1589 and by September that year was settled in Tintern.

Herbert was the author of several works himself, ranging from tracts on religion and some poetry, to the treatise on Protestant plantations in Munster. After the tragedy at St. Julian's, he would naturally want to help his wife come to terms with her loss. One reason for moving his library, the scene and cause of the tragedy, to Tintern could well have been the hope that it might help to assuage her grief. But at the same time it would also provide a foundation for the seat of learning he established.

No doubt his known interests in the hermetic tradition as well as science and mathematics would have been reflected in it. The astronomical details included on the early Byrom drawings and the brass plates made at the wireworks are typical of the world picture that would have been expounded at the College. Because of the very nature of the subjects studied such an institution would have been regarded as very special, calling for special gifts in those overseeing it. Eventually that was to dictate Richard Herbert's 'sale' of the estate to Thomas. In that way he showed himself true to the values and beliefs of his grandfather; beliefs also shared, as Dame Frances Yates has demonstrated, by the early Stuart princes and princesses, including Charles I whose cause Richard had espoused.

Against this background the presence of Sir Francis Bacon in the area is suggestive of fresh possibilities. Conflicting theories continue to attempt to account for his death and burial. What has never been open to dispute is his long-held dream of establishing a totally new experimental approach to learning. What can now no longer be ignored are his undoubted connections with the wireworks at Tintern, his friends in the locality, and his own house, Mount St. Alban's, cheek-by-jowl with St. Julian's.

We have seen how close and constant the third Earl of Pembroke's relationship with Bacon was. Three other Herberts, all brothers and close kinsmen to the Earl, also had connections with Tintern. These were Edward, Lord Herbert of Chirbury, Sir Henry Herbert and the poet, George Herbert. Edward was a handsome favourite of both the ageing Queen Elizabeth and later King James. Bacon could not fail to notice him at court. Edward, of course, was also the father of Richard Herbert of Tintern Parva.

The second brother, Sir Henry Herbert, deserves attention at this point. He has a particular relevance to the College, for he held the post of Master of the Revels for nearly 20 years. He took charge in 1623, the year the First Folio of Shakespeare's plays was published. His office would have brought him naturally to Bacon's attention, especially in the light of Bacon's love of theatrical entertainment. The Master of the Revels was one of the most important figures in the Elizabethan theatre. He was the means by which the sovereign exercised a close control over the plays. From the practical beginnings of supervising the making and storing of properties and costumes for Court entertainments, the role of the Master became one of a censor. He decided what was 'convenient to be shown before her Majestie'. In 1622 the current Master, Sir George Buck, was removed from office for incompetence by the Lord Chamberlain, who, at the time, happened to be William, third Earl of Pembroke. Buck's successor almost immediately sold his position to Sir Henry Herbert who remained Master until the theatres were closed down in 1642 with the outbreak of the Civil War. Henry considered his position gave him the right to license every kind of public entertainment in the country, demonstrating yet again the characteristic Herbert delight in power.

Moreover, the wireworks was the source of the brass plates for the theatre drawings in John Byrom's collection. In addition to the plates, the Science Museum catalogue of the George III Collection contains replicas of geometrical solids in brass. Given their provenance they, too, may well at one time have been part of the material used for instruction at the College. The philosophy and mathematics inherent in them is an integral part of the hermetic tradition and therefore a major component of any conceivable syllabus. Other drawings in the Collection, such as those concerned with the work of John Dee, also come within the range of ideas studied and championed by Sir William Herbert of St. Julian's, the founder of the College.

The importance of the third brother, George Herbert, to us lies in the fact that he was himself a writer of fine religious poetry and has left us his opinion of Bacon as a poet. George Herbert's collection of poems entitled 'The Temple' was an immediate success when published in 1634, the year following his death. He was one person with whom Bacon shared his interest in writing poetry. Bacon translated several of the Psalms into English verse and published them in 1625. It is the only book of verse that bears his name and is dedicated to his 'very good friend Mr. George Herbert'. The dedication indicates the debt Bacon felt he owed Herbert for his advice:

> The pains that it pleased you to take about some of my writings I cannot forget which did put me in mind to dedicate to you this poor exercise of my sickness ... Your affectionate friend, Fr. St. Alban.

By then Bacon was in disgrace and removed from office. The following year Bacon died and an anthology of poems written in Latin was published in his memory. Not all of them are signed but amongst those brave and honest enough to acknowledge their friendship was George Herbert. This was all the more to his credit since Herbert chose this moment to change the direction of a career that had already shown great promise. Despite his appointment as University Orator at Cambridge which was an acknowledged step on the way to public office, he turned instead to the Church's ministry and became a deacon. (His living was given to him by the Earl of Pembroke.) Herbert's tribute is interesting because of the picture he gives us of Bacon's gifts. It is not the legal authority nor the founding father of modern science that he mourns. It is the tribute of one poet to another.

> Long a heavy illness made you groan,
> With weakening foothold upon life you clung;
> What Fate intended now is plain. Alone
> In April could you die, that sole
> The weeping flower and plaintive nightingale
> Might celebrate the funeral of your tongue.[1]

We should also consider the surprising presence in the neighbourhood of Tintern Parva of mathematicians of the calibre of Henry Billingsley. Henry Billingsley studied first at Cambridge and then Oxford, where his tutor was a well-known mathematician and former Augustinian monk called Whytehead. His name appears on one of the geometrical drawings in Byrom's collection and the 'Schweighardt scrapbook'. The drawing carries written instructions on the division of a circle based on 'Whitehead's' (*sic*) direction. Later Billingsley moved to London where he became a wealthy merchant and played a prominent part in public affairs. According to the antiquarian Anthony Wood, Whitehead spent his last years in Billingsley's household and bequeathed him a valuable collection of manuscripts. Billingsley's love of mathematics found expression in the first English translation of Euclid's *Elements of Geometrie* in 1570. To this translation John Dee wrote a ground-breaking Preface. It is significant that even when he was an alderman in London (1585) and Lord Mayor (1596), Sir Henry Billingsley kept an estate in the area.

Billingsley's interest in property in Tintern came after the publication of the translation and before his civic success in London. In the 1580s Sir William mortgaged two manors near Tintern to Billingsley and it looks as though Billingsley may have decided to share his love of mathematics by teaching it for a while at Sir William's College. The College may have seemed an ideal setting also in which to explore the new knowledge outlined by Sir William's mentor, John Dee, in that Preface. In addition Tintern provided an excellent forum for Bacon's advocacy of new experimental approaches to learning.

If the College dealt with subjects regarded with suspicion by orthodox scholars, or propounded a revolutionary methodology as Francis Bacon did in *The Advancement of Learning*, then the students, like those envisaged by John Dee for his unrealised academy, needed to be reassured by an atmosphere of safety and discretion. Dee had described one possible site for his unrealised academy as 'the more commodious for the secret arrival of special men'. The site in Tintern Parva could be approached unobtrusively by water and the slipway next to the churchyard.

At this juncture we must pause to look at the Schweighardt scrapbook. I have written about this already in *The Byrom Collection* and *Kingdom for a Stage*. It is important because it is one of the only three known sources of geometric drawings similar or identical to Byrom's.[2] It was instrumental in helping to establish their provenance in the first place and in the search for the origins of the brass plates connected with them. Some fifteen drawings have become part of the assemblage in this unique volume, now in the British Library.

It takes its title from a printed German text called *Speculum-sophicum Rhodo-Stauroticum*, written by someone using the pseudonym 'Theophilus Schweighardt'. There is no name of the printer or place of publication, just the date: 1618. We cannot assume that the text was published in Germany simply because it is in German. Copies of it exist as a separate treatise entire in itself. However, the particular copy referred to here has been bound into a unique volume that came to the British Library either from the Royal Library of George II or of his wife, Caroline of Anspach. It is perhaps best regarded as a scrapbook because it also contains a number of original drawings, separate prints and geometrical figures related to drawings in John Byrom's collection. These are not interleaved with the text. Nevertheless, the printed text contains hand-written markings in the margins that are also to be found on drawings in Byrom's collection. This indicates that the volume was once part of the same resource as Byrom's. A number of the illustrations are emblematic, telling a moral tale, at times in a somewhat cartoon-like way. Because of this they belong to a style of allegory called a 'ludibrium'.

The Schweighardt scrapbook contains some beguiling examples. A reader new to it must take care. Its sequence of pictures can so easily be dismissed as quirky, but they repay careful study, for it is a very considered compilation. The pictures surrounding the printed text are the work of several artists. Some of them appear to have been positioned strategically. The main focus of the scrapbook, of course, is the printed German text but everything that has been added in the way of mounted pictures, prints and geometric drawings is concerned with intellectual and spiritual activities. The last words of the Preface to the printed text are in Latin. They translate as follows: 'From our centralleanic Museum I wrote this on March 1st, 1617.' The following pages give reason to believe that the 'Museum' referred to is the College at Tintern and the activities associated with it.

The title page of the text gives the name of the writer as 'Theophilus Schweighardt Constantiens' and the last word 'Constantiens' is explained in German: 'by the grace of God and Nature *unchangeable forever*'. The author's initials, 'T.S.C.', appear above the head of a man in an illustration. Thus the illustration is linked firmly with the text although it is placed *after* it in the book. It is not accompanied by any explanatory notes but tells its story through symbols.

One's eye is immediately caught by the central image of the engraving – a Tabernacle positioned above ground, on a mound or small hill, beneath which are two caves. Standing between the archways into the caves is a pedestal with the inscription 'Hinc Sapientia' meaning 'Here is the source of Wisdom'. On top of this pillar is the figure of a female, pregnant and winged. Her womb displays a foetus-like figure allied to symbols of the Sun and the Moon. Is this to tell us that her offspring will encompass all knowledge under the heavens? In the left-hand cave is a youth, in the right-hand cave stands 'T.S.C.' himself.

Towards the top, inside the Tabernacle, the figure of 'T.S.C.' is repeated, this time kneeling, with arms outstretched towards the heavens. From a table by his side rise clouds of incense. The small cupola at the top of the

13. Schweighardt, 'The Tabernacle'

Tabernacle contains the Hebrew letters for J.H.V.A., the name of Jehovah. This reminds us that the Tabernacle was the portable sanctuary in the form of a tent in which the Israelites carried the Ark of the Covenant. The Ark, a chest, was the most sacred symbol of God's presence among the Hebrews. It was carried from Mount Sinai to the promised land of Canaan and eventually placed in the Holy of Holies in the Temple built in Jerusalem.

The youth in the left-hand cave is standing in water, fishing and holding what looks like an eel in one hand which he is about to put in the pot he carries in the other. A book lies open on the riverbank with the Latin word for labour (with connotations of effort and energy) written across it. The boy faces towards the pregnant statue and could almost be said to be offering up his work to the figure of Wisdom. In the background of this fishing scene another image reinforces the idea of hard work. A woman can be seen on the river bank with a circular tub busy washing. The eel-like fish the boy has caught gives the picture a special relevance to Tintern. The Wye at Tintern became famous as a place to fish for eels and elvers and has remained so to the present day. Perhaps the boy and the woman are included to remind us that honest manual labour is the means whereby some serve God and find fulfilment. (Interestingly each of them is working either in or with water.) The cave on the right represents the alchemist's cave with various pieces of equipment on a circular table including a pair of scales and the words 'arte' and 'natura' above it, showing how the learned work through art and nature to achieve an awareness of the Godhead.

Closer examination shows that the picture comprises two halves. The lower half depicts a 'parergon'; the upper half the 'ergon'. The letters of both words are deliberately divided. 'Parergon' is split between the pregnant woman's wings. The word is taken from classical Greek. A 'parergon' is a work or task that is subsidiary or secondary to some other work, or 'ergon'. 'Ergon' is the important work. (In Greek it meant a man's employment or business.) Here the 'ergon' is clearly communion with God, depicted by the man kneeling in prayer. We are being told that man's most important duty is service to the Godhead. He is the point of all our labour, manual or intellectual, the goal of all our learning. The letters of 'ergon' are carefully divided to the left and right sides of the Tabernacle. As we ponder on this, we become aware of the artist's little joke, a serious jest, a 'ludibrium'. The kneeling figure stretches out his arms to the heavens and in doing so includes within his gesture the two letters 'E.R.', Elizabeth Regina. The final syllable 'gon' may well be another linguistic jest, since at the time the engraving was first published the Virgin Queen was dead.

Such close reading is warranted when a picture is obviously emblematic and full of details that might easily be missed. For example, to the right of the right-hand tent peg on the Tabernacle, just distinguishable from the rocks behind, sprouts a branch of an acacia tree. The acacia has a long history as a symbol. The ancient Egyptians honoured it as one of the plants from which funeral wreaths were made. The Hebrews are said to have planted a sprig of acacia at the head of a grave. It is still a part of Masonic practice. Slight as the branch is, it is an important clue. It seems that at one level we are dealing with a grave, and that all the works of T.S.C. are underground.

These works may well be carried out underground, i.e. in secret, but from the holiest of motives. The symbol of a grave and the more localised suggestion of Tintern in the figure of the fisherman narrow the setting down to the possibility that this is St. Michael's riverside churchyard. The Baconian links I had already established with Tintern reinforce that possibility. Therefore, we also have to consider that T.S.C. may well be Francis Bacon himself.

Moreover, the Preface gives the date of 1 March 1617 and that was a momentous month in Bacon's career. On 15 March James I returned to Scotland for the first time since his succession. Lord Chancellor Bacon was left in charge of the country in his absence. This was a high point in his worldy ambitions. The Schweighardt 'tabernacle' illustration makes clear the sacred nature and purpose of his intellectual aspirations.

Since that illustration was a print and therefore *not totally exclusive*, one wonders who would have received a copy of this engraving. One answer to that may be found in another illustration from Schweighardt, one that serves as a frontispiece to the text. Dr. Frances Yates includes it in *The Rosicrucian Enlightenment* with the following comment:

> This print (frontispiece) shows a peculiar building above which is an inscription containing the words *Collegium Fraternitatis* and *Fama*, and is dated 1618. On the building, on either side of its door there is a rose and a cross. We are therefore presumably now beholding a representation of the Invisible College of the R.C. Brothers.

Dr. Yates comments further on this strange print:

> A hand proceeding from a cloud around the Name holds the building, as on a thread, and the building itself is winged, and on wheels. Does this mean that the winged, moveable, College of the Fraternity of the Rosy Cross is Nowhere, like Utopia, invisible because non-existent in a literal sense?[3]

I would suggest rather that the allegory means that this College is moveable in the sense that it exists in the minds of the scholars who are able to move from one place of learning to another to expound its teachings. Thought is winged and not confined to one institution. The illustration is a print preaching an ideal that could be established anywhere by the 'brotherhood'.

This print may be looked at as a companion piece to the first one we looked at of the tabernacle with the initials of T.S.C. (They both appear in the same volume.) Like so many other emblematic drawings it operates on several levels. Looking at it carefully, the winged building with a well in front of it uncannily reproduces the position of St. Michael's Church with the the 'tomb X' (the tomb that first aroused my interest) in front of its west door. In the left background, the engraving contains an image of Noah's Ark perched on a mountain top, a reference to Nurtons, positioned half way up a hill, deliberately included to be seen from this view of St. Michael's. This was the site of the earlier form of Invisible College founded by Sir William Herbert of St. Julian's. This idea may not be as fanciful as it first appears. A clue can be found in a diary written in 1855 by the wife of the local doctor at Tintern, Jenny Audland, who was related to the residents at Nurtons at that time. The entry reads simply 'Noah's Ark' and nothing else. Not another word in explanation.

The story of the Flood and Noah's Ark from the Old Testament is familiar to many. Not so well known, however, is the importance of Noah's Ark to Freemasons. According to legend, Noah discovered the 'stone of foundation' and placed it in the ark as an altar. Later he erected it as an altar to the Deity. Noah's dove is also a masonic symbol.

> He sent forth a dove three separate times: the first time the dove, finding no resting place, quickly returned; the second time, she returned with an olive-leaf, which showed that the tops of the olive trees were now exposed; but the third time, the waters having receded, she returned no more. The dove is an emblem of peace and good fortune.[4]

In the engraving two doves can be seen leaving the Ark. The date 1618 is written clearly at the top and that is significant. For that is the year the third Earl of Pembroke inherited the title 'Grandmaster of Freemasonry' from Inigo Jones. Moreover, because of the letters patent of 1553, the Earl had already inherited the site of St. Michael's when he succeeded to his father's title in 1601.

It would appear that both the engravings we have been looking at have allegorical associations with the Rectory of St. Michael's and Sir William Herbert's College.

That College was the realisation of an ideal. In this connection we should note, too, that Ben Jonson describes this same illustration in his masque *The Fortunate Isles*, 1625, and links it, albeit satirically, with an 'invisible' Order associated with actors.

14. Schweighardt illustration (note detail of Noah's Ark)

Sir William Herbert intended his College to unite his students into a brotherhood of scholars. His twin principles were religion and science: the reformed religion of the Anglican settlement and the beginnings of experimental chemistry. The hermetic tradition, in some areas discredited, still had its place. No doubt, too, did the cryptography of Dee and Francis Bacon. Herbert was more enlightened than many of his contemporaries. Very able intellectually and a devout Christian, his conscientiousness as an MP can be judged from the fact that he served on nine separate committees concerned with a wide range of matters. Moreover his College at Tintern should be seen in the wider context of a European movement for reform in both education and politics. One theoretical model for a college is presented in the Schweighardt treatise. Other models were proposed not just for colleges but also for communities, and well-intentioned people attempted to turn theory into practice.

In 1619, one year after the Schweighardt text was published, the German theologian and Rosicrucian writer, Johann Valentin Andreae, published his *Description of the Republic of Christianopolis*. In his book Andreae describes a fictional city in which science, engineering, and Christian piety go hand in hand to form an ideal society. Andreae's theories were put to the test by the formation of a group of people devoted to Christian and intellectual renewal. Unfortunately the outbreak of the Thirty Years War led to its collapse. But in 1628 there was an attempt to revive the idea, this time in Nuremberg. War and the unsettled state of Europe had not destroyed the dream of a Utopia. Both these attempts can be seen as developments from and variations on Sir William Herbert's College at Tintern Parva and ideas Bacon expressed in *New Atlantis*. This is not altogether surprising since Andreae and Bacon were contemporaries.

People are bound to ask what happened to the College? How could it disappear without trace? The Civil War, the defeat and death of Charles I, and the establishment of the Commonwealth were sufficiently cataclysmic to bring about its closure. Like any living institution, it would change in form and purpose over the years and was destined to end with the Restoration. Even before then, however, the mathematical and scientific pursuits were being taken over by the scholars we associate now with the Invisible College. The esoteric studies of John Dee and the new scientific disciplines advocated by Francis Bacon were part of the intellectual heritage of men like Robert Boyle and culminated in the foundation of The Royal Society in 1660. Six years later, Thomas, perhaps in preparation for his return to York, gave twenty manuscripts to the Bodleian Library, among them a manuscript copy of John Wycliff's translation of the Bible. The gift is a reminder of the richness of the source of learning he had at his disposal.

CHAPTER EIGHT

Francis Bacon

Despite the calls on his time in London, Sir Francis Bacon must have been able to spend some considerable time in Tintern and the surrounding area. His duties as a leaseholder of the wireworks would provide a reason for him to visit the village but I believe his real interest was in supervising the highly precise process of creating the mass of information etched and engraved on the brass plates and other brass figures by expert engravers of the calibre of Theodore de Bry. This was a highly complex and important procedure, since some of the master plates depict a world of information in the sense that they depict a vision of the universe held together by geometrical laws. As I said earlier the astronomical details included on the Byrom drawings and the brass plates *made at the wireworks* are typical of the world picture that would have been expounded at the College.

Bacon's involvement in Tintern was only one aspect of his life. The fruit of his extraordinary intellect found expression first through the law and then in his legacy of philosophical writings. Leaving aside his interest in the theatre and in poetry, his philosophical works remain the foundation of his reputation today. We cannot do justice to them all within the scope of this book, but if we look at the most important, we can begin to understand why his work played its part in the foundation of the Royal Society in 1660. The chemist Robert Boyle thought highly of him. The French Royal Academy of Science acknowledged the importance of his emphasis on the need for experiment and observation. In Germany Leibnitz declared, 'We do well to think highly of Verulam, for his hard sayings have a deep meaning in them.' Today, while debate still continues about his complex character, he is still honoured as one of the founders of the revolution in the experimental sciences.

His major writings appeared after the accession of James I. We must remember this in connection with the timing of his activities in Tintern. *The Advancement of Learning* was written between 1603 and 1604 but did not appear in print until late in 1605. It was dedicated to the king who is addressed with the most fulsome praise. James I was recognised for his literary and scholarly tastes across Europe as well as in his own kingdom.

15. Francis Bacon

In dedicating the book to him, Bacon no doubt hoped for a personal reaction to the ideas he proclaimed. He set out boldly to review what he considered was wrong with the existing state of learning and education in the country and suggested a programme for reform. As a reformer, eager to reach as wide an audience as possible, he decided to write in English, not Latin. First of all he treats learning in the broadest sense as intended for the development of man as a whole. He rejects the futile theorising of the followers of Aristotle, 'shut up in the cells of monasteries and colleges'. Their fondness for useless subtleties and distinctions did little more than 'spin out unto us these laborious webs of learning which are extant in their books'. Too much learning of this kind, he opined, can make men 'perplexed and irresolute'. Real learning should teach us 'how to carry things in suspense without prejudice till they resolve'. Bacon's fundamental approach of questioning the evidence before his eyes is now taken for granted, but in his day was revolutionary. It was good to doubt, not to accept simply what one was told. 'If a man will begin with certainties he shall end in doubts, but if he will be content to begin with doubts, he shall end in certainties.' This approach led him to encourage the *practical* application of knowledge and stress the importance of experiment. In doing so he showed he possessed one of the truly original minds of his day.

This is best seen in the *Novum Organum*, published in October 1620 and described by Bacon as 'a new logic, teaching to invent and judge by deduction'. Written in Latin, still the universal language for international debate, the book was an elaboration of ideas set out in his fable *New Atlantis*. Those ideas had been revised year after year, according to Bacon's chaplain (Theophilus Field), going through at least twelve versions before reaching their final expression in this work. The frontispiece states that it was part of his *Instauratio Magna*. This was the great dream of Bacon's life: to write the Great Instauration or, in simpler terms, the Great Renewal. It was conceived as a thorough re-examination of scientific method and investigation. Never completed in itself, the *Novum Organum* was planned as a major part of the overall scheme. It developed Bacon's attack on the abstract theorising of the old Aristotelian school:

> The sciences which we possess come for the most part from the Greeks... Now the wisdom of the Greeks was professorial and much given to disputation; a kind of wisdom most adverse to the inquisition of truth.

In other words, such a method could split hairs in debate but not bring you any nearer to the truth. Bacon, on the other hand, champions the necessity for fresh observation of the world around us and for practical testing.

> Those who have handled sciences have been either men of experiment or men of dogmas. The men of experiment are like the ant; they only collect and use: the reasoners resemble spiders, who make cobwebs out of their own substance. But the bee takes a middle course; it gathers its material from the flowers of the garden and of the field, but transforms and digests it by a power of its own.

The whole argument of the *Novum Organum* is the importance of observing nature and comparing results from experiments with what one really sees to extract 'causes and axioms'. Bacon's love of gardening and plants is one of his most endearing characteristics. His prescription for the study of the germination of seeds expresses clearly his new 'scientific' approach.

> We must ... observe (as we may easily do, by taking out day after day the seeds that have lain in the ground two days, three days, four days and so on, and carefully examining them) how and when the seed begins to puff and swell, and to be as it were filled with spirit; secondly how it begins to burst the skin and put forth fibres, at the same time raising itself slightly upwards, unless the ground be very stiff ... In the same way we should examine the hatching of eggs, in which we might easily observe the whole process of vivification and organisation.

Novum Organum, too, was dedicated to James I, but the king confessed that the book was 'like the peace of God, that passeth all understanding'. An Oxford scholar, Henry Cuffe, said acidly that 'a fool could not have written such a work, and a wise man would not'. Cuffe saw the audacity of Bacon's methodology. It implied a criticism of so much established thought – where would such questioning end? We have only to remember the bloody divisions already caused by religious reformers to see how far ahead of his time Bacon's thinking was. While it is true that he himself never made any great scientific discovery, his interest in the application of knowledge can be seen in his design for an acoustical levitating machine.[1] His dream of a 'College of Inventors' was not realised but he laid down the foundations of the modern experimental method and had moments of inspired vision that led to great advances later, such as his realisation that when we look at a clear night sky there might be 'as regards our sight of heavenly bodies, a real time and an apparent time'.

Apart from his philosophical writings there is, of course, Bacon's collection of *Essays*. After circulating for some months in private they first appeared in print in 1597. That edition contained just ten essays; by the time he published the third edition in 1625 they numbered fifty-eight. They are the work by which Bacon is most widely known and mark an important stage in the development of English prose. He ranges widely in subject matter, writing on Death, Ambition, Gardens, Friendship, Superstition and Revenge. He writes in short, clear sentences graced with images which catch his thought in flight. Many of the beginnings especially compel us to read on: 'God Almighty first planted a Garden'; 'Men fear Death, as children fear to go in the dark'; 'Suspicions amongst thoughts are like bats amongst birds, they ever fly by twilight'.

Pausing to reflect on Bacon's written works and the extraordinary range of his intellect, I also reviewed the public offices he held. Having been constantly frustrated in his ambitions during Elizabeth's reign, he hoped for better things from her successor. The new reign began promisingly enough for Bacon when he was knighted on 23 July 1603, in the royal garden at Whitehall. However, he found himself one of three hundred so honoured that day to celebrate the king's coronation. Together with the knighthood the king granted him a pension of sixty pounds. For a man of forty-two this was very small beer compared with the rewards he saw lavished on others. His progress up the legal ladder was impeded by the success of his great rival, Edward Coke, who was now Attorney General and the jealousy of his powerful cousin, Robert Cecil, who had already attained the highest office as Elizabeth's Secretary of State. Four years elapsed before Bacon was made Solicitor General in 1607 with a salary of a hundred pounds a year. But the position was worth about a thousand pounds in fees and incidental benefits. In 1613 with some careful manouevering he managed to get Coke moved upstairs to be Chief Justice of King's Bench and in the subsequent reshuffle got himself appointed Attorney General. Coke was furious and rounded angrily on Bacon: 'Mr. Attorney! This is all your doing. It is you who have made this great stir.' Bacon's reply revealed his suavity and wit. 'Ah! my Lord. Your Lordship all this while hath grown in breadth. You must now grow in height, or else you would be a monster.'

In June 1616, at the age of fifty-six, he was made a member of the Privy Council, an honour he had so longed for. His power and influence increased accordingly just as Chief Justice Coke fell from grace. Further honours followed: he was made Lord Keeper of the Great Seal in 1617 and then Lord Chancellor and Baron Verulam. His final distinction came in 1621 when, at the age of sixty, he was raised one degree higher to become Viscount St. Alban.

Throughout his life Bacon demonstrated a fatal weakness that undermined his stature. Despite his undoubted intelligence and the breadth of his knowledge he was not good at handling money. He lived constantly beyond his means, and extravagantly so. The extravagance only increased with his advancement. Little wonder then that in 1606, at the time he was begging the Solicitor Generalship from his cousin Robert Cecil, he

16. Alice Barnham

married a young bride of fourteen. He himself was forty-five. Alice Barnham came from a family of wealthy drapers. Bacon had first noticed her when she was eleven and in his words 'a handsome maiden to my liking'. Looking at the disparity in their ages it is obvious that her fortune must have been the great attraction.

It is also obvious to any student of Bacon's life that he planned long and hard to achieve his ambition to reach the office of Lord Keeper, once filled with great distinction by Sir Nicholas Bacon. Everything was considered carefully, even his marriage. As one would expect from a man who spent his whole life dealing with the law, he was just as careful in making his will. He became ill towards the end of 1625, and, after making his will in December, soon added a codicil to disinherit his wife. The will was carefully worded to assert his own worth along with a dutiful submission to the inevitable.

> I bequeath my soul to God above. My body to be buried obscurely. My name to the next ages, and to foreign nations.

The words 'My body to be buried obscurely', so often quoted by his biographers, now took on a different meaning for me. Was it possible that here Bacon was referring to an obscure churchyard in Tintern Parva, fully aware of the ambiguity of these words? It would have been in character for a man who was interested in codes and who chose at times to sign his name with the cipher 'C'. The tomb at St. Michael's had lain unnoticed for centuries. If it were connected with Bacon, surely there would be papers somewhere to indicate who owned it? Whatever one's doubts, we have to recognise that there is a mystery about his death and burial. We noticed earlier the alleged absence of any remains at Gorhambury.

I continued looking for any further clues there might be among papers in the public domain. The State Papers Domestic for 1626 contain the following entry on p. 307 for April 10: 'Whitehall, Lord St. Alban is dead and so is Sir Thomas Compton.' That is all. The coupling of two separate deaths in one line of official reporting and nothing more. The *fact* of the death is mentioned, not the date. Little else is so straightforward. In the light of the inconsistencies mentioned earlier I had to continue my search. I was still wary of making a decision one way or another about Francis Bacon.

He was a man of exceptional gifts who, despite disappointments and setbacks, had always striven to use those gifts in the service of his sovereign. Elizabeth for the most part chose not to make much use of his talents. In James he found a more sympathetic monarch and was able to deploy his legal skills and acute mind in the king's cause and to his own credit. His philosophical writings show him to be ahead of his time. All that is agreed. However it is necessary to look briefly at his downfall. He was accused of accepting bribes and imprisoned. I do not propose to go over ground already well tilled, but Bacon's fall from favour raises issues that must be addressed.

By 1621 King James was ruling more and more through his most cherished favourite, George Villiers, now Marquis of Buckingham. The House of Commons had already become increasingly resentful at this and eventually their resentment spread to include Bacon who, seeing Buckingham's star rising at Court, had made a friend of him. The House of Commons set up the 'Committee for Inquiring into Abuses in the Courts of Justice' and on 14 March that year allegations of bribery and corruption were brought against Lord Chancellor Bacon. Gradually, to Bacon's horror, the charges mounted. It may well be true that it suited the king and Buckingham to sacrifice Bacon to the Commons to divert hostility from themselves and the abuse of monopolies. Bacon attempted, by direct acknowledgement of certain practices considered acceptable at the time, to rebut the charge of corruption. Then he sought to minimise the consequences of his behaviour by a confession and humble submission delivered to the Lord Chief Justice on 30 April. He protested that avarice had never been one of his vices and that his present poverty and debts were almost proof of this. He appealed to the members of the House of Lords to temper their judgment with mercy and to intercede for him with the king.

In answering twenty-eight particular charges Bacon used three main arguments to justify his behaviour. The first was to claim that he had already passed judgment by the time he received gifts from the litigant so the gift could not have influenced his decision. The gift was 'for favours past, and not in respect for favours to come'.

Secondly, he declared that certain gifts were presented on days when it was perfectly acceptable to give them, such as New Year's Day. This being so, he had not checked to see whether any case concerning his benefactor was concluded or still pending. Thirdly, he maintained that some charges involved servants who had received gifts of money without his knowing and that he had sometimes failed to ensure the regularity of their conduct. He confessed that this was 'a great fault of neglect'. All these arguments are debatable. Perhaps what strikes a modern reader most forcibly about the charges is the readiness with which people admitted that they had given Bacon bribes without receiving favourable judgments in return.

Nevertheless Bacon's punishment was a fine of £40,000 and imprisonment at the king's pleasure in the Tower. In addition he was deemed unfit for any future public office, 'nor to come within the verge [twelve miles] of the court'. Because events had reduced Bacon to ill-health the king refrained from sending him immediately to the Tower. His enemies, however, persisted and towards the end of May he left York House for the Tower. Imprisonment was what he dreaded most and he wrote on 31 May to Buckingham, almost demanding his release the same day. He protested that he had always been a good servant to the king, a loving friend to Buckingham and a dispenser of sound and sensible counsel. On 2 June he was released. From the Tower he was sent to the home of Sir John Vaughan.

The year 1621, which had begun with such promise, turned into a disaster for Bacon. His whole life was turned upside down, his public career ruined and his health badly affected. Sir John Vaughan was Comptroller of the Household to Prince Charles; his house was at Parson's Green in Fulham. At first the change to the 'sweet air and loving usage' was very welcome after the few days in the Tower.[2] Bacon wrote movingly of his gratitude to Prince Charles for saving him from imprisonment.

He was still hopeful of being able to serve the king and James indeed consulted him about the proposed reform of the Courts of Justice. Bacon readily gave his advice and used this as an opportunity to beg the king to 'give me leave to stay at London till the last of July'.[3] James replied, however, that it was his wish that Bacon should go to Gorhambury. This he did on 23 June.

Bacon had been heavily fined and already owed money. The situation was serious and he wrote to Buckingham, Prince Charles and a number of prominent courtiers begging for help. One of these, Sir Thomas Erskine, Lord of Kelly, succeeded in getting his confinement repealed. On 13 September Bacon received a warrant 'for the space of one month or six weeks' to go again to Sir John Vaughan's house at Parson's Green 'for the settling of your estate and taking order of your debts' and because 'at this time your broken estate of health requireth that you be near help of physicians'.[4]

Later the king reallocated Bacon's fine 'unto such persons as he himself shall nominate'. In effect this allowed Bacon to decide which of his many creditors should be paid the fine at the expense of the rest. James also granted him a 'coronation pardon' releasing him from liability from all past offences 'with an exception nevertheless of the sentence given in our high Court of Parliament'.[5]

Seeking more concessions in the autumn, Bacon got permission to return to York House. Loving the place where he was born and had lived as Lord Chancellor, he was loath to leave, begged to stay for Christmas, but was refused and sent back to Gorhambury.

Sir John Vaughan was not someone I had come across earlier in Bacon's life. Why did he appear now? Why was it to *his* house that Bacon was sent on his release from the Tower?

Sir John Vaughan was the MP for Carmarthen in 1601 and again from 1620 to 1622. He had been knighted originally in 1599 by the Earl of Essex for services in Ireland but that honour had been revoked by Queen Elizabeth. He received his second knighthood from James I in February 1616/17 and as Comptroller of the Household accompanied Prince Charles to Spain on an embassy concerned with his possible marriage to a Spanish princess.

Vaughan was elevated to the peerage as Baron Vaughan of Mullingar (1621) and later Earl of Carbery (1628). His family claimed descent from the Welsh princes of South Wales. His son, Richard Vaughan 1600(?)–1686 married Lady Alice Egerton, daughter of John, first Earl of Bridgewater. Lady Alice was the sister of two other Egerton daughters whom I had noticed earlier, Mary and Magdalene. Mary married Richard Herbert of Tintern Parva, the son of Mary Herbert and Edward, Lord Herbert of Chirbury. It was this Richard who had 'sold' the estate to Thomas Herbert. Thomas in turn had married as his second wife Elizabeth, the daughter of Magdalene Egerton. Thus, by some extraordinary twist of fate, one of the sisters, Mary, married the man who sold Tintern Parva Estate and the daughter of another sister, Magdalene, married the man who bought it.

Reflecting on Bacon's imprisonment, I noted that the man instrumental in obtaining the license for his release was one Sir Thomas Erskine. Who was he? Erskine enters history in 1600 by helping to save the life of King James in Scotland. For this he was rewarded later with an earldom. Later still, he appears on the fringe of our story as the fourth husband of Bacon's mother-in-law, Dorothy Barnham. That relationship and his good standing with the king made him a most suitable intermediary at this crucial moment in Bacon's life. The king undoubtedly had the greatest trust in Erskine. Who better to plead Bacon's cause? But if Bacon took care over his choice of envoy, equally careful thought would have been given as to who should have custody of him on his release from the Tower.

The role of Sir John Vaughan looked more like that of a protector than gaoler. But the relationship between the two men was a long-standing one. Both had different concerns with Tintern Parva. Bacon's interest, as we have seen, went back at least to 1611 as a shareholder in the wireworks. Sir John Vaughan had links with the area through his marriage to Catherine Catchmay, a member of the family who at one time leased part of Tintern Parva Estate where Sir William Herbert set up his College.

Bacon and Vaughan were linked in other ways. Sir John Vaughan had a brother, William. Both men studied at Jesus College, Oxford. William married twice. By his first wife, Catherine, he had a son, whom they christened Francis. The boy died young and Catherine died in 1608 when their house was struck by lightning. In 1610 William joined a company of merchant adventurers that included Sir Francis Bacon among the investors. To them James I granted 'considerable territory in Newfoundland for purposes of colonisation'.[6] Unfortunately William's hopes of making a fortune were dashed by the severe winters that devastated the colony. By his second wife, Anne, he had a son, Edward, who married Jemima Bacon, the daughter of Nicholas Bacon, thus continuing and strengthening the Vaughan–Bacon relationship into a later generation.

There are other indications of the respect Francis Bacon retained with the Vaughans. William Vaughan wrote several books and developed an interest in medicine. In 1600 he published *Naturall and Artificiall Directions for Health derived from the best Philosophers as well Moderne as Ancient*. This went through various editions. The fifth, published in 1617, was dedicated to Sir Francis Bacon; the sixth, published in 1626, to William, third Earl of Pembroke. It is perhaps significant that, after the 'death' of Bacon, Vaughan chose to dedicate the book to him. In Vaughan's mind the two men, Bacon and Pembroke, were linked and appropriately so in this context. Finally, Sir John Vaughan's own son Richard had a son christened Francis.

Despite searching, I was unable to discover any close connection between Sir Thomas Erskine and Sir John Vaughan. Nor had I seen him mentioned as connected with Alice Barnham's mother before this time. What seems to have happened is that, in the weeks before Bacon's imprisonment, King James tried to persuade Erskine, who had lost his own wife in April 1621 (two days before Bacon submitted to the charges brought against him) to pay court to Alice Barnham's mother, Dorothy, who had herself been recently widowed. Dorothy was a very wealthy woman. Her last marriage had been notoriously unsettled. After the death of her husband, Sir John Pakington, James may well have considered her wealth a suitable 'reward' for the man who had saved his life. Unfortunately another suitor pipped Erskine to the post and Dorothy married Robert Needham, Viscount Kilmorey. Nevertheless on *his* death in 1631 Erskine did become Dorothy Barnham's fourth and final husband. Reviewing this course of events I could not help feeling that James may well have had another motive in proposing the match. If Erskine had succeeded earlier in his suit in 1621, he would have been a trusted presence in a household from which he could report on the activities of the disgraced Lord Chancellor.

Alice Barnham is, in herself, a figure of some interest.[7] She is a very shadowy person during her life with Bacon for little is known of their relationship. At the time of Bacon's trial she was living with him at York House. Alice appealed on behalf of Francis for them to be allowed to stay in order not to lose all status in the eyes of the City. Both Alice and her mother appear to have been of volatile temperaments. Dorothy, as we saw, married four times. Alice married for a second time eleven days after Bacon's death in 1626. Her new husband was Sir John Underhill, who had joined the household as gentleman usher to Francis in 1617. From this it is quite clear what Alice's relationship with Underhill had been earlier. Their married life was marred by constant disputes over property and money, so much so that in 1631 the dowager Lady Alice Egerton appears to have arranged to have one of her servants placed as an informant in Alice Barnham's household. His name was Robert Turrell or Tyrrell. Later Turrell claimed that he joined the household as a gentleman usher to Alice Barnham. She, in turn, persuaded him to become servant to her husband. So it looks as if Turrell not only reported back to the dowager Lady Egerton about Alice Barnham but may have spied on Underhill also for his vehemently disenchanted wife.

The dowager Lady Alice Egerton had begun life as the daughter of a wealthy Elizabethan wool merchant, Sir John Spencer. Her first husband was Ferdinando Stanley, Earl of Derby. Beautiful and vivacious, she was the third wife of Sir Thomas Egerton, Lord Chancellor to Queen Elizabeth for twenty-one years. Frances Stanley, her second daughter by Ferdinando, married John Egerton, a son of Sir Thomas from his previous marriage. That union produced the three Egerton sisters, Mary, Magdalene and Alice, whose connections with Tintern we have already noted.

Ferdinando Stanley had been one of the members of Bacon's exclusive group, the Knights of the Helmet. From this beginning, I believe, can be traced a very protective attitude on Lady Alice's part towards Bacon in later life. We can sense her hand in the interventions in the household of Alice Barnham and John Underhill. I see her, too, as a guiding influence in the marriages of the three granddaughters to 'Tintern' men, each of whom was able in his own way to be a help and support to Francis Bacon.

There were compelling reasons why Alice Egerton should be so disposed to Bacon. In 1616 Bacon had given £8,000 to Lord Chancellor Egerton, (now Lord Ellesmere) for his retirement. This has been calculated in today's money as the equivalent of £4 million.[8] There were no automatic pensions for state servants. The king sent a message to Lord Ellesmere through Bacon that he intended to give him an annual pension of £3,000 (£1,500,000), but Ellesmere was terminally ill and survived the news by a mere half hour.

Lady Alice Egerton would have been fully aware of Bacon's generosity to her husband in the last days of his life. Doubtless, too, she would have remembered Bacon's help and support years earlier during the protracted legal wranglings over Ferdinando Stanley's estate. *Lancashire Funeral Certificates*, edited by T.W. King and F.R. Raines, describes how, after

Francis Bacon

Ferdinando's death, Lady Alice commenced her lawsuit against his successor, the sixth Earl of Derby:

> On the 23rd September 1594, Mr. Michael Doughtie, servant of William, earl of Derby, and Mr. Hugh Ellis, servant to the lady Alice countess dowager of Derby, deposited in the presence of Francis lord Bacon and others, a trunk containing family evidences, in the custody of sir Thomas Egerton, afterwards lord Ellesmere.

What was the result of these preparations?

> The profound legal and judicial ability of sir Thomas Egerton, afterwards the lord chancellor, secured for the dowager countess of Derby and her daughters a larger proportion of the old hereditary estates and titles of the Stanleys than any of the parties interested in them had originally anticipated.

There was reason enough here for her to seize any opportunity that came her way to help Bacon in turn. Furthermore, in 1600, Sir Thomas Egerton, now a widower of sixty but still handsome

> married, for his third wife, the accomplished dowager lady Derby, who at that time was noted for her vivacity and great personal charms; although she was no longer the youthful *Amaryllis* of Spenser, having attained the age of 44 years.[9]

The dowager Lady Alice Egerton was a patron of some of the leading writers and poets of the day. As late as 1635 she continued this role. About that year Milton's pastoral poem *Arcades* was written in her honour and presented to her at her home at Harefield by some of her grandchildren. Considering her indebtedness to Bacon for the part he played in securing both her financial and personal well being, I think this beautiful and compelling woman was one of the mainsprings in engineering his 'disappearance' on 9 April 1626.

Like all churches in Monmouthshire, St. Michael's came under the administrative responsibility of the Bishop of Llandaff, whose official palace was at Mathern, only six miles from Tintern. It was his responsibility to oversee and maintain the flow of Christian doctrine throughout the diocese. From 1619–1627, a crucial time in this story, the bishop was Theophilus Field, a man who also warrants our attention.

First of all, there was his position and authority as the local bishop. Secondly, on a purely personal level, he had a brother, Nathaniel, who was an actor and happened to be a member of what had been Shakespeare's company. In addition there was another Field, Richard. He was a printer who hailed from Stratford of all places and consequently knew Shakespeare well. He was responsible for printing the first three editions of *Venus and Adonis*, as well as the first edition of the *Rape of Lucrece*. Richard Field and Shakespeare had lived close to each other in the Blackfriars quarter of London. Moreover, Richard Field was a friend of Francis Bacon and is known to have visited him at his country retreat at Twickenham Park, where the two men could discuss in private, with like-minded friends, the degrees of Masonry and the publications of the Rosicrucians. Lancelot Andrews, a prime mover in the preparation of the Authorized Version of the Bible, was another member of this inner group. A trio of Fields, connected by blood or business, or both, with each other and either Shakespeare or Bacon, raises all sorts of questions for anyone attempting to unravel the mystery of Tintern.

For example, if we look a little closer at Theophilus Field we find another surprise in store. After a successful career at Cambridge, he rose from serving as a country vicar to be chaplain to James I. This brought him into contact with Francis Bacon and when Bacon became Lord Chancellor in March 1617, Field was appointed his chaplain as well. The close intimacy this position implies makes him a figure of some interest to us, especially since, in one of the many letters written by John Chamberlain, there is one dated 2 June 1619 which describes Field as acting as 'a sort of broker' for Bacon.

In October of the same year Field was promoted to be Bishop of Llandaff. What is more interesting still is that Field's departure from Llandaff (and thus the end of his responsibility for St. Michael's) coincided with Bacon's 'death' in 1626.

In 1621 Field was impeached by the House of Commons for bribery before his elevation to bishop i.e. during his time as Bacon's chaplain. (Bacon was to face a similar charge himself soon.) Field's defence against the charge of bribery was successful but the Commons still required the Archbishop of Canterbury to issue an official rebuke to him. In an act of political humbug the Commons also asked the Archbishop to admonish him as a private individual, not as Bishop of Llandaff – to avoid bringing scandal upon the Church. We should not be surprised, then, that Field was promoted to a *richer* diocese, St. David's, in 1627, and later still to Hereford. His later career need not concern us but his relationship with Bacon does. His years as Bacon's chaplain may well have been to Bacon's advantage in a way that has not been appreciated. It could explain the lack of any intervention from church authorities to prevent the activities in the churchyard at St. Michael's that were discussed in Chapters Two and Four.

At this stage it might be useful to pause and review the findings to date. Already there seemed to be a procession of figures linked with Tintern or the surrounding area and with Francis Bacon. First and foremost there was the brilliant figure of his business partner and fellow theatre lover, the third Earl of Pembroke. There was the grand presence of the Earl of Worcester dominating the landscape from his castles at Chepstow and Raglan, and his wife Anne ready to take charge of the wireworks. Then there were the three Herbert brothers, George, Edward and Henry, associated with him through poetry, property and plays; the two Field brothers, Theophilus and Nathaniel, chaplain and actor, and their printer namesake, Richard. Finally we have Toby Matthew forever a friend publicly showing his support yet a recusant, hiding at times in disguise at nearby Raglan. When we turn to Bacon himself, we are once more faced with the mystery of his death and above all his burial at ... which St. Michael's? Near which St. Albans? In Hertfordshire or Monmouthshire? Coupled with the tomb decorated with 'C's at Tintern Parva and the absence of any signs of an interment at Gorhambury – the ambiguity of two churches and two homes cannot be simply brushed aside. Was this ambiguity deliberate? It was certainly convenient for anyone wishing to confuse his enemies. It could be seen as an evasive tactic by someone dismissed from high office through trumped-up charges, disillusioned by the endless game of patronage and place-seeking, someone prepared to wait for the judgement of posterity.

The existence of the two churches dedicated to St. Michael was just the beginning of the problem. There are, I knew, at least sixteen such in modern-day Gwent. There were other causes for disquiet. Apart from the empty tomb at Gorhambury and the anonymous tomb at Tintern Parva I was bothered by glaring inconsistencies in accounts of Bacon's fate. According to different sources he died in four different places. An extraordinary feat even for someone with his formidable talents! He is said to have died at Lord Arundel's; at the house of a friend, Dr. Perry; at the home of Sir Julius Caesar; and at the home of his physician, Dr. Winterborne. When I thought of this quartet of settings my attention was caught by the name of Sir Julius Caesar.[10]

This man's career straddled the reigns of both Elizabeth and James I. We noted earlier his involvement in the management of the wireworks at Tintern. Furthermore a letter survives from Sir William Herbert of St. Julian's appealing for his help over the misappropriation of corn in the area. So his links with Tintern are clear.

Caesar was born in 1558 and died in 1636. His father, Cesare Adelmare, was an Italian who migrated to England about 1550 and eventually became physician first to Mary and then Elizabeth. Both queens addressed him as Caesar and this was adopted by his children as their surname. Julius was his eldest son and studied law at Oxford and Paris. He rose by degrees to become Master of the Rolls, but he first met Francis Bacon in 1576 when they were in the entourage of Sir Amias Paulet who was sent by Elizabeth as Ambassador to the King of France for three years. Francis was fifteen at the time, Julius a youth of eighteen. This time abroad was both civilising and instructive at a formative period in their lives. Years later Bacon chose to recall 'three of my young years bred with an ambassador in France' as a recommendation to James I. Those years also laid the foundation of a life-long friendship with Caesar.

Caesar lacked Bacon's legal brilliance but he was that rare thing in the Elizabethan and Jacobean courts – a man of absolute integrity and, unfortunately for himself, of most generous instincts. In 1584 Elizabeth appointed him Judge of the Admiralty Court, but, characteristically, without a regular salary. Because the suitors in this particular court were usually poor seamen or foreigners Caesar was regularly reduced to relieving them out of his own pocket. His generosity was legendary. Fuller describes him as practically

> the almoner-general of the nation. The story is well known of a gentleman who once borrowing his coach (which was as well known to poor people as any hospital in England) was so rendezvoused about with beggars in London that it cost him all the money in his purse to satisfy their importunity, so that he might have hired twenty coaches on the same terms.'

Fuller concludes:

> Sir Francis Bacon, Lord Verulam was judicious in his election when perceiving his dissolution to approach he made his last bed in effect in the house of Sir Julius.[11]

So there it was – Bacon's 'last bed' was ' in the house of Sir Julius'. This version of the authorised end is understandable when one realises that Sir Julius was at that time a neighbour to the Earl of Arundel in Highgate where Bacon is said to have taken refuge at the onset of this last illness. Sir Julius lived nearby at Muswell Hill.

The paths of the two men were constantly crossing both professionally and privately. In 1620 the Attorney General, Sir Henry Yelverton, was suspended from office on suspicion of wrongdoing and Caesar, as a member of the Star Chamber, was one of the judicial authorities called in to review the evidence with Bacon. The following year, 1621, when Bacon was in disgrace, the king appointed Caesar as one of the three liquidators to sort out Bacon's debts with his creditors. Later, in 1625, the year before he died, Bacon nominated him as one of the supervisors of his will, ,describing him as 'my good friend and near ally, the master of the rolls'. In the end the relationship had become a family one. When Sir Julius married for the third time in 1615 the bride was Bacon's niece, Anne, granddaughter of Sir Nicholas Bacon, and Sir Francis Bacon gave her away. With all this evidence of their closeness to each other, to suggest that Bacon died in the arms of Julius Caesar would in no way be stretching the bounds of credibility.

Bacon's personal involvement with Tintern was now over, but the legacy of his new approach to science and learning remained and grew in importance.

Four years later, almost to the day, another major figure was destined to end his ties with Jacobean Tintern. That was William Herbert, third Earl of Pembroke. He had succeeded in due course to the ownership of the Rectory of St. Michael's bestowed on his grandfather by Edward VI in 1553. On 10 April 1630, Earl William died in the most extraordinary circumstances. The facts were recorded by his kinsman, Thomas Herbert, future owner of Tintern Parva Estate and its hermetic college, in his *History of the race of Herbert*.

> This noble Lord, the night before he dyed, supped at Fishers Folly without Aldgate with Lady Lucy Countess of Bedford, Countess of Devonshir, Mrs Murray with severall other Lords and Ladyes, and some of the company discoursing upon the vanity of this life, the certainty of death, and the incertainty of the hour of death; The Earl tould the company that God Almighty had kept secrett the end of mans life, that he might be prepared – in continuale expectacion of it. But says he I would have no way trust in the presumpcions of Judiciall Astrology, for I bless God that I am now in as good health as ever I was in my life and have no simptons of death or other malady; Nevertheless my Fathers Chaplain being one very studious in naturall philosophy, at my Birth calculated the horoscope of my nativity, and found that I should end my life this day; The company agreed with the Earl as to the fallaciousness of that study, and a little before midnight parted; But being come to Baynards Castle and in Bed, he began to complain, and growing worse the Countess rung a silver watch or bell, which being heard, the servants hastned to know the occasion, and found the Earl dead of an Imposthumo or Apoplexy; Lamentable were the cries of his good Lady and Family and no less the sorrow of all that knew him; I heard our gracious King Charles the first say, when the news was brought to him of his good Earls death, he was never more surprised or fuller of anguish and sorrow for the death of any of his servants or Councillors than for him; For he was a Father to him in affection – faithful and prudent to him in Advice, an honnour to his Court and family, not sparing his own Estate, which was great (£30,000 p.anno as I have heard Mr Halesworth his secretary affirm) to honnour the King.[12]

The supper took place on 9 April, the anniversary of Bacon's death. With the conversation turning to the 'vanity of life' and 'the hour of death', one would not be surprised if Bacon and his demise were very much in the minds of those present. Thomas Herbert was to have dined with the Earl next day but with his patron dying in such strange circumstances, he decided to leave London for France and spent more than a year travelling on the Continent.

Like so many others, Pembroke's passing raises a number of questions. We have seen this with Bacon. Deciding where Bacon had died was one thing; discovering where he was buried was a different matter altogether.

That problem leads unexpectedly to another very close to Bacon, one concerned with the last days of his mother. Over the years many Baconian scholars had indicated that, like her son, she would have been buried at Gorhambury. But surrounding both these burials there is a mystery with claims that there is no physical evidence at Gorhambury for the burial of either Lady Anne Bacon or Sir Francis. Not surprisingly, this has led to much speculation and many conflicting claims.

The present study, initiated from the Byrom Collection and information thrown up by that investigation, led me to look again at a letter frequently quoted by scholars when discussing Lady Anne's last days. It has been used in various ways depending on the brief of the writer concerned. The letter was written by Bacon himself at the time of his mother's death to Sir Michael Hickes, secretary to Lord Burleigh, Bacon's uncle. (Bacon's mother and Lady Burleigh were sisters, Anne and Elizabeth Cooke respectively.) I knew of the letter but its contents assumed a different level of importance in the implications it had for the vexed question of Lady Bacon's burial place.

The letter was written on 27 August 1610 and the most extensive quotation from it can be found in Jardine and Stewart's biography *Hostage to Fortune*. The letter is part of the Lansdowne Collection in the British Library.[13] Its authenticity is beyond doubt.

> It is but a wish and not any ways to desire it to your trouble. But I heartily wish I had your company here at my mother's funeral, which I purpose on Thursday next in the forenoon. I dare promise you a good sermon to be made by Mr. Fenton, the preacher of Gray's Inn; for he never maketh other. Feast I make none. But if I mought have your company for two or three days at my house I should pass over this mournful occasion with more comfort. If your son had continued at St. Julian's it mought have been adamant to have drawn you; but now if you come I must say it is only for my sake.

It was the sentence referring to St. Julian's that suddenly took on a new significance, because it showed that Bacon must have been writing from nearby Mount St. Albans, Monmouthshire: the words 'here' and 'at my house' refer to Mount St. Albans near St. Julian's in Monmouthshire. St.

Albans, Gorhambury, Hertfordshire, does not make sense in this context. In 1610, the year the letter was written, William, the son of Sir Michael Hickes mentioned here, would have been about 14 years old. Living at 'St. Julian's' were Mary Herbert, her young husband Edward Herbert and their family; they had married in 1598. As a child Mary, daughter of John Dee's friend Sir William Herbert of St. Julian's, used to play with Dee's son, Arthur, when they were neighbours at Mortlake. Years later, the son of Burleigh's secretary was spending time with the same family.

The Herberts of St. Julian's owned Tintern Parva Estate (Nurtons) in 1610. Next to it, as we know, stood another church dedicated to St. Michael.

Lady Anne Bacon, a woman of formidable talent and character, had disappeared from public life some years earlier because of her ill health. Bacon appears to have used Mount St. Alban's as a refuge for his ailing mother towards the end of her life. Since her final resting place is unknown, could she, too, have been buried at St. Michael's, Tintern Parva?

Bacon's plea for the companionship of Sir Michael Hickes at this particular moment reveals a very tender side to his nature. He had just lost his mother, for whom he had been caring for some eight years. He had also lost his aunt, her sister Lady Burleigh, and Burleigh himself. His brother, Anthony, was long dead. Bereft of all his close family ties, he evidently thought that Sir Michael Hickes was one person whose company might be of some comfort. There was to be no great funeral feast, just the presence of his close friend to see him through this bleak occasion.

CHAPTER NINE

Intellectual Brotherhood

THE MYSTERY SURROUNDING Francis Bacon's death and burial has preoccupied writers for over four hundred years. Some biographers do not recognise that there is a problem and deal with his life accordingly. Others have attempted to deal with the inconsistencies presented to them but have never been totally satisfied with the result of their labours.

My search for first sources had led to the single sentence we looked at earlier in the State Papers Domestic for 10 April 1626: 'Whitehall, Lord St. Alban is dead and so is Sir Thomas Compton.'

Such a bald statement was provoking. Devoid of any attendant facts, the announcement is coupled with the death of another man. The name of Sir Thomas Compton does not leap off the page with the shock of instant recognition that comes with Bacon's fame. This announcement of his death is unworthy of such a public figure. One can be forgiven for thinking it was intended to reduce Bacon's status in history.

Indeed the entry brought me back once more to John Byrom, custodian of the theatre drawings that had led me to Tintern in the first place and a man who, ironically, brought with him problems similar to those surrounding Francis Bacon. Aspects of both men's lives have been forgotten, ignored or deliberately suppressed.

In May 1994, within weeks of the publication of *The Queen's Chameleon*, a photographer I had used for some of the illustrations and whose firm was aptly named 'Byrom Studios' was approached by a book dealer from Brecon, anxious to be put in touch with me. He had in his keeping an original eighteenth-century pocket diary written in what he thought was Byrom's shorthand. Among the few words he had recognised was the name of Ralph Leycester, a close confidant of John Byrom whom I mention on the very first page of the book. Eventually the bookseller sent me photocopies of some of the opening pages of the diary to enable me to check whether the shorthand was Byrom's and to assess the nature of the contents.

Ralph Leycester subscribed to learn Byrom's shorthand and I soon established that the diary dated from 1725 by which time Leycester had learned the system. My attempt to purchase the diary turned into a prolonged game of cat and mouse. It seemed to belong to a third party who wished to remain anonymous; the bookseller himself, being sure now of my interest, became curiously elusive. On one occasion I made five separate telephone calls to him and it was becoming extremely difficult to bring the negotiations to a successful close. This only happened when a relative, who lived not far from the bookseller's premises, acting on my behalf strolled into his office one morning to enquire what the state of play was. A copy of *The Queen's Chameleon* was visible on the desk in front of him. After this intervention I obtained the manuscript at the highest price it could be sold for without the owner being obliged to provide proof of provenance. I happily sent my cheque to Wales and it was duly cashed in Yorkshire. Strange as all this was, the price was well worth it.

I still do not know how the bookseller came by the MS, but the correspondence over the purchase has been carefully documented even to the cashing of my cheque. The appearance of the diary so close to the publication of the biography seems a clear indication that the owner was aware of its potential importance and wanted me to have access to it. His wish to remain anonymous was intriguing but could simply have been a desire to protect a much-valued privacy. The months that followed were spent in carefully transcribing the shorthand. The period covered, 1725–26, was of special interest for it coincided with a gap in Byrom's own detailed daily journal.

This is not the place to reproduce Leycester's diary in full, but it is necessary to refer to one episode that took place in June 1726. The importance of this for me was that it confirmed the thesis presented in *The Queen's Chameleon* that Byrom had been involved in a liaison with Princess Caroline, consort of the future George II. One day the complete manuscript will be published in traditional orthography. For our purposes it is sufficient to say that Ralph Leycester is clearly using Byrom's shorthand to record events he considered too dangerous to recount in conventional English. In effect the shorthand is, as Byrom himself intended, a secret language. Byrom taught it privately to the great and the good and did not publish the system during his lifetime. It thus remained a private code. Within that code Leycester further disguises the narrative by using fable and parable. (Byrom himself used a sequence of poems as the medium in which he could relate the course of his affair with Caroline.) Among Byrom's many pupils were the twin founders of the Methodist movement, John and Charles Wesley. Charles Wesley's journals remained a locked book until finally transcribed in 2008.[1]

Leycester's diary records that on the night of 14 June 1726 he was 'at Paul's churchyard at the club'. This was the Goose and Gridiron, where a distinguished group of Byrom's friends called the 'Sun Club' used to meet in a room underneath the meeting place of one of the early Masonic lodges. From this group Byrom later formed his own exclusive 'Cabala Club'. During the evening at the 'Sun Club' a fellow member, George d'Anteney, produced a written account entitled 'The sins of dogs and other animals'. Leycester records the content as if it were a fable about dogs, but the context shows that in reality it is an account concerning the discovery by the king of Byrom's adulterous behaviour.

Byrom's shorthand, then, was useful for recording things in secret. Those who used it had a need to ensure secrecy for one reason or another. Byrom found it profitable to travel from Manchester to London each year to teach his system to pupils who no doubt had perfectly good reasons for acquiring such a skill. Some undoubtedly had a need to cover their tracks. One such was the Rev. Montagu Bacon (1688–1749), a direct descendant of Sir Nicholas Bacon, Lord Keeper of the Great Seal in the reign of Elizabeth I and father of Sir Francis Bacon. Montagu Bacon was understandably proud of his distinguished forebears and was impassioned when he spoke of them. It would be perfectly natural for them to figure frequently in the conversations he had over the years with Byrom.

Byrom made the acquaintance of Montagu Bacon early in his London career. They were near contemporaries and both products of Cambridge. Bacon earned for himself a reputation as a scholar and critic. In 1743 he became rector of a church in Leicestershire but was soon removed to confinement in a house in Chelsea because of his political leanings. His unfashionable and dangerous views were passed off as a temporary mental derangement but the close supervision insisted on for proper medical care recalls his famous ancestor's release from prison into house arrest under the care of Sir John Vaughan.

Montagu Bacon is first mentioned in Byrom's journal in March 1724/5 and the last recorded entry is in May 1737. So, for a period of twelve years, he is to be found in the circle of Byrom's university friends. All seemed to share a common interest in shorthand and some, like Montagu, were evidently interested in ciphers. One reason for this was that many of Byrom's closest friends were either Freemasons or Jacobites. Some, like Byrom himself, were both. At times Byrom used the nom de plume 'Francis Freeman' where 'Freeman' was a reference to his being a Freemason. Records held by The United Grand Lodge of England reveal he was in fact a member of the Swan Lodge that met in Long Acre.

Byrom often discussed shorthand with Montagu Bacon, not just his own system but others as well. They met in Bacon's own rooms, in the rooms of mutual friends, 'in the park', in coffee houses and inns, in Westminster Hall and the Court of Requests. They breakfasted together;

17. John Byrom

they supped together. Montagu was just one of the shorthand pupils Byrom drew from a long list of distinguished families. Many of them referred to him as the 'Grandmaster of Shorthand'.

It should not surprise us that Byrom was interested in Sir Francis Bacon. He was a brilliant linguist with a keen interest in language fostered by his development of shorthand, and his library contained several of Francis Bacon's works, including a 1633 edition of *The Advancement of Learning*. In this work Bacon openly talks of codes; in particular he mentions

> a contrivance, which I devised myself when I was at Paris in my early youth, and which I still think worthy of preservation.

Moreover, in his diary for 6 May 1731 Byrom recounts a meeting at the Royal Society with one Dr. Peter Shaw. Shaw was physician-in-ordinary to George II but, more to the point, he was preparing an abridged edition of Bacon's writings that appeared two years later. On this occasion Byrom notes:

> Dr. Shaw spoke to me about Bacon's cipher, Omnia per Omnia, which he said was in *The Advancement of Learning*...

It is clear from his diary that Byrom met Shaw frequently in the two years leading up to his edition of Bacon. Byrom's interest in Bacon's ciphers is then a matter of record. Peter Shaw also found time to prepare an edition of *The Philosophical Works of Robert Boyle* that appeared in 1725. Intriguingly, Boyle is said to have been the owner of the brass plates connected with some of the drawings.

The serious researcher enters the world of codes and ciphers with some trepidation. It is a perilous domain full of pitfalls and for that reason feared by some and derided by others. Inevitably anything associated with secrecy and conspiracy brings with it uncertainty and unease. Perfectly rational people can become suddenly impatient, even irate, at the mere thought of codes. Yet the need for them in times of war for instance goes without saying. When I embarked on seriously learning Byrom's shorthand, I got a little insight into this world because it was like learning a dead language. I was fortunate enough to have the help of Sir James Pitman who arranged for me to have access to the collection of shorthand material that he had donated to the Library of Bath University.

Byrom in his Journal mentions the work of a seventeenth-century expert on codes, John Falconer. He does so in association with Bartholomew Close and matters related to some of the geometric drawings. The references intrigued me greatly. So much so that it became one of my ambitions to see a copy of his book. The catalogue of Byrom's library printed for private circulation in 1848 contains a copy of John

Falconer's *The Art of Secret Information, disclosed without a Key, with Rules for decyphering all manner of Secret Writing* published in London in 1685. It is perhaps better known by its Latin title *Cryptomenysis Patefacta*. Since Byrom's library had been deposited at Chetham's Library in Manchester, I looked forward to seeing his own copy with the possibility of any annotations he had made personally. Unfortunately, but perhaps not surprisingly considering the nature of the book itself, Byrom's copy was not available for study. The librarian informed me that a number of books listed in the catalogue had never been received by Chetham's. This appeared to be one of them. My disappointment at this was lessened when I later found a copy in the rare books collection of the British Library.

There I was able to study and copy the contents for several days. First and foremost I noted that the correct full title of the text was *On the Art of Secret Information disclosed without a Key containing Plain and Demonstrative Rules. Printed for Daniel Brown at the Black Swan and Bible without Temple Bar, 1685.* In the preface Falconer dedicates the book to 'the Earl of Middleton, Secretary of State for the Kingdom of England'.

Falconer acknowledges the skills and devices of 'Lord Verulam' (in other words Francis Bacon) in formulating ciphers. The book is clearly a comprehensive and very valuable manual on cryptography – far more valuable than I realised at the time, for after the publication of *The Queen's Chameleon* I received a most interesting letter from a reader.

From it I was able to fill in a great deal of the background of John Falconer's family, and towards the end of the letter I learned that:

> *Cryptomenysis Patefacta* published after Argyle's execution in 1685, and at the height of Monmouth's rebellion obviously carried the high hopes of its author. However, it was probably never fully appreciated until the second half of this century when, as a result of the concentrated effort we made to break enemy codes and ciphers in WW II, it was rediscovered. Today it is held to be the product of an acute and experienced, practical mind. In 1966 it was said to give what seem to be the earliest examples of the most widely used modern French military, Japanese diplomatic, and Soviet spy ciphers.

My correspondent knew much more about Falconer's manual than I did. My interest had been strictly historical and I was surprised to read this twentieth-century evaluation of its efficacy. It helped me to place it in the mind of John Byrom. I had studied it originally to gain a better understanding of the methodology and mythology used by Byrom in his ciphers. As I progressed further with my work, Falconer's code book took on a fresh and wider relevance.

When I had been studying Falconer's work in the British Library I had noticed that the 'Falconer Papers' included other fascinating items of information that made him even more intriguing. For example: 'This John Falconer was entrusted with the private cipher of James II, whom he followed to France, where he died.'

The 'Falconer Papers' also included a reference to and an extract from John Byrom's own Journal:

> Remains of John Byrom, Vol 1 part 2 page 517. anno 1731. We came next morning (June 4) to Whitchurch to Mrs. Falconer's where we had cider, mead and cowslip wine: Miss Cork, Mr Yates and Sons were there: went with us to the Church which was like our new church. Mrs. Falconer showed us a letter from Thomas Falconer from some part of Ethiopia. [This son, Thomas Falconer, had died a year before this date and shortly after his return to England.]

Byrom's acquaintance with Falconer's descendants indicates the degree of his interest in Falconer's work.

Ciphers were becoming a recurring theme in the progress of my research. First and foremost there was Francis Bacon's interest in codes, then Falconer's classic manual, followed by John Byrom's own shorthand and his interest in the ciphers of both these men. Then there had been my discovery of the work carried out by Dr. Orville Owen in deciphering the ninth edition of Sir Philip Sidney's *Arcadia*. That had led Owen to spend fifteen years investigating the river Wye in Chepstow. I was then introduced to the figure of Colonel Fabyan, a textile millionaire in Illinois, one of whose many interests, codes, led him to build up a very large collection of editions of Bacon's works. This in turn led to his becoming associated with Owen's work in Chepstow. Colonel Fabyan was a man of many parts; he was involved in a number of military projects before and during the First World War. He put his laboratories at Riverbank at the government's disposal and set up the first military code school in the US. His contribution was officially recognised by the American government in 1993 and one of his chief cryptanalysts, William Friedmann, succeeded in breaking the famous Japanese 'Purple Code' during the Second World War. As I traced my way through all these labyrinthine activities one thing became clear. Although codes brought with them a hint of the bizarre, they also made a genuine and valuable contribution to a nation's security. The world of codes could not be dismissed altogether as rubbish. It is significant that among the many books on ciphers in Colonel Fabyan's library was Byrom's shorthand manual.

Byrom himself was a secret Jacobite, concealing his tracks so carefully that he did not suffer the fate of many Stuart supporters after the failure of the Jacobite rising in 1745.

John Byrom had led me to Tintern in the first place and now seemed to be hovering in the background, never very far away, both his public and private life inextricably woven into the story. In the western part of the churchyard at St. Michael's stands a monument to members of the Watkins family in the area. Three of the four sides have weathered badly and the names recorded for posterity's gaze have disintegrated. Some on one side are still visible and as I contemplated them I remembered the role played by past members as Tylers, or gate keepers, in lodges of Freemasons. More to the point I recalled that, when I discovered the rent books which recorded that Byrom had rented a property just off the Strand and conveniently close to Leicester House for his assignations with Princess Caroline, one William Watkins was also renting rooms nearby from the same landlord – the Dukes of Bedford. Watkins proved to be a name that loomed large in Welsh Jacobite circles.

Byrom had rented the house in secluded New Round Court in the name of Thomas Siddal, his fellow-Jacobite from Manchester. Siddal was privy to Byrom's involvement both with Caroline and the Stuart cause, but never betrayed his trust. In the end Siddal paid for his part in the '45 uprising with his life, while Byrom escaped undetected. Hence the anonymous letter sent to the Duke of Newcastle at the time of the trial of the rebels in which it was claimed that Siddal knew enough to save the heads of twenty men. Nine members of the Manchester Regiment of Stuart volunteers were sentenced to death and in July 1746 they were taken to Kennington Common in London in three sledges, each drawn by three horses. Siddal was in the second sledge with two others: Thomas Deacon and David Morgan. Each of the nine in turn was first hanged, taken down while still alive, disembowelled, quartered and beheaded. It was to honour the memory of these men that Byrom wrote the moving epitaph in the shorthand manuscript that recounts the course of his ill-fated liaison with Caroline.

> Our townsmen now that they are dead and gone
> Leave Heaven to pass the honouring sentence on,
> Martyrs are not still, he who keeps the keys
> Of its blest gates may open if he please.
> Strive to get in thyself, ne'er mock I wrote
> On the wrong side, to keep thy neighbour out.

This tribute is fraught with guilt on Byrom's part for escaping the punishment exacted from others. But the lines can have a wider application. They commemorate all who are loyal to their beliefs whatever the cost.

But that is not all. Travelling with Siddal to their gruesome end was David Morgan, like his name Welsh through and through and hailing from the borders of Glamorgan and Monmouthshire. Morgan became known as 'the Welsh Jacobite', but he was not the only Welshman to support the Stuarts in their attempts to regain the throne. Many in Wales had become disillusioned with the Hannoverians and looked back with sympathetic nostalgia to the Stuart past. Among the most important aristocratic supporters was the fourth Duke of Beaufort whose family had displayed a hereditary devotion to the Stuart dynasty. Another great landowner who could count on the almost feudal loyalty of his retainers was Sir Watkin Wynn. Both men were too powerful to be touched by the authorities but were prepared to risk everything for the Jacobite cause. Two descendants of Sir John Vaughan, custodian of Bacon on his release from the tower, also left Wales to join the rebels.

What is important for us to note here is that David Morgan and Florencia Morgan, wife of Sir William Herbert of St. Julian's and chatelaine of Tintern Parva Estate, shared a common ancestry. They could both claim descent from Sir Thomas Morgan of Pencoed Castle in Monmouthshire and David Morgan was clearly linked with dynasties concerned with St. Michael's Church and events around it. As we have seen earlier, a shared pedigree counted for much, bringing with it inherited loyalties. In addition some very good marriages had allied the Morgans to two of the wealthiest and most influential families in the principality. Accordingly, David's father saw to it that his son's education befitted his rank and he was sent to Christ Church College, Oxford, where he matriculated in 1714 although he did not take his degree. This may have been because his political sympathies already lay with the Stuart cause. The following year, 1715, saw the first attempt to regain the throne led by the 'Old Pretender', Prince James Edward Stuart.

Soon after this, Morgan went to London to study law and was called to the Bar in 1721. After his father's death he gave up this career and retired to the family estates in Wales. We do not hear much of him again until the second Jacobite rising in 1745, led by the 'Young Pretender', Prince Charles Edward Stuart. Events show that Morgan must have been kept fully informed of the young prince's preparations *before* his advance into England. In November 1745, accompanied by a servant and an unnamed friend, he rode from Monmouthshire to Preston where he joined the Prince on 27 November. He offered his services as a political adviser to him and the offer was immediately accepted. This suggests that there had been some previous communication between the two parties. Thereafter Morgan was called the 'Pretender's Counsellor'.

He accompanied the prince and his army to Manchester where they arrived on 29 November. Eyewitnesses describe him as riding by the prince's side, mounted on a bay horse and giving 'all the directions about everything'. At Derby during a most critical juncture of the rebellion, the Scottish Lords in attendance on the prince advised returning to Scotland. Morgan was furious and urged that the rebel troops should advance into Wales where he knew the prince would have great support. Morgan's advice was not heeded and so he parted company with the army near Leek in Staffordshire on 7 December. Travelling with a guide to Stone, he was soon arrested and spent the next seven months in prison waiting to be brought to trial. In July 1746 at Southwark he, along with sixteen other prisoners, was charged with high treason.

Morgan was the last to be tried and complained that some of the condemned men could have given evidence in his favour. But it was too late, and on 22 July he was convicted. In earlier years he had been criticised for having a haughty, turbulent disposition, but on the day of his execution, since there was no minister of religion in attendance on either of the other Jacobites to be hanged that morning, he read prayers and pious meditations to them before mounting the scaffold himself.

Despite refusing to take the Oath of Abjuration when he completed his degree at Cambridge and thereby sacrificing any chance of a public career, Byrom escaped the consequences of his own Jacobite sympathies. He managed to steer a path through the preparations for the '45 uprising and the presence of the prince and rebel troops in Manchester. His shorthand pupils were not chosen for their political sympathies. Indeed he taught nobles close and loyal to the king, although, as we shall see, Jacobites did find the system useful for passing on news in secret. Byrom's discretion paid dividends; at no time was his own life in danger.

After the collapse of the '45, the Young Pretender took refuge in Paris and ignored King Louis XV's request to leave France quietly in return for a pension. In November 1748, Byrom received a long and detailed account of the eventual arrest of Prince Charles in Paris. He read the account, written in shorthand, to a group of friends at Rothmell's coffee house in London. The group included Charles Stanhope, who later asked Byrom to transcribe it into traditional writing since he was still not fluent in the system.

The report is anonymous but evidently written by someone with sufficient standing to obtain information directly from the Marquis de Chatelet, Governor of Vincennes Castle, where the Prince was initially held prisoner, and from several French and Scottish nobles who had played a part in the drama. Byrom saw the original account in traditional writing before any public version was published. Displaying his usual caution he translated it into shorthand. This is yet another reminder of the value to Byrom and his pupils of a system of communication which was both speedy and discreet. It enabled him to state that, 'The Prince was in the Palais Royal bound with a rope like a common criminal'. Such a telling detail was later considered treasonable and left out of the 'official' report.

Byrom showed amazing dexterity in playing a double role during and immediately after the rebellion. His links with the Jacobite cause are clear and bring him within the circle of Jacobite supporters not only in Manchester, but also London and Wales. If the Young Pretender had decided to march to Wales rather than retreat to Scotland the support awaiting him there might well have prolonged the rebellion considerably, even if it was ultimately doomed to fail. As I pondered on this, I was struck again by the different facets of Byrom's links with Monmouthshire. His image produced a kaleidoscopic series of reflections – first came the brass-works, the source of the plates for the theatre drawings. They in turn lit up the figure of Francis Bacon, whose Jacobite descendant, Montagu Bacon, was for a time a member of Byrom's circle. Stuart loyalties reflecting from the shared fates of David Morgan and Tom Siddal showed Byrom in another perspective. As all these figures rotated in my mind, fresh family alliances continued to emerge linking apparently separate dynasties.

At the time of the '45, the rector of St. Michael's Church was Mallet Bateman and the patron was John Curre, grandson of a Berkshire man who had moved to Monmouthshire to manage the estates of the first Duke of Beaufort. The family had prospered and John Curre married Elizabeth Fielding, the only child and heir to the owner of large tracts of Tintern Parva Estate. One of the few memorials decorating the walls of the nave of St. Michael's is dedicated to her memory. The long-standing and profitable association of the Curres with the Beaufort dukes is an indication that they, too, were Jacobites. The Jacobite cause came to the very heart of the area I was interested in.

Papers placed at my disposal by the Woods concerning the history of Nurtons show clearly that Elizabeth Fielding had inherited the properties from her grandfather, Edward Fielding, who was a prosperous merchant in Bristol engaged in exporting tobacco to Ireland. Fielding rose to be an Alderman in the city and inevitably had close connections with the Merchant Venturers. This company of entrepreneurs was very much involved in financing the foundation of Bristol Infirmary.

John Curre remained patron at St. Michael's until his death in 1775. From 1768 to 1804/5 the rector was Thomas Edmonds.[2] As we saw earlier, it was the Edmonds family that had inherited Tintern Parva Estate through the widow of Sir Thomas Herbert. Now, years later, the name Edmonds appears again in another guise. An indenture concerned with Tintern Parva and dated 1808 mentions a John Edmonds Stock as owner of the estate but living in Bristol, where he was a physician in general practice.

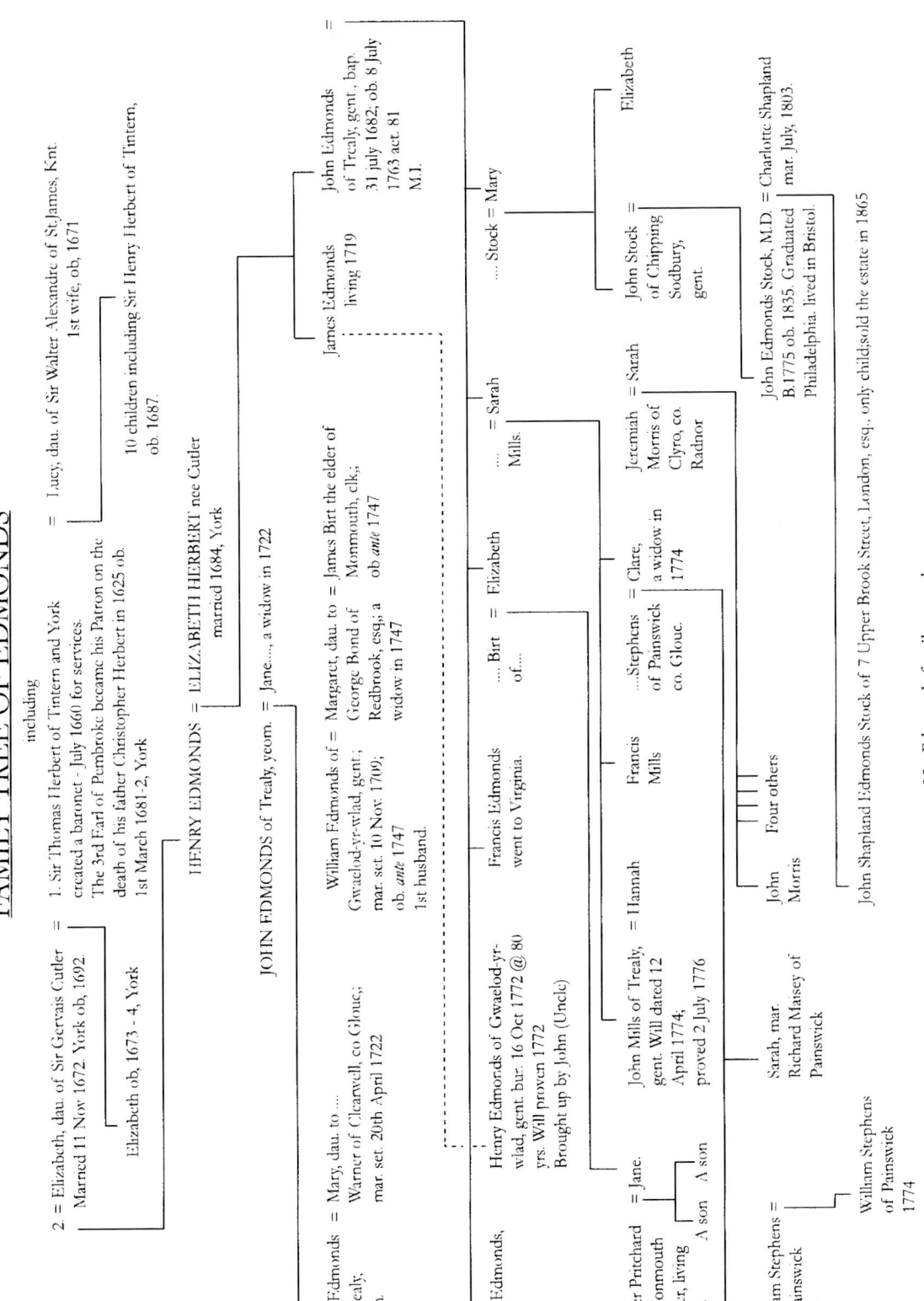

18. Edmonds family genealogy

His father had made a fortune from a paper warehouse in Bristol and sent him to Edinburgh University to study medicine. Here, in 1793, John Edmonds Stock, an eighteen-year-old student, fell under the spell of the French Revolution, then at its height. This was the year that saw the execution of King Louis XVI, the beginning of the Reign of Terror and the worst excesses of the Revolution. This meant that all radical thinkers throughout Europe were now viewed with fear and suspicion, a threat to national stability. Undoubtedly many idealists longing for change in England, Ireland and elsewhere on the Continent saw the Revolution as an inspiration. In Edinburgh, Stock became involved with two leading Scottish republicans, Robert Watt and David Downie who were part of the 'Pike Plot', a plot to seize control of Scotland. Their plans were discovered in May 1794; they were arrested, convicted of high treason and condemned to the same gruesome fate as Morgan and Siddal in 1745. However, Watt had his sentence commuted to transportation for life in return, it is thought, for giving evidence against Downie. Downie was Stock's friend and Stock, too, was accused of treason and would have been executed along with him, if he had not fled to America, where he took refuge in Philadelphia.

Whatever drew him to this city, his flight saved him. Stock finished his medical studies in America, graduating at Philadelphia at the turn of the century. After seven years he returned to England and the charges against him were dropped because of his youth at the time of the plot.

Stock's priority was to re-establish himself in this country and regularise his affairs, domestically and professionally. In 1803 he married Charlotte Shapland from Gloucestershire and set up a medical practice in Bristol, first in Park Street and later in Royal York Crescent. While he was building up his practice he turned his attention to his property interests in Tintern. On 19 May 1808 he appeared before the annual Court of the Manor of Trellech held at Troy House, the residence of the Duke of Beaufort, to lay claim to his properties in and around Tintern Parva. The following year we find him there again when he gives up his rights to all these lands

> except the Messuage and Lands called Norton [*sic*] which is not intended to be hereby surrendered but to be excepted and reserved unto the same John Edmond Stock.

What was it, I wondered that made him hold on to Nurtons above all his other properties?

Contemporary evidence shows that Stock was a good medical man, in some ways ahead of his time. A year after opening his practice he became associated with one of Bristol's most famous and forward-thinking practitioners, Dr. Thomas Beddoes, who had set up an institute to study diseases of the lungs. Beddoes also worked at Bristol Infirmary. Stock published a Memoir in his honour in 1811, the year he himself was elected to the Infirmary staff.

Thomas Beddoes was also a man of strong political passions, a man who pursued not only scientific but also ethical interests, sometimes both together, as when he wrote medical pamphlets on the importance of hygiene. In 1798 he established his Institute in Clifton and the engineer James Watt constructed the apparatus, but it did not achieve the results Beddoes had hoped for. He was forced to abandon another dream – that of a purpose-built lecture theatre – because he was accused of being a Jacobin, a supporter of the godless instigators of the French Revolution. This made him abhorrent to orthodox believers on the Infirmary Committee. It is obvious that Beddoes and Stock were linked by both medical and political sympathies. The resentment caused by Beddoes's beliefs must have reminded Stock of the dangerous consequences of his own youthful aspirations.

Stock was a man of great energy with a strong sense of social commitment. He became actively involved in philosophical and political clubs in Bristol. He joined the 'Bear Cubs' Club' where he led discussion on several topics. One of these, in 1809, was devoted to Thomas Chatterton, the Bristol-born poet who died in poverty after taking arsenic at the age of eighteen.

Apart from the Bear Cubs' Club, Stock also joined the 'Anchor Society', an established charitable institution, and in 1816 he became the President. Among its many activities the Anchor Society helped to raise money for University College. His membership is another indication of Stock's enlightened social views.

In America Stock had been a Unitarian, a branch of non-conformist Christianity that believes in the unity of the deity and allows freedom of opinion about the divinity of Christ. Stock's non-conformity is understandable in the light of his early political enthusiasms. Philadelphia, where Stock had settled, had been founded by the Quaker William Pitt, as a refuge for those persecuted for their religion. Many Welsh Baptists had migrated there. During his seven years in the city Stock had become a pillar of the Unitarian community. However, after his return to England, Stock's religious views changed and he was converted to a belief in the Trinity.

This caused some stir back in America: Stock found himself forced to write to a Unitarian minister in America explaining what had led him to change his belief and he resigned from a Dissenters' group in Bristol, the 'Lewin's Mead Society'. Stock's letter to his American friend was somehow misquoted and his views misrepresented. So he felt it necessary to explain his conversion accurately and *publicly* to the editors of *The Christian Herald*. In doing so he may well have had in mind the animosity caused by the radical views of his youth and did not want anyone to be under any misapprehension about his present religious convictions. Today, when religion does not play such a major part in people's lives, it may be difficult for us to understand the pressure it exerted upon society through institutions like the Church and universities. Even today, within Freemasonry, there are specific Orders such as the Templars that require members to believe in the Trinity of God the Father, the Son and the Holy Ghost.

In this regard Stock's death sends out a somewhat confused message. Clearly as a youth he was easily influenced in championing a radical cause. He was also a free-thinker in religion. After his return and a pardon for his earlier political views, he was influenced again, this time by a sick minister he was attending. So, he conformed and accepted the divinity of Christ. One of the pall bearers at his funeral in 1835 at the Lewin's Mead Burial Ground was Richard Smith, a surgeon at Bristol Infirmary and a leading Freemason. Freemasons tend to be supporters of the Establishment. Smith actively encouraged some of his pupils and hospital colleagues to become Freemasons. Stock may have been one of them. Yet he was still buried in the cemetery in Bristol associated with non-conformists. Does this mean that at heart he had remained a free-thinker?

This question has a bearing on his attitude to Tintern Parva. Stock returned to Bristol and displayed an orderly attitude towards his land holdings at Tintern, disposing of some but clinging to Nurtons. Whatever reasons he had for selling off parts of his land evidently did not apply to Nurtons. We should ask ourselves why, especially since he continued to reside in Bristol himself to pursue his medical career. What over-riding influence induced him to hold on to the much-reduced estate? Before attempting an answer, we should, perhaps, also note his relationship with the Rev. John Mais.

Stock was already on the staff of Bristol Infirmary when Mais, a curate at St. Mary Redcliffe Church, became a student of Mr. Hetling at the Infirmary and was later reprimanded for his role in body-snatching in 1822. This misdemeanour did not prevent him from becoming chaplain at the Infirmary in 1825, nor from being appointed rector at Tintern Parva in 1827. Clearly he would have been well known to Stock, who remained on the staff of the Infirmary until the end of January 1828. He then continued in general practice for another seven years. At no time does he seem to have objected to the very flexible arrangement Mais had for his pastoral visits to St. Michael's. What could dictate such an 'indulgent' attitude? Surely some higher purpose or more important duty took precedence over customary procedure.

What happened to Nurtons? Who lived there while Stock was in Bristol? Other members of the Herbert dynasty from York, by name Place and Tireman, settled at Nurtons and occupied the main residence from circa 1805 to 1852. Dr. Stock himself appears to have had only one son, John Shapland Edmonds Stock. He was a confirmed bachelor whose chosen career, the law, took him to London where he practised as a barrister before becoming Recorder for Exeter. By 1861, when he made his will, he had dropped Edmonds from his name, apparently to indicate some kind of closure on his part, and by 1856 he had formally relinquished all responsibilities and ties with the estate. His remaining holdings in the area, three farms, were sold off in 1865. By then the estate had been purchased by the Rev. Robert Vaughan Hughes who added the patronage of St. Michael's to the possession of Nurtons. That, as we saw in Chapter Three, raised all sorts of questions about his intentions.

CHAPTER TEN

Chains of Command

ALL THE DATA accumulated in the previous chapters suggested to me that there was some sort of legacy in the tiny churchyard of St Michael's. Although there were gaps in the story, it began to look increasingly likely that there were people who were privy to this legacy. That seemed a fair conclusion to draw from the way in which Christopher Heath's name appeared to have been associated with a much older burial site with which he had no obvious family connections. Moreover I felt I should not ignore completely the investigations carried out by Dr. Owen and others at nearby Chepstow. Such energy! Such expertise! The determination shown over the years was evident in the press reports. The failure of that enterprise should not deter other searches in the area.

The tombstone itself consists of three sections. The topmost section is the one bearing the inscription. It also differs from the other two in being made from imported, not locally quarried stone. If Heath's name had indeed been added as discreet and respectful camouflage, it was all the more reason for me to persist in my search. The churchyard containing the tomb had for centuries been part of Tintern Parva Estate and the owners of that estate displayed a blood-related continuity down to the time of Dr. Stock and his son.

The rector when the inscription was added was, as we know, the Rev. John Mais. He was the incumbent at St. Michael's and received the incumbent's stipend for over forty years. Yet he appears in only one census of Tintern – that for 1861. He did not live in a house as grand as 'Nurton House'. There lived Catherine Tireman, a relation of the Stocks, described in the census as 'a gentlewoman from London' reigning over a household that consisted of a family of four servants and the servants' three children. Mais had a much more modest dwelling at 'No. 1, Tintern Road'. By then he was seventy-one and described as 'married'. Yet we find him living without his wife and cared for by an unmarried female aged 21, from Redbrook, Gloucestershire, a small village just a few miles away. Thus, she was local to the area, not someone he had brought from his home in Bristol. The picture conjured up is of an elderly man living a frugal existence in a small house looked after by an unfamiliar young woman. Yet this is difficult to square with other facts we know about him at this time.

He had three grown-up daughters and all of them were married at St Michael's Church. First there was Alicia Maria who married in June 1859, secondly, Mary Frances married in April 1864 and, finally, Elizabeth Anne who exchanged vows in April 1867. These weddings were spread over an eight-year period, culminating in a marriage service conducted by the Bishop of Newfoundland. That was surely no mean affair. So, we are driven to ask, how were these occasions arranged? Where did the families of the brides and grooms stay before the weddings? How did Tintern at that time accommodate the inevitable guests? The only record of a dwelling we have for Mais in Tintern does not answer any of these questions.

The second of these marriages took place in 1864, the year the inscription was added to the 'Heath' tomb. It is unlikely that any possible deception was initiated by Mais himself at the age of seventy-four. By that time of life he was more likely to be acting on someone else's instructions or, at least, express wishes. Was there a particular person or group with influence over him or with whom he felt obliged to acquiesce?

The 1861 census occupied a lot of my thoughts. In it Nurtons was listed as 'Nurton House'. In the 1841 census it had been called 'Nurton Priory'. Was this change of name indicative of some deeper, hidden, change in the function of the house? It was being called a priory when John Mais was the rector at St. Michael's. The church was now separated from the estate by the new road to Monmouth and five years later, in 1846, it was practically rebuilt. Whatever its state, however neglected it might have become, there were evidently still sufficient parishioners to justify the continuation of the appointment of a rector and, as we have seen, Mais remained rector until 1871.

Historically, apart from its original meaning of a religious foundation in the Roman Catholic church, a 'priory' was the name for an administrative unit within a larger unit or 'Tongue' in the Templar/Hospitaller organisation. Was this a clue? Was the inclusion of the word 'priory' a deliberate intention to revive this association, or simply a reflection of the Gothic revival in architecture with its fashion for 'abbeys' and 'castles', mirrored in the historical novels of Sir Walter Scott? Moreover, after the Dissolution of the Monasteries, the Knights Hospitaller of St. John were also disbanded, but it is known that certain families retained an interest in and loyalty to the Order.

1871 was also the year Robert Vaughan Hughes gave up all rights as patron of St. Michael's and split up the estate once more, selling Nurtons to a family called Cruttwell. It does look as if the association of Vaughan

Hughes with estate and church was tied in with the career of John Mais. In this context we should consider that the Rev. Robert Hughes added the name Vaughan to his own when he married his first wife. Vaughan is a name with both literary and spiritual resonances and added substance to plain 'Robert Hughes'.

Throughout the history of Tintern Parva the families associated with it are all suggestive of order and pedigree. By adding Vaughan to his surname, Hughes was in effect declaring his worthiness to be master of the estate and to fulfil any obligations that role might bring. His right to the name came from his maternal great-grandmother. But that was not all. Bradney, in the family pedigree, lists her as 'Elizabeth Vaughan of Cemmaes' – an alternative spelling for Kemeys and a word rich in historical associations for both the county and our story.

There are two parishes in Monmouthshire connected with this name. Both are on the bank of the river Usk. The one higher up the river is called 'Kemeys Commander' after, it is said, a Norman soldier, Payne de Kemeys, who conquered Gwent about 1091 and was rewarded with the lordship of the area. The second parish is further down the river and so became known as 'Kemeys Inferior'. From Norman times until 1700 'Kemeys Inferior' was the seat of the senior line of the Welsh branch of the Kemeys or Camois family. Another branch later adopted the name Kemeys-Tynte.

After the Dissolution of the Monasteries, the manor of 'Kemeys Commander' was held by William Morgan of Llantarnan, the father of Florencia, wife to Sir William Herbert of St. Julian's, the owner of Tintern Parva Estate, and remained with his descendants until the Civil War. According to Archdeacon Coxe in *A Tour in Monmouthshire*, 'Kemeys Commander' was a 'commandery of knights templars of St. John of Jerusalem'. It is situated between Usk and Raglan. An Ordnance Survey map of Monastic Britain, 1954, shows the exact positions of all the commanderies in Britain. The key to the map defines a commandery as a 'camerae', an establishment of

> important 'Members' of the Templars or Hospitallers, which usually had one or two brethren of the Order at most and sometimes only lay bailiffs and chaplains. Many of these were also leased out privately from the 14th Century onwards.

From this it is clear that 'Kemeys Commander' was at one time a focus for activity by Knights Templar and afterwards by the Order of St. John Hospitallers. As we have seen, this Order, too, was suppressed by Henry VIII in 1540 in his attack upon the authority of the Pope. However, while the Order of St. John remained broken and in disarray in England, it still flourished in parts of Catholic Europe. Indeed loyalty to its aims remained among families traditionally linked with it in its prime in this country. For administration purposes the Order had become divided into Nations or 'Tongues'; the English 'Tongue' was made up of the Priories of England and Ireland. The Restoration of the 'Tongue' of England was a long-held dream. When Charles I married the Catholic Henrietta Maria of France a scheme was put forward to Rome to restore the 'Tongue' of England, but it came to nothing. The dream, however, persisted, even though England was clearly committed to a Protestant established church.

During the nineteenth century the idea of reviving the 'Tongue' of England gained fresh support. The crucial problem remained of how to adapt an ancient and military Order to the needs of a very different and rapidly developing society. This question exercised many Freemasons who were drawn to the charitable works exemplified by the original Knights Templar and Knights Hospitallers.

Eventually in 1841 the Order was re-established in England but it had no official standing. Even so, its humanitarian and charitable work won it great respect and increasing support. The Prince of Wales, later Edward VII, played a prominent part in the 'rehabilitation' of the Order. In 1881 he was elected 'Bailiff Grand Cross of the Sovereign Military Order of Malta' and in 1888 he was instrumental in Queen Victoria granting the English branch of the Knights Hospitaller a 'Royal Charter of Incorporation'.

It is evident from the official history, *The Knights of St. John in the British Realm* by Sir Edwin King and Sir Harry Luke, that faith in the restoration of the Knights in England was never lost. It is equally evident that support was strong amongst families connected with this story. Problems always arose, however, over the question of the return of the confiscated commanderies to subsidise the Order.

Nevertheless, members of leading local families in Monmouthshire shared the same hope. We can gauge this from the desire of certain families to keep alive their links with the name of Kemeys.

In this context we should take one more look at the Rev. Robert Vaughan Hughes. We know he was the last man to own the estate at Tintern Parva in its entirety. First, he gathered together parts of the estate that had been sold off. Then, he reversed this process, selling Nurtons in 1877 and the rest of the land in 1889. That year he added a codicil to his will witnessed by 'J. Vaughan Hughes M.D. Surgeon Major' who appears to have been a brother. He lived at 'Cemmaes Court, Hemel Hempstead'. Such an address far away from Monmouthshire indicates long-held family loyalties. Had both men been members of some larger 'brotherhood'?

The word 'brotherhood' immediately calls to mind Freemasons, who regularly refer to each other as 'brother'. I had been collecting Masonic material ever since I began studying the provenance and meaning of the

Byrom collection of geometric drawings. Many of the drawings contained symbols that had associations with the iconography to be seen within the craft of Freemasonry.

I soon learned that one of the abiding preoccupations of Speculative Masonry or Freemasonry is the documentation of its beginnings, its roots, both historical and philosophical. There were, I knew, among the Freemasons those who believe that some of their traditions derived from Knights Templar teachings.

Thomas Dunckerley, said to be the natural son of the Prince of Wales, later George II, and a physician's daughter, was a leading figure among the Freemasons of his day. In 1786 Dunckerley persuaded Grand Lodge to establish a separate Province for Bristol. He was invited to become Grand Master of the Knights Templar in that city. Although modern Freemasons do not claim to be descended from the Knights Templar, there was certainly in Bristol a group of Masons dedicated to that Order, a group which Thomas Dunckerley believed had existed since 'time immemorial'.

Against this background I was not surprised to read that in 1855 the Provincial Grand Master for all Monmouthshire was Charles John Kemeys-Tynte. By that time Freemasonry was sufficiently established for Kemeys-Tynte to authorise a public church parade through the streets of Newport of Masons in their regalia.

Charles John Kemeys-Tynte was a direct descendant of Sir Nicholas Kemeys who had died in 1649 defending Chepstow Castle for the Royalists on behalf of the Earl of Worcester. Charles John Kemeys-Tynte, MP for Bridgewater 1847-1865, was yet another member of this prominent Monmouthshire family to whom Vaughan Hughes was related. Another kinsman was Robert Jones Allard, a surgeon at Bristol Royal Infirmary who took the name of Kemeys on inheriting property from the family. The relevance of these Masonic–Kemeys connections for us is that they indicate a conduit for the continuity in a traceable form of Knights Templar influences in Monmouthshire. Those influences were important to Robert Vaughan Hughes and his brother and may well have had a bearing on his conduct towards Tintern Parva and St. Michael's.

We should not forget that at the time of the first national census in 1841, the estate house was described as 'Nurtons Priory'. The word 'Priory' does not appear in subsequent censuses. Was it dropped deliberately once the house was converted to a Victorian villa? There was certainly never an ecclesiastical establishment there ruled by a Prior. Did the name mean something different and imply that at one time the site was used to inculcate values that the commanderies once championed and that still held true for many, despite the suppression of the Templars.? The values and knowledge of the Templars gathered from their years in the Holy Land shared common ground with the hermetic tradition.

I recalled that Florencia Morgan's father had owned the manor of 'Kemeys Commander' and her family continued to own it until the Civil War. Her husband, Sir William Herbert of St. Julian's had, I believed, established his College at Tintern Parva. It had been a long-cherished dream – a dream shared by Francis Bacon. In the Introduction to his *New Atalantis*, Bacon writes of exhibiting to the reader a

> Modell or Description of a College, instituted for the Interpreting of Nature, and the Producing of Great and Marvellous Works for the Benefit of Men.

He called it 'Salomon's House' and this deliberate evocation of the biblical symbol of ancient wisdom casts Bacon in the role of a universal teacher.

Sir Francis Bacon was known to the early members of the College. He had a house nearby and showed his concern for the prosperity of the local community and efficiency of the wireworks. I believe the College attempted to practise some of his basic tenets such as the importance of experimentation. After his downfall and demise, his memory was still honoured by leading families whose sense of loyalty and pieties were strong and continued down the centuries, not only because of what he had achieved but for what he represented. In a very special and unexpected way the graveyard at Tintern became associated with him and his teachings.

The original buildings that constituted Sir William's College have undergone radical change, but within the existing structure tantalising hints of a grander past have been found. The present Victorian villa is somewhat misleading, but, fortunately, parts of the old gateway and the original boundary are still visible in the grounds, clear indications of the original stature of the buildings they enclosed. No documents concerned with the College have survived to tell us its history. That is partly due no doubt to the accidents of time, but mainly, I am sure, because it was decided as a deliberate policy to obliterate its existence.

The shadowy figure of the Rev. John Mais disturbs the veneer of rural rectitude that Vaughan Hughes strove to leave behind. The arrangement approved by the Infirmary Committee that allowed Mais three months' absence to carry out the duties of rector at St. Michael's was most peculiar. Was he absent for a *block* of three months or for particular months with special high days and festivals scattered through the liturgical year? The Minutes of the Infirmary are no help in clarifying this. The more likely arrangement would be one that coincided with events in the church calendar. In that way he would have been more able to accommodate the wishes of his patron, the Rev. Vaughan Hughes, and officiate at any rituals or ceremonials that Nurtons might have hosted. This would also interfere less with his duties at the Infirmary than a continued absence.

What we can be sure of is the major role of Robert Vaughan Hughes at this stage of the story, even if he were acting on behalf of a larger organisation. Our attempts to wipe out the past are seldom without flaw. Vanity, fear, a variety of emotions, prevent people from destroying evidence of past 'indiscretions'. A photograph, a packet of old letters, a phrase in a will, often reveal truths we would like to conceal. A distinguished lawyer once confessed to me his surprise at the number of times he had found such evidence in his clients' archives. It is the same here. 'Something' has been hidden, but not completely. The attempt to transform an anonymous tomb into a misleading marker and so deceive future generations has not succeeded. We should remember the words of Bacon himself about 'the inseparable propriety of time'. It is 'ever more and more to disclose truth'.

CHAPTER ELEVEN

Beneath the Surface

I HAD BEEN ABLE to satisfy myself about the origin of the brass plates for Byrom's collection of drawings, but, in doing so, I found myself enmeshed in an even greater mystery seemingly associated with the history of Tintern Parva for centuries. The unassuming church of St. Michael was a focus for much of this mystery and raised a number of questions, some of which have been aired in the foregoing pages. The strange iconography on the mysterious tomb led me to consider the possible impact of Francis Bacon in the area, the admitted uncertainty over the place of his burial and the likelihood of a connection between Bacon and the tomb. Documentary research, parish records (however incomplete) and family deeds all played their part in the search. Some preliminary and non-intrusive scientific investigation had even suggested that the mysterious tomb may not be a place of burial at all but some form of marker. But for what purpose? For more than a hundred years various accounts have appeared about missing documents/manuscripts associated with Francis Bacon. In the process of gathering evidence for my own work, I seem to have highlighted a continued interest in the area shown by certain groups, including at times the Sovereign, and even a desire to maintain control over specific parts of it. It became increasingly obvious that before proceeding further I should seek advice. The question was – where best to turn?

Since part of the story centred around a churchyard, I thought it wise to seek advice from someone versed in ecclesiastical law. This led me to Professor C.N. Doe, an expert on canon law and at the time an adviser to the Archbishop of Canterbury. He also happened to be the Director of the Centre for Law and Religion in Cardiff University Law School. Accordingly, I approached him as a private researcher through my solicitor, who outlined the nature of the problem facing us at St. Michael's. As one might expect, Professor Doe approached the matter by first addressing some basic assumptions. Foremost was the need to be sure that the area with which I was concerned was indeed consecrated ground. From that fact, once established, all sorts of rights and obligations would follow. Things a layman might take for granted or never need to consider suddenly became matters of prime importance. For example, how far *down* does consecrated ground extend? Who owns a grave? Who owns its contents? In what sense can these be 'owned' at all?

I should make it clear at once that my desire for legal certainty was in no way dictated by mercenary motives. If my researches into St. Michael's led eventually to the discovery of artefacts in the form of manuscripts or 'treasure', my chief concern was to know to whom such finds would belong. Other issues, such as how best to ensure their safe transfer to the rightful owners would be dealt with later, dependent on what, if anything, was found. Professor Doe enlisted the help of a team of academics from his law school to deliberate over the legal niceties involved in the enterprise. After deliberations that lasted six months, I received the following advice.

The church and churchyard of St. Michael are owned by the (Anglican) Church in Wales and are subject to its laws. Professor Doe's working party could find no documentary evidence of the consecration of the original churchyard, but I was assured that even in the absence of explicit records, 'as a matter of law, it must be presumed that the site of the original churchyard at Tintern Parva is consecrated'. When it came to considering how far consecration extends I was referred to the parallel consideration of what constitutes the extent of ownership of land in civil law: 'a well-known presumption that the person who owns the land owns everything up to the sky and down to the centre of the earth'.

One can see the importance of such a definition applied to unconsecrated land where, for example, minerals or fossil fuels might lie buried, but the ruling was also directly relevant to anyone wishing to carry out an archaeological dig on church land. This ruling made it clear that consecration did not cease at the depth of a burial. Far from it.

It was also necessary to know who owned any monument in a churchyard. As one might expect, this is the person who erected the monument and after his death 'the heirs or heirs in law of the person in whose memory the monument was erected; a monument expressly includes a tomb'. Again for me this was not just another academic nicety. It had practical relevance, for the owner has the right to bring an action of trespass against anyone removing or defacing a monument.

Having carefully established these fundamental points with the help of many legal precedents, the working party considered the question of who owns the contents of a tomb. We have to distinguish immediately between human remains and other contents. No one can own a body. The contents of a tomb remain the property of the original owner. After making a gruesome legal distinction between a body and a shroud the lawyers turned their attention to the question of treasure trove: 'It is commonly understood that property is not treasure trove if it was deliberately abandoned or accidentally lost.' From this, legal authorities have gone on to pronounce that 'objects buried in graves are unlikely to constitute treasure trove'.

That decision debars any claim on the part of any 'first finder', because

> If an object is not treasure trove, then prima facie it will belong to the original owner or his heirs. Subject to that an object buried in or attached to land or a building is in the legal possession of the owner or occupier of that land or building.

All these points had to be clearly established before I could proceed further with any investigation of the churchyard at Tintern Parva. My initial investigation carried out by Euroscan had been non-invasive and the rector had given his permission for that to take place. To go further was a very different matter indeed. So different that it was necessary to rethink the best way forward.

I took a long considered look at the landscape involved, remembering the changes that time had wrought upon it. In particular the west end of the church is a late addition and occupies what at one time must have been part of the churchyard. Indeed old tombstones from it form in a haphazard way the pavement of the aisle. Apart from the Tudor roses carved in the vaulting of the south porch there is nothing inside to indicate the age of the building. No vaults, no great windows, no statues. The few memorial tablets are on the walls of the mid-nineteenth-century extension and give few clues to its earliest history. The simplicity is stark and deceptive.

Yet the history of the area belies this modest edifice. The calibre of some early rectors hinted at something more important. The long sojourn of the peripatetic John Mais made one wonder what kept him there. The preliminary work of Euroscan had suggested a more intriguing past with the possibility of subterranean cavities. However, Euroscan had ceased to trade so I needed to engage another firm of geophysicists to examine the whole area afresh.

The physical area covered by the old churchyard has not changed. Beyond its eastern limit a twentieth-century extension has been created out of the neighbouring field. The original grounds of the church slope down from the Monmouth road to embrace the church, its ancient south porch and then a flat stretch along the riverbank. That slope on the north side is full of burials. The least populated part lies to the west, stretching from the nineteenth-century extension to the boundary wall at the western limit. This is comparatively empty when viewed alongside the northern slope and the original south porch plot. Moreover most of the graves are not old, apart from the 1616 stone we noted earlier and one or two dating from the seventeenth century near to the south porch. Despite the undeniable existence of a church dating back to at least the fourteenth century, there are no obvious signs of its earliest historical associations. One is bound to ask where, apart from the Rectors' list and the letters patent of Edward VI, the evidence for that history is to be found.

Since the church is built into a hillside one had also to consider the possibility of different levels in the churchyard. The only way to reach an accurate conclusion was to carry out another non-invasive scientific investigation of the area of most concern, namely the part in front of the west extension of 1846 up to and including the tomb of interest.

Accordingly the search was on for a geophysics company with the necessary experience. This led to Stratascan Ltd., a firm working mainly with archaeology and engineering. They are based in Worcestershire and so were within a convenient distance.

Proximity, however, was not the main factor under consideration. The firm had surveyed some impressive historical sites including Fonthill Abbey in Wiltshire, Hampton Court Palace, the Tower of London and Cardiff Castle. That spoke for itself. Accordingly in March 2004, Stratascan were commissioned to undertake a survey of the western end of the graveyard at St. Michael's Church, Tintern Parva. There are now a number of techniques to choose from for such work. Which, I asked, would be the most suitable for our purpose? The company's final report stated:

> Ground probing radar was considered to be the most suitable technique due to the depth requirement of the investigation, cluttered environment and constraints of size. To supplement this technique both magnetometry and ground conductivity (EM) surveys were also carried out.[1]

The combination of these three techniques led the geophysicists to conclude that much of the area surveyed consisted of made ground up to two metres in depth in places over what may once have been an exposed ground surface. Within that area they had found anomalies that were 'inconsistent with the use of the site as a graveyard'. Moreover,

> A number of discrete anomalies have been found towards the western side of the site. Their positioning around the grave referred to as Tomb X may be significant.[2]

Many other anomalies were found which were thought likely to be burials. Even so, it was clear from the survey that the site was certainly worth further investigation. The signs of infill and different levels called for some archaeological investigation, and it was suggested that this should take the form of three separate trenches in areas not associated with graves.

The archaeological team chosen to carry out this investigation was suggested by Peter Barker, Managing Director of Stratascan: Cambrian Archaeological Projects Ltd. based in Powys, Wales, also had an established record of proven worth. Its director, Kevin Blockley, had over 27 years' experience as an archaeologist at a wide variety of sites including Canterbury and Salisbury Cathedrals, Westminster Abbey, Lambeth Palace and the sunken gardens at Aberglasny.

Following a site meeting, C.A.P. Ltd. were asked to make an archaeological evaluation of possible non-burial anomalies located by Stratascan in the churchyard. Accordingly a Specification for the excavation of three trenches, each measuring 3 metres long and 1 metre wide was prepared. Trench 1 was to be adjacent to the stone boundary wall at the western limit of the graveyard. Trench 2 was to be dug at the foot of the tomb of interest. Trench 3 was to be excavated at the 'foot of graves adjacent to the churchyard path' almost opposite the west door of the church.

Having reached agreement on these points, it was now necessary to apply to the church authorities for a 'Faculty' – official permission for the work to be carried out. The petition was dispatched, as customary, with the support of the rector and the Parish Council to the Chancellor of the Diocese of Monmouth, early in September 2004. Since the proposed archaeology was to be carried out in places where there was no likelihood of disturbing any burials the application seemed to be reasonably straightforward and the Faculty was granted on 7 December 2004.

As it was now nearing the end of the year, the likelihood of poor weather, the Christmas holidays and high tides on the river Wye at the winter solstice were all factors to be taken into account in deciding the first favourable opportunity for the excavation. It was arranged for the period 31 January–18 February 2005. For the most part the weather was kind and work proceeded with little disruption except towards the end when the displaced soil was being reinstated.

Cambrian's precise objective, as stated in the final report, was:

> To determine the extent, nature and character of possible cavities or voids located on the geophysics plot and to assess the quality and date of any archaeological remains present with specific attention being paid to establishing a chronology of occupation for the site.[3]

Each of the three trenches was then dug by hand in the positions described earlier. The removal of the topsoil level revealed a similar context in all three trenches. This was a layer of plaster and mortar deposits at depths varying between 0.1 and 0.3 metres that appeared to relate to 'the rebuilding of the church in 1846, possibly being spread around the graveyard as a levelling deposit'.[4]

The Hidden Chapter

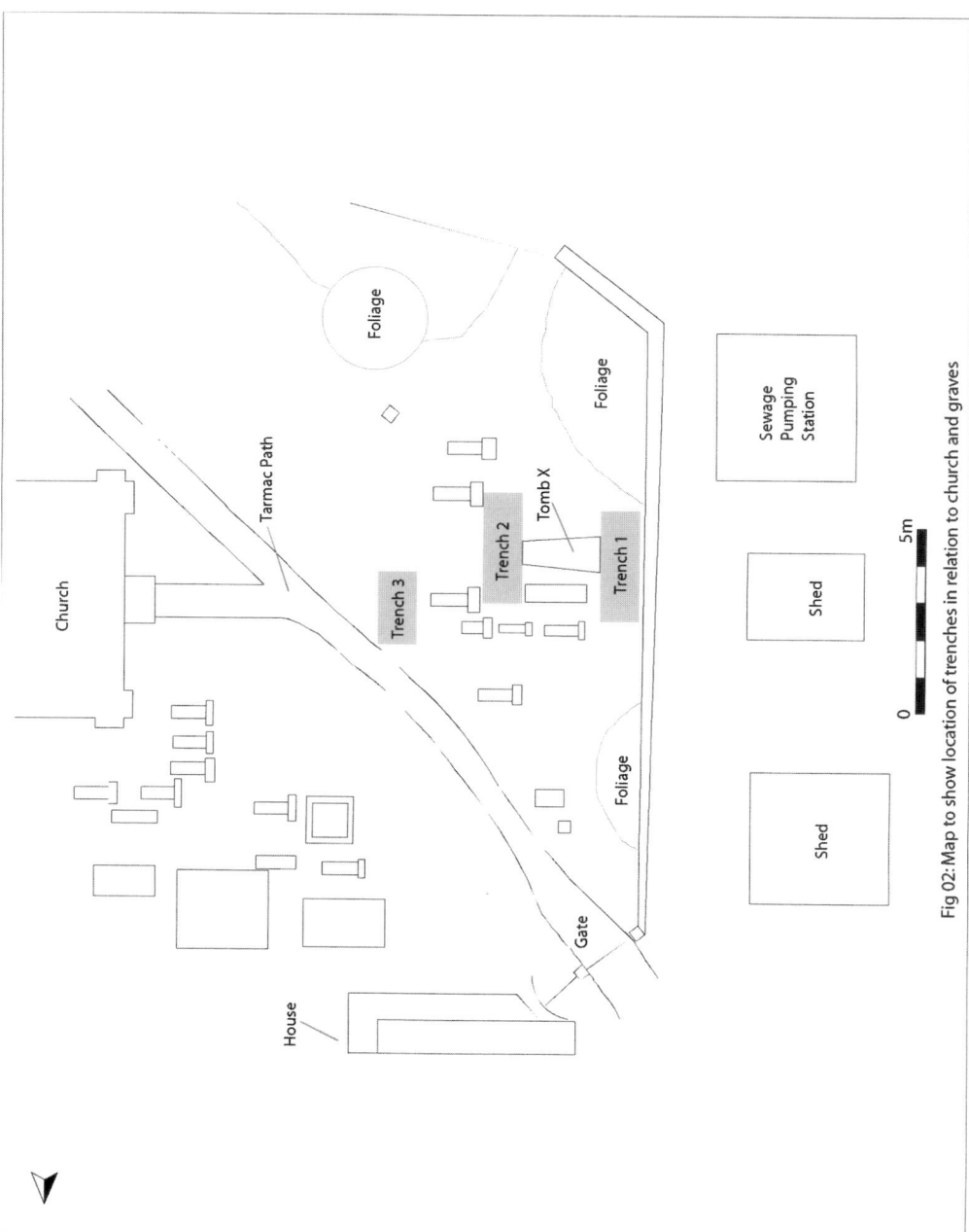

19. Three trenches (Cambrian Archaeological Projeccts Ltd.) St. Michael's Church. CAP Report No. 359)

The excavation produced some interesting results, one or two quite unexpected. The first of these was the discovery in Trench 1 of a 'rough wall consisting of roughly hewn blocks of sandstone and quartz conglomerate' butting up to the existing boundary wall below the level of the topsoil and thin layer of plaster. Further excavation showed that the boundary wall, which also serves as the retaining wall for a disused slipway, appears tied into this wall 'perhaps utilising the large pre-existing wall as its foundation'. The composition of this newly discovered wall is colloquially known as 'pudding stone' because the presence of different coloured pebbles in the matrix resembles a Christmas pudding. It was confidently dated to the thirteenth century, thus pre-dating 1348, the year given for the first incumbent on the list of the church Rectors. Medieval pottery found close to the pudding stone wall has been dated between *c.* 1250 and 1500.

The depth of the trenches did not exceed 1.68m (five and a half feet). At that depth the archaeologists encountered the water table. The pottery mostly consisted of domestic vessels and roof ceramics and all were of medieval date. Some seven pieces of cook pots and eight jugs were similar to finds at Tintern Abbey. Three jug sherds originated from the kilns at Bristol Redcliffe, operating *c.* 1250–1500. Perhaps the most exciting find amongst the pieces of pottery was in Trench 3 (nearest the present path to the west door). Here were found three sherds of mid-second-century Roman Black Burnished Ware originating from Dorset. Here, too, was a single stakehole cut into the natural reddish fine soil, evidently a support for some form of structure.

In addition to these finds, the discovery of widespread industrial deposits led the archaeologists to state in their report that

> The presence of such large amounts of industrial iron slag, fired clay furnace lining and charcoal was rather unexpected. It seems likely that this industrial activity on the site dates from the Roman period.[5]

Cambrian Archaeology Projects Ltd. suggested that this unexpected amount of slag might be responsible for the earlier geophysical readout being 'somewhat anomalous'.

It was also possible to conclude from the deposits that this was at one time a Roman site used to produce domestic ware rather than military implements for the local markets and towns. This was of real interest because no other Roman sites have been identified in Tintern, although the presence of the Roman garrison at Caerleon is well documented and within distance for such a commercial undertaking to flourish. A piece of pottery, dug up some twenty-five years ago at Nurtons, was identified as part of a Roman mortarium, a creamy white bowl, used for grinding seeds and mixing paste. Robert Trett, former curator of Newport

Museum, described it as 'standard kitchen ware made in Oxford', dating it to AD 240–300. Kevin Blockley agreed it was intended for domestic use. So the use of the site during the Roman occupation was now clear and filled in part of its lost history, but we had found no signs of its earliest use as a place for Christian worship.

Adding to the mystery, Trench 2 had produced further revelatory data. What appeared to be a grave cut for Tomb X interrupted the geological structure of the landscape. As the report says:

> Tomb X proved to have no supporting vault structure beneath it although the presence of a cut and disturbed fill consistent with that of a grave was highlighted. The proposed presence of cavities within the natural geology was neither proved nor disproved, although the presence of natural, undisturbed, soil at the base of all three trenches does suggest that the presence of any such cavities (though unproven) can be assigned to natural geological activities.[6]

I found the overall archaeological evaluation unsettling because there had been no tangible conclusions from which one could move forward. The findings of what was described as a 'grave cut' certainly did not fit in with my own researches. I had noted that the cut itself appeared to carry on further down than the five and a half feet investigated in the immediate trench area. The Burial Records of St. Michael's Church state that a single burial should be at a depth of five feet. Was this a shaft of some kind that had been filled in or, possibly, a well? The commemorative stones sitting on the surface were an interesting mixture. The two flat ledgers were of local stone, but the engraved stone on the top was not. Hefty as it was, it had been imported. There was evidently more work to be done here. And so it has proved. The information discovered and collated since the archaeological dig has more than recompensed my initial unease over the report.

Even so, the findings from the excavation formed a new and valuable archive. I was delighted to be able to arrange for all this material to be deposited at Chepstow Museum in April 2007. The archive consists of all the records of the work in progress and is now a permanent contribution to the national archive of the Roman presence in Wales. The findings in fact were the first evidence of a Roman presence in Tintern.

The conclusions about the Roman use of the site were exciting in themselves. The depth of the excavation stopped at the water table and the archaeologists were prevented from digging down further in the trenches. This was frustrating because it had not been possible to prove or disprove the presence of cavities on the site. Nevertheless the suggestion in the report that any such cavities '(though unproven) can be assigned to natural geological actions' was entirely compatible with a layer of impermeable rock below the water table known to exist between Symonds Yat and Chepstow. Tewdric's retreat 'among the rocks of Tintern', would most likely have been a natural cave, not man-made, and could well have had other uses later.

Two thousand years of history had been uncovered within the small compass of the three trenches. The Roman industrial workings were a precursor of the development of the wireworks of the Elizabethan age. The possible presence of St. Tewdric, king and martyr, preceded the foundation on the same site of a Christian church prior to St. Michael's. The two disciplines of philosophical enquiry and practical experimentation that came together in the design and building of the Elizabethan playhouse and the brass plates could be found in these beginnings. The past, in a strange way, seemed to foreshadow the future.

I had by now heard of another possible source of information apart from archaeology. There were photographs of a wall that went lower than the water table, associated with the boundary wall of the churchyard. It was inevitable that in time I should learn of a slipway down to the river Wye alongside the churchyard wall. People referred to it by name as 'Fryer's Wharf'. There is an old photograph of St. Michael's taken from across the river 'showing the wharf' in *Tintern's Story*. That stretch of the riverside is much changed, but there are still signs of something outside the church's western wall buried under rubble and rubbish. Evidently this slipway had been filled in, but I had been told of photographs that showed it empty of debris. These needed to be examined.

Accordingly a meeting was arranged with Mr. James Simpson and his wife Mary, the possessors of this precious photographic record. After I had explained the reason for my interest, Mr. Simpson was very cooperative and put at my disposal a selection of photographs of the slipway. His passion for the river soon became obvious and his knowledge of its history proved to be invaluable.

During our discussion he spoke of a second slipway across the river opposite the churchyard. It is not often visible because of the high tides, although it had been mentioned earlier by other local contributors. However, one day when the water level was at its lowest, revealing once more the remains, Mr. Simpson, with characteristic enterprise, went out in his boat to photograph the stones disappearing into the clear summer water. They are regular blocks of stone suggestive of a substantial structure – one so positioned as to be linked deliberately with Fryer's Wharf, the slipway by the side of the church.

The pudding stone wall uncovered by the archaeologists had been identified as medieval, dating from the 1300s. It looked very much as if that were the original churchyard wall and the one visible now above ground a later version. The two had been physically joined together, perhaps when the ground in front of the west door had been levelled. Fryer's Wharf slipway does not appear on the 1830 map engraved at the Ordnance Map Office at the Tower of London but its absence does not necessarily mean it did not exist before that time. It can be seen on a Tithe Map of 1844 for Tintern Parva parish, surveyed by P.E. Wanklyn for the seventh Duke of Beaufort, and now in the Badminton Papers at the National Library of Wales. Its description as 'Old Wharf' implies that it was already of some age two years before the western extension to the church was built. Common sense dictates its earlier existence, particularly as the second slipway on the Gloucester bank of the river was such a substantial structure. The two were evidently intended to be a unit and a purposeful part of the river at this bend in its course.

Mr. Simpson's direct and unvarnished account of the slipway and the surrounding area, given to me in May 2005, is included here:

> My family came to Brockweir in 1949 and I inherited from my father a keen interest in the surrounding area. My son, Richard, is following in my footsteps. One of my early memories was going with my father up to a dig at Chase House Farm, near Madgett on Tidenham Chase where the Forest of Dean Archaeological Society, headed by Dr. Scott Garrett, were excavating a Bronze Age barrow. The old maps show [that] near this area is Modesgate Camp, which I understand was an Ancient British camp. Offa's Dyke runs close by. By the time I left school one of my interests was the River Wye and its maritime heritage, and, with my boating activities, I was becoming very concerned about the loss of the riverside quays and slipways. I was particularly concerned about two slipways at Tintern, the loss of which deprived the local people of access to the river, an access they had enjoyed for centuries. One, sometimes referred to as the 'Abbey Watergate Slipway', was at the Anchor Inn, described in old maps as 'the Duke of Beaufort's Boathouse'. The other was at Fryer's Wharf in Tintern Parva.
>
> Some twenty years later, in 1995, I was still trying to revive river accesses in Tintern, so it was decided to have an exploratory dig at Fryer's Wharf. We got together a working party and the trench we dug revealed a cobbled slipway leading into the river. Whilst researching in the Gwent County Record Office, we had found that, in the 1910 Valuation Book, Thomas Charles Luff, clerk to Tintern Parish Council had entered 'Free Wharf' and 'open for the use of all who care to make use of it' for the wharf 'near the Church'.
>
> Apart from a sewage pumping station that had been placed over half of the slipway in the early 1960s, the way was clear of any permanent structure. As the weather and tides were favourable we decided to open it up. With the aid of a friend with a JCB digger and two days' fine weather, we had the

section of the slipway between St. Michael's Church wall and the sewage pumping station open.

We were conscious of the speculation of the whereabouts of Tintern Ford. Judith Russell, the author of *Tintern's Story* claimed the actual location as being Ash Weir, which is one of the many obstructions to navigation that had been placed in the river by Roger de Gomm, the Abbot of Tintern Abbey in the thirteenth century. We had become aware of the remains of another old slipway on the left bank opposite Fryer's Wharf, probably revealed in recent years because of the filling in of Fryer's Wharf (which had become known as 'the tip') throwing the course of the stream to the opposite bank. The approach to this second slipway on the Gloucestershire side of the river was a track, still visible but interrupted for a short distance by an old quarry. This track was believed to be the remains of an ancient road. It would seem that this slipway marked the site of an old Roman ford linking England and Wales since the river crossing is on the shortest route between Trellech and Madgett (Modesgate) and may have been the river crossing before the Roman bridge was built at Chepstow.

During the course of our dig my son, Richard, told me that the base stone of the old Tintern Wayside Cross, which was probably smashed by Oliver Cromwell's men, was placed on the wall (above the letter box) by the village well. This is adjacent to the old crossroads with roads leading off to Trellech, Tintern, the river and the Nurtons house. To the right hand side of the old road to Trellech via Whitelye is Coed Beddick Wood, which rises to a summit of 500 feet and overlooks the whole area into the valley below and the river crossing, which Richard remarked has to be the site of an ancient hill fort.

Before the monks came to Tintern there probably would not have been any weirs on the tideway. These weirs were put there by the monks to trap migrating salmon, which was one of their main sources of food.

The building of Ash Weir would have thrown the water level back upstream and so caused the loss of the ford at Tintern Parva. However, this did not affect the monks; they still had the Abbey Watergate crossing.

When I saw Mr. Simpson's photographs they showed a well-built stone wall, parts of which extend down to a depth of about 4.57m (15 feet) – some distance below the ground level of the churchyard and the depth the archaeologists had reached with their trenches. The adjacent floor was carefully laid with rows of setts gently sloping down into the river Wye. The whole had evidently been constructed with deliberate care.

The surprising depth in places of the churchyard wall has to be borne in mind when considering the archaeological report. The archaeologists had stopped digging at the water table (approximately five and a half feet), but evidently someone at some time had dug *far lower than that* close to the tomb of interest.

More of the history of the site of St. Michael's Church was emerging. The Rectors' list, however incomplete, starts in the mid-fourteenth century. The death of Tewdric takes us back to *c.* 595. The Roman industrial workings have been dated to *c.* 150-300.

One result of the Romanisation of South West Wales was the building of Caerleon, two miles from present-day Newport. This town grew up around the administrative headquarters of the Second Augusta legion and became the largest urban centre in Roman Wales. By the time of the industrial workings at Tintern Parva this part of the country was so pacified that many of the troops from Caerleon were dispatched north during the summer months every year to work on Hadrian's wall. The local natives, the Silurians, enjoyed the benefits of an extended period of peace and were able to invest in Roman-style dwellings with 'heated bath-houses, painted wall-plaster and mosaic pavements'.[7] The Roman workings at Tintern Parva churchyard were part of that prosperity.

Caerleon was also said to have been the site of a university. In *The History and Legends of Old Castles and Abbeys* the anonymous author writes:

> It is mentioned upon the authority of Geoffrey of Monmouth and Alexander Elsibensis, that at the time of the Saxon invasion [527–595] the university of this place contained two hundred philosophers, who studied astronomy and other sciences, and taught them to others. St. Julius and St. Aaron, two zealous evangelists, suffered martyrdom at this place.[8]

However uncertain Geoffrey of Monmouth's authority may be as a historian, this passage contains the factual detail of two Christian martyrs, Julius and Aaron, closely associated with this part of South Wales, and this adds credibility to the claim about a university at Caerleon. Indeed Caerleon was an ideal place for a centre of learning to develop. Julius and Aaron were two Romano-British converts to early Christianity in Wales. The likely time of their death together at Caerleon has been given as *c.* 303. A third martyr was St. Alban. Chapels were built in the locality of Caerleon dedicated to Alban and Julian. Both have long since disappeared. The main residence and estate of Sir William Herbert of St. Julian's takes its name from one of these early martyrs and Bacon's house at Mount St. Alban's takes its name from the other. Both houses remind us of the early Christian presence in the area. Certainly by 313, when Constantine made Christianity legal throughout the empire, Christianity was already established in Wales.

The area around Tintern was no exception. Two miles upstream from Tintern Parva a community was established on the banks of the Wye at Llandogo. The local church is dedicated to Oudoceus, Bishop of Llandaff and an early Christian saint. It was to him that Meurig gave land for an oratory at Mathern near the spring where his father Tewdric finally expired. The proximity of Llandogo to Tintern Parva and the two churches, one dedicated to Oudoceus and the other to St. Michael, together with the stories of a religious community at Llandogo and Tewdric's retirement to a cave at Tintern are indicative of the continuity of Christian worship in this area long before the present church of St. Michael was built.

Undeniably the site of that church occupies a strategic position. Bearing in mind that the Monmouth Road did not exist until the early nineteenth century, the church stood close to an important crossroads. The surviving signs of a slipway on each side of the river indicate a route from England across the river into Wales and up to Trellech, one of the most important medieval villages in South Wales. Once on the Welsh side of the river, this ancient road still turns left to follow the riverbank downstream to Tintern Abbey and Chepstow four miles further on. To the right, the road used to veer uphill towards Llandogo and then on to Monmouth, climbing past the former Abbey vineyard on the hillside, skirting the high stone wall and disused gateway of what was once Tintern Parva Estate. The crossroads stands outside the eastern boundary of the original Abbey grounds but there remains a sign of it in 'The Hospice', an old stone house on the 'Tintern side', which because of its name is thought to have been the site of the guest-house where monks offered hospitality to their visitors. So much of the area's past seems lost, yet intriguing clues remain for the persistent searcher. It seemed to hold a special interest for a select few down the centuries. The reason why still had to be determined.

CHAPTER TWELVE

Masonic Maze

When I first looked at the photographs of Fryer's Wharf and the boundary wall of the churchyard, I had been chiefly concerned with the depth of the wall in relation to the archaeological dig on the other side. But then I began to look at the regularity of the stonework and my attention was caught by one section in particular. Here the size of the stones was interrupted by two in particular that seemed larger. Indeed, the shape of one of these was noticeably different, but both seemed to cover more than two courses of stone. To begin with I could not be certain whether this was the result of some distortion caused by the perspective of the photograph. However, these two stones appeared to be different from the rest, so there was only one thing to do – to look at them in situ. They were positioned side by side near the entrance to the churchyard where the infill of rubble was minimal. This made it possible for me to photograph them head-on for record purposes. I had not been wrong. Mr. Simpson's photograph had been focused on the direction of the slipway running down into the river rather than on the boundary wall itself, and this gave a slight distortion to the stones under review. Even so the shape of the right-hand stone of the pair *was* as I had thought.

Broader at the top than at the bottom, the shape of this stone resembled that of a keystone in an arch, the chief retaining stone at the top of an arch or dome. That is its very practical function in building – to take the stress of an arch and hold everything in place. Although there was no actual arch in the wall supported by this keystone, its shape was unmistakeable and I knew that a keystone has symbolic associations for Freemasons. The stone to the left, I noticed, was square-shaped.

It was not long before I learned also of the symbolic importance in Freemasonry of a square-shaped stone called an 'ashlar'. This is a building stone whose main angles are right angles. Its shape is achieved by careful chiselling. The chisel, therefore, comes to represent a process of education. The ceremonies of Freemasons include two ashlars – one rough and one perfectly smooth. The first represents natural man, uneducated and unaware of his obligations to society. The smooth-faced ashlar, ready to be built into a wall, symbolises the cultured and educated man with an awareness of his duties to his fellow men.

Two Masonic connections seemed worth pursuing. So I arranged to show the photograph to the Rev. Neville Barker Cryer, a leading Masonic scholar and author of several books on Freemasonry. For a number of years he had been aware of the nature of Byrom's collection of drawings and had made valuable contributions to my earlier work. Our discussion proved illuminating, particularly his description of the purpose of a keystone.

> It is in fact the key to the entry of what lies beneath an arch or behind an arch, and in symbolic masonry it is indeed very often the case that, when the keystone is removed, light is then permitted to enter the area beneath or behind the arch and one is able to discover whatever lies there.

When this particular stone was measured, its width at the top was 16 inches and at the bottom 10 inches. The central measure from top to bottom was 12 inches. This recalled what has been described as a favourite mystery symbol of the Egyptians – an oblong 8 × 5 in dimension.[1] Proportionally the stone in the boundary wall was the same – 16 × 10. The dimensions of the keystone in the boundary wall seemed to be deliberate – especially in the light of a further comment of Neville Cryer:

> The dimensions of the stone are such that it very much resembles the kind of keystone that is used ceremonially though it seems to be twice the size of those that are used in ceremonies.

Rev. Cryer's analysis illustrated the process whereby the operative mason's work took on symbolic meaning. The keystone can be viewed as

> A token of the progress in the skill of a master craftsman in stone. It shows that he can now produce an item that has unusual dimensions – wider at the top than at the bottom and with sloping sides that are perfectly aligned to each other, as shown when you try to dissect it with a diagonal. It is a very definite mark of a craftsman's skill and as such, of course, it infers that the craftsman is at a stage for moving forward in his profession and trade. The stone in a sense means 'you can go on from here'.

Moreover, in symbolic masonry the presence of a keystone

> is always related to the entry into some chamber or vault in which there is some manuscript material. What, of course, is of greatest interest is that the keystone as it is mainly referred to in symbolic masonry is the key to a vault beneath Solomon's Temple.

The keystone in the boundary wall was only a few feet away from the first tomb of interest. Was its presence here symbolic, too, and more importantly when was the wall built? Later, during a radar survey of the boundary wall, pieces of Willow-pattern ware were found embedded in an exposed portion at the foot and served as useful indicators of the age of that particular section, dating it to the early nineteenth century. The church itself, we know, was altered and extended in 1846.

Byrom's collection of drawings was beginning to suggest even more intriguing associations. It contains one on thick card cut out into the shape of a cross that folds up into a cube and is concerned with the dimensions of the Holy of Holies, the innermost sanctum of Solomon's Temple. There are also drawings with 'The Ark of the Covenant' and other biblical references written on them. The latest date by which these drawings could have been completed is 1732. I knew that the Temple holds a place of prime importance in the rituals of Freemasonry. Here now, in the boundary wall of St. Michael's churchyard, I seemed to have stumbled across fresh evidence of that importance. The third Earl of Pembroke is described in *Burke's Peerage* at one point as 'the Grand Master of Freemasonry', and, as we know he owned the advowson and other rights to the church. However, he had died in 1630, so he must have been head of an earlier quasi-Masonic brotherhood pre-dating the foundation of the premier Grand Lodge in 1717. Be that as it may, we have already seen, too, that he had interests in the wireworks in Tintern and, through the letters patent granted his grandfather, in St. Michael's Church. It was not possible, therefore, to ignore the presence of two stones, keystone and ashlar, side by side in the boundary wall. Even though I was looking at it almost three hundred years after the death of the third Earl of Pembroke, there again seemed to be some sort of continuity here in the churchyard. What were the implications?

Already the discovery of a Roman presence on the site during the excavation of the three trenches had raised enough questions – but more were to follow. The archaeology had led indirectly to another unexpected find in the churchyard. When the dig was over the archaeologists filled in the trenches with the soil they had displaced. Towards the end of this operation one of them noticed that near the boundary wall the grass newly exposed from a pile of soil gave way to a rectangle of moss. The most likely object to interrupt the grass in such a way would be a ledger or flat-lying tombstone. On scraping a little of the moss away this proved to be so. The ledger had obviously been intended to be seen like the rest in the churchyard and, when it had been fully cleaned, revealed both a name and a date. It was a memorial to 'Ann', 'The Wife of William Watkins' who 'Died May – 1843. Aged 33'. The rest of the lettering, which looked like a pious epitaph, had faded badly and was now illegible. Major Cowell, closely associated with St. Michael's for thirty years and for much of that time one of its churchwardens, could not remember the stone ever being visible. The rector agreed that it should now be left exposed.

Curiously the ledger was positioned quite close to the keystone and ashlar in the boundary wall. The name 'Watkin' within the ranks of Freemasons and in Lodge history carries its own resonances. Other details on the ledger may be of some significance. I already knew of the existence of the 'Sir William Watkin Lodge' in North Wales, named after a famous eighteenth-century Freemason.

Sir Watkin Williams Wynn, 1692–1749, was a Tory MP for twenty-nine years and a persistent opponent of Sir Robert Walpole, the king's first minister. He was born Sir Watkin Williams but took the additional surname Wynn on inheriting the estate of his kinsman, Sir John Wynn. We met him briefly in Chapter Nine – a secret Jacobite and a Freemason who had helped the Stuart cause during the 1745 rebellion, but was too powerful to be charged. John Byrom recounts in his diary how he himself caused a great stir at a dance in the Manchester Assembly Rooms one April evening in 1750 when, at the request of his partner, he asked for a jig to be played called Sir Watkin's Jig. A number of army officers present viewed this almost as an anti-government protest, despite the fact that the Jacobite rising had been put down five years earlier.

Sir Watkin Wynn remained a hero to many of his fellow countrymen, giving his name not only to a dance but to a recipe for the 'Watkin Wynne [*sic*] pudding'. He claimed descent from the most important royal tribe of Wales, responsible for ensuring over seventy years of Welsh independence from the Norman invaders from 1094 to 1170. This was a lineage anyone could be proud of. Another ancestor had been a member of the household of Charles I, and loyalty to the Stuarts continued with Sir Watkin's own Jacobite sentiments. He died in 1749, but his son married a daughter of the fourth Duke of Beaufort, the other leading untouchable Stuart supporter in Wales and the owner of vast swathes of Tintern.

I bore all this in mind when the ledger with the name Watkins appeared unexpectedly after the archaeological dig. Its position relative to the boundary wall began to look strategic. William Watkins, the husband of Ann, came from Abergavenny, only twenty miles away from Tintern. One of his Jacobite uncles, John, had been forced to flee like other Stuart rebels to the New World. A number of the Watkins clan led colourful lives, each generation producing a William amongst its offspring. One of these was given the additional name 'Beaufort' as a reminder of the connection with the great ducal family.

Of particular interest to us at this point is a later William Watkins who was a Freemason and moved to North Wales where he served as Keeper of

The Hidden Chapter

Caernarvon Castle. The Constable of the castle at the time was the fourth Earl of Caernarvon, one of the most senior Masons in the kingdom. In 1872 he arranged for the meetings of the Segontium Lodge to take place at the castle in the room invariably set aside for royal visitors. William Watkins had the double distinction of being both Keeper of the Castle and 'Tyler' of this lodge, one of the essential offices in Freemasonry. The Segontium Lodge met in the castle for thirty-two years and William Watkins was Tyler for much of the time.

The office of Tyler is one of the greatest honours a Master can bestow on a brother Mason. Duties included the preparation of a lodge for meetings and ensuring that all the ceremonial materials special to that lodge were in the correct place. He often summoned masons to a meeting and it was his responsibility to permit only the duly qualified to enter the lodge, and to keep off intruders. His function made him both the gatekeeper and guardian of the lodge's secrets (whatever that meant). What intrigued me was that it was not unknown for the office of Tyler to be held by successive members of the same family. It may well have been the case with the Watkins Freemasons.

This seemed even more likely when I learned that two ceremonial caskets in two separate Welsh lodges, one in Abergavenny, the other in Caernarvon, had the same form of words inscribed on top, a not unusual feature according to the Rev. Cryer.[2] Such a link between a lodge in North Wales and an older one in South Wales is revealing. Indeed, the shared inscription may be the result of William Watkins moving from the south where the family had its roots to take up his duties at the castle in the north. The wording on the caskets reads as follows:

> Thus saith the Lord God. Behold I lay in Zion for a foundation stone a tried stone, a precious cornerstone, a sure foundation. He that believeth shall not make haste to judgement. Also evil I lay to the line and righteousness to the plummet.

The inscription emphasises the importance of the 'cornerstone' as a sure basis from which to build. I was aware that for some masons the term 'cornerstone' was interchangeable with 'keystone' and this served to emphasise even further the importance of the feature built into the church boundary wall at Tintern Parva. A monument close to the ledger and keystone records the names of several generations of Watkinses, and records show that there were members of the family in Tintern who worked as stonemasons.

All these facts, both historical and Masonic, increased my interest in the ledger in St. Michael's churchyard with the inscription in memory of Ann Watkins. Taken together with the discovery of what looked like two

Masonic stones in the boundary wall, the immediate area behind the Ann Watkins ledger and along part of the churchyard wall nearby called for closer scrutiny.

Accordingly, I commissioned Stratascan to carry out further non-invasive radar investigations on a small section of the wall. With the agreement of the rector that section was cleared of ivy and undergrowth to allow the survey to be done as accurately as possible. The survey was carried out on Wednesday 17 August 2005, a day blessed with warm, sunny weather. The face of the wall and the slipway floor and ground immediately behind it were surveyed by ground-penetrating radar. Later, the slipway floor and elevation were drawn, stone by stone, and photographed.[3]

When the exercise was completed and the data analysed it was clear that the survey had produced both valuable facts and intriguing data. First of all, the radar was able to give the thickness of the wall as 0.5m. Secondly, although a 'zone of complexity' behind the wall was revealed and attributed to 'rubble infill', it was later agreed that this could equally be caused by a continuation of the medieval pudding stone wall that had been revealed by the archaeology behind the tomb of interest and which appeared to be keyed into the present boundary wall. That would make sense since the medieval wall is considered to be the original boundary wall for the churchyard at its western limit.

Other reflections from the survey equipment proved more surprising. Two signals received from behind the keystone at different depths indicated 'a different make up to the wall at these positions'. In addition there was the find of a 'flat-topped feature' at a depth of 1.6m and some 1.5m behind the face of the retaining wall (i.e. within the churchyard) to the rear of the keystone. This was so unexpected that I felt it must surely be significant, although in a way yet to be determined. Despite its depth, this feature was almost level with the Roman remains discovered close by during the excavation of the trenches. What could be beneath the flat top? It had nothing to do with a burial.

Finally, and equally surprising, came the conclusion from the re-examination of the data collected from the nearby 'Watkins ledger' that 'it is felt that no burial lies beneath the ledger'. *If* there had been a burial then it would have taken place *before* the extension to the church was built in 1846 when the western end of the graveyard was raised and levelled in keeping with the building. If there had not been a burial there, then that, too, had implications. Had the ledger been placed there for some other purpose than to mark a burial?

Another step I could take without causing any physical disruption to the churchyard was to check the church records. So, I applied to the rector to

The Hidden Chapter

be allowed to look at the original entry in the Burial Register. The volume started in March, 1813.

Turning to the entries for 1843, I saw this particular burial listed as 'No. 130':

Name	Abode	Date	Age	Officiating Minister
Ann Watkins	Tintern	May 39th	33 years	G.T. Hall

I stared at the date for some time – May 39th – to make sure I was not imagining it. The figures were unmistakeably 3 and 9 and no attempt had been made to alter them. I looked at the other entries on the page. No. 132 recorded the burial of a child and a mistake had been made in the child's age. A correction had been made, the incorrect figure crossed out and the correct one written in its place. Moreover the correction had been initialled by the Minister responsible. I made a careful check through the rest of the pages of the Register and copied out exactly for my records from page 5 (1825) to page 51 (1904). There were not many mistakes and when they did occur, they were *all* corrected in the same way. The mistake was crossed out, replaced by the correction and initialled. This was after all an official document of great importance to both church and state.

Regularly throughout I could see the signature or stamp indicating that the records had been checked for the Bishop's Visitation, certifying that they were correct. No alteration had been made to this extraordinary date of May 39th. When I compared the entry with one in a typed list given to me earlier by the rector, I noticed that the date had been typed in as 'May 29' with no reference to the original '39'. The typist had presumed that it was a simple mistake of one figure. But the Officiating Minister was not a novice. He conducted five burials at St. Michael's that year and the page clearly shows that he had spotted and corrected an error in a child's age. At the time the rector was the Rev. John Mais. How such an error could be left on the page was questionable. In a typewritten entry one could assume that a finger had slipped from 2 to 3 on the keys. But this was handwritten.

Slowly but inexorably I was being pushed towards the thought that this 'impossible' date was deliberate. After all it was a nonsense number to enter in any register. Was it saying that because such a date does not exist the funeral did not take place? Was this bizarre use of 39 significant in a particular way? Was it intended as an easily recognisable code for some compromise or accomodation? That may seem absurd, but no more absurd than writing 39 as the day of a month.

This was no hasty conclusion and the date was not a detail I wished to overlook. I felt it important to get a copy of Ann Watkins's death certificate. That, I thought, might throw some light on the matter, and in an unexpected way it did. The certificate showed that Ann had died of consumption on the 'twenty-seventh May 1843'. It was issued some three weeks later, on 18 June. Yet, the typed version of the burials at St. Michael's Church 'corrects' the date of burial to 29 May – two days after the death and 21 days *before* it was officially registered. I found this conclusion troubling.

If '39' was not an aberration, the officiating minister, the Rev. G.T. Hall, knew what he was doing. And what he did deliberately was probably under instruction. No other date in these pages confounds our expectation or demands an explanation. Finally, and most puzzling of all, this date was not questioned or corrected when the Burial Register was examined during the next official Visitation.

When I reviewed all the facts surrounding the burial entry, I had to admit that they did not hang together coherently. Hoping to make more sense of them I decided to look at the census for 1841. This was the year Nurtons was described as a 'Priory' and it was just possible that a Watkins entry for that year might provide a clue to resolve the quandary. The death certificate of Ann Watkins described her simply as 'of Tintern Parva' and perhaps in this small hamlet that was all that seemed necessary. But there were other Watkinses in the immediate area, enough certainly to warrant a monument later to their modest dynasty. Could one of them add anything helpful? The 1841 census provided one minor surprise in that at that time Tintern boasted at least four hostelries. It was at what sounded like the latest of these, The New Inn, that I found an entry for William Watkins. Described as a mason, he was evidently living there with other lodgers amongst whom was one Ann Morgan aged 30. (The right age for her to qualify as 'Ann Watkins deceased' in 1843.) No doubt working in the locality, probably at the church, William married 'Ann Morgan' not at St. Michael's but at St. Mary's, in the nearby parish of St. Briavel's in Gloucestershire, on 26 September 1841. The wedding certificate states that his father, John Watkins, was also a mason.

Later in the Marriage Register at St. Michael's there is an entry recording the marriage of William's sister, Emma Watkins, in May 1852 to Charles Roach, the parish clerk. It seems likely from this that the Watkins men, both masons, were working on the alterations to St. Michael's Church for some years. John Watkins also witnessed his daughter's marriage and was still described as a mason. How long Charles Roach had been parish clerk one cannot say, but in his official capacity he would certainly have had access to the records and other church matters. So much was clear. Yet the facts surrounding Ann Watkins and the ledger remained perplexing.

Some months after I first saw the entry for 'May 39th 1843', I had an opportunity to speak to the rector about it. In a very matter-of-fact manner he described the date as a 'code' for the benefit of those in the church 'who knew'. In what way could this be a code? I knew that each ordinand for the Anglican church has to declare belief in the thirty-nine articles of faith before being received into holy orders. Therefore, 39 can be seen as a number of fundamental importance to an Anglican cleric. Did that account for the rector's prompt response? We did not pursue this matter further, but I felt convinced that the entry singled out this spot as special.

This was a defining moment for me. I had learned that Lady Anne Bacon, Francis Bacon's mother, played a major role in the introduction of the Thirty-Nine Articles. It was she who first translated from Latin into English the *Apology of the Church of England* by John Jewel in 1564. This book was highly regarded and the Archbishop of Canterbury, Matthew Parker, praised the excellence of Anne Bacon's translation in a letter addressed to her in a preface. There was in fact an idea to join it with copies of the Thirty-Nine Articles and for them to be deposited together in all the cathedrals and churches and also in private houses.

Given the various strands of the Bacon family's interests in the area and the close involvement of the Pembrokes in the site of St. Michael's Church during the same period, I felt sure that the unusual date of *May 39th 1843* in the burial register was deliberate and thus significant.

CAP Report No.359 photographs

Plate 1: Tomb X

Plate 2: Overview of Trench 1, Looking South, Scale 2m

20. Tomb X and pudding stone wall with measuring rod

CAP Report No.359 photographs (extract)

Plate 6: East Facing Section of Trench 2 Showing Mortar Banding Grave Cut and Charcoal Layer, Scale 2 x 1m

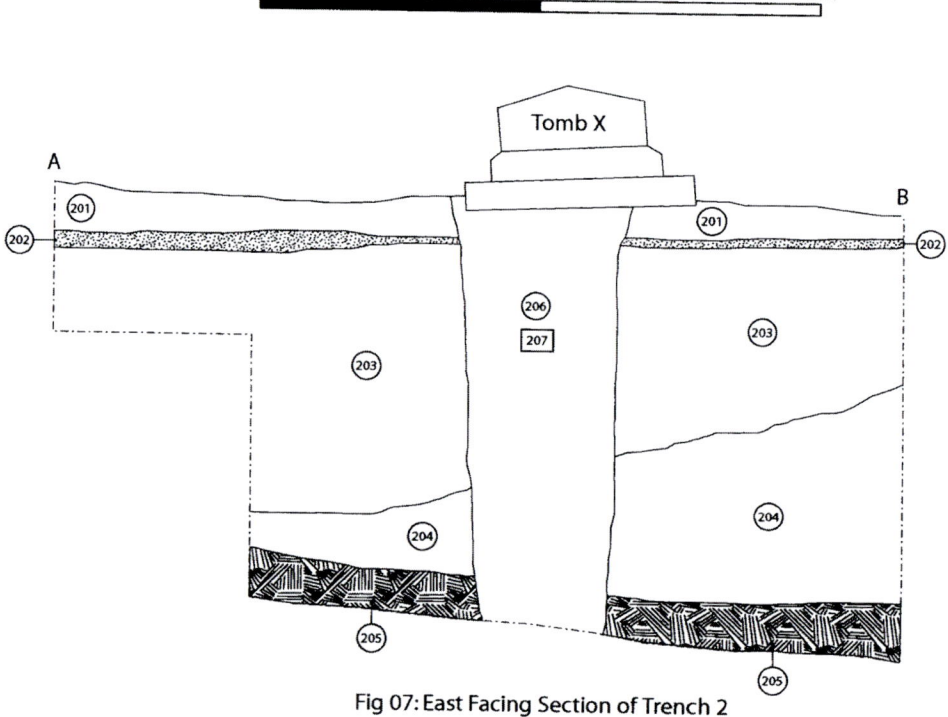

Fig 07: East Facing Section of Trench 2

21. Grave Cut photo and drawing (Cambrian Archaelogical Projects Ltd)

22. Slipway on English side of riverbank

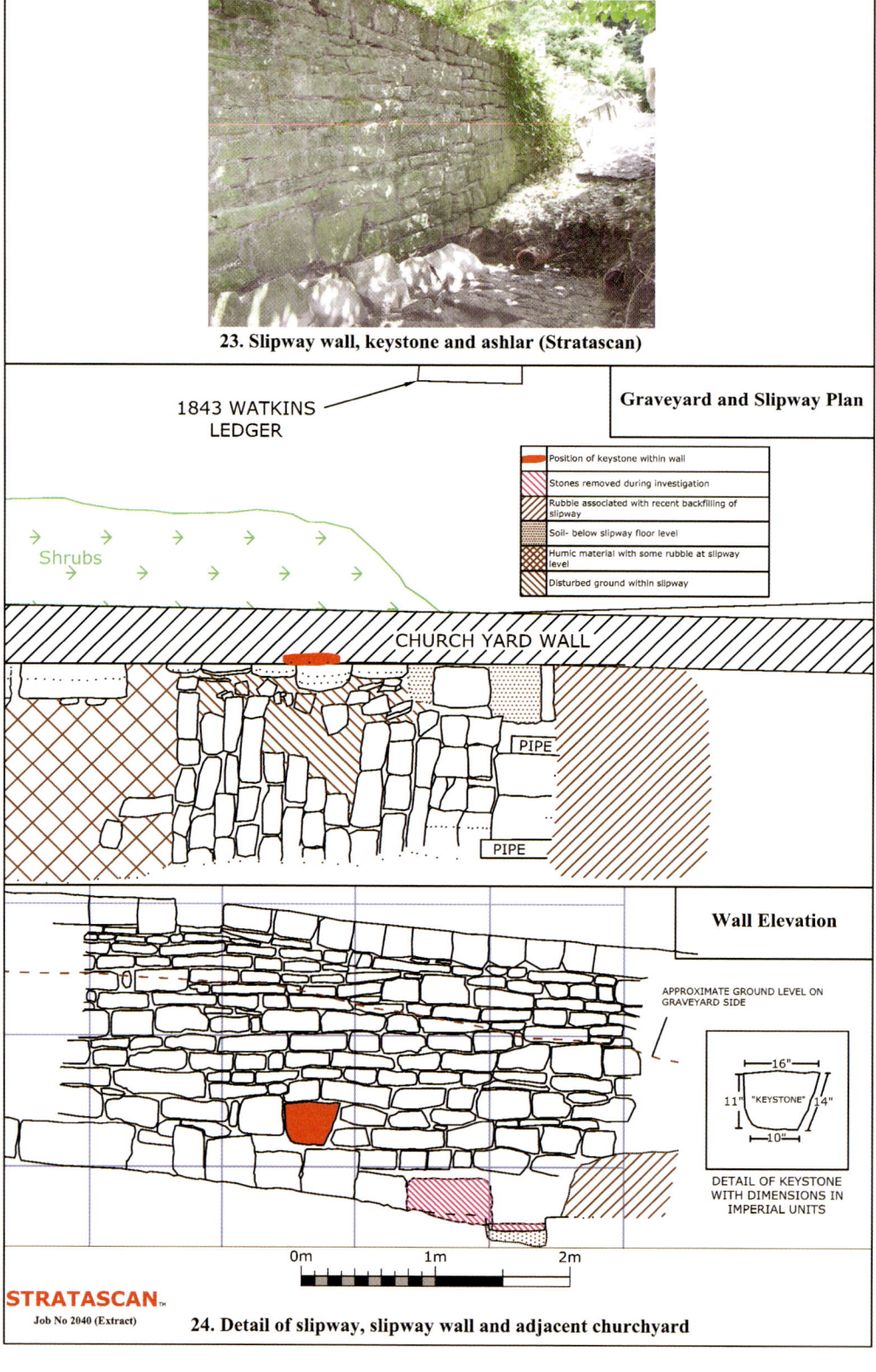

24. Detail of slipway, slipway wall and adjacent churchyard

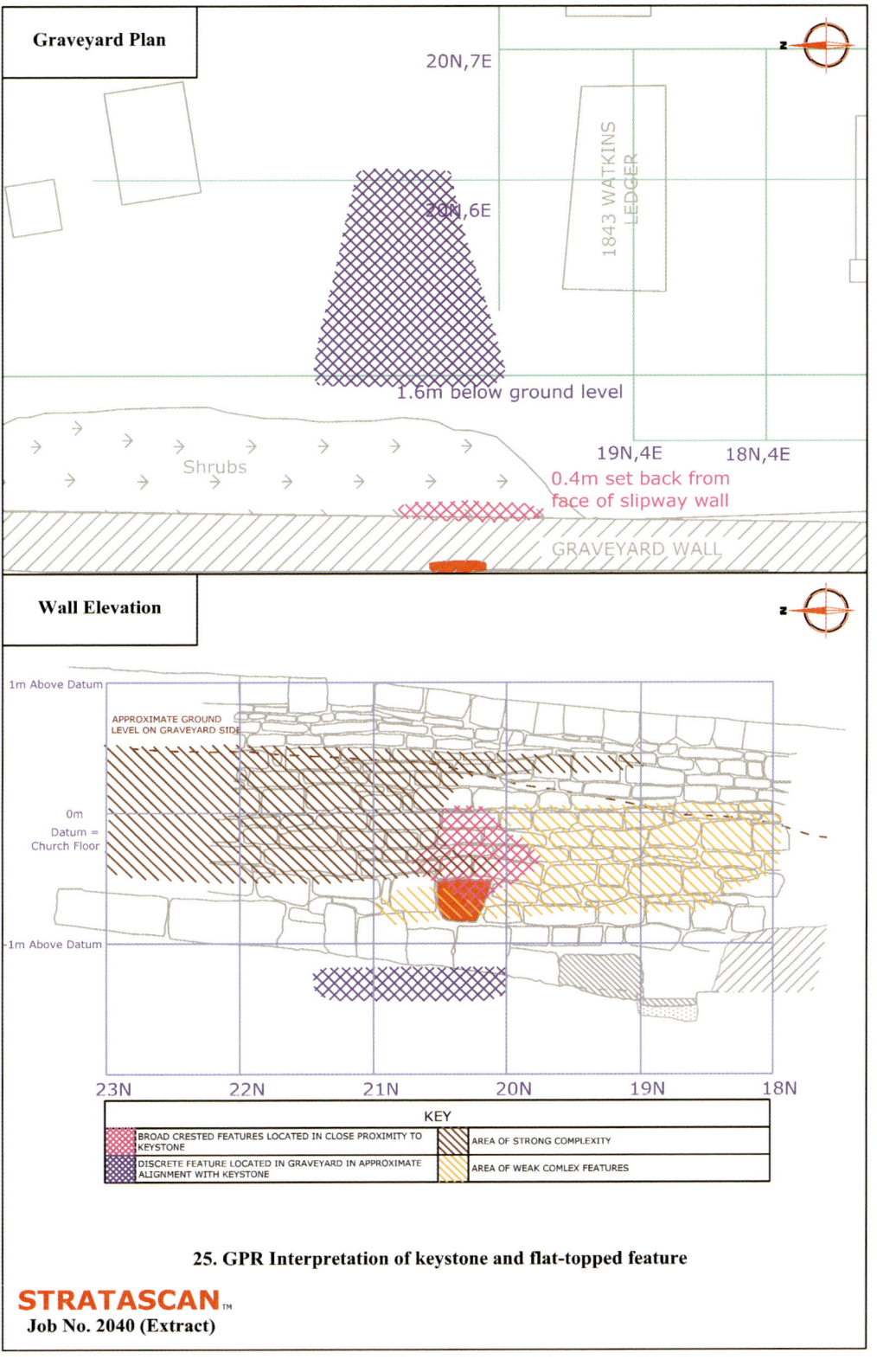

25. GPR Interpretation of keystone and flat-topped feature

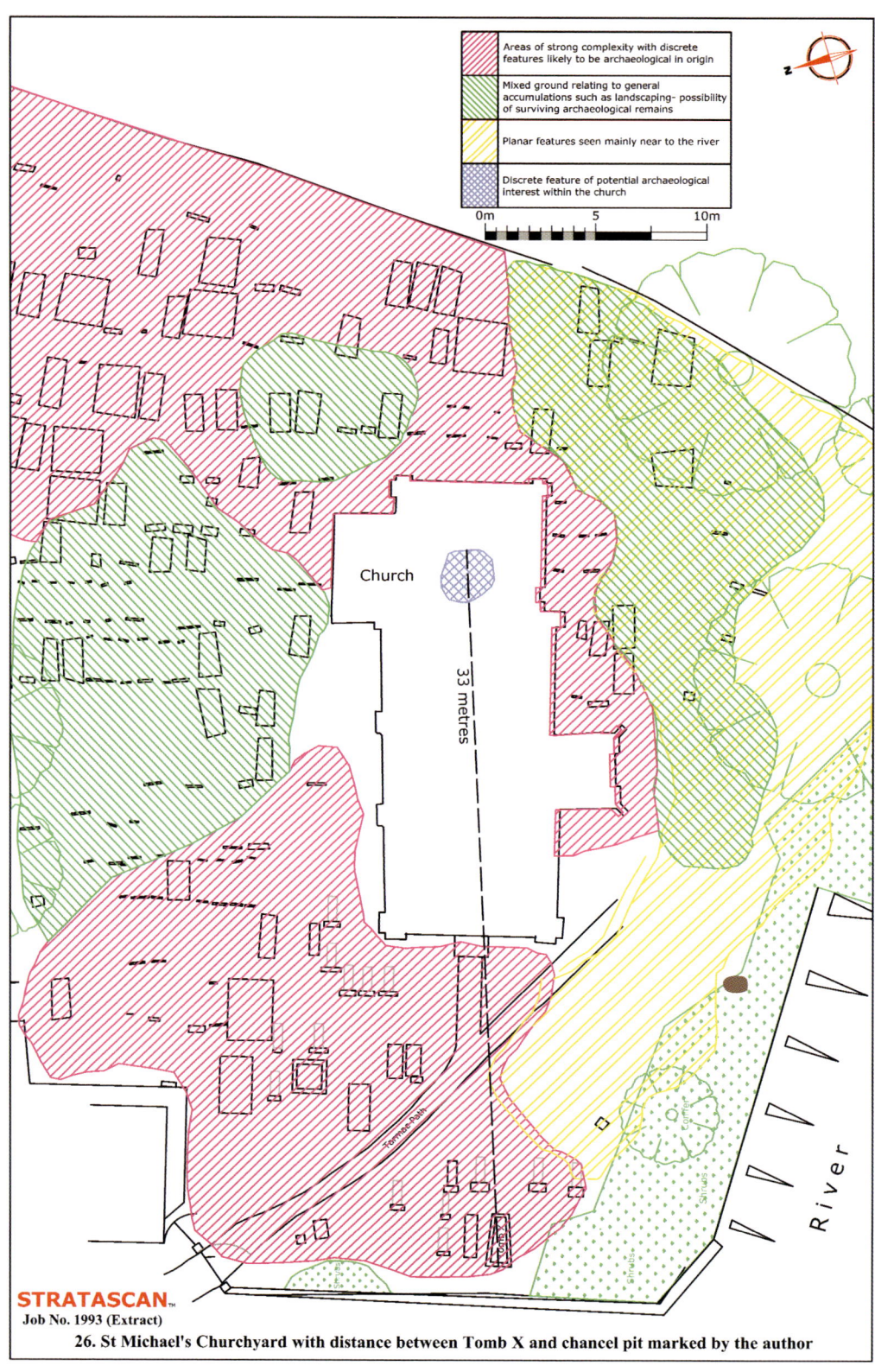

26. St Michael's Churchyard with distance between Tomb X and chancel pit marked by the author

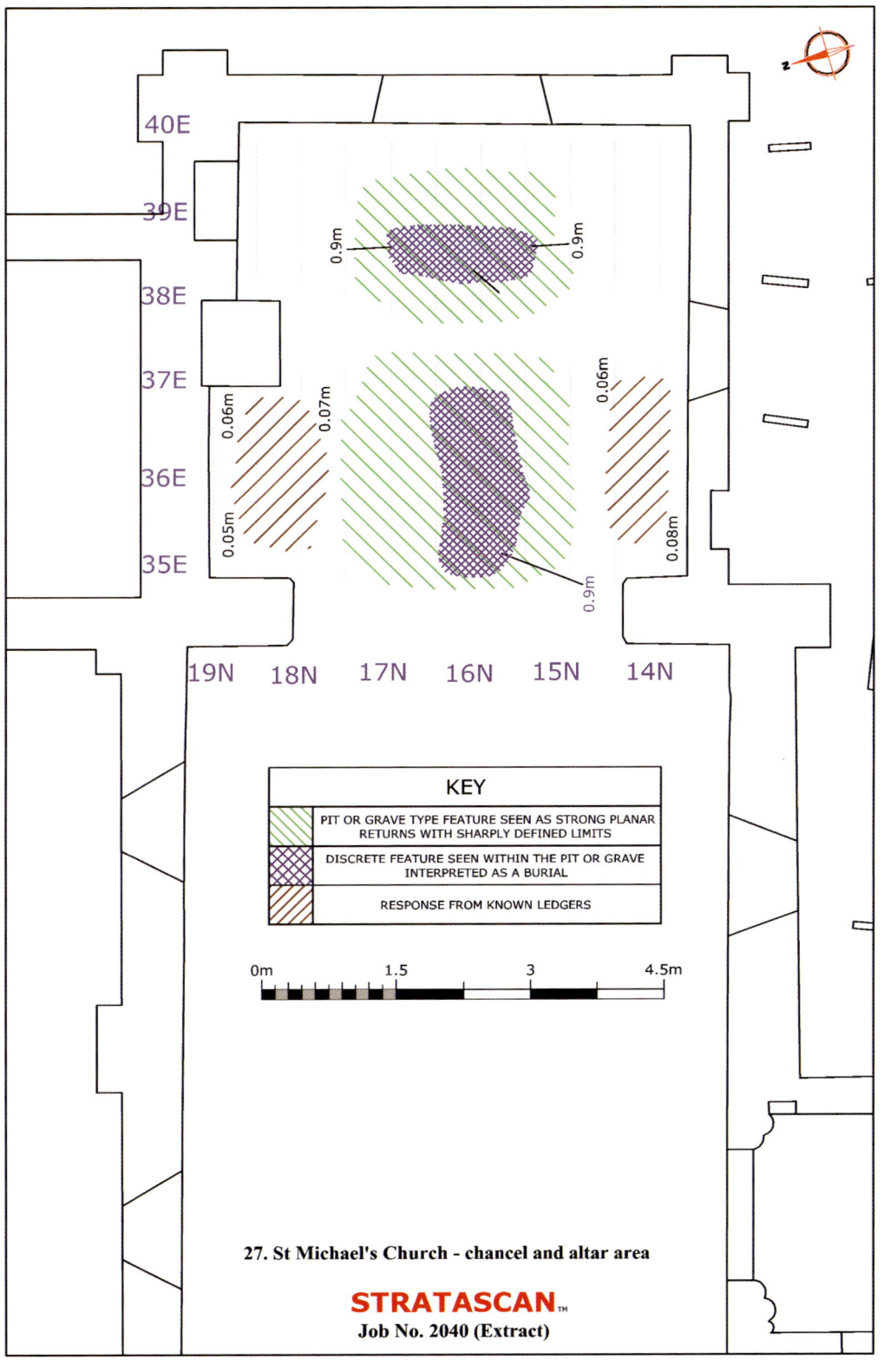

27. St Michael's Church - chancel and altar area

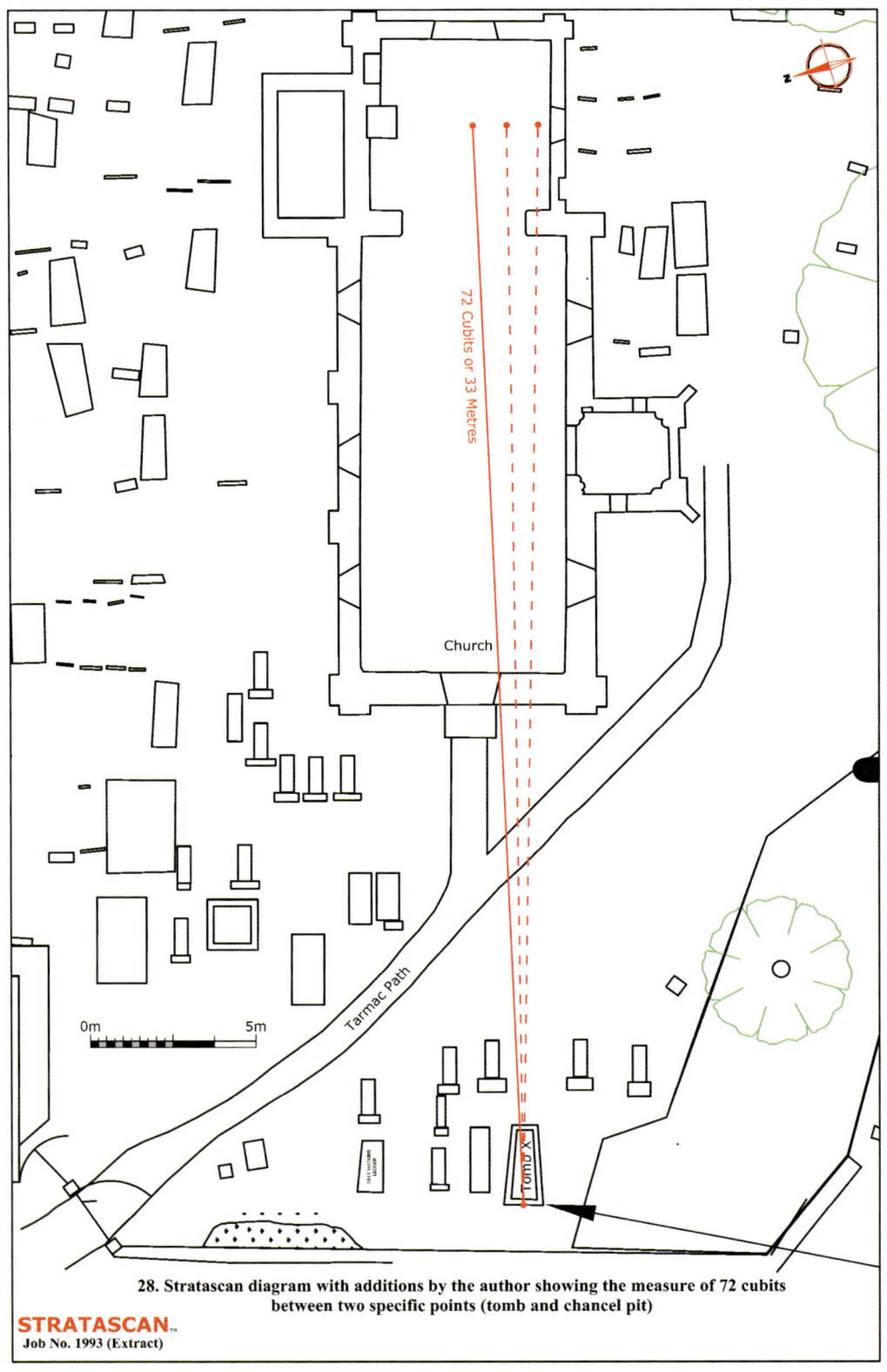

28. Stratascan diagram with additions by the author showing the measure of 72 cubits between two specific points (tomb and chancel pit)

STRATASCAN
Job No. 1993 (Extract)

CHAPTER THIRTEEN

Truth Lies Buried

ALL THE INVESTIGATIONS at St. Michael's were carried out with permission from the appropriate authorities. Helped by my solicitor, I had gained the Faculty approval as well as the cooperation of the rector, the Rev. Phil Rees, and the churchwarden, David Cowell. The first survey carried out in March 2004 had revealed anomalies in the western end of the churchyard 'inconsistent with the use of the site as a graveyard'. The three trenches dug in February 2005 proved that this particular spot had once been a Roman industrial site. That dig had led to the finding of the Ann Watkins ledger which resulted in another small survey in August the same year of a small section of the churchyard and the western boundary wall. This showed up a mysterious flat-topped feature at the level of the Roman remains and concluded that there was probably no burial beneath the Ann Watkins ledger. Intriguing as all this was, it left too many questions unanswered. Yet another non-invasive scan, this time to cover all the old churchyard and the little red standstone church itself, might help me to decide how best to proceed.

While the church is understandably a listed building and still serves as a place of worship for local parishioners, it lacks the amenities of plumbed-in drinking water and toilets essential for any prolonged and regular usage. This meant that the church was not in such constant use that an occasional visit with ground-penetrating radar was likely to cause any disruption to its usual services or the customary timetable of burials, baptisms or marriages. The rector, always cooperative, readily gave his permission. The results of the survey inside the church produced surprising data and it was repeated with different equipment to make sure there had been no miscalculations! The Rev. Phil Rees, David Cowell and Mrs. Cowell were all present when the findings were discussed.

The old churchyard covers an area of some 2,500 square metres and slopes gently from north to south before levelling out around the church and the banks of the river. As one would expect, the area stretching down from the lych gate to the north side of the church is covered with graves marked by headstones, edgings and here and there large stone chest tombs.

The Hidden Chapter

There are far fewer graves visible in the most western portion in keeping with the fact that this was ground levelled off for the extension to the west end of the church around 1846.

The extended church itself is still on an intimate scale and plainly decorated. The internal dimensions are approximately 20 metres long by 7 metres wide. The nave of the church contains pews mounted on a timber suspended floor. The air void beneath the pews may have been included as an aid to drying out the church, for it is subject to flooding at certain times of high tide. A swarm of bees has nested within the void for as long as parishioners can remember. However, this void did unfortunately limit the use of radar in these sections. The survey, therefore, mainly covered the length of the walkway down the centre of the nave, the south porch, the chancel and the vestry. The floor of the walkway and south porch is made up of flagstones and ledgers; the chancel floor is largely covered with plain red tiles inset with a central pattern of Victorian decorative tiles leading from the chancel steps to the altar.

The general survey of the site confirmed that the 'Roman iron working activity' found in the western end of the graveyard by the archaeology extended throughout the churchyard. The survey inside the church found a possible 'pit-like structure some 2 metres across in front of the altar'. This is a common place for burials in many old churches and cathedrals, so I was understandably excited by the news. Who or what could be buried in this prime position?

As was normal practice, Stratascan produced a series of plans of the site investigated, precisely to scale and including all relevant features in order to provide a visual context for the results of their survey[1]. Studying one of these drawings and calculating the distances between various objects delineated, I noted that the distance from the head of the tomb that had first engaged my interest and the furthest edge of the newly discovered 'pit-like structure' (the edge near to the altar) measured exactly thirty-three metres.

As readers will appreciate by now, this number had too many associations for me to regard it as a simple matter of fact. It quickly became even more significant when I translated the modern metre into biblical cubits: thirty-three metres equal seventy-two cubits. The number seventy-two is a constant in the dimensions of drawings concerned with churches and Elizabeth playhouses in John Byrom's collection. It was usually connected with interior walls or important acoustical positions. Here the seventy-two measure linked a commemorative stone visible in the churchyard with a feature hidden underneath the chancel floor. With this very much in mind, I felt compelled to ask Stratascan to check the accuracy of their calculations and equipment. They met this challenge head-on by surveying critical areas of the churchyard and chancel again with different equipment. (This is the survey mentioned earlier that took place in August 2005.) They came back with precisely the same figures. The distance *was* thirty-three metres or seventy-two cubits.

That was not all. The use of a different machine in the repeated survey produced a startling piece of fresh information. The definition from this particular piece of equipment was sufficiently increased to allow Stratascan to interpret the 'pit-like structure' as a 'grave containing a burial at a depth of 0.9m'. In addition 'a similar truncated feature' was found immediately in front of the altar. When I examined the plan containing these findings, I noted that while the 'burial' lay in the normal west to east position, the second feature was at right angles to it, lying north to south. Such an orientation in front of the altar was most unexpected. Like so much of the data I had now gathered from the site this brought its own flurry of questions begging for answers.

For the measurement to be meaningful in the survey, the distance measured had to be deliberate and not a chance coincidence. In that case, which came first: the pit-like structure or the tomb? The tomb includes the date of 1864 and that is considerably later than the date of the chancel which is the nucleus of the original cell-like church. (The Elizabethan section exemplified by the south porch was clearly attached to that cell and then the west extension added later still.) Moreover, the archaeological investigation and radar surveys together have shown beyond doubt that there has been a radical change in the topography of the western end of the churchyard. The original ground level was much lower – at the level of the Roman workings. When a visitor today walks from the west church gate to the west church door he is walking on in-filled ground. Certainly before 1846 the ground surrounding the '1864' tomb was much lower – lower even than the level of the pit-like structure in the chancel. The absence of church records does not help us. Nor is there any indication from any inscription in the chancel floor or on any plaque on the walls of who (or what) lies buried in the pit. The '1864' tomb seems to be a marker indicating a much earlier feature lower down and deliberately distanced from the chancel by seventy-two cubits as part of a philosophical and architectural concept.

Readers will remember that in the first chapter I drew attention to the use of numbers substituted for letters as a form of code and demonstrated that in one simple code we could replace all the letters in the surname Bacon with the number 33. It was also noted that the Science Museum has a handwritten catalogue dated 1770 which lists certain items in its possession that date back to at least 1570. It does not place them in strict numerical order, and brass plates associated with the Byrom Collection are listed as item 33 between items 39 and 36.

In this connection we need to be aware that in ancient science numbers were not simply indicators of quantity but, like letters, were endowed with symbolic qualities. Thus in ancient Greek the word for 'truth' is *aletheia* and its numerical equivalence is 72. In previous books I have shown that 72 has clear biblical, cabalistic and astronomical associations imbuing it in the minds of ancient philosophers and scholars with a special virtue. When I came to analyse the drawings associated with the Elizabethan 'Globe', it became apparent that everything in that playhouse took place within a square frame of 72 units out of which the theatre's circular design was created. It was against this background, and in the light of my work on the theatre drawings in Byrom's collection that had brought me to Tintern in the first place, that I now had to face the implications of the number 72 emerging from the data thrown up by the radar scan. There was nothing fanciful about it. The juxtaposition of ancient and modern minds in this secluded site was too extraordinary to ignore.

However disturbing such a conclusion might seem, it is in keeping with the repeated findings of the radar surveys of anomalies inconsistent one way or another with the use of the western part of the site as a churchyard. Moreover, as I was to discover later, we had not yet come to the end of those inconsistencies.

I had been working with John Byrom's collection of drawings for over twenty years and after constant study I knew many of them almost by heart. That acquired knowledge now proved invaluable in my detailed study of the plans produced by Stratascan. I was able to assimilate the information they contained with some assurance.

Moreover it seemed to me that a pattern was beginning to emerge from certain features in the plans which I recognised from drawings in the Collection. Years earlier I had separated off in the Collection a sequence of interrelated drawings concerned with the 'Rose' theatre. Now my memory or logic (call it what you will) made me place the radar drawing containing the 72 cubits measurement alongside two drawings I had identified with the Rose theatre. The scales of the two sets were the same and so complemented one another.

This being so, I had acetates made of the two Rose drawings. With every detail on them now transferred to transparencies, when I placed either of the Rose drawings on top of the Tintern Parva plans I could examine closely any possible relationship there might be between these representations of two totally separate areas – the churchyard at St. Michael's and the design concept of the Rose playhouse. I noticed almost immediately that the position of the marker tomb and what I had identified as the entrance to the playhouse coincided. Furthermore, a straight line of 72 units marked off in 9 groups of 8 dots extended from the entrance of the theatre along the centre of the drawing and ended at the point on the Tintern Parva plans indicating the position of the pit-like structure in the chancel. This correspondence between plots of two very different sites served to emphasise the importance of 72 as a unit of measure. Whether that use was practical or purely symbolic, I felt it should be carefully considered in assessing the history of St. Michael's Church. The Rose theatre was completed in 1587. Was there a connection between the owners of both sites during the sixteenth century?

The 72 measure is a key element in unravelling this. Part of an ancient but respected tradition of arithmetic with important symbolic associations, it would hardly be ignored in teaching the mathematics promoted in this country by John Dee and later by such disciples as Sir William Herbert of St. Julian's with his College at Tintern. The same tradition would be familiar to Francis Bacon. We should also remember that Dee was tutor to Robert Dudley, Earl of Leicester, and magus to Queen Elizabeth herself. For a while his influence was paramount and his reputation reached across Europe as far as Bohemia and Poland.

Evidence of this can be found in an engraving that originated in the Netherlands, published in a book in Amsterdam and illustrated by a poem. The reader can study the engraving for himself (see illustration 29).

The graveyard setting is emblematic and recalls the churchyard of St. Michael's and the tomb of interest at Tintern Parva. In the background, on the left, one can see an old abbey-like building in the distance reminiscent of Tintern's own monastic foundation. (Its position in the engraving is uncannily accurate.) The two figures suggest two men closely connected with our story. The one to the left is Sir Francis Bacon. In 1949 the American Masonic writer, Manly P. Hall came to the same conclusion.[2] We are helped in this identification by the roses decorating his shoes. The figure's right foot is displayed to show off the rose to maximum effect. This detail is crucial for it replicates the rose carved on Bacon's shoe on the statue erected to him in St. Michael's Church at Gorhambury, near St. Albans, Hertfordshire. In the engraving Bacon is receiving the lamp of wisdom from an old man whose features resemble those of John Dee. On the right, flowing down the page is a stream. This is intended to represent the 'underground stream' of the knowledge to be found in the hermetic tradition. Dee was an exponent and advocate of this knowledge allegedly rediscovered during the Renaissance. Below the stream we can see a shrub of acacia, reminding us of its use in the 'tabernacle engraving' we looked at earlier. Below the acacia, almost at the hem of the old man's garment, rests a shovel. Written on it is the letter 'C'. 'C' meaning a hundred, as we know, is the numerical equivalent of the words 'Francis Bacon'. This links the

The Hidden Chapter

29. Jacob Cats: *Lampada Trado*, 1655, Dee and Bacon

figure on the left even more strongly with Bacon. It also has relevance to the 'C's on the tombstone at Tintern Parva, although it cannot be taken to mean that the tombstone can be dated from this visual 'echo'.

The emblem, therefore, shows John Dee handing over the lamp representing his philosophy and teachings to his younger disciple, Francis Bacon. Between the two men lies an open grave. But the grave is not the end, for the light from the lamp casts its shadow as a definite triangle into the grave.

The title of the engraving is *Lampada Trado* or 'I hand on the torch' and the book in which it appeared is entitled *Alle der Wercken*. The author is Jacob Cats and the book was published in 1655. The pictures, or emblems, are used to illustrate moral homilies expressed in accompanying verses. The book was extremely popular and went through several editions in Cats's own lifetime. There is only one copy of the first, 1655, edition known to exist in Britain and it is in Glasgow University Library. Manchester Central Library owns a copy of the 1658 edition, but it is very different.

The differences are immediately obvious and very significant. Other engravings in the book have also been altered and made simpler but this one has been changed in a specific way. I include a copy of the 1658 version for comparison (illustration 30). It has been depersonalised in that features that could be said to identify the person of Francis Bacon have been removed. The rose has gone from the foot, and his ruff has been changed from an Elizabethan collar to a Puritan design. The shovel and the acacia plant have both disappeared; the symbolic Masonic dots on the lantern have been omitted. So, too, has the moon. The mystery of night has given way to the clarity of day. The church in the background has been stripped of any ecclesiastical features. It is simply a small building in an anonymous background in a different position, because the entire emblem is a mirror image of the 1655 version. It has been reversed.

These changes had stripped the scene of all feeling. It was bland and inferior. The 1655 version, on the other hand, so haunted me that I wanted to know more about the author. It was extraordinary that an engraving that looked so like a scene from Tintern hailed from Amsterdam. This had to be explained.

Jacob Cats was born in 1577 in the Netherlands and died on September 12, 1660. He is fondly referred to as 'Father Cats' because his volumes of verse and books of emblems made him immensely popular. Originally he had studied law at Orleans and practised at The Hague. He visited Oxford, Cambridge and London, and became an acknowledged expert in jurisprudence, rising to be a Chief Magistrate and, eventually, Keeper of the Great Seal in the Netherlands, the office equivalent to that held by Francis Bacon in England. He would have been aware of Bacon's eminence in this

The Hidden Chapter

30. Jacob Cats: *Lampada Trado*, 1658 (mirror image and changes), Dee and Bacon

country and that may have played a part in the presentation of the two figures in the 1655 engraving. Cats's background in the law equipped him with an international outlook which was put to good use in diplomatic missions to England, first in 1627 to Charles I and later in 1651/2 in an unsuccessful visit to Cromwell. Moreover, in 1635 he dedicated a collection of poems on marriage to the niece of Charles I, daughter of his sister Elizabeth, the ill-fated Queen of Bohemia living in exile in the Netherlands. By then Charles I had resumed the patronage of St. Michael's Church in Tintern Parva, after the death of the third Earl of Pembroke.

But Cats's acquaintance with England started much earlier and quite modestly. He had visited the country first in a private capacity when he was in poor health, and consulted a leading doctor in London. His Calvinist beliefs made him sympathetic to many contemporary Puritan writers in England. His legal training and international outlook made Bacon a figure of interest simply from a professional point of view. As we have noticed, Cats eventually held the same position as Bacon in the legal establishment of his own country. Moreover, he so impressed and charmed Charles I that the king knighted him. That is indicative of his rapport with the royal establishment.

The exiled Queen of Bohemia was a liberal patroness of men of letters and science, despite her straitened circumstances. She loved the theatre and as late as 1626 a group of actors called The King and Queen of Bohemia's Company was playing in London. To her a man knighted by her brother would be more than usually welcome. With Jacob Cats the queen could talk of an England they both knew. The Stuart princes, including Charles I, are known for their continued patronage of the new knowledge that came with the rediscovery of the hermetic tradition first championed in England by John Dee and then exemplified in other ways by Francis Bacon. It is not surprising that with so much discussion across Europe of new schemes for imparting knowledge, both Bacon and Dee would figure prominently as prophets and models. Writing to Bacon after his fall from grace in 1621 the queen said 'though your fortunes are changed (for which I grieve) believe that I shall not change to be what I am. Your very affectionate friend, Elizabeth.' Against this background it is easier to understand how Jacob Cats acquired the knowledge expressed in the iconography of his emblems, but expressed in one edition only. After 1655 all references were discreetly omitted.

The later engraving of 1658 looks like the result of a careful re-appraisal of the original. The purpose of the illustrations was to drive home the moral of the accompanying verses. They would normally be of a general application. Cats appears to have particularised the first version because of his knowledge of Bacon as the intellectual successor to John Dee. Perhaps he thought it better later not to draw too close an analogy with real people. By 1658 we were nearing the Restoration of the Stuarts in England and the diplomat in Cats might have wanted to avoid raising the embarrassing issue of James I's treatment of his loyal Lord Chancellor.

Both versions of the engraving have the following verse beneath, spoken by the 'John Dee figure', elaborating on the idea of handing on the torch. Translated from the Dutch, it reads as follows:

> **This light e'er now for me has shone,**
> **So now I give it you, dear son,**
> *The old man speaks*
> This light, my honoured child, the lamp of life,
> Was, from a Light on high, bestowed on me,
> That, for a time, it might our purpose serve.
> And so today, as to my closest friend, I hand it on.
> Having it long employed, and so progressed
> With measured steps, until my humble path had reached its end.
> Here, at the last, am I at this grave's edge,
> Where no light makes its way, nor torch disperse the gloom.
> Whilst you shall, from this day, pursue your path,
> Whether it be midst mountain peaks or in the coastland vales,
> On soft and yielding clay or barren shore;
> O'er rugged rocks or else on drifting sand,
> Keep to the road that's straight, avoid the artful ways,
> Walk down the middle of the street and pass the filthy alleys by,
> And whilst you still have youth, let not your footsteps stray
> But when your steps slow down take care you do not fall.
> Set out then, dearly loved, go forth, my son,
> Flesh of my flesh you were, e'er everyone discerned you.
> I have lived out my span, your journey's just begun,
> I must depart and go the way that all flesh goes.
> For this is the way of the world, the most astute remain
> Until they pass their torch to someone else's hand.
> Thus does swift time move on, and in its measured course,
> The fresh growth dost supplant the old growth of the tree.

Underneath the verses is a note explaining that the idea of handing on the torch comes from the athletic games held in classical Greece.

The second emblem (illustration 31) is also taken from the 1655 edition of Jacob Cats's book. The Dutch title translates as 'The Power of Truth'. Underneath is a sentence in Italian: 'Verita non puo star sepolta' or 'Truth cannot be kept buried'. The words in bold type beneath the illustration announce the theme of the lines that follow.

> **Though Truth here lies within the grave**
> **Yet what is hidden must emerge.**
> Though many there are who'd Truth suppress
> Yet still they will not have success.
> Here nothing's said that's sly or ill,
> No evil chatter, no voiced ill-will.
> If Truth's with evil tongues waylaid
> It may perforce seem grave-like laid,
> Yet barred from sight it still doth shine.
> For note this happy truth, though light decline,
> And Truth's pure power is thrust in cavern deep,
> We know that ne'ertheless it out will sweep
> To open up the grave and spread abroad its light,
> However strong and difficult the things it has to fight.
> For Truth, though violated, destruction can defy
> And though it may be wounded, the Truth just cannot die,
> It reaches up to be released, though some may troubled be,
> For Truth has been from days of old a daughter time sets free.
> This Truth that men do seek, without compulsion's strain,
> Shall spring to life as hardest rocks in a myriad of terrains.
> It shall burst forth as does the sun with rays across the skies.
> For Truth wherever it is found will not be bound but rise.[3]

Manly P. Hall has an illuminating comment on both this engraving and the verse:

> This rare and little-known engraving shows a radiant figure raising the lid of a tomb. This stone is labeled [sic] *Veritas*. The panel on the wall (difficult to read in the reproduction) contains 33 letters including the numbers, and states that truth died in 1626 ... The year 1626 is the supposed year of Bacon's death. This emblem relates to the resurrection of the esoteric doctrine from its secret tomb; that is, the Society dedicated to its perpetuation through concealment.[4]

The iconography is straightforward. Truth, personified in the figure of a woman, is lifting the stone from above her tomb. Light pours out into the darkened surroundings. These will now be illumined by Truth. The writing on the tablet gives the date 1626, the year usually given, as Manly Hall comments, for Bacon's death. But this tablet, meant to represent the public conception of things, is not the whole 'truth'. Truth may have been buried but cannot *remain* so – and we see her emerging. We are reminded of the lines in *The Merchant of Venice*: 'Truth will come to light; murder cannot be hid long; a man's son may, but, in the end, truth will out.'[5]

This emblem is separated in Cats's book of poems from the earlier one

The Hidden Chapter

31. Jacob Cats: *Verita*, 1655, Chancel Tomb

showing Dee and Bacon, but the date 1626 has been deliberately included to tie the allusion directly to Bacon. Moreover, the reference to a 'cavern deep' in the context of Truth's cave strengthens the relevance of the message to the tomb at St. Michael's.

Once again, the photograph of the emblem has been kindly supplied by Glasgow University from their 1655 edition. However, I also checked the 1658 edition held by Manchester Central Library and discovered that the tablet and inscription seen on the wall in the first edition *have been omitted from this later version*. Again the particular has been made general. In other words for later editions any reference to Bacon has been removed.

The 1655 *Lampada Trado* has an important place in this story because of the clues I believe it contains, clues pointing to the churchyard at St. Michael's. It is not so much the persons depicted but the setting in which they have been placed that convinces me. The most persuasive clue is the letter 'C' drawn on the shovel on the right. In moments of doubt this image returns to reassure me that the engraving contains certain truths about Francis Bacon. I have studied the 'C' motif here and on the tomb itself. On the shovel it is one, ornate, swirling letter; on the tombstone it is repeated

"A clear synopsis of the whole Science"
(translated from the Latin quote on the reverse side.)

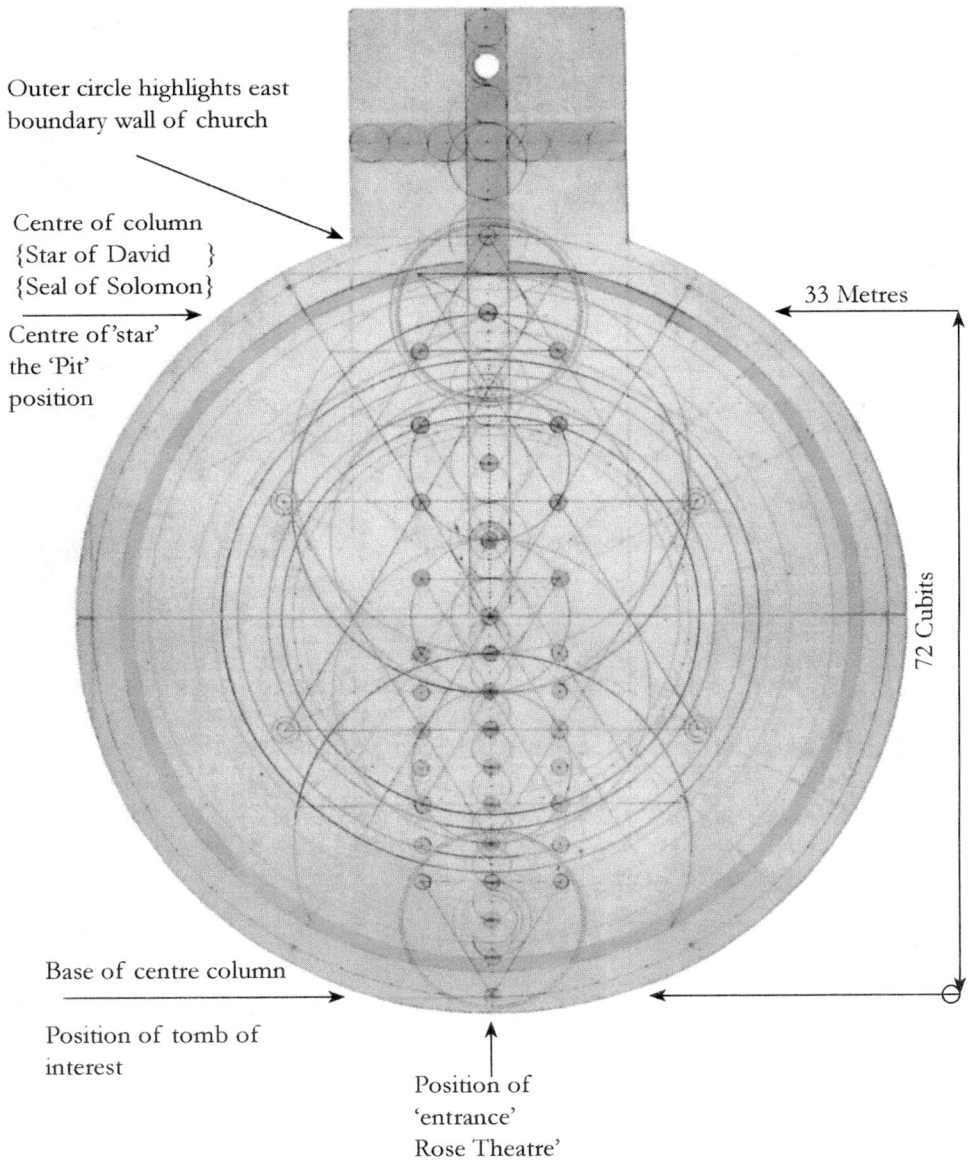

The geometry highlights strategic positions.

The 33 and 72 measures appear to correlate with the two main features in the Cats illustrations

32. John Byrom, Geometric Drawing, 'Rose' sequence

again and again, eight times in all, at the head and the foot.

However, the rest of the engraving has so many apt allusions to the data I had already collected that I am compelled to say that, in the end, the inclusion of the shovel leaves little to the imagination. Moreover it has to be considered with its 1655 companion piece *Verita no puo star sepolta*. The two form a pair and *Verita* depicts the chancel of the church. The detail in both provides the link, just as the physical distance of 72 cubits on the ground links pit and tomb.

So, the two engravings bring us back to Tintern Parva. Their messsage is clear. *Lampada Trado* speaks to us across the centuries of a legacy of knowledge. The *Verita* engraving goes further and states explicitly that truth of that knowledge cannot be buried forever. Interestingly, this 'truth' is recorded visually in the Byrom drawing (see illustration 32). Some secret hovers around St. Michael's Church. It appears to have been of surpassing importance to its guardians. Whether the nature of that secret changed or evolved it is not yet possible to say, but, as we have seen, the immediate area has been of continued concern to the highest in the land.

CHAPTER FOURTEEN

Stranger than Fiction

It was now the beginning of 2006. Throughout the six years spent researching the history of Tintern Parva and the surrounding area I had been subjected to a bewildering succession of surprises and some tantalising clues. Hoping for enlightenment I turned once more to the scant documentation St. Michael's had to offer.

I looked again through the typed list of burials the rector had given me. There was no layout of the old churchyard, plot by plot, with graves numbered and named. The local amateur historian Mr. Woolven had been a pioneer in mapping many old churchyards in the area. The church owes him a debt for his labours, but his list, confined to 'Monumental Inscriptions' as opposed to graves is, alas, incomplete. It does not for some strange reason include the alleged '1864' memorial. I knew, too, that a number of stones might have been moved over the years to make it easier to cut the grass. But the church list extracted from the Burial Register would at least tell me who was buried there, even if the grave itself was not marked by any monument, ledger or tablet. Because of the peculiar arrangement surrounding the appointment of the Rev. John Mais and the burial of Ann Watkins, I was particularly interested in the nineteenth century and studied every entry from 1813 to 1889. The list was chronological but did not include the names of officiating ministers. Even so, it was sufficient for my immediate purpose.

The first ten pages did not contain any names with any special connections to my work, but towards the end of the list, on page 11, I came to one that suddenly stood out. The date was 9 February 1888. The name was 'Elizabeth, Lady Francis Russell' and her address was given as St. Anne's (*sic*), Chapel Hill. The Russells are one of the great aristocratic families of England, both as Earls and later Dukes of Bedford. One member of the family had already featured in the history of Tintern in the shape of Anne Russell, Countess of Worcester. She had taken direct control of certain responsibilities at the wireworks in 1630, and was in addition a cousin of Francis Bacon. That had made her doubly interesting. Dee, too, as one might have guessed, had known members of the Bedford dynasty. A diary entry for 22 January 1577 records 'The Earl of Bedford came to my house.' This was an earlier 'Francis' Russell, the second earl, a prominent politician and diplomat. He was also godfather to Francis Drake who was about to embark on his voyage around the world. His visit to Dee may, indeed, have been connected with that voyage.

It was the second earl's son, 'John' Russell, who was the father of Anne, Francis Bacon's cousin. So, the three names 'Russell', 'Bacon' and 'Dee' were already connected in my research. The appearance of 'Elizabeth, Lady Francis Russell' in the burial register for 1888 made me pause. The names 'Francis' and 'John' occur repeatedly down the generations of Russells. One Lord John Russell was Prime Minister twice in the mid-nineteenth century. I was surprised to learn that a member of this prolific family had lived in the village and been buried in St. Michael's churchyard. The house 'St Ann's' can still be seen on the lower slopes of the hill above the main road, looking down towards the great west door of the ruined Abbey. Taking its name from the former chapel at the Abbey entrance, its long lancet windows are a reminder of its monastical past.

The burial entry sent me hurrying down to the churchyard to find her grave. Standing before the west door, my attention was drawn to a double grave to the left of the church, fenced off by small iron railings formed into Norman arches. Inside the enclosure stood two stone crosses side by side like sentinels, their bases lost in the long grass hiding the inscriptions. The double grave appeared to be almost square and had been dug into the sloping hillside, where one side had been built up to provide a level surface for the memorial. Parting the grass I was able to read on Lady Russell's tomb her address – 19, Marine Parade, Dover. I had never before seen a grave with the address of the deceased on it and I noted it was not the one in the typed register. The companion stone gave the name of her husband as 'John Loraine Baldwin' with the additional information that he had served as 'Warden of Tintern Abbey'. This was the first reference I had seen to a 'warden' at the Abbey. It was presumably an appointment made by the owner, the Duke of Beaufort, lineal descendant of the Earl of Worcester on whom Henry VIII had originally bestowed the monastery when it was dissolved.

As with practically every new fact that came my way, these two names brought with them a long train of questions. Who was Elizabeth, Lady Francis Russell and what was she doing being buried in Tintern? According to the cross on her grave she had lived in Dover. No doubt her husband's duties as warden brought her to Wales. I noted at once the French resonances of Baldwin's middle name, but, however tempting it was, I could not allow myself to digress from my first line of enquiry at the time. It was enough for the moment to assume that she had lived some time at Dover but had moved to Tintern when her husband took up this post. Perhaps she had homes in both places.

She was evidently very conscious of her status as a member of the Russell family. For although married to Baldwin, she retained the name and courtesy title of 'Lady' as a former member of the Russell dynasty. This she was entitled to do, and having once been married to a Lord she evidently had no intention of being diminished to a mere 'Mrs'. It was 'Francis', the masculine form of the name, not 'Frances', that she bore. Which of the many Lord Francis Russells had she married? The family archivist at Woburn, the ducal family seat, was unable to find a likely candidate. So, for a while, my efforts to trace this Elizabeth and her particular Francis were strangely, almost ridiculously, frustrated. Enquiries with Dover Public Library were no more successful. They could only tell me what I already knew, that she was married to J.L. Baldwin.

I eventually found her first husband amongst a flotilla of Russells listed in a biographical index of British naval officers in the nineteenth century. He was 'The Honourable Lord Francis John Russell' born in 1808 and one of the thirteen children of the seventh duke. Not surprisingly, he was sent to sea at fourteen years of age and rose to the rank of Captain, dying in 1869. But he had indubitably married in 1844 an Elizabeth Peyton, the daughter of an Anglican minister. He had married at thirty-six and died twenty-five years later at Maidenhead in the parish of Bray, Berkshire. There were no children from the marriage and his naval duties meant that he was frequently away at sea.

But Lady Elizabeth does not appear to have lived in the straitened circumstances of many nineteenth-century naval wives. On the contrary, when she applied for the letters of administration to deal with her late husband's effects, she was living in London in Wilton Street, Grosvenor Place, a highly desirable address by anybody's standards. Nor was she destined to suffer the indignity of living on a small pension. Elizabeth, Lady Francis Russell, I soon learned, was very wealthy in her own right.

In July 1873, now aged fifty-one, having been a widow for not quite four years, she married Baldwin. He was born in 1809, making him sixty-four at the time. This seems a rather late age at which to venture into matrimony for the first time and his address on the marriage certificate is given as the Alexandra Hotel, an indication perhaps of a bachelor life lived in hotels (no doubt very good ones) and clubs. They were married at St. Paul's, Wilton Place, the bride's parish church in Belgravia, since her address was still Wilton Street. The space on the certificate for 'rank or profession' is left blank after her name for it is clear from her title. No more needed to be said. Baldwin describes himself as 'Esquire', that is – a cut above a mere gentleman, even if he were unfortunate enough not to have

33. John Loraine Baldwin

a title. They belonged to an age and society conscious of rank and determined to maintain its subtle distinctions. The surnames of the four witnesses come from the highest ranks of late Victorian society – Peyton, Russell, Ponsonby and Thynne. The couple were becoming more interesting with every detail I came across. Elizabeth died in February 1888, fifteen years into the marriage; Baldwin survived a further eight years until 1896, dying at the age of eighty-seven. Lying in stately isolation within their carefully railed off double plot, perched above the path to the church door, they still seemed to assert their prominence in this modest setting. It was time to look a little more closely.

According to the inscription on his gravestone Baldwin was appointed Warden of the Abbey in 1873, the year he married, by its owner the eighth Duke of Beaufort. The magnificent ruins had by then become a favourite destination in the fashionable rural tourism inspired by the Lakeland poets. It appears that the wardenship carried with it the residence of St. Ann's, which had been largely rebuilt. This provided a suitably dignified establishment from which Baldwin could carry out his duties. His reign of twenty-three years earned him the affectionate title of 'Bishop of Tintern'.

But John Loraine Baldwin had cut a dash in society long before 1873. The son of an army officer of good family, he was a founder member of the 'I Zingari' Cricket Club. One night in July 1845, two very good Harrovian cricketers, the Hon. Frederick Ponsonby (later Earl of Bessborough) and his brother, Spencer Ponsonby, together with another player, R.P. Long, were invited by Baldwin to dine after a match at Harrow at the Blenheim Hotel in Bond Street where they decided to form a cricket club made up solely of gifted amateurs. It was decided that this particular club was not to have its own cricket ground but should seek to promote the popularity of cricket by playing matches at country houses whose owners liked to include a game to entertain their guests. They christened the club I Zingari because that is the Italian for 'the Gypsies' or 'Wanderers'. The name, it is claimed, came from the wine-heated brain of R.P. Long, who immediately after pronouncing it fell into a deep sleep.[1]

The four men drew up the rules very much under Baldwin's guidance and next day informed twenty of their friends that they were now members and another that he was to be Perpetual President. This was the beginning of a club still in existence today and with a fine reputation in the history of English cricket. What interested me however, was that Spencer Ponsonby was one of the witnesses to the Baldwin–Russell marriage nearly thirty years later. Baldwin was evidently good at keeping friends. Furthermore, the man chosen to be the club's first Treasurer and Auditor was the Hon. Robert Grimston.

Robert Grimston (1816–1884) was no dilettante. Apart from being a solid cricketer he was someone who saw the potential of telegraphy. After studying at Cambridge and Lincoln's Inn, he eventually joined the boards of a number of electric telegraph companies and in 1868 became chairman of the company which opened up the telegraph route to India. But it was his pedigree that intrigued me. He was the fourth son of the first Earl of Verulam and his early years were spent at Gorhambury, the Grimston family seat which had once been the home of Francis Bacon. He died unmarried at Gorhambury in 1884 and was buried in the family vault at St. Michael's Church, St. Albans. The Grimston family connections with Bacon are too strong to be ignored.

Built originally by his father, Sir Nicholas Bacon, Gorhambury was loved by Francis and he embellished it lavishly when he inherited it from his brother, so much so that John Aubrey declared 'When his Lordship was at his country house Gorhambury, St. Albans seemed as if the court had been there, so nobly did he live.'[2] On Bacon's death the house passed to his secretary, Sir Thomas Meautys, who had married Anne Bacon, a granddaughter of Sir Nicholas. He it was who erected the monument to Bacon in St. Michael's Church, showing him seated and with a rose carved on his shoe. (This is the statue alluded to in the allegorical engraving of Dee and Bacon by Jacob Cats.) In turn Sir Harbottle Grimston married the widow of Meautys and bought Gorhambury from the family in 1652. According to Aubrey:

> This October, 1681, it rang over all St. Albans that Sir Harbottle Grimston, Master of the Rolles, had removed the coffin of this most renowned Lord Chancellor to make room for his owne to lye-in in the vault there at St. Michael's church.[3]

This story is part of the mystery surrounding Bacon's death and burial. If it is true, could it be that this led to the re-interment of Sir Francis Bacon at Tintern Parva? His involvement with the wireworks is an established fact; folklore gives him a house nearby. Was he buried for a second time at St. Michael's near St. Albans, but this time in Monmouthshire? Sir Thomas Herbert, who was responsible for the funerals of Charles I and the Earl of Worcester, died in March the same year. His Tintern estate included the site of the College where I believe the ideas of Dee and Bacon were studied. Herbert's loyalty to the king was exemplary. Had he, before his own death, been involved in finding a new resting place for Bacon once Harbottle Grimston had taken over Gorhambury and embarked on his programme of re-building? I wondered, too, whether some of Bacon's lost manuscripts had been buried with him or secreted at St. Michael's earlier. The uncanny duplication of those two names, St. Michael's and St. Alban's, that we noted in the first chapter would have amused and delighted him.

I felt sure that the Grimston–Bacon–Gorhambury connections would have been known to John Loraine Baldwin. It would have quite simply been a topic of mutual interest between Robert Grimston and Baldwin. Both men were products of Christ Church, Oxford, and friends for at least forty-five years. The Baldwins were proud of their pedigree as we noticed from the inclusion of 'Loraine' as John's second name. Indeed the 'Gorhambury connection', if we may call it that, could hardly have escaped the attention of Baldwin's wife since her family, too, was related to the Bacons. Francis Bacon's nephew, Sir Robert Bacon, married Ann Peyton, a direct ancestor of Elizabeth, Lady Francis Russell. How much did Elizabeth know about the mysteries that accrued around Francis Bacon and his legacy? It is not clear how long Baldwin knew the wealthy widow before they married, but she retained her title as a public reminder of her station in life. Both as wooer and wooed and husband and wife, they would have talked of their families and that surely included Aubrey's story of Bacon's unseemly ejection from the Grimston family vault. The Peytons themselves were another distinguished dynasty with considerable wealth. When I looked at the interconnections closely, there was little wonder that Elizabeth Peyton's first husband was the son of a duke. The naval captain, Lord Francis John Russell, was fortunate to have won her hand; John Loraine Baldwin even more so.

We are dealing with a society acutely conscious of its genealogical roots and family alliances. The list of members of the I Zingari Club itself was based on the close ties of blood, school and status. All this made the appointment of John Loraine Baldwin to the 'wardenship' of Tintern Abbey more than a sinecure, a pleasant gesture by a ducal friend. Francis Bacon seemed to hover around the arrival of this autocratic newcomer with his aristocratic wife to the rural charms of Tintern. His hidden presence, his final resting place may have played a significant part in bringing them there.

It is time to add a little colour in the cheeks of J.L. Baldwin. He is remembered for more than his help in founding the Zingari cricketers. He is forever associated with the development of the game of badminton. This takes its name from the family seat of the Dukes of Beaufort in Gloucestershire where Baldwin was a frequent guest. It began as the ancient game of battledore and shuttlecock, and by the middle of the nineteenth century was being played in many English country houses. The story is told that Baldwin joined in a game of battledore and shuttlecock being played in the great hall at Badminton by some of the eleven children of the seventh Duke. He suggested that the shuttle should be hit away from rather than towards opposing players and this was how the game of badminton was born.

One set of rules was devised in India about 1870 but Baldwin's alleged contribution is very credible, since in his bachelor days he was a popular figure in London society and responsible for drawing up the rules for various card games including short whist, écarté and bezique. His meticulous mind was at its best performing such tasks. Not for nothing was he called 'The King of Clubs'.

Baldwin was a man of independent means, enjoying sufficient inherited wealth from his father to free him from the need to pursue a profession. His family background, Westminster School and Christ Church, provided him with a natural circle of friends with which to make his way in society. Wit and a theatrical skill did the rest. The humour for which he was famous may seem rather dated now but was typical of his age. The rules of the I Zingari Club were playfully worded but symptomatic of the affluence and assurance of the talented amateur. At one point the name of the secretary was given out as 'A. Secret'. Modern readers may groan at this, but Baldwin was a multi-talented man, an excellent rider at 'four in hand', an accomplished card player and an admired amateur actor. Many members of the Zingari were also part of a theatrical group calling themselves 'The Old Stagers'. Baldwin played a prominent role in the amateur theatricals that were the nightly accompaniment of matches played during Canterbury Cricket Week. This tournament, of course, was timed to take place just at the end of the London season. In more serious mode, he played a leading part in the re-organisation of the Turf Club in Piccadilly. Interestingly, in 1858 he founded a music club whose members had genuine musical merit. Someone christened it the 'Pig and Whistle' and an anonymous female friend presented him with a sculpture in silver of a pig with a whistle round its neck. A man who loved punning, Baldwin might well have appreciated a sly reference to Bacon in the 'pig'. I could not help wondering if the gift came from Elizabeth, Lady Francis Russell. She could easily have known Baldwin during her first marriage and been loved as a friend long before their marriage. The sculpture was either a most lucky find or a commission by someone wealthy enough to share such a joke, and Elizabeth certainly was. All in all, Baldwin was a very popular figure, cleverly caught in a brilliant caricature by 'Spy' in one of his series of satirical portraits of prominent contemporaries.

Elizabeth, Lady Francis Russell was a worthy partner to this man. Her father, the Rev. Sir Algernon Peyton, fifth baronet, was the rector of Doddington in Cambridgeshire from 1811 until his death in 1868, a period of fifty-seven years. Her mother Isabella Anne Hussey was equally well-born, being the daughter of Thomas Hussey, MP for Galtrim, Co. Meath, Ireland and granddaughter of Horatio Walpole, first Earl of Orford. Doddington was an attractive parish and at that time joined with two other parishes, March and Benwick, making it the richest living in the Church of England. With a handsome stipend added to the family's existing wealth, it is not surprising that Sir Algernon Peyton served his parishioners for over half a century. When he died he left a considerable fortune to his two surviving sons, both major-generals, and Elizabeth. Her first husband, alas, died within three months of her inheritance. It was John Loraine Baldwin who eventually benefited from Elizabeth's prosperity.

When Elizabeth was born in 1821 her father had already been rector for ten years. Even so, she was not baptised at Doddington but at Brandon in Suffolk where the Peytons had estates of their own. At twenty-four, she married Lord John Russell, having spent the first part of her life in Doddington. On the north wall of the chancel of the parish church there is a brass tablet erected in memory of her and her brother Algernon.[4] But she was not buried at Doddington, despite the fact that her father's remains lay in the vault. She kept her first husband's title but was not buried with him. Her main home, after London, appears to have been Dover, yet although she died there, she was not buried at Dover either. Her body was taken back by a somewhat circuitous route to Tintern Parva and buried in St. Michael's churchyard, where eight years later she was joined by her second husband. On the surface that may seem perfectly reasonable. However, Tintern Parva's remoteness from Elizabeth's immediate family roots led me to wonder whether there was an additional reason that made this a very special resting place for these two people.

The image of the two crosses side by side struck me as a little unusual. Why two separate ones? Why not one large cross inscribed with both their names, the usual practice with shared graves? There was, of course, an interval of eight years between their deaths and Baldwin could hardly leave her grave unmarked. But two crosses side by side seemed to say something about their relationship. They spoke of companionship and genuine affection, but also a certain independence. At any rate there was no joint monument after his death. This may seem trivial, but small details can turn out to be very significant. So it proved with these two crosses.

Elizabeth's death at Dover, at her home in Marine Parade, was very sudden. According to the *Cambridgeshire Times*, she had been to London to attend the wedding of her nephew, a Captain Peyton, and afterwards paid a short visit to her brother Sir Thomas Peyton, who was too ill to attend the wedding. She appears to have picked up some influenza-like infection from him, for within a few days of returning home she was taken ill herself and died on 2 February 1888, her husband at her bedside. This makes it likely that the two crosses were Baldwin's decision, after her totally unexpected demise.

This man was meticulous and, as we have seen, found his true metier as

The Hidden Chapter

a rule-maker. He delighted in detail – down to the colours and insignia he invented for the I Zingari Club. His lifelong friend, Robert Grimston, evidently had similar qualities for him to be chosen for that most delicate job of all in any club – treasurer and auditor. Baldwin gave himself the role of club archivist, keeping a record of its activities in a handsome scrapbook that runs to twelve volumes and is now housed in the library at Lord's.[5] At Lord's, too, hangs a portrait of him seated in a Bath chair with the two Ponsonby brothers behind him. The portrait is a testament to the impact Baldwin had on the club over fifty years. Robert Grimston died before him, in 1884, but his intimate knowledge of Gorhambury and Bacon's loving associations with the house must have become an open book to Baldwin through the long years of their friendship. The I Zingari Club drew from the cream of British society; three of the first twenty-one members were earls. Others were equally blue-blooded. Baldwin's secluded grave in a churchyard that had already revealed unexpected finds became even more of an enigma. Could Francis Bacon be part of the solution? Perhaps a wider look at the friendships Baldwin and his wife had enjoyed might provide an answer.

The next step was to consult the leading daily papers to see what reports they contained of the deaths of Elizabeth and her second husband. I did not doubt that there would be obituaries of J.L. Baldwin. 'Spy's' gallery of caricatures was a guarantee of that. But Elizabeth, Lady Francis Russell? What might the papers tell me about her? Had she led a public life or been content to exercise her influence more discreetly as a figure in good society? The latter seemed to be the case because I had difficulty in finding out very much about her from the newspapers. Of course, *The Times* carried an announcement of her death. On Saturday 4 February 1888, it said simply:

> On 2nd Feb. at 19, Marine Parade, Dover, Kent. Elizabeth, Lady Francis Russell, wife of John Loraine Baldwin.

That was all. I looked at editions for several days following, but she had not merited an obituary notice. Things were very different for her husband. Eight years later, on Saturday 28 November 1896, *The Times* announced:

> On the 25th Inst. at St. Ann's [sic] Tintern, John Loraine Baldwin of 19 Marine Parade, Dover, only son of the late Lieut. Colonel John Baldwin of Eltham and Dover, in his 88th year.

This was followed on Wednesday 2 December by an obituary notice:

> The funeral took place of Mr. John Loraine Baldwin at Tintern yesterday. The chief mourners were Miss Daniell, neice, Mr. Ernest Peyton, brother-in-law, and Miss Harcourt and Mr. C.F. Millett, cousins. And the friends present included the Earl of Cork, the Marquis of Worcester, Lord Edward

Somerset, and many others. A number of the villagers followed in the procession. Wreaths were sent by the Duke of Cambridge, the Hon. Spencer Ponsonby-Fane, the Duke and Duchess of Beaufort, Mr. Augustus F.M. Spalding, the 'I Zingari', the Earl and Countess of Londesborough, Countess Grosvenor, Baron and Baroness Deichmann, Lord and Lady Llangattock, the Countess of Guildford, the Dean of Hereford.

A royal prince (George, Duke of Cambridge) and a clutch of coronets were proof enough, if more were needed, of Baldwin's social eminence. Setting aside this grandson of George III (until very recently Commander-in-Chief of the British Army), some of those coronets gleamed brighter than others. One in particular caught my eye with a dazzling relevance. The Earl of Cork was Richard Edmund Boyle, the ninth Earl. It was his famous ancestor, Robert Boyle, who had once owned the brass plates from which the Byrom geometric drawings were printed. It was those drawings that had brought me down to Tintern originally in my pursuit of their provenance and the site of the Tintern brassworks. I had discovered that Francis Bacon had been a shareholder and one directly involved in running the wireworks. The way the wheel had come full circle seemed almost incredible. My sense of Bacon's involvement with the 'King of Clubs' and his burial increased with the thought of a Boyle standing by his graveside.

The public records system in this country is an invaluable resource. Public libraries, and civic and county record offices, house countless archives waiting for the researcher. I turned to the local newspapers for any accounts of the funerals they might contain. The paper covering news from Tintern in the late nineteenth century was the *Chepstow Weekly Advertiser*. It was published on Saturdays and the issue for 11 February 1888 carried a straightforward announcement of Elizabeth's death at 19, Marine Parade, Dover. The following week, however, gave a detailed account of 'the funeral obsequies [of] the lamented lady wife of Mr. J. Loraine Baldwin, the custodian of Tintern Abbey'. The account, written with a conscious respect for class that is now a thing of the past, can be seen in full in Coda Two. The facts of her birth and marriages are as given earlier. But there are other details we should note at this point, particularly the matter of her two addresses and the manner of her burial. The notice states:

> She married, secondly, in 1873, Mr John Loraine Baldwin, and resided certain portions of each year with him at his charming bijou residence at St. Ann's, Chapel Hill.

Later we are told:

> The body, which was enclosed in a shell in a massive brass-mounted coffin of best polished oak, arrived at Chepstow from Dover by the 2.47 pm train, accompanied by two or three immediate relatives, with their attendants.

Dover it seemed had been Elizabeth's main home, which she left at *specific times* to join her husband at his much smaller residence at Tintern. The phrase 'certain portions of each year' seems to imply fixed and regular periods rather than randomly timed visits. As it turned out, Elizabeth had commitments that required her presence in Dover and even London. Curiously enough, Dover had also been the home of Baldwin's father.

The journey her coffin took was not as simple as the *Chepstow Weekly Advertiser* would have us believe. One week after her death, on 9 February, it left Dover at 5.30 in the morning for Charing Cross and was then transported across London to Paddington Station. From there it travelled to Chepstow; the total journey took nine hours. Finally it was transferred to a hearse

> provided by Mrs. Garret, of the Beaufort Arms Hotel for conveyance to Tintern, whither it was attended by her husband, Mr. J.L. Baldwin, General Peyton (brother), General Wynn, and some members of the household.

I am not morbidly addicted to graveyards or funerals, but it is important for the reader to get a clear picture of the events of this day. The newspaper account is ambiguous.

We do not know who left Dover before dawn with the coffin. The most likely person was the funeral director from Dover itself appointed by Baldwin. (We shall come to him later.) We only know who *arrived* with the coffin at Chepstow in the middle of the afternoon. The husband, now aged eighty, would understandably join the cortege at Chepstow. The two generals and their attendants may well have joined the train at Paddington, unless they had travelled from their homes on a previous day. The coffin then had to be received, mounted on the hearse and proceed at an appropriately stately speed to Tintern. The drivers could hardly navigate the twisting rises and falls of that road at much speed. The month was February, the journey slow and the procession stopped outside the 'charming bijou residence' to be met by 'the workmen in the employ of Mr. Baldwin, and the domestics of the establishment'. Local gentry with their carriages also accompanied the procession or might have already gone ahead to wait in the church. We are told further that 'at the gates of the churchyard there was a large assembly of residents of Chapel Hill and Tintern and the vicinity'. The seating was not for them. At least an hour and a half must have elapsed from the arrival at Chepstow to the entrance into St. Michael's, so that the service began at about four o'clock in the afternoon. In February that would still allow some daylight but dusk would soon descend upon the scene, quickly turning to darkness. It is important to bear this in mind. The organisation and timing of the funeral was notably efficient, characteristic of Baldwin's attention to detail and orderliness – and, perhaps, the most fitting final tribute he could pay his wife. The only other point I would draw attention to at this stage is the description of the grave itself. The Chepstow reporter (possibly the undertaker) states:

> Wreaths, crosses, and other floral tributes of most magnificent and the choicest of flowers were in such profusion from friends far and near that not only the coffin but the grave, *a large square one bricked and cemented*, were covered completely, as also was the grass for some distance surrounding it.

We do not need to list the names of the mourners or those who sent flowers. It does, however, provide us with one fact – that Elizabeth, Lady Francis Russell was the Dame President of the Dover Habitation of the Primrose League. That office and its duties looked like one reason for her spending part of each year in Dover.

The Primrose League took its name from its association with Benjamin Disraeli. Queen Victoria sent a wreath of primroses to his funeral with a handwritten note in which she described them as 'his favourite flowers', and thus it came to be the name of an order devised in 1883 to promote Conservative principles. Each member signed the following declaration:

> I declare on my honour and faith that I will devote my best ability to the maintenance of religion, of the estates of the realm, and of the imperial ascendancy of the British Empire: and that consistently with my allegiance to the sovereign of these realms, I will promote with discretion and fidelity the above objects, being those of the Primrose League.

According to Winston Churchill, at its height the League had a million paid-up members. It was organised in lodges which were deliberately given the quaint name of 'habitations'. It was, as one might expect, hierarchical, with titles and decorations that its members could earn. At one time it had more support than the British trade union movement. By 1912, however, its decline had begun. 'The imperial ascendancy of the British Empire' passed with the end of the Second World War and the League was eventually wound up in 2004. Ladies had been included from the beginning, and during her last years Elizabeth Russell played her part in helping to run the Dover Habitation. In recognition, the 'Dames of the Dover Habitation' sent a wreath of primroses; and the 'Knights' one of primroses and violets to her funeral.

Dover, I learned, was also the site of a religious foundation dedicated to Radegunda. On the hills just outside stand the ruins of an abbey built in 1191 that flourished until the Dissolution. I found this a strange echo of

Monmouth's own early history, for Radegunda, as we know, had been revered in a chapel at Usk, visited yearly by pilgrims from France. There were not many churches dedicated to her in England. How odd that she should be here also, looking down upon Dover like a guardian spirit. Eleanor of Aquitaine, too, I recalled, had built a chapel in her honour in France. The saint was a reminder of spiritual values and good works. Apart from her social status and polish, Elizabeth Russell had been loved and esteemed for her 'good works and kind and gracious sympathy' by the people of Tintern. There was something reassuring about this statement in the paper – a welcome reminder of constants across centuries of changing fortunes and fashion.

Eight years later, on another winter's day, 1 December 1896, John Loraine Baldwin was laid to rest next to her in even more imposing circumstances.

Again we are indebted to the *Chepstow Weekly Advertiser* for a full and fascinating account. Since Baldwin died in Tintern there was no need to transport the body from Dover or anywhere else. However, the funeral was conducted by the same firm that had dealt with his wife. We are told that the arrangements 'were admirably carried out by Messers Flashman and Co. of Dover (undertakers to Her Majesty), under the personal superintendence of Mr. J. Relf'.

That this firm should be Queen Victoria's undertakers is indicative of the style with which Baldwin made his final exit. The stage management was again impeccable, even spectacular, the weather being the only eventuality beyond Messers Flashman's control. It was, after all, December.

> Rain commenced just previously to the cortege starting from the house to the church, and fell heavily during the whole of the ceremony. The procession was headed by the local police, then followed the hearse containing the coffin, which was literally hidden from view by the magnificent wreaths lying around it, and immediately behind the hearse walked the deceased's valet, who had during a lengthy servitude become greatly attached to his master. In the rear came a long line of mourning coaches, then members of the Trellech, Llandogo and Tintern Friendly Societies with which the deceased had associated himself from time to time, and following these additional empty coaches sent by sorrowing friends.

Apart from the additional coaches there were nine at the front of the procession. The service was conducted by the rector, assisted by eight other clergy. One wonders how they all managed to find a place to stand within the confined space of the chancel which also had to accommodate a surpliced choir, a cornet player and an organist.

The chief mourners were General Peyton (brother-in-law), Miss Daniell (niece), Miss Harcourt (cousin) and Mr. C.F. Millett (cousin). Amongst those who were present at the graveside were the Marquis of Worcester, Lord Edward Somerset, the Earl of Cork and Orrery.

These and a very long list of friends who sent wreaths testify to Baldwin's social success and popularity. However the weather is never a respecter of class and the old cliché 'rain stopped play' had a cruel aptness for this highly respected cricket lover. The second hymn, 'Peace, Perfect Peace', was to have been sung over the grave, 'but the rain was by this time descending in such torrents that it had to be abandoned'.

The account contains an interesting description of that grave:

The brick vault built for the reception of the remains was tastily lined with white chrysanthemums, moss and evergreens. The site of the grave *was adjacent to* that of the deceased gentleman's late consort, the Lady Francis Russell, who died 8 years ago, her tomb bears the following inscription: 'In loving memory of Lady Francis Russell, wife of J. Loraine Baldwin, 19 Marine Parade, Dover, in her 67th year on 2nd February, 1888.' [Emphasis added]

We must remember, too, the use of a double coffin, as for Elizabeth.

The remains were encased in two shells, the outer coffin being of dark polished oak with handsome brass mounts, the breastplate bearing the following inscription: 'John Loraine Baldwin, born 1st June, 1809 died November 25th 1896 in his 88th year.'

Such double coffins were fashionable in the late nineteenth century for important funerals. And there is no doubt that this one was important. Elizabeth's funeral was more complicated to arrange because she had died at Dover, yet in the event proved to be simple by comparison to Baldwin's. His was simple to arrange but the occasion itself was much more elaborate, even theatrical. He had been honoured with the friendship of the Prince of Wales, and H.R.H. the Duke of Cambridge visited his home in Marine Parade whenever his duties took him to Dover. This implied certain obligations. Although Mr. J. Johnson, an undertaker in Chepstow, supplied the double coffin, the rest of the arrangements, including the interment, were organised from Dover despite the distance. Later, however, circumstances made me think that there might have been a reason for this.

CHAPTER FIFTEEN

The Charade

THE PATIENCE OF the attentive reader must be rewarded. We have witnessed two funerals at close quarters and the reason for this must now be made clear. We are not engaged on a social history of burial customs, although we have spent a considerable amount of time in and around one particular church. The origin of this enquiry was, as I have frequently reiterated, the search for the origin of the brass plates for certain geometric drawings in John Byrom's collection. Those drawings had once, it is believed, belonged to Robert Boyle. He is the father of modern chemistry, the man who played a crucial role in the transition from medieval alchemy to modern science.

He follows in the footsteps of Francis Bacon (as the *Lampada Trado* engraving foretold) and by the pursuit of experiment and observation helped to free 'Natural Philosophy' from the dead hand of past authority and open up the pursuit of scientific knowledge to honest and unyielding enquiry. The contributions of Boyle (1627–1691) and Isaac Newton (1642–1727) are twin glories in our intellectual history and influenced the development of science worldwide. The geometric drawings and the role of John Byrom as their custodian have to be placed properly in this context.

It was therefore with some degree of excitement that I found that a direct descendant of Boyle had been one of the chief mourners at the graveside of John Loraine Baldwin in 1896: the more so since Baldwin's wife was linked by her ancestors to the family of Francis Bacon. Was this simply a quirk of fate? The previous pages document why I believe the church and churchyard of St. Michael's evoked deeply held allegiances and interest down the centuries. Some of these clearly predate, and are therefore unconnected with, Boyle and Bacon. But, again and again, the site seemed to exert a special attraction for different reasons. The experience was like listening to a resounding fugue by Bach. The Boyle variation on the theme of continuity now emerged like a leading motif, growing in richness as it approached its climax.

The graveyard had already been the source of several surprises. Its history had proved to be unexpectedly varied. The archaeology had indisputably revealed its previous use as a Roman industrial site and at a lower level than is visible today. The pudding stone wall had been uncovered inside the slipway wall as a thirteenth-century boundary, but again at a lower level. Inset horizontally into an angle in this wall is a metal pipe that has not been accounted for. We do not know where it begins or ends. The three exploratory trenches had enabled me to envisage something of the earlier topography of the western part of the churchyard. A large area of it had obviously been raised during the extensive rebuilding programme around 1846, but documentation was sparse. The 'simple' church and its graveyard were becoming more complex with every fact I discovered. When Stratascan informed me of the presence near the Watkins ledger of a flat-topped feature also at a level similar to that of the Roman workings, that was confirmation of a major piece of landscaping.

Now, suspecting that Baldwin's middle name, Loraine, was a declaration of his family connections with the French Lorraine dynasty, and alerted also to his connections with the Boyle family and Lady Russell's connections with the Bacons, I was forced to consider whether the small area enclosed by rails was part of the anomaly-ridden area underground that had already been documented. Was this brick-lined vault to be considered inside or outside the area of research? Its position relative to the Watkins ledger, the original 'tomb of interest', the boundary/slipway wall and the chancel can be seen in illustration 43. Would it repay examination as the chancel, the slipway wall and the Watkins ledger had? Could the keystone in fact mark an entrance that led to a structure that *included* the vault? The double vault might prove to be another in the series of questionable sites we had encountered in the church and graveyard. I could not leave the job half done. (The unsuccessful investigations in the early twentieth century at Chepstow were quietly beginning to become an issue for me. With my own discreet explorations a hundred years later, five miles up river, I seemed to be rubbing shoulders with the chief figure of that investigation, Francis Bacon himself and the owner of the Chepstow site – the Duke of Beaufort.)

Pondering on the double vault led me to consider other forms of burial. Apart from traditional crypts in churches and cathedrals, where else were bodies interred at this time? Already, as we have seen, with the rise of the medical schools body-snatching from churchyards had become a national scandal. In addition urban churchyards had declined to undignified, unsanitary, squalor.

The first response to this problem came with the opening of the General Cemetery of All Souls, Kensal Green, London in 1833. This was planned along radically new lines, inspired by the garden cemetery of Père Lachaise in Paris, opened in 1804 and soon renowned for its beautiful landscaping and monuments. Eventually Kensal Green became the most fashionable place to be buried in London. This was due to becoming the burial place of three royal figures: the Duke of Sussex (brother of George IV) in 1843, his sister Princess Sophia in 1848 and finally the Duke of Cambridge (grandson of George III) in 1904.

Kensal Green now arranges conducted tours since, apart from the graveyard, there are Georgian catacombs and impressive individual mausoleums, including those of the same three royals. I recalled that it was this Duke of Cambridge who was a close friend of Baldwin. I read again the words in the Chepstow *Biographical Sketch*:

> There is, therefore, little occasion for surprise that he was honoured by the friendship of the Prince of Wales and the Duke of Cambridge or that on the official visits of the latter, as Commander in Chief, to Dover – the permanent home of Mr. Baldwin – His Royal Highness never failed to make a complimentary call upon his old acquaintance.

Could it be that Baldwin had planned a similar resting place below ground for himself and his wife in Tintern – that among the impermeable rocks there lay a similar vault? Was that the reason why the Queen's own undertaker was employed for these two interments so many miles from his base at Dover and eight years apart?

A non-invasive GPR investigation might provide an answer to my questions. Without it my data would be incomplete. So, with the permission of the rector, the Rev. Philip Rees, now retired, I commissioned Stratascan to look again at this small section of the graveyard in September 2006.

As with the earlier surveys, I arranged a meeting in Tintern Parva to receive the report of the investigation and invited the late Major David Cowell, the former churchwarden with whom I had dealt from the beginning of my interest in St. Michael's, and the rector, who, unfortunately, was unable to attend. Stratascan was represented by one of its project officers and the Managing Director, Peter Barker. At the meeting great care was taken in explaining the findings.

After reading the funeral accounts in the preceding chapter, the reader will be surprised to learn that:

> The fragmented discrete anomalies identified within the railed grave area do not correlate with the burials as suggested by The Chepstow Weekly Advertiser in 1888 and 1896, as there is no (substantive) evidence of two large coffins or brick vaulting within the radar data collected in this area. This may suggest that the anomalies identified within the radar survey relate to some other form of activity taking place.'[1]

Both funerals were so very detailed in their organisation and such public events that it was not possible at this stage to reconcile this with the two newspaper accounts. The Chepstow paper reported two burials, eight years apart, side by side in the same double grave.

The meeting had been held on 29 November 2006. Peter Barker suggested that it would be useful to know what material was used for the inner 'shell'. We had descriptions of the outer coffins. Both were of oak and both had brass mounts and name-plates on them. Yet traces of these two materials were not found. Peter Barker knew of respected authorities from whom he could get reliable information. Accordingly, on 6 December, he wrote to Julian Litten, Ph.D, FSA. I include the relevant part of his email below:

> We have some good eyewitness accounts of two burials in one double grave that took place in the late 19th Century. They could be described as high status burials.
>
> I am trying to find out about the type of coffin that may have been used. The account refers to an inner shell within a substantial outer oak shell. It also mentions a brass plate on the top of the coffin onto which the occupant's name had been engraved.

Dr. Litten replied as follows:

> The inner shell would either be of elm or oak, depending on the date of the burial. As a rough guide, elm was preferred until about c.1870, after which oak became fashionable for both the inner and the outer case.
>
> It was common practice – and still is – to put a name-plate on the outer case. Indeed, it is not at all unusual to come across an additional name-plate on the inner coffin as well.

Peter Barker also consulted Bill White, Curator at the Centre for Human Bioarchaeology at The Museum of London. He replied as follows:

> The description you have suggests an inner shell or coffin made of lead, inside an outer shell of wood – a fairly common arrangement in the 19th century. There were also triple-shelled coffins: the same thing but enclosed in an outer lead coffin. An inscription bearing some biographical information on the coffin's incumbent was also provided quite often, especially for 'high status' burials. If the 'breastplate' is indeed made of brass there is a good chance that the inscription will still be legible. Sometimes they were made of lead or of iron, plated which could corrode badly and make the inscription frustrating, difficult or impossible to read.

The comments on the brass name-plates were particularly interesting. They should have survived but the radar showed no signs of them. Equally, as Peter Barker informed me in a later email:

> If the Russell coffins were indeed lined with lead, then we would get very strong responses in the radar returns. As you know we are not seeing strong responses.

The views of both experts had to be considered seriously in any assessment that was to be made now of this puzzle.

I knew from Professor Doe at Cardiff University that no one owns a body. I knew, too, that the Church is not responsible for the removal or disappearance of a body from its churchyard. But after very careful and prolonged debate I felt that this was not a case of body-snatching.

My main reason for this was that Queen Victoria's undertaker, Messers Flashman and Co., had been responsible for both burials.

But that left me with an even greater mystery. If the survey had identified 'a number of anomalies that do not correlate with those of Christian burials', what has happened to the two coffins one would expect to find at a depth of around six feet? This was the question that I had had to face over the Ann Watkins grave and the tomb of interest, but those were very modest burials in comparison. The high-status funerals of Elizabeth Russell and J.L. Baldwin had been commemorated in a substantial manner. The two crosses still stand in their original enclosure, bordered by a fence of Norman arches. There are no outward signs of the inroads of time. A single ledger is sometimes so weakened that safety demands its removal to another position. It was the visible permanence and deliberateness of the duplication in this monument that made the missing evidence more puzzling for me. So, Stratascan looked at the site again.

Having made certain technical adjustments to their equipment they were able to gain even more information:

> The alteration of the range settings of the antenna from 60nsec (September 06 survey) to 100nsec (April 07 survey), a different gains calibration and possibly the conditions of the site have provided us with a more informative data set from within the Russell / Baldwin grave. When the new dielectric constant is applied to the September 06 data set a number of weak anomalies possibly relating to the two burials are discernible at a depth of around 0.9m.[2]

This was only one of the curious features to emerge. A depth of 0.9m is shallow for a grave – a little under three feet, when the usual depth for a burial is around six feet.

The findings brought other surprises. The *Chepstow Weekly Advertiser*

The Charade

34. The double grave of John Loraine Baldwin and Lady Francis Russell

describes the grave in its first report as 'a large square one bricked and cemented'. The second account states that, 'The brick vault built for the reception of the remains was tastily lined with white chrysanthemums, moss and evergreens.' A vault by definition implies some sort of cavity – hence presumably the brick-lining. But from the data gathered in the radar survey there appears to be no such cavity. The reflections are from filled-in ground and that seems to argue against a vault. Why build a vault and then fill it in with soil? At both funerals the ground immediately around the graves was dressed and covered with flowers. Yet the second account, written eight years after the first, distinctly describes the grave as a vault.

The graves would have been dug by local labour under instruction from Messers Flashman and Co. The double grave was clearly planned at the time of Elizabeth's interment. In other words the general physical features were fixed in 1888. Baldwin's funeral differed from Elizabeth's only in scale and up-to-the-minute details such as the mourners likely or able to be present and the steps required to meet their needs in attending.

Peter Barker understood my real concern to establish the truth, and Stratascan had carried out the supplementary survey to confirm the accuracy of the earlier survey of September 2006.

The geophysicists had expected that the caskets 'made from substantial

GRAVE			KEY	
Left	John Loraine Baldwin ob. 25 Nov. 1896	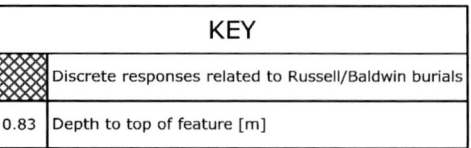	Discrete responses related to Russell/Baldwin burials	
Right	Lady Francis Russell ob. 2 Feb. 1888	0.83	Depth to top of feature [m]	

"Two burials are discernable at a depth of around 0.9m." (Stratascan)

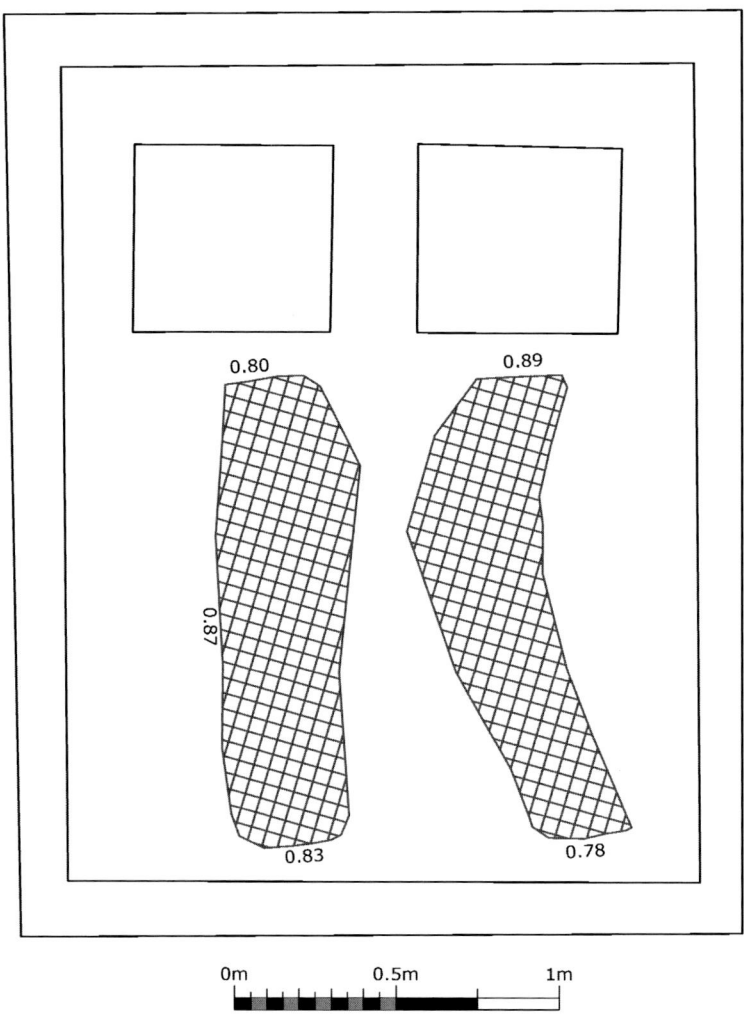

STRATASCAN™
Job No. J2222 (Extract)   35. Two burials

timber' might still be intact. These caskets were double coffins, one within another. Air voids would be expected to be present in the results of the survey, 'but the strength and character of the returns seen within the grave are not entirely consistent with this'.

Furthermore:

> Air voids would still be expected with these anomalies and we stand by the interpretation that the strength of the anomalies within the data does not seem strong enough to be related to air voids. These anomalies also do not have the characteristic 'Focused Ringing' effect often associated with air voids.

Stratascan were unable to offer an explanation for the difference between the two shapes shown in Figure 2 of the April 07 Survey Report (illustration 35). They insist that the shapes are 'a representation of the feature beneath the surface'. And we must accept that.

We need to bear in mind that these anomalies occur at around a depth of three feet and that the Baldwin/Russell coffins were substantial in size and style. The *Chepstow Weekly Advertiser* described Lady Russell's oak coffin as 'massive'. Baldwin's would hardly be inferior. Furthermore, they may well be still intact, yet, as the Conclusion of the April 07 Report states, 'there is little evidence of the bottom of the grave cut within the radar data'. The discrepancy between the two 'shapes' at such an unusually shallow depth leaves me feeling uneasy. I reported the findings personally to the rector and warden on 24 May.

These factors, combined with the absence of strong signals for air voids and the 'Focused Ringing' effect, make me doubt that the burials suggested at this depth in the report of the April 07 survey are those of J.L. Baldwin and Lady Russell. The findings are so unusual that they seem to me rather to indicate that the double grave was re-used at a later date for two other burials. If that were the case, it would explain why the geophysicists never found evidence of a 'vault'. It would have been filled in. Such a burial would be less likely to be discovered within a railed enclosure than in the open area of the graveyard.

What then are we to make of the possible 'absence' of the caskets of Baldwin and his consort? They are either buried lower in the double grave or they are not. The evidence for this did not show up in the earlier survey of September 2006. Hence the conclusion of the findings at that time. If they are not buried there, some individual or group must have been party to the 'charade' of the funeral and organised an alternative resting place for this couple. In this respect we should remember the description in the Chepstow paper of the brick vault 'lined with white chrysanthemums, moss and evergreens' and the heavy downpour that forced the curtailment of the service at the graveside.

This thought made me look at the mourners gathered around Baldwin's graveside. Apart from close relations and the local gentry with whom he was on visiting terms, the most important were two members of the Beaufort family, the Marquis of Worcester and his brother Lord Edward Somerset and the Earl of Cork and Orrery. We know of the Boyle connection through Cork. That indicated how important past family links were. The Marquis of Worcester was interesting in other ways. Henry Somerset was the heir to the dukedom and Baldwin's connection was initially explicable through his friendship with the family, frequent visits to Badminton and his influence in helping to shape the game played in the family home. After being educated at Eton, the Marquis joined the Royal Horse Guards and served as an Aide de Camp to Queen Victoria. The most intriguing fact about him for me was that as ninth Duke of Beaufort he became closely involved with Dr. Orville Owen in his excavations in the bed of the river Wye at Chepstow during the early 1900s, looking for missing Bacon manuscripts. The ghost of Bacon was here again hovering around. Lord Edward Brudenell Somerset was new to me – but not for long. What I was to learn of him made him a figure of unexpected interest.

In an effort to make sense of the incomprehensible, I struck out in another direction. Perhaps the wills of both Elizabeth and J.L. Baldwin held clues. Who had benefited from the fortune Elizabeth had inherited from her father? Certainly not her first husband. Who, in turn, benefited from Baldwin's demise? Elizabeth had no children by either of her marriages and, so far as I knew, Baldwin had no such claims that could be made upon him. They had lived their life together in great style – what happened in the end to all that wealth?

CHAPTER SIXTEEN

Where There's a Will ...

THE DETAILS CONTAINED in a will reveal a lot about the testator. Some wills are exhaustive in their detail; others say very little. Even so, that little can be important. So it was with Elizabeth, Lady Francis Russell.

The will was made three years before her death, on 4 May 1885. At the time she was sixty-four years old, so there is nothing unduly premature about the date. John Loraine Baldwin was seventy-seven that year. Certainly, one might expect him to make a will as well since his wife was younger and would in normal circumstances be likely to outlive him. Since she died first, there is no evidence that in 1885 he made a will out of concern for her future well-being.

Elizabeth's will is expressed in fourteen lines. The crucial section states:

> I hereby devise and bequeath all my property real or personal and as to any part thereof over which I may have any power of appointment by any deed, will settlement or other instrument I appoint the same unto my husband the said John Loraine Baldwin absolutely. And I appoint him sole Executor of this my Will.

It was witnessed by her butler at Tintern and her solicitor C.F. Millett, 1, Old Palace Yard, Westminster, London.

Although, as I learned later, there were other blood relatives living, none was a beneficiary. Her entire wealth went to her husband, who was the sole executor. She died on 2 February 1888 and was buried a week later on the 9th. Probate was granted to her husband on 21 February, nineteen days after her death and twelve days after her funeral. Just like the funeral, the will was dealt with most expeditiously. The bare facts tell us little, except that Elizabeth made no provision for the possibility that her husband might die first. That was worth more than a passing thought. The gross value of her personal estate was £30,382 18s 11d. In today's money that sum would make her a millionaire. By the close of February 1888 her affairs were all settled. The total absence of bequests of jewellery or any other personal possessions strikes a poignant note and emphasises the suddenness of her end.

The Hidden Chapter

We must now turn to the last wishes of her husband in 1895. Apart from all his pecuniary bequests, John Loraine Baldwin certainly made provision for his friends out of the contents of his house and garden. One of the peculiarities of his will was that it was witnessed and signed in the presence of the manager and hall porter of the Great Western Hotel, Paddington, London. He arranged to do this on 19 May 1895, eighteen months before his death. By then he was eighty-six and, without the company of any friend or relative, formalised the final disposition of his wealth in a hotel room with two of its staff as witnesses. The scene suggests a frailty and isolation in stark contrast to the full and active life he used to live. It was as if he had set out alone for London and, venturing no further than the railway station, returned home when the business was completed. What could London offer him now?

The reality was very different. Baldwin was not as frail as we might think. Despite being confined to a Bath chair, he was well enough to attend a three-day match against the Gentlemen of England at Lords the following month, June, to mark the fiftieth anniversary of the I Zingari club and also celebrate the jubilee of the Old Stagers. That makes the hotel signing more intriguing. Baldwin was a millionaire and related to the solicitor. Why did he not simply ask Millett to visit him in Tintern and conduct the business in the comfort of St. Ann's? After all, Millett was to receive a very large bequest for his legal services and could have accomplished the journey more comfortably than a man in an invalid chair. The solicitor certainly spared Baldwin the journey to his Westminster office and came to the hotel instead, but since travelling to Lords presented no problem for Baldwin next month, one is led to wonder whether he chose the hotel out of a desire for secrecy. (None of his precious Zingari friends was asked to be a witness.) Subsequently he added two codicils, both in August 1896. He does not appear to have travelled for those. But he had already made the major provision for his effects twelve months earlier. It was now a matter of minor adjustments. The first codicil was witnessed by two friends and neighbours from the Chepstow area, the second by his doctor and butler in Tintern. By then his health must have been failing and he was anxious to have everything in order.

Such is its detail that the will runs to over three pages of closely typed A3 paper. Apart from the main bequest there are gifts of money to twenty-two individuals, the poor of the two adjacent parishes of Tintern and Chapel Hill and the Society (not yet Royal) for the Prevention of Cruelty to Animals. This amounted to a total of £3, 000. There were gifts of £50 each to the five offspring of the eighth Duke of Beaufort. He remembered his cousin's children including one, Cyril Baldwin Harcourt, who was Private Secretary to the Archbishop of Canterbury. And he did not forget his faithful gardener. Most intriguingly, there was his generous bequest of £1,000 to his solicitor. This man, Charles Frederick Millett, was another Loraine cousin and the same solicitor who had drawn up Elizabeth's will eleven years earlier. I noted that Millett had not attended her funeral, although he was charged with dealing with her affairs. However, he was very much in evidence now, not only at Baldwin's graveside but also as his sole executor.

Probate was granted on 9 January to Millett. The gross personal value of Baldwin's personal estate, calculated in April 1897, was £36,996 10s 7d. After the payment of all these bequests, funeral expenses, debts and any other expenses incurred by the will, he states:

> I give all the rest and residue of my property To my dear cousin Elizabeth Alice Annie Harcourt and I appoint her my residuary Legatee.

What interested me most when I first studied the will was the provision he made concerning Lord Henry Edward Somerset, the fourth and youngest son of the eighth Duke of Beaufort:

> And further Upon trust in the event of my friend the said Lord H. Edward Somerset being appointed Keeper of Tintern Abbey in succession to myself to give hand over and transfer to the said Lord H. Edward Brudenell Somerset all my effects other than money or securities for money which may be in and about my residence at Tintern and the gardens attached thereto Provided always and I hereby declare that it is my will that in the event of the said Lord H. Edward Somerset predeceasing me or not being appointed my successor as Keeper of Tintern Abbey that the trust hereinbefore created in favor of the said Lord H. Edward Somerset shall wholly fail.

It was this arrangement that required two codicils. In the first codicil Baldwin had made provision for Lord Edward's wife and eventually their son, provided Lord Edward had been appointed Keeper of Tintern Abbey within six months of his death. Lady Edward was to hold the chattels from St. Ann's in trust for her son who would own them absolutely on reaching the age of twenty-one. The second codicil confirms the bequest to Lady Edward and her son in the event of her being made Keeper of Tintern Abbey in lieu of her husband. Baldwin was evidently concerned about who should take over the office of Keeper, although, of course, it was not in fact his to give. In the original will he thinks only in terms of Lord Edward Somerset and perhaps made the bequest in the hope that it would persuade the Duke to nominate him as the next Keeper. The house at St. Ann's, as we know, went with the post and Baldwin was evidently prepared to leave it fully furnished for Lord Edward or his wife. In the light of the mystery surrounding the graves, I had to consider the possibility that he may have had some other purpose.

In the event, Lord Edward died within the six months, so all these provisions came to nothing. His wife remarried surprisingly quickly, and left the Beaufort family circle. Lord Edward's death was registered on 19 May 1897. He had died at Stoke Park, Stapleton, Gloucestershire, aged forty-four, from typhoid fever on 17 May. Spread by a species of salmonella, typhoid fever is commonly caused by poor hygiene in the preparation of food or from a source of poor sanitation. Stoke Park was a country mansion belonging to the Duke of Beaufort. The eighth Duke and his wife had already retired there, handing over Badminton and all its responsibilities to his eldest son and heir, the Marquis of Worcester. The Duke died in 1899 and Worcester succeeded as the ninth Duke. He it was who sold estates in Monmouthshire including the Abbey, its lands and woods to the Crown between 1900 and 1901, comprising 5,333 acres in total.

The scene of the Marquis and Lord Edward, standing together at Baldwin's grave, is coloured in hindsight by the unfulfilled aspirations of the friend they mourned. Lord Edward, a major in the army, had been appointed by Queen Victoria as a member of the Honourable Corps of Gentlemen at Arms, an ancient bodyguard of the British sovereign formed originally in 1509 as a mounted escort to protect Henry VIII in battle. By the nineteenth century its duties were confined to ceremonial occasions such as the State Opening of Parliament, state visits and similar royal functions. Baldwin had chosen him in preference to any of the other Somersets to succeed him as Keeper of Tintern Abbey and, if not Edward, then his wife. Did both Queen Victoria and Baldwin see the same characteristics in him – an exceptional loyalty and reliability? Furthermore, the office of Keeper of Tintern Abbey had brought with it for Baldwin residence at St. Ann's. He clearly wanted that for Lord Edward, too, devising a Trust for all his precious glass, furniture and papers including, surely, choice possessions of his late wife, Elizabeth.

Baldwin must have had a serious reason to make these provisions. Since the revelations about the double grave, nothing, I felt, could or should be taken for granted. Indeed, perhaps it was not simply the Abbey that was the concern for Baldwin, but also St. Michael's churchyard, where he himself was to be interred. Could that have been the real centre of interest for Baldwin as it appears to have been for others in the past?

In attempting to work out what actually happened, I noticed a curious repetition of the date 19 May. It was the date Baldwin made his will at the Paddington hotel and it was the date his friend the Marquis of Worcester, future ninth Duke of Beaufort, was born in 1847. But 19 May had a far more dramatic significance for the Beauforts. The Duke's ancestor, Henry

Somerset, second Earl of Worcester, played an important part in helping Henry VIII with his divorce from Catherine of Aragon, his marriage to Anne Boleyn in January 1533, the coronation in June that year and the subsequent christening of their daughter, the future Queen Elizabeth I. Before the marriage Henry VIII had created Anne Marchioness of Pembroke, bestowing on her lands in Monmouth that included Tintern Parva. When the king grew tired of her, Anne was accused of adultery with several men, one of them, Sir William Brereton, who happened conveniently to be married to the sister of the Earl of Worcester. Worcester was one of the judges appointed to try the queen whose marriage he had supported, and he found her guilty. Anne was executed at the Tower of London on 19 May 1536. The charge was possibly false but the men allegedly involved were executed on 17 May. Anne's execution two days later was followed in September the same year by the dissolution of Tintern Abbey. As a reward for his unquestioning obedience Henry gave the Abbey and its revenues to Worcester the following year, 1537. This episode is crucial to the rise of the Worcesters. Down the centuries the Abbey ruins were a visible reminder of how they rose to power – by Anne Boleyn's execution. Unswerving loyalty to another monarch, Charles I, led to the Somersets becoming Dukes of Beaufort.

John Loraine Baldwin's closeness to the eighth Duke and his family is well documented. Beaufort anniversaries would be important to him. In Baldwin's eyes 19 May would be an appropriate day to make a will in which he provided so carefully for the future of the Duke's youngest son. All it required was to arrange with his solicitor, Millett, for that to be the day the will was witnessed and signed. Was the lawyer, too, aware of the relevance of 19 May to the Beauforts? For it shortly became the date when Lord Edward's unexpected death was registered. That death occurred uncannily on the anniversary of the execution of Anne Boleyn's alleged lovers.

Neither of Lord Edward's elderly parents who were living at Stoke Park at the time caught the disease from which he died, although, of course, it is not transmitted from person to person like influenza. The eighth Duke died two years later in 1899 and the widowed Dowager Duchess lived on until 1906. So the source of the infection remains unknown. However, Edward's death was extraordinarily unfortunate in its timing. He died twenty-five weeks after the death of John Loraine Baldwin – within the half year stipulated in Baldwin's will for his appointment as Keeper. Since that appointment had not materialised, the Trust set up in his favour was deemed to have 'failed'. Accordingly, neither Edward's widow nor his son inherited anything from St. Ann's. Lord Edward's own will reveals the modest amount of money he possessed. It totalled £25 and he had already received £50 from the estate of J.L. Baldwin. Lady Edward, as we saw, ensured her future by marrying a second time. The 'chattels', as the codicils decreed, reverted to the residuary heiress, Elizabeth Harcourt.

In his will Baldwin refers to her as his 'dear cousin', but it was in fact her mother who was first cousin to him. She was Gertrude Charlotte Lucas, born in 1823 at Newport Pagnell, Buckinghamshire. This small town was the site of the first cricket game played by the I Zingari. The club was founded in July 1845 – late in the season for any matches to be arranged. Gertrude was still living at home and the family connection may have helped Baldwin to organise a last-minute fixture in August. It was symptomatic of Baldwin's approach to arrange fixtures through family, friends and aristocratic connections. The following year Gertrude Lucas married George Simon Harcourt of Ankerwycke Estate, Hertfordshire, and between 1846 and 1863 she gave birth to ten children, four girls and six boys. Elizabeth Alice Harcourt was the youngest of the girls and the one Baldwin chose as his main legatee. He left £300 to each of her sisters and £50 to each of her brothers who survived him, except the eldest, Otto, who, according to some records, had emigrated to Australia. When Baldwin died Elizabeth Harcourt was thirty-six and still unmarried. Nevertheless, something about her persuaded Baldwin to leave her a large fortune.

Elizabeth Harcourt had evidently also caught the attention of the solicitor, Charles Frederick Millett. He had drawn up the wills of both Elizabeth, Lady Francis Russell and John Loraine Baldwin. As Baldwin's sole executor he knew exactly his intentions and wishes. Should we be surprised, therefore, that a little over ten weeks after Baldwin's funeral, these two married? Or that, only days prior to the marriage, Millett performed an intriguing legal service for his future bride by drawing up a Trust in the interest of her unborn children? In the light of that, no one could accuse him of fortune hunting. Millett's legal foresight had carefully pre-empted any suspicion of that.

Millett's handling of Baldwin's affairs and his subsequent marriage calls for close scrutiny. Both Baldwin and his wife would have chosen a solicitor of the highest repute and Millett's offices at Old Palace Yard, Westminster in 1885 and in Great George Street in 1895 are indicative of his standing and success. Even so, we are bound to ask what sort of man he was and what motivated his actions. Born in 1838, into a wealthy family, he was already forty-seven when he drew up Elizabeth, Lady Russell's will in 1885 and approaching fifty-seven when he drew up Baldwin's. He was unmarried, so, from the moment that Baldwin signed his will in the Great Western Hotel, Elizabeth Harcourt was bound to be an object of interest to him. If he had not known her earlier he had eighteen months to meet and cultivate her before Baldwin died. It certainly looks as if he did just that. They shared the same carriage at the funeral. Even if he had known her beforehand she had not done anything to persuade him earlier to abandon his independence. At fifty-eight years of age bachelors are seldom ready to sacrifice their independence except in a very good cause. The timing of Millett's marriage does not hint at an ardent autumnal romance, but suggests rather hard-headed calculation.

The reason why Elizabeth Harcourt was not already married may not be immediately clear. But she was one of four daughters (all spinsters) with six brothers, whose widowed mother was living off a provision made at the time of her own marriage. It looks as though there was no money for dowries for any of the girls even if they had been acknowledged beauties. Nobody came along to sweep any of them off their feet into a loving marriage. John Loraine Baldwin evidently felt some pity for them for, as we saw, he left each £300, a small consolation compared with Elizabeth's inheritance. But pretty or plain, Baldwin chose Elizabeth as his heir and Millett sat up and took notice.

The marriage certificate makes this clear. On February 11 1897, less than three months after Baldwin's death and one month after being granted probate, Millet married Elizabeth Harcourt at St. Stephen's Church, Kensington. Elizabeth's address is given as St. Mary the Virgin, Dover – her local parish. Her mother owned a house locally in Camden Crescent. Millett's address is given as St. Stephen's, South Kensington, evidently his parish. Notably it was in his parish that the banns were read and the marriage took place. So the banns were first read one week after he had been granted probate. One of the witnesses to the wedding was Percy Barnes. He, I learned later, was the solicitor who drew up the Trust for any children that might come from the marriage.

Millett hailed from a family settled originally near Penzance, Cornwall. He was the third of twelve children, six boys and six girls born to his father, who early in his marriage moved to Droxford, Hampshire. This man, another Charles Millett, served with the East India Company, rising high within its ranks at a time when it had ceased to be a trading company and become an administrative arm of the British in India.

As a young man of twenty-two Charles Frederick was living at home with his parents in Grosvenor Street, London, in a household that maintained sixteen servants including a footman, under-footman and even a page. This in no way encouraged a life of indolence and self-indulgence. On the contrary, ambition marked out several of his brothers. One, Montague, joined the Bengal Infantry at eighteen, saw service during the Indian Mutiny (1857) and took part in the capture of Lucknow. By the time he retired he had reached the rank of Major General. Two others chose careers in the forces. Charles Frederick may have settled on a safer career in law, but did so with equal success.

At the same time it cannot be denied that the family was never less than affluent and as a bachelor Charles Frederick remained steadfastly a fixture in the family home. But the death first of his father in 1873 and then his elder brother in 1876 left him as head of the family. By the time he married, only two of his five brothers were still living. It was to this household that he brought his bride and in this house that their first child was born. So, both before and after marriage, he was supported by a contingent of domestic staff on a scale now inconceivable. As late as 1901, for instance, four years into his marriage, his own household in Carlisle Mews was managed by six female servants. (Strangely not a manservant in sight.) Does this help to explain his pursuit of Elizabeth Harcourt? Was it to ensure the continuance of a very comfortable lifestyle? Of course, we must not forget the Trust set up before the marriage to protect any children they might have. This does not remove the suspicion of an element of calculation, but there may have been another more altruistic reason as well.

After first gaining a degree, he was articled to a firm of solicitors and by the time of his father's death in 1873 was sufficiently experienced to be chosen over his elder brother as one of two executors. The other was William Thackeray Marriott, a barrister and evidently a man of great capability for he was later appointed twice as Judge Advocate General and in that capacity acted as legal adviser to Queen Victoria. Charles Millett senior's will was a complicated affair, setting up various Trusts for his wife and children. Having held an important post in the East India Services and being very wealthy, he would understandably have chosen his executors with care. Indeed Charles Frederick Millett may well have worked professionally with Marriott before his father engaged the barrister's services.

As befitted the eldest surviving son and head of the household, Charles Frederick Millett collected and kept together certain items that reflected the history and standing of his family. First and foremost was what he called the 'Millett Plate' – silver and electro-plated articles bearing the Millett coat of arms, a silver cup presented to his grandfather, George Millett, a 'large sea-piece' by Pocock of a fleet of ships of the East India Company which his grandfather had commanded, a gilt inkstand presented to his great-grandfather William Baldwin, a barrister, and last but not least a portrait of the same William Baldwin by Romney. In addition there was the 'Daniell Plate', an inheritance of swords and medals from his Daniell forebears. The safekeeping of these items was a matter of concern. Upon his wife's death his eldest son was to inherit the 'Millett Plate', his second son the 'Daniell Plate'. He was to the end conscious of his Baldwin inheritance – both from his great-grandfather William and the wealth of John Loraine Baldwin through his wife. Little wonder that they christened their first son Charles Baldwin Millett.

The Millett family on this evidence was clearly a pillar of the Establishment. The law, army and civil service were the context in which they had sought excellence for over two hundred years. The detailed care of John Loraine Baldwin's will was reflected in Charles Frederick Millett's own final Testament. Could such a man knowingly be associated with a funeral that was in one sense a charade? Who indeed could be suspected of any deception? The undertaker, Mr. Flashman, came with the commendation of his appointment to Queen Victoria. Could one doubt his role? My dilemma was considerable. The findings of both radar surveys seemed difficult to reconcile with the two sets of people most immediately concerned with winding up Baldwin's affairs. Yet there must be an explanation of this extraordinary contradiction.

Flashman, of course, withdrew from the Tintern scene, as one would expect, the moment Baldwin's funeral was over and his services were no longer required. His representative, Relf, returned to Dover and we hear no more of the firm. Millett's involvement with Tintern lasted a little longer. First, there was the matter of Lord Edward Somerset's possible succession as Warden, the attendant wait for a decision, and Lord Edward's death. Only then could a final decision be made about the contents of St. Ann's and the fate of any of the staff who had been retained until the matter of the Wardenship was clear. All except two, the cook and a kitchen maid, were dismissed. They were local girls from St. Briavels on the Gloucester side of the river Wye. Millett found places for both of them in his London household.

The most important landowner in the area remained the Duke of Beaufort, who had handed over the responsibility for his vast estates to the Marquis of Worcester, who succeeded as ninth Duke in 1899, within two years of Baldwin's death. He will forever be associated with Dr. Orville Owen's excavations at Chepstow in the bed of the Wye every summer from 1909 for several years. Owen was convinced that he had found a code in the plays of Shakespeare and works by other Elizabethan writers that proved Francis Bacon was the true author of Shakespeare's work. Later he convinced the ninth Duke sufficiently for Beaufort to allow Owen to go ahead with his excavations. I was intrigued by this story because Owen linked Bacon with the Chesptow area and the Byrom theatre drawings had led me to discover Bacon's link with the Tintern wireworks close by.

The sensation that I seemed to be going round in circles was reinforced when I considered that the Crown in the person of Henry VIII had once given Tintern Abbey to a Somerset Earl of Worcester while a later Somerset Duke of Beaufort had sold the Abbey lands back to the Crown in 1900. This circular pattern of events seemed almost ominous in some indefinable way. Either voluntarily or unwittingly the ninth Duke of Beaufort, by his disposal of the Abbey lands, had placed himself outside the concerns of Tintern and St. Michael's churchyard. This could be an indication that he was unaware of anything untoward about the funerals of Lady Russell and J.L. Baldwin and their double grave. Yet later he was fully conversant with the purpose of Dr. Owen's investigations – to recover Bacon's lost papers and other documents connected with the Elizabethan period. After all, the duke's own birthday was an annual reminder of the grim events that were the origins of his family's great wealth.

While I was assessing the duke's role in this story, I was sent a copy of *The Shakespeare Code* by Virginia M. Fellows (published 2006). In the process of describing Dr. Owen's attempt to uncover the cipher the author refers to another American, 'J.B. Millet [*sic*] of Boston'. This man visited Dr. Owen's workshop in Detroit at least three times between February 1893 and December 1895 to investigate the cipher wheel that Owen used to discover Bacon's code. Apart from recounting his response to what he saw at the workshop, she does not say any more about J.B. Millet himself. The surname made me wonder if he could be connected in any way with Charles Frederick Millett and activities taking place in England.

I discovered that J.B. Millet was a book illustrator whose brother Francis Davis Millet was a well-known artist. Francis was a great friend of Mark Twain, who attended his wedding, and Twain was one of the most famous supporters of Bacon's authorship of Shakespeare's plays. One interest common to the two Millet brothers and Mark Twain was evidently 'the Shakespeare question'. In later life Francis Davis Millet settled at Broadway, Worcestershire, fifteen miles from Stratford-upon-Avon. Curiously the house he lived in was 'Russell House' and that name brought other echoes, for in 1885 Elizabeth, Lady Francis Russell made her will with the help of her solicitor, Charles Frederick Millett. As if this was not enough I learned that F. D. Millet made his will the same year.

Francis was a man of many talents. Immediately after graduating from Harvard University, in 1869 he moved to Boston to study lithography while working on the *Boston Advertiser*. Later he designed two stained-glass windows for Memorial Hall at Harvard,[1] and was responsible for several murals in public buildings in America. He was also skilled with his pen both as a translator of Tolstoy and as a journalist, working as a war correspondent for newspapers in New York and London. Tragically, he died on his way home to America when the *Titanic* sank in 1912. He was sixty-six at the time.

It is difficult to know how interested his brother Josiah Millet, the Boston book illustrator, was in Orville Owen's activities at Chepstow, but he must have been aware of them. The excavations had now been under way for three summers and his interest in Owen's deciphering would surely make him want to know if the excavations proved that Owen's claims were right. The excavations after all were well publicised in the press. Certainly Baldwin's solicitor, Charles Frederick Millett, could not help seeing it in his daily newspaper. Baldwin, his wife's fortune, and the Beaufort family were too closely connected for him to be indifferent. The presence of three Millets hovering around the Shakespeare question does suggest a common interest. Had I assessed the nature of that interest accurately for all of them, or was there more to learn?

This question raised itself with more urgency when I learned that on the *Titanic* was another, younger, Harvard man and wealthy American book collector, Harry Elkins Widener. At the age of 27 he was already the enviable possessor of a copy of the First Folio of Shakespeare. Widener had been visiting England with his parents to add to his collection of rare books and purchased a copy of the second edition of Francis Bacon's *Essays*. The night disaster struck the *Titanic*, the philanthropic Wideners had given a party in honour of the ship's captain. A fellow Harvard graduate, Francis Davis Millet, then at the height of his career and travelling first class, would certainly have been one of the Americans invited to the party. Later that same night Harry Widener helped his mother into one of the lifeboats and then stood back. There is a story that he was about to enter a lifeboat himself when he remembered his precious new Bacon purchase and went below to collect it. He did not survive. His mother did and later gave two million dollars to build a library at Harvard to house her son's collection. It continues to grow to this day and is a major part of the university library. The presence in the margins of this mystery of elements that keep referring back in one way or another to Shakespeare or Bacon has to be recorded.

The conundrum surrounding St. Michael's graveyard will only be solved by keeping a balance between a scrutiny of detail and the wider context. Looking at the list of Baldwin's friends who sent wreaths to his funeral I noticed it included the 'Dean of Hereford'. He was the Honourable and Very Rev. James Wentworth Leigh, a member of the Leigh family of Stoneleigh Abbey, Warwickshire, by the 1870s the largest landowners in the county.

After spending his earlier years as a minister very much on home ground at rural livings in Stoneleigh, Stratford-upon-Avon and Leamington, James Wentworth Leigh was in charge of a London church in fashionable Bryanston Square before being appointed Dean of Hereford, two years before Baldwin's death. He would therefore know Baldwin both as a figure in London society and through the I Zingari Club. The Leighs had a private cricket ground at Stoneleigh Abbey and invited the I Zingari to play there. The Dean's brother, Edward Chandos Leigh in fact became Club Secretary to the Zingaris. In studying Baldwin I was not surprised to find links between his aristocratic friends and cricket. But the

Leighs brought me back again to Shakespeare. Admittedly they were a Warwickshire family. At one time the library at Stoneleigh Abbey is said to have contained four copies of Shakespeare folios and that did seem to show a more than ordinary interest. The family have steadily deposited a considerable archive of both personal and estate papers dating from the twelfth to the twentieth century with the Shakespeare Birthplace Trust.

Again we need to remember the importance of pedigree and the legacies that high birth can bring. Amongst the Leigh ancestors we find Sir Thomas Leigh, the first baronet. He married Katherine Spencer and Ferdinando Stanley married her sister Alice. Ferdinando was linked with the Elizabethan acting companies and that may be one source for the interest of the Leigh family in Shakespeare and the acquisition of the folios. When Ferdinando died his widow Alice married Sir Thomas Egerton, the Lord Chancellor, friend and mentor of Francis Bacon. The Egertons, as we saw earlier, eventually forged links with Tintern Parva Estate. These pedigrees and alliances, uniting now in the figure of the Dean of Hereford, added their own colour to the picture I was getting of John Loraine Baldwin's circle.

I noticed that the Dean sent the wreath in his official capacity as 'Dean of Hereford' rather than as a friend. This reminded me that Hereford was the see once ruled by Bishop Thomas Cantilupe from 1275 to 1282. The last Englishman to be canonised before the Reformation, he had been Provincial Grand Master in England of the Knights Templar, and the Templars contributed to the building of Tintern Abbey. St. Thomas Cantilupe was one of the most trusted advisers of Edward I and his integrity in dealing with affairs of both church and state was legendary. In Chapter Five we noted the great interest Edward I had in the development of Tintern Abbey, confirming grants to it even on his deathbed. We saw, too, his own family connections with the area through his daughter Joan, as well as his association with Westminster Abbey. In this context, the Dean's wreath can be viewed as a dignified reminder of Baldwin's long association with Tintern Abbey as well as his friendship with the Leigh family.

The funeral arrangements for John Loraine Baldwin were meticulous. The stage was carefully set for a public and genuine outpouring of affection and respect. Heritage and loyalty seemed to dictate the choice of this special spot in St. Michael's churchyard. Nevertheless the burial appears to have ended in ambiguity. The shallow depth of the findings in the double grave does not fit with normal burial custom. Nor would it be expected in such a high status funeral. J.L. Baldwin and his consort must have known the ultimate resting place for their remains. Can we conclude, therefore, that running alongside and through the spectacle was a deliberate, if innocent, undercurrent of deception? Where was the truth of this matter to be found?

CHAPTER SEVENTEEN

Pedigree and Power

I DID NOT EXPECT to find a solution in the pages of any book. Bradney's voluminous *History of Monmouthshire* does not deal in riddles and uncertainties. Any inaccuracies it may contain are inaccuracies of fact, not fiction. The local newspapers were clearly unaware of anything untoward at the time. It became a question of hunting for clues among the personal experiences of individuals – aspects of behaviour that might reveal something new. So I returned to the Millett–Harcourt marriage and studied the details on their marriage certificate. This time it was the name of one of the witnesses that opened up a fresh avenue of enquiry and turned out to be a most important step forward. It was a name entirely new to me, that of Sir Lambton Loraine. Where had he sprung from to appear suddenly in St. Stephen's Church, Kensington, and formally sign the register?

I would not have been quite so surprised if his name had appeared among the mourners at either Elizabeth, Lady Russell's funeral or Baldwin's. But it did not. He is not included in the list of the sixty-eight individuals and groups who sent wreaths. Yet here he was giving meaning and weight to the 'Loraine' in Baldwin's name. Searching for more information, I learned that he was the eleventh holder of a baronetcy, Lorraine (*sic*) of Kirkharle, created in 1664. Eventually one 'r' was dropped from the name and Sir Lambton Loraine as the head of the family wrote a history of the pedigree of Loraines in the UK, printed in 1902. I could not believe my good fortune that over a century later a copy of the *Pedigree and Memoirs of the Family of Loraine of Kirkharle* was to be found in Manchester's splendid Central Library. At this stage in my investigations it was like manna in the desert. The index included references to John Loraine Baldwin and there was even a portrait of him. The book runs to 428 pages and the meticulous recording of family minutiae made compelling, sometimes chilling and, by the end, sad reading. The baronetcy became extinct with the death of Sir Lambton's younger son and heir, Sir Percy Loraine, in 1963. There will not, I suspect, be many copies in the public domain. It was intended solely for private circulation to members of the Loraine dynasty and related families.

The Hidden Chapter

Millett, Harcourt marriage certificate with highlighted sections.

Married after Banns by
August Lichfield

Witnesses:
Gertrude Harcourt   Lambton Loraine
Claude H. Millett   Percy Barnes   Otto Harcourt

36. Marriage Certificate

Pedigree and Power

Loraine begins his account by claiming the family's descent from Lothar, eldest son of the Holy Roman Emperor Charlemagne. The Norman-French Lorraines came over with the army of William the Conqueror and settled in Northumberland, taking up residence near the Scottish border at Kirkharle. One of the first Lorraines to make his mark in England was a priest, 'Robert de Lorraine'. He became Bishop of Hereford in 1079 and remained in office until his death in 1095. He was a distinguished scholar and his tomb can be seen near the choir in Hereford Cathedral.

But the account of the earlier history of the family on the Continent is dotted with such names as Godrey de Bouillon and the de Bar family. As we saw in Chapter Five, Edward I's daughter, Eleanor, married Henri, Count de Bar. Sir Lambton Loraine confidently associates his family's origins with Lorraine in France and its emergence from Lotharingia, part of the Holy Roman Empire. While not providing every step in the pedigree, he is concerned to show the history of his forebears as far back as the Carolingian rulers of the tenth century and the creation of the hereditary Dukes of Lorraine. The blood of Charlemagne flowed through their veins and, so he believed, through his. Charlemagne, of course, had married a Merovingian princess to strengthen his hold on the Kingdom of the Franks. However remote these events may seem to us, at the beginning of the twentieth century they were important to Sir Lambton Loraine in establishing the true dignity of his lineage. I began to realise that the Loraine dynasty brought another dimension to Baldwin's connection with the Tintern area.

Baldwin's kinship with Sir Lambton Loraine was through his mother, Elizabeth Loraine, and the baronet has his place in the unravelling of Baldwin's affairs. First and foremost he was a naval man. Born in 1838, he joined the navy at the age of fourteen. After three months he went to sea and first saw active service while still a cadet. In 1858 he served on the royal yacht *Victoria and Albert*. This brought him into close contact not only with the queen but also the Prince of Wales and the Duke of Cambridge, both friends of Baldwin. He served on a number of ships around the world, from the Mediterranean to the Pacific, in North America and the West Indies 'in defence of British honour and interests'.

In 1873, while sailing in North American waters, he hastened to Cuba, then fighting for its independence from Spain, and intervened to put an end to the execution of the British and American crew of a Cuban ship. On his way home to England in 1874 he was given the freedom of New York for this timely action that also helped to prevent a war between America and Spain. He left the Navy the same year with the rank of Post Captain and settled in London to the life of an aristocratic bachelor, except for a

37. Sir Lambton Loraine

38. Sir Percy Loraine

brief spell at sea again in 1878. That year he married, and divided his time with his wife and children between London, Hertfordshire and Suffolk, but had no connection with Wales.

A thoroughgoing Tory, he was deeply affronted by a Warrant from the Crown subordinating the rank of baronet. He was elected by his fellow baronets to defend their ancient privileges. His *Memoirs* conclude with a petition to King Edward VII on his succession to the throne after the death of Queen Victoria in 1901. It reviews the history of the rank of baronet from its institution by King James I in 1611 and the 'place precedency and privileges' of baronets as originally created by James. The petition points out that the rank and dignity of baronet had been lessened by decrees of Queen Victoria and pleaded that in future dignity should be protected and strengthened by the title 'Sir' being replaced by 'Lord' to avoid confusion between a knighthood and a baronetcy, a knighthood being awarded for the lifetime of the holder, a baronetcy being hereditary. Today the arguments and distinctions put forward by Sir Lambton Loraine may strike one as the height of elitism. Nowadays very few baronetcies are awarded. Loraine's conviction of the importance of his rank may seem antiquated to us, but it meant that the documentation of his pedigree was exhaustive. This helped me understand the network of alliances that have played an important part in this complex tale.

Having spent his youth and early manhood at sea, Lambton Loraine was not a cricketer, but that did not stop him attending the jubilee celebrations of I Zingari in 1895. Baldwin had helped create the club and that was reason enough. Writing about him, Lambton Loraine was clearly proud that Baldwin added to his Loraine pedigree the consummate social skills of the 'King of Clubs'. This earned him the privilege of being included in the family portraits in Loraine's *Memoirs*. The two men met regularly, certainly in London around the time Baldwin was discreetly making his will in the Victorian grandeur of the Great Western Hotel at Paddington. This makes his absence from the funeral more surprising. He did not attend, send an empty carriage or even a wreath. Yet he went to the Harcourt–Millett wedding and officially witnessed it. Both Elizabeth Harcourt and Charles Frederick Millet were members of the Loraine dynasty, too. Accordingly, Sir Lambton Loraine's signature seems almost like a seal of approval from the head of the family. Perhaps he saw this alliance as one way for the Loraines to regain some of the power and wealth they had lost in the past?

What bearing did all this have on the mystery of the double grave? I reviewed the events following from the death of John Loraine Baldwin – his will with its insistent codicils; the death of Lord Edward Somerset frustrating Baldwin's wishes; the Harcourt–Millett marriage ensuring the destiny of the remaining residuary legacies. To me this sequence did not seem random and was suggestive of some sort of power struggle. Furthermore that struggle in some extraordinary way was concerned with whatever lay beneath the churchyard at St. Michael's. The anomalies that science had revealed in the Baldwin double grave, the 1864 tomb and the flat-topped feature held part of the answer.

The Loraines were a Northumberland family. Anyone studying the Loraine pedigree either in the detailed 1902 *Memoirs* or in the more visual form of a family tree cannot fail to notice a cluster of deaths in the mid-nineteenth century which removed *five* baronets in rapid succession over a period of *two* years. They start after the death of the fifth baronet, Charles Loraine, in 1833 and continue with the deaths of his three sons William, sixth baronet, in 1849, Charles Vincent, seventh baronet, in 1850 and Henry, eighth baronet, in 1851. These were followed by two uncles: William, ninth baronet, who also died in 1851 and John Lambton Loraine who died in 1852, the tenth baronet and father of Sir Lambton Loraine himself. During this period of rapid change, in 1851 John Loraine Baldwin was staying with another Loraine, his uncle, the Rev. Loraine Loraine (*sic*) Smith in his vicarage at Passenham, Bucks. Baldwin's life was different. He and his father lived in southern counties of England. In London Baldwin had founded the I Zingari club in 1845 and his own social success was in striking contrast to the declining fortunes of the head of the Loraine dynasty.

What had they all got in common apart from the right to a succession that at this period in the Loraine family looked liked a death sentence? We are dealing with six baronets; all except the eighth were Freemasons. Two of them held very senior appointments: Sir Charles, the fifth baronet and Sir William, the ninth. Sir Charles held the rank of 'Grand Prior to H.R.H. the Duke of Kent's Encampment of Masonic Knights Templar of St. John of Jerusalem'. This is recorded with some pride in the family *Memoirs*. Sir William Loraine, the ninth baronet, in 1824 became only the second person to be appointed Junior Grand Warden of the United Grand Lodge of England. (The only other person so honoured was a son of the Royal Duke of Sussex.) In fact the fifth, ninth and tenth baronets were all installed as Knights Templar during their Masonic careers.

Sir Charles was baronet at a critical time in the family history, during the later stages of the Napoleonic War. As Sir Lambton Loraine cryptically puts it:

> it is to be feared that the troubles arising from this banking business often harassed his domestic circle when the nation was rejoicing over the victories of Trafalgar and Waterloo.[1]

'This banking business' refers to Sir Charles Loraine's involvement with a private bank, the Tyne Bank, operating in Northumberland. Ten years elapsed between the battles of Trafalgar (1805) and Waterloo (1815) and that is an indication of the seriousness of the problem. In 1815 local banks in Durham and Yorkshire failed because the depletion of bullion aggravated by the length of the war led to a shortage of silver currency. The run on several banks naturally caused alarm elsewhere and Sir Charles was involved with his banking partners in reassuring customers of the Tyne Bank of the safety of their assets. These the bankers guaranteed, and hoped to meet those guarantees without having to sell any real estate.

Unfortunately the optimism in Sir Charles's case was not justified and in the end he was forced to sell the estate at Kirkharle where the Loraines had lived for four hundred years. How it affected his role with the Masonic Knights Templar is not clear to me (although I noticed two later baronets were also Masonic Knights Templar). It was a low point in the family's fortunes. The failure of the bank may have had worse consequences than Sir Lambton Loraine knew about or was prepared to acknowledge publicly. Indeed, one can be forgiven for thinking that the swift succession of these deaths was suspicious, although Loraine himself refrains from saying so. But whereas he is frequently able to record the precise moment of a birth, he provides a seemingly innocent cause for only two of the six deaths. The seventh baronet died from an internal abscess, the tenth, Sir Lambton Loraine's father, from intestinal inflammation. It was only three months earlier that Lambton Loraine had joined the Navy. Ironically, a posting to five years in the Pacific as a teenager may have saved him from a fate similar to that of his predecessors. So, what are we to make of all this and where did John Loraine Baldwin fit into the scenario?

Sir Lambton Loraine had two sons. The elder was Eustace Broke Loraine, born in 1879. After Eton he was commissioned in the Grenadier Guards and took part in some grim encounters with the Boer army, by 1900 in retreat before the British troops under Field Mashal Lord Roberts. Loraine endured a hard campaign fighting the Boers who adopted guerrilla tactics following the collapse of the Boer government. After his return to England Eustace was greatly impressed by the French pilot and aircraft designer Louis Bleriot, the first man to fly the English Channel from Calais to Dover on 25 July 1909. Eustace obtained permission to train as a pilot with the newly formed Royal Flying Corps and became very enthusiastic about the future of aviation. Three years later, on 6 July 1912, he died when his aircraft crashed on Salisbury Plain. A stone memorial was placed at a crossroads near Stonehenge to mark the site. Tragedy had struck the Loraines again, for this gallant and glamorous figure was the heir to the baronetcy. After his death the family was never the same again. His younger brother Percy was the last to succeed to the title.

The death of Eustace came just three months before the sinking of the *Titanic*. It is not surprising that this catastrophe should directly affect characters in our story. So many wealthy, talented and influential people were lost that the disaster was seen as proof of the puny power of mankind, helpless against fate. Thomas Hardy gave expression to this idea in his poem 'The Convergence of the Twain' where he describes how the iceberg was being silently fashioned at the same time as the ship was being built. They were twin halves of a collision that jarred two hemispheres.

Disasters, great or small, do not stop progress although they may alter its direction. By 1912 Tintern had changed. The Baldwin funeral was by now either a faint memory or forgotten. The new railway station gave greater access to the area for visitors and tourists. The Abbey was the main attraction, St. Michael's remaining deceptively modest by comparison. At Chepstow Dr. Orville Owen energetically continued his series of excavations with the support of the Duke of Beaufort. In London the Millett–Harcourt marriage had produced both a daughter and an heir. Meanwhile Sir Lambton Loraine, still fighting to maintain the family's honour, had written to the Minister of War, asking why Eustace's bravery on active service in West Africa had not been officially rewarded with the D.S.O. recommended by his Commanding Officer. He was now looking to Percy to reinvigorate the name of Loraine.

Percy was born in 1880 at the family home in Montagu Square, London. This means that at the time of Baldwin's death and the Harcourt–Millet marriage he was seventeen. His father had hoped that after Eton Percy would follow him into the Navy. But he had other ideas. From an early age Percy had insisted, 'I want to be an ambassador.'[2] Diplomacy was to prove his forte, rather than warfare. So, he went up to New College, Oxford, to study history and languages in preparation for a career in the Diplomatic Corps. Nevertheless he had inherited his share of the family's patriotism and courage and soon interrupted his studies to enlist in the army and serve, like his brother, in South Africa against the Boers. Percy also knew the cost of guerrilla warfare at first hand, getting shot through the knee. Despite being offered a regular commission several times, he held to his earlier ambition and, still only 21, returned to New College to complete his studies. Over six feet tall, well-proportioned with dark hair and pale blue eyes, intelligent and naturally good at games, he combined aristocratic elegance with a beguiling melancholy. The Diplomatic Service provided an ideal setting for his talents.

He entered the Service as an attaché in 1904. In those days candidates were required to have a private income of at least £400 a year. So, until promoted to the rank of Third Secretary at a salary of £150, they were unpaid. His first three posts were Turkey, Persia and Italy. He was fortunate that Constantinople proved to be an excellent training ground. Within two years he was made Third Secretary and transferred to Persia in 1907. In 1909 he moved to Rome where he served under a very civilised and intelligent ambassador, Sir James Rendell Rodd, who in his youth had won the Oxford Newdigate Prize for poetry and known artists of the calibre of Whistler, Burne Jones and William Morris.

Rome was a stimulating experience for Percy. He thought of turning to writing but realised that he lacked the imagination of an original thinker. His strength lay in his ability to master the intricacies of a problem, an invaluable gift in the career he had chosen. On a more personal level he remained shy and reserved. In Italy in 1910 he met 'a quite beautiful and charming' American woman from New York. They met again in Paris and London but she was married. He confided to his diary that 'she is the only woman I have ever met towards whom I feel capable of an infinite faithfulness'. The lady in question returned to America and Loraine's reserve became more marked, to a degree that many who did not know him well found disconcerting.

After a very short spell in Peking he was posted early in 1912 to Paris, still as Second Secretary. Despite his obvious reserve he was soon caught up in the social life of the city. He became friends with the Ambassador's secretary, Reginald Bridgeman, and through him met Jean Cocteau, then in his early twenties. Cocteau was working with Diaghilev's Ballet Russe, now taking the city by storm. The two men became good friends. Cocteau, who lived opposite the British Embassy, was frequently popping into Bridgeman's office to entertain the staff with the latest gossip. At this time Percy took a flat where he was looked after by a married couple. In his diary he describes the lavish décor:

> I did the walls of the sitting room with a rose and gold Italian damask and the walls of the wee dining-room, as it was badly lit, with a golden-yellow French damask, that took your eyes away from the dark ceiling. And on the walls I hung Japanese coloured prints…[3]

The expense alarmed his father who wrote to the Foreign Secretary, Sir Edward Grey, to ask why diplomats were not housed abroad at the Government's expense. But Percy was not totally devoted to a life of pleasure. When his brother died he tried to set up a fund to carry out research into the risks of flying. This was intended to be a lasting memorial to Eustace. But despite gaining some influential support, in the end the project came to nothing. When Percy was disappointed at being overlooked for promotion in Paris, his anger moved Cocteau to use his friendships at the Embassy to speak on Percy's behalf. He could not hope to influence matters but this does show his appreciation of the abilities of Percy, who was eventually consoled with promotion to the Embassy in Madrid.

The death of Eustace had also been a promotion but of a different kind, within the family. Percy's mother had brought to her marriage a new estate at Bramford near Ipswich. This was the first land the Loraines had owned since losing Kirkharle. Percy was proud of his background and his father's *Memoirs* were a testament to the Loraines' standing down the centuries. As the only surviving son and successor to both title and land, Percy saw his career as a sure way to add lustre to the family. Cocteau could well understand. The very name 'Lorraine' had connotations for any educated Frenchman. Cocteau's father had been a prominent lawyer and the drive to excel, even astonish, distinguishes Jean's career. He was sensitive to the rise of his own family. One of his maternal uncles had himself been an ambassdor. Cocteau was aware of pedigree when it mattered. That awareness helped to cement the friendship of the two men and they continued to correspond long after Percy left Paris.

While Percy was in Madrid, his father died, in May 1917. In his will he expressed the hope that Percy would 'assist in gathering together and recording future family events and add as may be necessary to the family pedigree at Herald's College'. Percy went to England for the funeral. He was now thirty-seven years old, the last in the long line of Loraine baronets and still unmarried. He would regard his father's wishes as a solemn duty with its implied hope that the dynasty would continue. Before returning to Madrid, he was summoned to breakfast with the Prime Minister, Lloyd George, to discuss his Intelligence work. His reputation as a diplomat was now deservedly high. After the signing of the Armistice in 1918, he was again seconded from Madrid, this time to be part of the British Delegation at the Peace Conference in Paris.

We do not need to follow Percy Loraine through every posting. His time in Paris has a particular relevance for our story and the reader should know that he was an extremely able diplomat. His time as Ambassador to Turkey (1934–1940) is generally regarded as the peak of his career. Modern Turkey had just been born and Loraine formed a very positive personal relationship with its creator President Ataturk. On a more personal level he finally married in October 1924, but it became a matter of deep regret that the marriage brought no children and therefore no heir to the baronetcy. In the end his career meant less to him than the racehorses he started to breed after his retirement in 1941. In May 1961, at the age of eighty, he died.

A footnote to Cocteau's diplomatic friendships was added when he came to London in 1959 at the request of the French Ambassador to paint a mural for the church of Notre Dame de France. This was the religious centre of the French community in London in Leicester Place, off Leicester Square, and was being rebuilt after being badly damaged in the Blitz. The mural can be seen behind the altar. Cocteau, now seventy, included a portrait of himself as a young man in the foreground to the left of the cross.

Cocteau had finally settled in the small village of Milly-la-Forêt outside Paris, where he decorated the Chapel of St. Blaise. This was to be his final resting place. On the wall behind his tomb is another mural, drawn the same year as the one in London. Its most distinctive feature is a large triangle which frames a head of Christ wearing a crown of thorns. For the Christian the triangle represents the Trinity of Father, Son and Holy Ghost. Cocteau had studied the paintings of Dürer for the set and costumes of his play *Bacchus* (1951), and Dürer's masterly use of triangular space in 'The Adoration of The Holy Trinity' clearly influenced his own paintings, as his diaries show. Certainly, the emphatic triangle in the Milly mural is an indication of Cocteau's interest in the esoteric tradition.

I made a note of Cocteau's use of the triangle because of the dated triangular drawing in the Byrom Collection that we looked at in Chapter Four. I felt that Cocteau's work might throw additional light on the geometric drawings. The latest date on any of the drawings is 1732. But certain of the earlier ones clearly had an esoteric element in them, particularly those associated with John Dee and his alchemical symbol the Monas Hieroglyphica. Others bore the traditional designs of the cabalistic Tree of Life.

All this increased my interest in the area around Tintern because I believed the plates from which some of the earlier drawings had been printed had been made at the wireworks. But what was most surprising at the time was the importance the area seemed to have had for several ruling monarchs. Moreover those monarchs had close and prolonged links with France and leading French families.

For example, one of Edward I's daughters, Joan d'Acres, married Gilbert de Clare, one of the most powerful landowners in the area. Among her possessions was a church at Llanishen dedicated to St. Dennis, the French 'national' saint, whose abbey in Paris became the resting place of the Christian Meroviginian kings. They, of course, are linked with Radegunda to whom the priory at Usk was dedicated, so long an important site for French pilgrims. Another of Edward's daughters, Eleanor, married Henri Count de Bar. That name, too, I had come to associate with the Lordship of Usk (which included Tintern Parva) and other parts of Monmouthshire. These marriages may have been dictated in part by reasons of state, but they also mark a personal attachment to this part of South Wales. The de Bars later married into the ducal house of Lorraine, and in the first chapters of his *Memoirs* Sir Lambton Loraine goes into some detail about his family's connections with the House of Lorraine and the de Bars. Such genealogical claims would intrigue Cocteau.

Since Cocteau was consciously using geometrical forms for symbolic purposes in his art, I felt I should look again at his relations with Percy Loraine. Did their friendship include a shared interest in the esoteric tradition? Cocteau's use of dreams and the unconscious in his work is well documented and in keeping with an interest in the occult. But it was the age-old symbol of the triangle on the chapel wall at Milly close to his tomb that intrigued me most – as it is intended to intrigue everyone who sets eyes on it. The triangle's rich, symbolic associations convinced me that Cocteau's prolific imagination and keen intelligence would find fertile soil in the pedigree of a friend like Percy Loraine, whose family claimed descent through the Dukes of Lorraine from Emperor Charlemagne.

I looked again at the head of the figure at the bottom right of the mural in the Church of Notre Dame in London and the head of Christ in the mural above Cocteau's tomb at Milly-la-Forêt and noticed a similarity between them. Painted in the same year, could the two heads have been modelled on Percy Loraine? I had been able to study two photographs of Percy. One, taken from the family *Memoirs,* shows him as a young man in army uniform and is reproduced for the reader (illustration 38). The other is a portrait by T. Geraldy painted in Paris in 1913 when, at the age of thirty-three, Percy first met Cocteau. The photograph of this portrait is still in copyright and unfortunately I have been unable to trace the descendants of the executors of Sir Percy's will for permission to reproduce it, but it can be seen in Gordon Waterfield's biography *Professional Diplomat.* If the reader studies these two photographs, particularly that of the portrait, he may be able to see the likeness I thought I had recognised. As the leaflet available from the London church reminds us, Cocteau's gift for likeness was 'quite remarkable'. Was this a final tribute from the artist to a man whose abilities he admired and respected?

Cocteau's hermetic interests appear to have included the ancient Jewish mystical tradition of the Cabala. Patrice Chaplin describes meeting Cocteau in the Catalan city of Girona in 1955 when, as a young girl of fifteen, she took part in a film Cocteau was making in the city at the time. In her memoir *City of Secrets* (2007), she recounts how her curiosity drove her to peer through the windows of a deserted building behind Girona cathedral where she saw Cocteau taking part in some form of ceremonial ritual.[4]

Girona took its name from a former Roman citadel, Gerunda. Overrun

The Hidden Chapter

in turn by the Visigoths and Moors, Charlemagne finally re-conquered it in 785 and made it one of the original fourteen countships that formed Catalonia. Early in its history Girona had a flourishing Jewish community. From the twelfth century until 1492, the city was one of the leading centres of cabalistic learning in Europe. Amongst the illustrations reproduced in her book, Patrice Chaplin includes two drawings based on triangles with associations that I recognised as cabalistic.

One of the dates on the Byrom triangular drawing was 1414. I learned later that in 1414 the King of Aragon gave the title 'Prince of Girona' to his eldest son, Alfonso, as a symbolic unifying gesture for his kingdom. The kings of Aragon at this time, together with the Counts de Bar and René d'Anjou all figure proudly in the labyrinthine pedigree constructed by Sir Lambton Loraine for his *Memoirs*.

1154 is another date on the triangular drawing and, as we saw, 1154 was the year Henry II was crowned in a ceremony deliberately designed to evoke memories of Charlemagne.

The earliest date on the same triangular card was 713. That date was associated with the constant power struggles within the Merovingian kingdom that finally led to its downfall; and the arrival of the Carolingians in the person of Charles Martel, father of Charlemagne. The Cathedral at Girona claimed to possess a throne used by Charlemagne, the man who had freed the city and established Catalonia before becoming the first Holy Roman Emperor. For me all this pointed to common strands of history providing other links in the intellectual pedigree of the drawings with Girona, Charlemagne and the Cabala.

Cocteau's presence at a private ritual in Girona may link him with the Cabala tradition and help to explain the importance he places on the triangle as a visual symbol in, for example, the mural at Milly and his painting of the Temptation of Christ (1951), constructed on a background of differently coloured triangles.

The deserted house and its abandoned garden had once been the talk of Girona. Debussy was just one of its many visitors. Was there, I wondered, some connection here, hitherto not fully understood, involving two prominent French artists and the Cabala?

The relevance of the Cabala to the Byrom collection can be seen in various examples. One of the theatre drawings is connected with part of the tiring house roof that jutted out over the stage of the playhouse. This was the 'Heavens' painted with the signs of the zodiac and emblems of the old Ptolemaic cosmology. A winch enabled actors or stage properties to be lowered from an opening in the ceiling onto the stage below.

The drawing of the winch appears to be a working drawing showing its position in the upper storey of the tiring house. The paper has been torn across the bottom beneath the design but fortunately the fragment containing the writing that accompanied it has miraculously survived and contains a reference to 'the Cabalists' when describing the cosmology of the 'Heavens' depicted on the roof. The drawing also contains small images of triangles in its explanation and is evidence of the cabalistic thought that lies behind the design concept of the Elizabethan playhouse.

The Cabala, originally a Jewish system of meditation, was incorporated into a new medieval Christian philosophy by Ramon Lull (1232–c. 1316). Lull was a Catalan living and writing when Girona was at its height as a centre of Jewish thought. It was his dream to unite the basic principles of Christianity with Moslem and Jewish knowledge and wisdom.

An element common to both Jew and Christian was a devout interest in the Temple of Solomon. For both sets of believers it was the first permanent home of the God who had brought the Jews out of bondage. He dwelt in its innermost part, the Holy of Holies. Accordingly it has been an object of reverent study for centuries, becoming in the process an important element in Freemasonry. In April 1720 the Earl of Pembroke visited the home of the antiquarian William Stukely to see Stukely's drawings of Solomon's Temple. Six years later, Sir Isaac Newton made his own plan of it from the description in the Old Testament. He also appears in Sir Lambton Loraine's will, as we shall see later in the chapter.

And there are faint echoes of the Temple, too, in the later life of Sir Percy. When he retired from the diplomatic corps to concentrate on horse racing, his most successful horse was Darius. (It won the 2000 Guineas at Newmarket in 1954.) Sir Percy named the horse after Darius I of Persia, to commemorate the happy years he had spent as Ambassador to Turkey. The name was meant to bring the horse good luck. But Sir Percy would know from his time in the Middle East that Darius the Great was the Persian ruler who allowed his Jewish subjects to rebuild Solomon's Temple.

To the onlooker the public world of Sir Percy Loraine was one of brilliance, glamour and style. Postings to exotic embassies in Europe and the Middle East were undoubtedly enriching to any intelligent, receptive mind. Elegance disguised the pressures; decorum masked the sense of power discreetly wielded. How satisfying it must have been. Yet at the end there was disappointment, and even, following a quarrel with Churchill, a sense of injustice. So, at the last, he resembled his father and the feeling of outrage that had led to the meticulous documentation of the Loraine family *Memoirs*. The feeling of desolation Sir Percy revealed in retrospect reminded me of St. Michael's and Tintern Parva. Despite its association down the centuries with important or colourful figures, the church and the surrounding area had slipped out of history. No one could tell now what had happened there.

A sense of déjà vu quickened my intuition and made me turn to the wills of the last two baronets. The fact that Sir Lambton Loraine was not only Baldwin's friend but also a kinsman, together with his presence at the Millett–Harcourt wedding, gave me a glimmer of hope. There might be legacies in his will and his son's that could explain the silence that had fallen on St. Michael's after the impressive spectacle of John Loraine Baldwin's funeral.

Sir Lambton Loraine died on 13 May 1917. His will was proved the following November. It runs to six pages of close typing, and, as one might expect from the author of the *Memoirs*, is meticulously detailed. It names three executors who were also the trustees: his wife, Frederica, his only surviving son, Percy, and David Augustus Bevan, a lawyer and cousin – another member of the Loraine bloodline. The wishes it expresses are clearly those of an upright and proud man. His first concern, rightly, is for the welfare of his wife who brought money and land to their marriage. Thereafter he distinguishes throughout between legacies and 'heirlooms', the latter forming a category on their own. Characteristically, too, he ensures the safekeeping of the remaining copies of his *Memoirs* so that it may continue to be presented to relatives and 'genealogical authorities'.

His mode of living and social status can be seen in many of the personal items mentioned, such as his sporting guns, fishing tackle, and his 'fur coat and its case'. Fortunately some of the heirlooms are specified individually too. They included his pictures, miniatures, paintings of shields, armorial documents, and family seals. One or two remain intriguingly vague, such as 'The contents of my iron safe at Bramford Hall the same having family historical value, and the gilt Main Trunk of H.M.S. Niobe.' All his papers had evidently been carefully filed away ready for this day. His naval papers are not simply mentioned separately but subdivided into their different postings. His estate papers are distinct from the Petition to King Edward VII. He left nothing to chance. He even specifies the 'five or more chests' in which these heirlooms were kept. Perhaps the most intriguing individual item was 'the lock which I possess of Sir Isaac Newton's hair'. This had come into the Loraine family in 1872 through a descendant of Sir Isaac's niece, Catherine Conduitt. Some Newton manuscripts that were originally with it had already gone to New College, Oxford, where Sir Percy later studied. Why had the lock not gone with them? What compelled Sir Lambton Loraine to keep it? Newton was not related by blood. The lock appears to have had some deep significance that prevented him from parting with it. Where, I wondered, is that listed item now?

The most poignant item specified was 'the mahogany framed armchair in which my father died'. That sad news had reached him when he was a still a boy training for the sea at Plymouth.

Sir Lambton Loraine's self-appointed role as family historian made him also the keeper of its secrets. Through the trustees he provided for the future of the heirlooms in every imaginable contingency. In the event, since Percy had survived him, the heirlooms, including all the papers, went to him. An inventory of them was taken, and a copy signed by all three trustees was to be given to and kept by Percy. What, I wondered, did the written archives contain and would Percy's will tell us what had happened to them?

Forty-four years later, on 23 May 1961, Sir Percy Loraine died. His executors were Francis James Rennell, a stockbroker and Trustee of the British Museum, another stockbroker, John Henry Bevan and his solicitor, Cecil Alfred Sherman. The will was drawn up originally in 1955 but two codicils were added later. What caught my attention immediately was the name Bevan. He was the son of David Augustus Bevan, Sir Lambton Loraine's trustee. John Henry Bevan's presence as one of Sir Percy's executors is another example of the Loraines' almost obsessive concern with continuity. In the event John Henry Bevan turned out to be a fascinating man in his own right.

After making immediate provision for his widow, Sir Percy's main concern was with the regalia of his baronetcy. These included 'the Banner bearing the Arms of Loraine of Kirkharle', his baronet's badge, the insignia of a Knight Grand Cross of the Order of St. Michael and St. George, and the insignia of all other orders and medals awarded to him. Even though he was the last Baronet of Kirkharle, the records of his rank and dignity mattered. I was concerned to discover what had happened to the heirlooms so carefully listed in his father's will. None was mentioned directly but there was one very interesting provision in Clause 9:

> I give Sir Pierson Dixon all documents belonging to me which deal with or concern matters affecting the course of my life and my official career and work including all letters or correspondence (not merely personal or private) and the texts or copies of all speeches articles broadcasts publications and drafts of or notes for projected publications and a copy of my father's book 'Pedigree of Loraines of Kirkharle' Upon Trust to arrange for and supervise the publication within three years after my death in such form and manner as he shall think most appropriate of a book or books preferably of a biographical nature.

Sir Pierson Dixon was a fellow diplomat, although some twenty years younger. They knew and admired each other for over thirty years. At the time of Percy's death, Pierson Dixon was Ambassador to France. In April 1961 he had invited Percy and his wife to Paris to spend a weekend at the Embassy. For Percy the prospect of seeing Paris brought back happy memories. Accepting the invitation he wrote, 'Four wonderful years were mine – The last two of the peace, the first two of the war.' Later, on 22 May, the day before they were due to fly, Percy developed a slight temperature. At first it was planned for Lady Loraine to go on ahead and Percy to follow, but his condition worsened and she telephoned Paris to call the visit off. Percy's condition deteriorated rapidly and two hours after the phone call he died. Writing in *The Times* three days later, Dixon praised the excellence of his judgement, which he likened to wisdom, and concluded: 'Whether directing the activities of a large embassy or the affairs of his racing stable he was essentially a man of action. Everything he did was first-class.'[5]

Sir Percy's will was drawn up on 9 February 1955 at the office of his solicitor, 2, New Square, London. In it Sir Pierson Dixon's address is given as 'The Foreign Office, Whitehall' since neither Dixon's address nor Loraine's death could be predicted. Did that mean that all the private and public papers intended for Dixon did in fact go to the Foreign Office? Whether they did or not, Dixon, for some reason, did not carry out Percy's wishes. Despite Dixon's publicly expressed admiration, it was left to someone else to write Loraine's biography. The time limit of three years set by Percy may not have been realistic for a working Ambassador. Moreover his nomination as the author of the projected biography was an interesting departure from Sir Percy's usual practice in that he was not a Loraine either by birth or marriage.

Sir Pierson Dixon himself died on 22 April 1965, aged sixty-one. Four years had elapsed since Sir Percy's death and the time limit had passed. Sir Pierson Dixon's own biography *Double Diploma* written by his son, Piers Dixon, was published three years later in 1968. The book gives a compelling account of his father's career and contains a brief but telling diary entry from September 1946 when Sir Pierson Dixon was attending talks in Paris with the Foreign Secretary, Ernest Bevin. The entry reads: 'Amusing dinner at the Embassy. Jean Cocteau after dinner sat on a sofa drawing unicorns.'[6] This may seem at first an odd thing to record, but perhaps it was not so odd after all. The entry provides us with a fleeting glimpse into Cocteau's mind. The grand occasion and formal diplomatic setting was an appropriate one in which he could deliberately doodle with the image of this fabulous creature. The unicorn has both alchemical and heraldic associations. Its inclusion in the Royal Arms of Scotland is a visual claim for the purity of a dynasty that unites virtue and blood. In this context we are reminded of Cocteau's friendship with Sir Percy Loraine and the Loraine family's belief in the importance of pedigree. Dixon's keen eye noticed Cocteau's behaviour and chose to record this detail above all else from the business of that evening. Interestingly his son, Piers, also chose to include the incident in the biography.

Pedigree and Power

We have come a long way in our search for the Loraine family papers, proudly collated by Sir Lambton Loraine, dutifully preserved by Sir Percy and entrusted to Sir Pierson Dixon. What had become of them? It was the turn of Sir Percy's trustees to be scrutinised, in particular his cousin John Henry Bevan who first appears at the age of eight in the family *Memoirs*. Bevan differs from the other two trustees because he was a blood member of the Loraine family. The others were not, although Rennell, predictably, was related by marriage. He was a cousin of Sir Percy's wife, Louise Stuart-Wortley. These are important distinctions, as is made clear in Sir Percy's will where (in addition to two legacies for his services as an executor and trustee) John Henry Bevan is named as the residuary legatee if he survived Lady Loraine.

In drawing up the arrangements for the projected biography Sir Percy stipulated that

> the said documents and the benefit thereof and of all arrangements to be made by Sir Pierson Dixon in respect of the said book or books shall be held in trust as part of my residuary estate.

That suggests that Sir Percy's papers did not go immediately after his death to the Foreign Office en route to Pierson Dixon. More likely the trustees instead kept custody of them. But since the period 'of three years within my death' had elapsed and no book had been published, then the Trust would have been deemed to have failed and the papers would revert as part of the residuary estate to the residuary legatee, in this case John Henry Bevan.

It was important to find out what had happened, for I was convinced that there was a good chance the Loraine family papers would contain evidence that explained the conflict that had led to the frustration of John Loraine Baldwin's plans for the Wardenship of Tintern Abbey. Legally the papers should have been transferred to Bevan. He should own them. Did he?

John Henry Bevan was a man of many talents. The *Dictionary of National Biography* makes no bones about it, describing him as 'intelligence officer and stockbroker'. He possessed undoubted courage and in the First World War was mentioned twice in dispatches and awarded an MC. In the Second World War he served at home to even greater effect. Bevan was placed in charge of a controlling section that worked next to Churchill's Operations Room in London. Its task was to oversee a systematic programme of organised deception on a vast scale. Bevan's wartime career was the stuff of Hollywood films. Audacious, dangerous and successful, the work for which he was responsible made a decisive contribution in fooling Germany's secret agents throughout the war and in particular helped to bring off the Allied landings in Normandy in 1944. According to the *DNB*, he possessed 'the necessary combination of imagination, initiative, resilience and sound military instincts to say nothing of personal charm and persuasiveness'. Years had to elapse before the story of his department could be told. According to the novelist Dennis Wheatley who worked with him in the London section, one of his greatest assets was 'an extraordinarily attractive smile'. Wheatley wrote an account of their wartime exploits, *The Deception Planners*, published in 1980, after his own death.

I could understand how Bevan became the residuary legatee. Sir Percy had no heir himself and the family connection with Bevan was important. In addition, Bevan's personal qualities made him an ideal candidate to maintain the family honour. He soon showed that in the matter of Sir Percy's biography. After Sir Pierson Dixon died, Bevan, as one of the executors, made sure the life was written and chose Gordon Waterfield, a member of his wartime team and author of several books on the Middle East, to write it. Entitled *Professional Diplomat*, the biography finally appeared in 1973.

Bevan himself died in December 1978 and according to *The Daily Telegraph* left £252,740. This appears to be the only fact about his 'estate' on record in the public domain. I was not interested in his personal wealth, only the possible whereabouts of the Loraine papers that had been used in the biography, the copyright of which, I noticed, belonged to 'the Executors of the late Sir Percy L. Loraine Bt.'. Two generations of Bevans had provided executors for two generations of Loraines. For that reason alone I thought it a potentially profitable line of enquiry. However, when I applied through the usual channels for a copy of John Henry Bevan's will I was told it had not been published. Most wills, with the perhaps understandable exception of such people as the Sovereign, are usually in the public domain. However, in this case, although the total amount of his personal wealth has been published, other details of his will are not available. Bevan or his executors may have had good reason to arrange this. Nevertheless it meant that my search for the Loraine papers in the public domain had ended at a closed door. So, apart from anything else, what had happened to the lock of Isaac Newton's hair?

CHAPTER EIGHTEEN

Eternal Triangles

During the Second World War John Henry Bevan spent much of his time planning deception after deception. He was the master of throwing enemy agents off the truth by any credible diversion he and his team could devise. In 1943 he asked Dennis Wheatley to write a history of the section's wartime work. Later, when someone showed him the unfinished draft, Bevan commented, 'This won't do at all, Dennis. No one will want to read all this nonsense about the sort of people we were.' This typifies his modesty. It was the operations that mattered, not the people who carried them out. Only when both Wheatley and Bevan were dead was this account published. That his will is not in the public domain should not surprise us. He had only to plead 'reasons of state'. That would be sufficient to keep all sorts of information hidden. The trunks and cases of Loraine documents would be 'lost' among the masses of material he had gathered in the course of his work and that, in his judgement, should not be divulged. He had done his duty by his cousin, Sir Percy Loraine, twelfth and last baronet, in seeing that the biography was published.

Waterfield's biography of Percy Loraine was entitled *Professional Diplomat*, since for the most part it concentrates on the public figure rather than the private individual. Today a biographer might also be interested in the possibility of a shared interest in the esoteric between Sir Percy and Cocteau.

Certainly it was important to the Frenchman and as such would surely have featured in many conversations during Percy's years in Paris. In the first volume of his diaries entitled *Past Tense*, Cocteau describes the progress of a large painting he started in September 1951. The subject was *The Temptation of Christ on the Mountain*. On 16 September he writes, '...when I get back from Paris I'd like to paint a big canvas *Jesus tempted by Lucifer* where all the forms would be inscribed within triangles.'[1] He draws a sketch of the painting's construction which includes notes on the colours he was proposing for the different triangular forms. He 'pondered each millimetre of this canvas' and while the ordering of space is an essential element of any painting's creation, Cocteau's overt emphasis on triangles in *The Temptation* reinforced my conviction that in this painting and in the Milly mural he was demonstrating how a truth could be expressed visually through forms 'inscribed within triangles'.

By 1951 Percy Loraine's horse Darius, a two-year-old that he had bred, was waiting to astonish the racing world with its success. For a while Darius filled Percy's letters and his life. The name recalled his time as Ambassador in the post that made him an acknowledged expert on the Middle East. While in Teheran, Lady Loraine formed a lasting friendship with Hilda Arfa, the English-born wife of a distinguished Persian. As Hilda Bewicke she was the first English dancer to be recruited by Diaghilev for his ballet company. Highly intelligent and with a gift for languages, she was a vivacious link between Percy and Cocteau, reminding the diplomat of his days in Paris. Cocteau in turn was very much involved with another Darius. Darius Milhaud was an avant-garde composer much influenced by Cocteau, who inspired his protégé to compose two ballets for Diaghilev's company. Cocteau first knew Milhaud when he was a student in Paris at the same time as Percy Loraine was setting out on his diplomatic career. Cocteau's published diaries show that in 1951 he was preparing a series of programmes for radio and deliberating whether Milhaud should write the music score. That Darius was a name important to both men for such different reasons was almost a grace note to their friendship.

It is clear, then, from his diaries, that Cocteau's interest in triangles was not a passing one. In the Byrom Collection a number of the drawings are actually cut out in the shape of a triangle and used to convey different kinds of information. In the Westminster Abbey triangular drawing it is immediately obvious that the Chapter House, where the secular business of the Abbey was conducted, lies outside the triangle. The triangle is concerned solely with what lies within the religious confines of the building, and aptly so. As we know, for the Christian the equilateral triangle is a convenient symbol for the Trinity. Robert Fludd used triangles to convey his idea of the construction of the universe. Three of the five Platonic solids are composed of equilateral triangles. Cocteau's interest in triangles shows a familiarity with the geometrical element of the esoteric tradition.

That collection also contains a drawing on which is inscribed the Cross of Lorraine, familiar today as the rallying sign of the Free French forces during the Second World War. However this form of the cross was originally adopted by René d'Anjou as his personal emblem when he became Duke of Lorraine. For some years Cocteau's Paris address was the fashionable Rue d'Anjou and that name would have special resonances for him.

The Loraine pedigree was important also to John Loraine Baldwin. Since birth his middle name was a constant reminder of the dynasty to which he belonged. We examined his aristocratic connections at length in Chapter Fourteen. He, therefore, could claim descent from the premier families of France. That linked him, too, with the Norman overlords that we know once ruled Monmouthshire, built a castle at Goodrich, a priory at Usk and an abbey at Tintern. I felt certain that a deep sense of family history was inherent in his assumption of the role of Warden at the Abbey and his decision to be buried at St. Michael's.

The same reasons had motivated Elizabeth, Lady Francis Russell earlier. Her descent from Sir Nicholas Bacon was to me another powerful factor that needs to be taken into consideration. Nothing would have been easier or more natural than for her to be buried at Dover, the couple's main home, in a graveyard full of Russell kin, but her connection with Francis Bacon's family and his associations with Tintern outweighed all that. Baldwin's anxiety to ensure that Lord Edward Somerset succeeded him as Warden stems from the same sense of lineage – the line of Worcester overlords put in place by Henry VIII. At the end of all my searching I was compelled to accept that if the anomalies at the depth of three feet in the double grave were too shallow to be connected with the burials of J.L. Baldwin and Lady Russell as the second radar survey would have us believe, then there were only two other explanations. Either Baldwin knew that the double grave was not to be their last resting place and had planned for it, or someone else had determined to frustrate his plans. The first alternative seemed the more likely, but, whichever of them turned out to be correct, concern for the control or ownership of Tintern Parva down the years owed much to lineage and the loyalty it inspired.

A similar concern for lineage is seen in Charles Frederick Millett. He had been responsible for the wills of Elizabeth, Lady Russell and John Loraine Baldwin. It was his marriage to Baldwin's legatee, Elizabeth Harcourt, that was witnessed and in effect sanctioned by Sir Lambton Loraine. Millett had Loraine blood in his veins, as did his wife. Millett's own will shows the same careful concern for heirlooms as Sir Lambton Loraine's with its attention to the 'Millett Plate', the 'Daniell Plate', and the Romney painting of his great-grandfather William Baldwin. While it is true that wills are designed to deal with heirlooms, the point here is that Millett's heirlooms indicate his own family connection with John Loraine Baldwin. Moreover he appears to have wished that awareness on to his eldest son in giving him 'Baldwin' as his middle name. What is not clear is whether as a blood relative of Baldwin, as well as being his legal adviser for years and the husband of Elizabeth Harcourt, he saw himself in a stronger position as a potential custodian in Tintern than Lord Edward Somerset.

Somerset's right to a custodial role came through the Beaufort family's historic ownership of Tintern Abbey and its lands. But times were changing. By the time of Baldwin's death, the eighth Duke had already handed over his responsibilities to the Marquis of Worcester who, when he eventually became the ninth Duke of Beaufort, dispensed with most of the family's holdings in Monmouthshire.

With the funeral of Baldwin over, Millett left Tintern to return to his law practice in London. He died in 1917, just weeks before Sir Lambton Loraine who had witnessed his wedding. By then Millett was living in Bexhill-on-Sea, Sussex. By the time his wife died in 1923, she had moved to Eastbourne. It is clear that shared and tangled loyalties went deep with the mourners at John Loraine Baldwin's funeral.

We have to remember that the extraordinary mystery of the double tomb in St. Michael's churchyard was an incidental by-product of my search for more information about the Byrom drawings. That search had repeatedly thrown up groups of historical figures with close involvement with the area.

The legend of St. Tewdric and his hermit's cave hovers around Tintern Parva and endows the site of St. Michael's Church with importance from an early date. Devotion to the cult of St. Radegunda at the nearby Priory at Usk added to the spiritual resonances of the area and for four hundred years a great abbey towered over the landscape. The temporal power of the Norman invader was exercised from Goodrich Castle as a constant reminder of a French presence. That presence could also be seen in the church at Llanishen, dedicated to St. Dennis, patron saint of France, whose abbey in Paris is rich with Merovingian associations. Standing on land owned by Edward I's daughter, Joan of Acres, the church exemplifies, too, the Plantagenets' policy of keeping ownership of much of the land close to their own family. Even with changes of royal dynasties, Tintern was considered a valuable prize. Henry VIII wooed Anne Boleyn with it, before bestowing the Abbey on the Earl of Worcester. In turn, his son, Edward VI, gave St. Michael's as a reward to the Earl of Pembroke.

The reign of Elizabeth I saw the emergence of the wireworks in Tintern and the attempts to produce the first brass in the kingdom. This brought Francis Bacon into the area as an active shareholder anxious to see the venture succeed. At the same time we have the foundation of a college for hermetic studies at Tintern Parva Estate by Sir William Herbert of St. Julian's. I believe Bacon was personally involved in this venture and that St. Michael's Church and neighbouring area may be part of the mystery that surrounds his death. It was the tomb in the churchyard decorated with the ornamental 'Cs' associated with Bacon that first caught my attention and led in part to the discoveries recounted in the previous pages.

But other influences have been at work at St. Michael's. The gateway at the western entrance of the churchyard reveals another presence we have

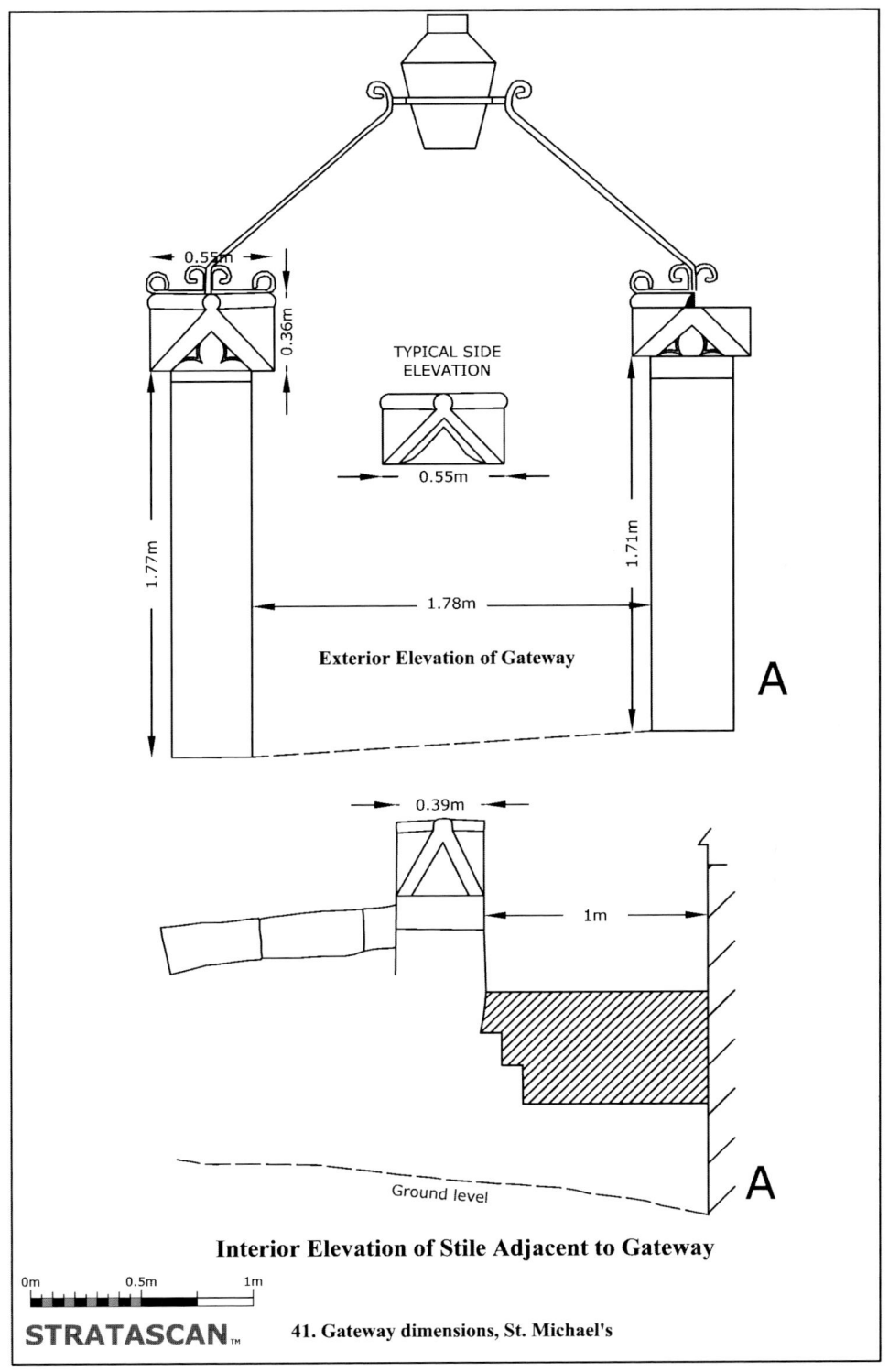

41. Gateway dimensions, St. Michael's

to consider. Two stone pillars support the gateway itself above which hangs a lantern in the shape of a keystone. A third pillar stands to the right, next to an old stile built into the end of the slipway wall. This can be easily missed because it is partially hidden, especially in summer, by trees and bushes. Each pillar is crowned with a copestone bearing four carved representations of a pair of dividers – a prime Masonic symbol.

When the two pillars supporting the gates were measured we discovered that their height, 1.77 m (or 70 inches) was practically the same as the distance between them – 1.78m. They had been designed to contain the space of a square. With Masonic iconography on the pillars I suppose I should have expected no less.

I have already discussed the symbolic associations concerned with the keystone in the slipway wall in Chapter Twelve. The pillared gateway positioned so near seemed to stress those associations and their significance. The Watkins commemorative family monument now highlighted further for me the role of the 'Tyler' or 'gatekeeper' in Masonic lodges. The Watkins family had performed the role in known lodges for years.

When I showed photographs of the gateway to the Rev. Neville Cryer he immediately recognised the iconography and was prepared to comment.

> … I think quite frankly, apart from the top of the pillars, the most striking feature of this particular entrance is the creation of a metal arch with a light at the top. Now the light, of course, could have been of any design you like. It could have been square, circular – and yet it is in the shape of a keystone and is in the very position that it ought to be, namely at the apex of an arch. It really is most singular that such a design should be at the entrance of a site that we know already has connections with both Operative and Accepted Masonry. And I can only believe that this gateway was specially and purposely designed to have connections with not a few who lie buried in this particular churchyard.

The Burial Register at St. Michael's that I had seen begins in 1813. It is evident from a few graves in the old churchyard that there were earlier interments. But the 1813 Register marks a new beginning in some way. 1813 was a crucial year in the formal development of Freemasonry not just in England, but throughout English Freemasonry worldwide. That year two long-standing rival groups, the 'Antients' and the 'Moderns', were finally reconciled and formed 'The United Grand Lodge of Ancient Freemasons of England'. The Dukes of Beaufort had played an important part in this process. The Masonic symbolism of the pillars at the gateway to St. Michael's reflects the dividers visible at the apex of the Tudor south porch roof and may have been intended to celebrate this historic accommodation. Did the Burial Register of 1813 mark the same event? The enigmatic keystone and ashlar placed side by side in the boundary wall are possibly indications of the Brotherhood's involvement with the church. They had been positioned sufficiently close to each other to ensure their significance was understood by the initiated. Those outside the Brotherhood would be none the wiser.

The secrecy surrounding Freemasonry is legendary. Symbols and signs form part of their hidden language. In recent times Freemasons have become more open as an organisation, more accessible to enquiries from outside their ranks. The nature of my quest over the years has forced me to access what records are available.

However, now it seemed as if my enquiry was taking on a different kind of reality. I had been disappointed that John Bevan's will was not available for public inspection. I could understand that the years he spent running the Deception Unit might make him, in Dennis Wheatley's words, 'obsessed by security'. Discretion about family secrets would be paramount to such a mind. But that could now be a serious impediment, for Sir Percy's will might well include facts relevant to some important figures connected with my research, among them Sir Isaac Newton. Paradoxically, the more I uncovered, the more there was that needed to be explained. The Baldwin/Russell grave was just one phenomenon that left questions waiting for answers. There were, moreover, always implications arising from the presence of Francis Bacon in the area, his involvement with the wireworks and the Baconian iconography on the tomb that had sparked off my original interest.

I mentioned the decoration of the pillars to Elsa and Adrian Wood during the same visit and they were able to tell me that there were pillared gateways in the vicinity with the same decoration! These were the entrances, rear and front, to a mansion, high up on the hills at Cleddon near Trellech. Accordingly, I was taken next day by the Simpsons up the narrow lanes to photograph them. Solemn and majestic, these pillars were not, like the ones at St. Michael's, made from single blocks, but rose in layers of dressed stone, looking, if anything, all the grander for that. Their caps, too, displayed dividers on all four sides. Yet clearly the statement they made at this remote spot would be recognised only by those 'who had the understanding'.

CHAPTER NINETEEN

A Twist in the Tale

Cleddon and its residents

Bradney's account of Cleddon says little about the area itself and when he turns to the history of the house he begins it late in the day. The reader senses that he knew more than he was prepared to include.

The Amberleys

> Cleddon ... was sold ... to Lord Amberley, the eldest son of earl Russell the Victorian statesman, who came here with his wife to reside. The estate comprised 87 acres, of which 63 were woods and plantations. Lord and Lady Amberley were both possessed of views on life in strange discord to those of the simple-minded people among whom they settled, and strange stories are told of their proceedings and of the upbringing of their children ...[1]

When I read that Viscount Amberley was the son of Earl Russell I immediately thought of Lady Francis Russell who had lived in Tintern and been buried at St. Michael's Church. Her first husband, Lord Francis Russell, was Earl Russell's brother and this made her Viscount Amberley's aunt. Her husband, the naval sea captain, had died in 1869. Amberley bought Cleddon the following year. Three years later Lady Francis took up residence with her new husband, John Loraine Baldwin, at St. Ann's, when he had been made Warden of the Abbey.

These two branches of the Russell dynasty had been neighbours in the most fashionable part of London and were now neighbours again in this remote part of Wales. Lady Francis had been a Russell for twenty-five years and retained her Russell surname and title after her second marriage. Even with a marked difference in age the two couples would have visited each other. Cleddon is only about three miles from Tintern, near Trellech.

Bradney's account of the Amberleys' lifestyle is misleading in its brevity although his reticence is understandable in the context of contemporary Victorian culture. Katharine, Lady Amberley was born into a well-known Liberal family, the Stanleys of Alderley, Cheshire. Her father had been a minister in Palmerston's government. So both husband and wife had grown up in a progressive tradition. Moreover, they were devoted to each other, although they shocked people by espousing such causes as the extension of the vote, birth control, women's rights and general education.²

When they moved to Cleddon they called the house 'Ravenscroft'. The change of name is not simply suggestive of the presence of birds in the nearby woods. By this time the raven had acquired an aura of mystery and romance in popular imagination from the widely read poem *The Raven* by Edgar Allan Poe, first published in 1845. The poem made him a household name in America. As it so happened, in 1867 Kate and her husband visited Boston where Poe had been born. So perhaps we should not be too surprised that when the Amberleys' third offspring, a boy, was born at Ravenscroft he was christened Bertrand. The name is said to come from ancient French roots meaning 'bright raven'. This boy, Bertrand Russell, grew up to become one of the best-known English philosophers of the twentieth century.

The Amberleys had visited Boston to meet the city's famous radical thinkers. The encounter strengthened their own activities on behalf of women's rights in this country. This eventually earned Kate a public snub from royalty. Bertrand Russell tells the story in his autobiography. At a garden party given by the parents of the future Queen Mary the Duchess of Cambridge exclaimed loudly:

> Yes, I know who you are, you are the daughter-in-law. But now I hear you only like dirty Radicals and dirty Americans. All London is full of it; all the clubs are talking of it. I must look at your petticoats to see if they are dirty.³

Despite this appalling rebuke, the Amberleys' advanced views did not alienate them entirely from aristocratic society. Kate kept a journal which tells us much about life at Ravenscroft. Early after their arrival the Duchess of Beaufort accompanied by her son Lord Henry Brudenell Somerset and Lady Westmoreland called to celebrate Kate's son, Frank's, fifth birthday. The Duchess arranged to let them have access to the woods bordering the grounds so that they could walk there if they wished. The Amberleys were also invited to lunch at Troy House, still in use as a residence of the Beaufort family.

This branch of the Russells had strong links with the Beauforts. A direct ancestor of Lord Amberley, Anne Russell, had married the fifth Earl of Worcester, stout defender of Raglan Castle during the Civil War. As we noted in Chapter Six, that fierce loyalty to the Stuarts led eventually to the elevation of the Earls of Worcester to the Dukedom of Beaufort. His wife, this same Anne Russell, was the cousin to Francis Bacon who took over the running of Tintern Wireworks at a difficult time in its history. In addition, Elizabeth, Lady Francis Russell, as a Peyton, could claim descent from the Bacon family.⁴

The Amberleys arrived at Ravenscroft in July 1870 and were very happy there to begin with, enjoying life on the small estate and in the countryside around. But Kate was horrified at the meagre state of local education and went to church just once. Thereafter she resolutely stayed away. Lord Amberley, an agnostic with a reverend sense of doubt, spent his time writing political articles and a comparative study of different faiths, *An Analysis of Religion*, published after his death in 1876.

They brought with them a son, usually called Frank, and a daughter, Rachel. Bertrand was born in 1872. Two years later his mother and sister both died of diphtheria. Not being a believer, Kate had asked to be buried in the grounds of Ravenscroft. The tomb for her and Rachel lay in sight of the house. Viscount Amberley seems to have had a delicate constitution, for he died of bronchitis in 1876 and was buried with them. The two boys, Frank, now 11, and Bertrand, 4, were taken from their unorthodox guardians to live with their Russell grandfather at Pembroke Lodge, London. He also removed the three bodies to the family vault at Chenies in Buckinghamshire. So the Amberleys were gone, and 'Ravenscroft' at some point became 'Cleddon' once more.

The stone-dressed pillars capped with dividers link the house in some way with St. Michael's Church, but when was that link made? The Amberleys' tenure had been short, six years in all. What we know of their interests and pursuits does not suggest they were responsible for building the gateways. One of the property's attractions seems to have been its potential as a sanctuary surrounded by mature trees and walls already in place. So who was the previous owner?

John Roberts Esq.

Bradney gives us few facts but they are significant. He states:

> Cleddon belonged during the first half of the nineteenth century to John Chapman Roberts, a captain in the Royal Monmouthshire Militia, who died 17 May 1859, aged 81. In 1870 it was sold by captain Roberts' executors to Lord Amberley …

Two things caught my attention straight away. First, yet another event occurring on 17 May, and secondly the gap of eleven years between the death of Captain Roberts and the sale of his property by the executors. Eleven years seemed a long time for a house to be empty. Was it in fact empty all that time?

Roberts appeared to have owned the house for the better part of fifty years. What had brought him to this remote spot? The census of 1841 describes him as 'a man of independent means'. Certainly he would have had to purchase his commission in the first place and no doubt, as was the

Cleddon Hall

Tintern Parva: Churchyard/Slipway

42. Gateways

custom then, when not on active service he would have been reduced to half pay. In all probability his army pay was not his sole income. Facts I learned about his regiment seemed to confirm this.

The Royal Monmouthshire Militia owes its origin to Henry VIII. Monmouthshire was one of several new counties he created after the Dissolution of the Monasteries. In 1539 troops were mustered there in his desire to control and tax Wales. These eventually became the Militia and were loyal servants of the Crown. Their role was to preserve law and order.

The Militia Act of 1757 empowered the Lord Lieutenants of the counties to raise men by ballot for a period of three years' service, but the well-off were allowed to pay for a substitute. Successive Dukes of Beaufort commanded the regiment which had its headquarters at Monmouth Castle. The local gentry purchased their commissions 'to maintain their social standing'. I was intrigued to learn that the Militia were also known as the 'Monmouthshire Royal Engineers'. The duties that earned them that title might have had a bearing on John Roberts's captaincy and his residence at Cleddon. This seemed a distinct possibility when I read about the workings under the house and in the grounds.

I learned of these from a volume celebrating Trellech at the beginning of the new millennium. Contributors inevitably drew on the past and one, George Taylor, was owner of Cleddon at the time. I was interested in what he had to say about the water supply to the house. This comes from a well no longer accessible.

> All the water for the house is drawn from a well sited below the Hall. A tiled cover matches the main floor tiles. Below that is a cut stone slab. From beneath where the servants' staircase used to be, a low stone lined passage or duct enters the main well shaft some four or five feet lower than floor level, quite a steep slope. [This shaft is] about seven feet in diameter, approximately forty feet deep, beautifully cut dressed stone to the bottom.

Moreover, Mr. Taylor goes on to say

> There is another well just outside the old coach house, unlike the one in the house this is cut out of the solid rock, just a few feet near the top bricked up.

This, too, is about seven feet in diameter.

> The bottom was thick clay, but the interesting thing was that about eight feet from the bottom a cut out high enough to walk along had been hewn from the solid rock to a point about twenty five feet below the coach house, presumably for extra storage[5]

Both wells are feats of substantial engineering, particularly the second. Bearing in mind the modest size of the original house one can only wonder at the scale of these workings. One is forced to ask who built them and for what purpose. The diameter of the wells and the additional stonework seem an extravagant use of engineering skills for a domestic dwelling. All we know of Cleddon before Captain Roberts is that it was the site of a small inn kept by a poacher, Job the Outlaw, still active in 1810. The majestic pillars at the front entrance suggest the property had another function at some time. The dividers could not be ignored. They surmounted both entrances, at the front and back, and were intended to make a statement.

When the Amberleys moved in, their building activities were confined to an extension for their son, Frank, at the back of the house, a conservatory and other minor internal modifications. They seemed to concentrate more on developing the gardens. Accordingly, the extraordinary structures below ground must date from at least the time of Captain Roberts. His long service in the Monmouthshire Militia would provide him with the manpower necessary to develop such features and a means of training the soldiers under his command.

What more do we know about him? A search through public records produced a will, and one that proved instructive. It was made and signed the day Roberts died. In fact a codicil was also signed the same day, leaving £50 to a local shopkeeper whose honesty had impressed Roberts. It seems a sign of lucidity that he was capable of making this addition at the very end. Roberts left his home, 'Cleddon Lodge', to his two executors, Henry Gosling, a banker, and John Endell Powles, solicitor. Both men had family homes which, I learned later, they continued to live in. It looks, therefore, as if Cleddon remained unoccupied, or was used for other purposes. It was sold, as we know, eleven years later, to Viscount Amberley.

Roberts did not die at Cleddon but in Church Street, Monmouth, at the home of Annabella Williams, the unmarried sister of the Very Rev. Thomas Williams, Dean of Llandaff. How long he had been there we cannot say, but one senses some degree of compassion for a sick and elderly acquaintance. Moreover, his presence in Church Street was not an act of charity towards a poor man. He left handsome bequests to the family of his first wife and, in addition to Cleddon Lodge, owned a working farm which he bequeathed to one Thomas William Oakley. Gifts of money were also left to a local surgeon and a medical dispensary.

Roberts would be a figure of some repute in Monmouth on several counts. As a long-time resident at Cleddon Lodge, he was a member of the local squirearchy. His career as an officer in the Monmouthshire Militia would earn him additional respect and, incidentally, help him to hone the engineering skills required by the Militia, something he seems to have done on his own estate. It would have meant regular contact with the regimental commander, the Duke of Beaufort, and the Freemasonry of the county, both regimental and civilian. It is therefore significant that during his residency Cleddon was called 'Cleddon Lodge'.

The Masonic insignia on the two entrances to the estate suggest a specific loyalty. When owners later than the Amberleys changed the name back from 'Ravenscroft' to 'Cleddon' they called it 'Cleddon Hall'. That may have been in part to signify a break with past Masonic allegiances.

Roberts strikes one as a solitary figure. He married twice but either both marriages were childless or any offspring predeceased him. Did he become increasingly reclusive after the death of his second wife, living alone except for one domestic servant in a ten-bedroom house set in eighty-seven acres? He had been responsible for building the 'pretty drawing room' and 'very good dining room' described by Kate Amberley. Both are reminders of his marital hopes, together with a Coat of Arms to be seen on an outside wall. In the end it was left to his Masonic friends and activities to provide a meaningful social life and sense of continuity. A career in the army accustomed him to a life of discipline and his duties as a magistrate showed a readiness to dispense justice. He seems, then, to have been an exemplar of unquestioning authority and order. We do not know his final resting place. Yet the date on which he died, 17 May, was the date the alleged lovers of Anne Boleyn were executed and the date when Lord Henry Brudenell Somerset, Baldwin's hoped-for successor, also died. As far as Tintern is concerned, 17 May has some curious associations.

Masonic Monmouth

Detailed research has shown that Captain Roberts's executors and main beneficiaries, Henry Gosling and John Endell Powles, were almost certainly Freemasons. Thomas William Oakley to whom he left the farm was also a solicitor and a Freemason. It is clear that Roberts moved in a select group within the Brotherhood.

Records of Masonic meetings in Monmouth date from 1768, and in 1814 the Monmouth Militia, with its headquarters in the local castle, was granted permission to hold its own military lodge, but for some reason the Masonic licence was withdrawn in 1822. Cleddon was ideally placed for the members of the lodge to continue to meet under the protection of Captain Roberts. Eventually Freemasonry in the town became centred around the 'Loyal Monmouth Lodge' which grew in size and status towards the middle of the century.[6] It is perhaps fitting that the house where John Roberts died was close to the unobtrusive heart of Masonic Monmouth. It is a key to the importance he had in the eyes of both ecclesiastical and Masonic colleagues. It seems to have been more than a coincidence that John Roberts spent his last days with the sister of the Dean of Llandaff, in a house where the two worlds of Church and Freemasonry could meet.

The Established Church has a tradition of sympathetic appreciation of Freemasonry, because it is aware that English Freemasonry has never been subversive in the way that some Masonic movements on the Continent have been. Rev. Neville Barker Cryer is an example of the accommodation possible between Church and Brotherhood. His dual role makes his comments on the Masonic signs on the pillars at St. Michael's Church and the keystone and ashlar in the church boundary wall of particular value.

From photographs of the pillars he concluded that 'This gateway was specially and purposely designed to have connections with not a few who lie buried in this particular churchyard.' About the keystone and ashlar he was even more specific. In symbolic masonry, he says, a keystone 'is always related to the entry into some chamber or vault in which there is some manuscript material'. Moreover, the keystone is mainly associated with 'a vault beneath Solomon's Temple'.

The reader will understand how a series of anomalies revealed by non-invasive ground-penetrating radar in both St. Michael's Church and the churchyard had made me wonder where symbolism ended and fact began. But the discovery of John Roberts nearby at Cleddon in a house with Masonic gates and strange workings underground is a factor we have to consider because of the Masonic gateway at the church. Does his presence lend weight to the idea of some kind of attempt to recreate physically symbolic aspects of Solomon's Temple?

The Temple of Solomon is central to the beliefs of Freemasonry. Solomon is looked upon as Master. The building of the Temple as described in the Old Testament, the mysteries it enclosed, and the rituals enacted therein, are important to them. John Roberts would have been dedicated to a serious study of the Temple. What the current owner of Cleddon describes as a 'servants' staircase' beneath the hallway floor at one time may have had a different purpose. Since the underground workings seem excessive as a water supply, could the stairs have been a simpler version of 'the winding staircase into the middle chamber' described in the First Book of Kings? Were they built to lead to a small complex engineered by Roberts where ritual practices were enacted by members of the Brotherhood to gain a greater understanding of the Temple? A lodge at Cleddon was likely to have been a private one. Such lodges are not unknown; one met in the Crypt under York Minster during the late eighteenth century. Although I have found no record of one at Cleddon, the unmistakeable symbolism of the gates suggests such a hypothesis is not unreasonable.

Cleddon After the Amberleys

Mystery of one kind or another persists around Cleddon. According to Kate Amberley's diary she and her husband were shown round the house on their first visit by 'the owner, Mr. Morris', about whom nothing is known. After the deaths of the Amberleys, the house was sold again. Writing in 1913, all Bradney was prepared to say was

> After this Cleddon obtained further notoriety in being the residence of the marquis of B..., son of the Duke of M..., and the countess of A... who ran away together and were the cause of a celebrated trial for divorce.[7]

The current owner, writing more than a hundred and twenty years after this liaison, writes openly about the residency of Lord Blandford and Lady Aysleford at Cleddon and blames it for a gap in the history of the house: 'The shame in those times was so bad that, as far as I can find out, the deeds and references to the place were destroyed, this is the reason for the gap in the information...'[8]

The Marquis of Blandford was the son and heir to the seventh Duke of Marlborough and became involved in a major scandal with the wife of another aristocrat. It is unfortunate that he deliberately set out to destroy any records of his stay at Cleddon before leaving and going to America.

In 1880 Cleddon Lodge was sold to Arthur Bosanquet, a member of a distinguished Huguenot family from Dingestow. He changed the name of the house back to 'Cleddon'. From then on records exist of the different owners, but none of them needs concern us.

The Church

Roberts's move from Cleddon to Monmouth was dictated by his failing health. The choice of Annabella Williams's house is worth pondering. Her brother was Dean of Llandaff, the chief administrator of that ancient cathedral. The Church in Wales is a creation of the early twentieth century and in 1859 Monmouth was still part of Llandaff diocese; so were St. Michael's at Tintern Parva and the church at Mathern. Annabella's brother was in effect next in importance to the bishop who was responsible for every parish in the diocese. Two of these concern us closely: Mathern because it is the final resting place of St. Tewdric and St. Michael's because I believe it conceals the cave where Tewdric had once lived as a hermit.

We saw in Chapter Three that the bishop's official home was near the church in Mathern for nearly 400 years. We also know that the Rev. Robert Vaughan Hughes, a nearby resident, took a prominent, almost aggressive, part in the refurbishment of Mathern parish church and was patron of St.

Michael's for fifteen years. The rebuilding and repair of churches in the diocese came under the diocesan architect, John Prichard. In that capacity he would be responsible for the extension to St. Michael's and the landscaping of the western limits of the churchyard. This array of ecclesiastics and their servants suggests a degree of involvement by the Church in the mystery of Tintern Parva, equal to the interest displayed by Freemasons and certain members of the aristocracy.

The letters patent of 1553 granting the Rectory of Tintern Parva to Pembroke and Clarke is a key document in that the power to 'innovate' enshrined in it declares the importance of the site. The king's aim was to protect it in perpetuity through the custody of successive Earls of Pembroke. But we know that the importance of Tintern Parva to the Crown began long before 1553 – in the twelfth century. William Marshall, supreme chivalric knight of his age, was a noted benefactor of the Abbey at Tintern and after him William de Valence, Henry III's half brother, had ruled the area in the king's name from Goodrich Castle. Royal involvement continued through several reigns.

The archaeological dig at St. Michael's revealed a pudding stone wall and fragments of pottery dating from the thirteenth century and the Roman period. This provides evidence for a much earlier slipway than the present boundary wall suggests. There is also the intriguing matter of the commission Dee undertook for the Duchess of Northumberland to write a treatise on tidal waters the same year the Earl of Pembroke was given the Rectory and Church of Tintern Parva. Dee had joined Pembroke's household in 1552. He was then recommended as a tutor to Northumberland's son, Robert Dudley, the future Earl of Leicester and favourite of Elizabeth I. (Pembroke and Northumberland were both friends and rivals.) Dee was soon writing *The True Cause and account of Floods and Ebbs*.

In 1570 Henry Billingsley published his translation of Euclid. For this Dee wrote a lengthy Preface, revolutionary in its advocacy of applied mathematics. Dee's association with Billingsley had a direct bearing on Tintern. First Billingsley was a tenant of Sir William Herbert of St. Julian's and then mortgaged property from him in the Monmouth area. Billingsley, I believe, was active in Tintern as a mathematician involved with Sir William's College even before his successful career as a merchant in London. As he achieved prominence in the City the outdoor playhouses were beginning to flourish.

At the same time Dee's reputation began to decline. Even before Elizabeth's death he was being attacked as a 'conjurer' and 'caller of Divels'. Sincere but naive attempts to communicate with angels destroyed him. By the time he died in 1608 there were few to defend him. James I had succeeded Elizabeth and *The Tempest* was performed for his daughter Elizabeth's wedding in 1612.

This play has a bearing on aspects of Dee's career, and his friendship with Sir William Herbert. Herbert, as we have seen, was a keen student of Dee's treatise *Monas Hieroglyphica*. In this work Dee writes of man's spiritual transformation through a command of the natural magic of the universe. Little wonder that he is thought to have been the model for Prospero in *The Tempest*, who lives in a 'poor full cell', a master of occult arts:

> … graves at my command
> Have wak'd their sleepers, oped, and let em forth
> By my so potent art …

Prospero's boast is reminiscent of the slander that beset Dee. The theme of regeneration is close to Dee's innermost ideas and Prospero's cell recalls Tewdric's cave among the rocks at Tintern. Interestingly the geological strata around the area contains a layer of impermeable rock below the water table where that cave could have been created naturally in the rock. Unfortunately the topography at St. Michael's has been changed radically. Only through the archaeology do we get an idea of the original ground level at the west end of the churchyard and what might lie below.

According to my Masonic consultant, it would be something substantial, possibly modelled on the Temple of Solomon. I was mindful of his opinion when the last rector, the Rev. Rees, told me that the first time he entered the church, its basic outline reminded him of the Temple of Solomon. For long enough scholars have likened the Elizabethan theatre concept to temples and there happen to be Rose theatre drawings that contain clearly the geometry of a six-pointed star – the shape of the Seal of Solomon. When I had overlaid the transparency of one drawing on top of the excellent Tintern Parva plan produced by Stratascan in August 2005, the result, described in Chapter Thirteen, had been a revelation.

The Rose Theatre and St. Michael's Church

If we look at the drawing again, we can see that the Seal of Solomon falls directly on top of the oldest part of the church. The significance of this must be explained. The Seal of Solomon, basically two triangles intertwined, symbolises the ancient hermetic formula 'as above so below'. On this Rose drawing part of the shading is coloured more deeply to distinguish between 'above' and 'below'. It suggests a structure below ground that mirrors *geometrically* what is above. We should also note that, when overlaid on the Tintern Parva plan, the Rose drawing encompasses within its outermost circle the old slipway, showing that had to be included in any deliberations.

Repeating the overlay procedure only confirmed what I had seen before. The geometry of the Rose drawing highlighted the position of the tomb X and the position of the burial in the pit-like structure found inside the chancel. These remained fixed features in the plan of the church – two points determined long before the final extension of the nave in 1846. But this time I also noticed another point picked out by the overlay of the Rose drawing. Following the line that marks the horizontal diameter of the large circle, from the centre of the circle towards the left, the eye comes to rest at 'point A'. This marks the place on the Stratascan plan of the Baldwin/Russell double tomb built in the nineteenth century. Since the Rose drawing existed long before that tomb, the inclusion of 'point A' in the drawing indicates a point important in its geometry. Seeing that the geometry, when overlaid onto the site of St. Michael's, highlights salient features in the geometry of the *site* as well, we are forced to examine the significance of this third match. Was Baldwin's choice of this place for his double tomb nearly three hundred years later accidental or deliberate? I believe it to be deliberate. For me the extraordinary results of the two radar scans of the double tomb confirm that John Loraine Baldwin knew the importance of that particular spot. Not for one moment did he imagine anyone would later question what lay beneath.

On the Rose drawing 'point A' is balanced on the other side of the horizontal diameter with a similar figure. This may well indicate another point of importance on the church site and remains an area deserving further interest.

Even so, the matching of the Rose drawing and Stratascan plan has important implications for the provenance of the theatre drawings in the Byrom Collection. In Chapter Four we looked at the triangular drawing in the Collection which can be superimposed on the ground plan of Westminster Abbey. Since significant features of the Abbey have remained constant for centuries, a number of points on both the ground plan and the triangle can be seen to correspond. Although the topography at St. Michael's Church has changed with time, particularly with the extension of 1846, the preservation of the original chancel remains a fixed point of departure from which other dimensions can be calculated.

For example, from it we discover the distance (72 cubits) to the position of 'tomb X'. We know what an important measure symbolically that is and a burial in the chancel focuses the eye on the place where 72 cubits lead us. Indeed 'tomb X' marks a place of importance on the church site just as the matching point on the Rose drawing indicates the entrance to the original theatre in London. When the Rose drawing is broken down into its constituent elements – circles, squares and triangles – the pattern of triangles demonstrates in another form the correspondence between the theatre drawing and the church site. The drawing is commemorative. The Rose Theatre was built in 1587, the year Sir Philip Sidney died. His sister, Mary Sidney, was the wife of the second Earl of Pembroke, owner and custodian of the site of St. Michael's Church. Theodore de Bry, the Huguenot printer and engraver from Liège, was responsible for the engravings of Sidney's funeral procession through London. He was also, I believe, the man behind the visual presentation of the concept of the playhouses in the geometrical format that we see in the Byrom theatre drawings.

The correspondences we have been looking at confirm the relationship between the wireworks at Tintern Parva, where the first brass was made in this country, and the brass plates in the Science Museum. That in turn adds to our understanding of the presence of Sir William Herbert's College at Tintern Parva, on the site described in the first census of 1841 as 'Nurton's Priory'.

I felt that now I had come full circle. The letters patent allowing Pembroke and Clarke to 'innovate' seemed also to have liberated other individuals to innovate also with, for example, the Elizabethan theatre design and, on a more mundane level, the encouragement of new skills at the wireworks. But I was left wondering why an awareness of these developments in the area had not emerged earlier. Had the history of local events and people become so fragmented that their impact and importance were forgotten? Who had kept this secret history alive?

John Loraine Baldwin

The supreme guiding figure that emerged in the latter part of the nineteenth century seemed to be John Loraine Baldwin. In his person flowed the blood of the ancient House of Lorraine and he was aware of that legacy. We must not allow his London nickname 'King of Clubs' to mislead us. He was more than a dilettante of the world of cards and cricket. He used both these activities as a means to infiltrate the highest levels of society and exercise a form of control. People deferred to him in their most susceptible moments – when they chose to relax. By gaining acceptance of his rules and regulations for innocent pastimes such as whist and badminton, Baldwin acquired a quiet, unostentatious but genuine pre-eminence. This brought him the close friendship of the Duke of Beaufort, 'uncrowned king of Monmouthshire' and a leading figure in Freemasonry.

Conscious of his Lorraine blood, Baldwin married in his sixties the wealthy Elizabeth Russell, descendant of Francis Bacon.

Her social position as a member of the Russell family was assured; the large fortune she inherited from her father reinforced her independence. Yet she agreed to marry Baldwin and whatever she owned became his. Her will is astonishing in its total concentration on Baldwin. Not one female relative or friend is singled out for a bequest. Is that symptomatic of their relationship? The biographical sketch of Baldwin included with the report of his funeral is carefully, almost dutifully, written and gives us a clear picture of his influence and popularity. The jocular gift of a silver 'pig and whistle' obviously had undertones recognisable to some of his friends; otherwise the joke would have been pointless. But the circumstances surrounding the making of his will seem to me most revealing.

I went over the facts again. His will was made on 19 May 1895, in the hotel at Paddington Station. It named Lord Edward Somerset as the man he wished to inherit St. Ann's and with it all Baldwin's and his late wife's possessions. The bequest chimed in with the hope that Edward Somerset would succeed him as Warden of the Abbey. But, as we know, Somerset died on 17 May 1897 before he could inherit. His death certificate was issued on the inauspicious 19 May.

It was his brother, Lord Adelbert Wellington Fitzroy Somerset, who succeeded as ninth Duke of Beaufort on 30 April 1899 at the age of fifty-seven. The death of Adelbert's father had been preceded by those of a sister in February and Brudenell in May 1897, and these three deaths so close together seem to have had a severe effect on him. Adelbert had been born on, of all days, 19 May, and, soon after succeeding to the dukedom, he began to divest the Beauforts of their lands in Monmouthshire. Yet he did not lose interest in the county. On the contrary, he is the Duke famously associated with the American Dr. Orville Owen in the series of excavations on the banks of the Wye at Chepstow mentioned briefly in Chapter Sixteen.

Dr. Owen

Owen's work has been dismissed and largely forgotten because he did not find what he was looking for at Chepstow. Yet when other backers dropped out, the millionaire George Fabyan did not. He was the owner of Riverbank Laboratories in Illinois, where his interest in ciphers led him to establish a school of cryptography that produced the first military code breakers for the US government. Fabyan built up an impressive library of first and only editions of Elizabethan authors. He became convinced that Shakespeare's plays were the work of a society of Rosicrucians but died before he could complete his thesis.[9]

Twenty-eight years after his death Robert Sherwood, a solicitor employed by the *Encyclopeadia Brittanica*, was busy investigating the Fabyan–Owen story. I myself was given a copy of the official history of Riverbank by Ian Taylor, a broadcaster and publisher in Canada and a contributor to the book. He suggested that I should investigate the same story for any possible relevance to my researches.[10] One of the strongest critics of Owen's deciphering was William Friedman. Friedman worked for Fabyan and the fact that Fabyan still supported Owen may be due to the recognition of something of genuine value in Owen's deciphering. Unfortunately in 1995 Sherwood also died, before he had completed the book he was planning. What conclusions he might have come to remain unknown. But he is one of a long line of Americans caught up by the Shakespeare authorship question. It is a line that includes, as we have seen, Mark Twain and his two Millet friends.

The Byrom theatre drawings had led me to Tintern in search of the place where the brass plates for some of them had been made. Much that I learned in the process was, to say the least, unexpected. But Tintern had been instrumental in helping me with the provenance of the concept behind the theatre drawings. That can now be proved through what I might call the Pembroke–Sidney drawings: the Rose drawings. The geometry of particular drawings is replicated in St. Michael's Church and the churchyard as we saw in Chapter Thirteen. The mysterious dimension of 72 units inherent in the geometry reappears in the measure of 72 cubits or 33 metres between the tomb of original interest and a pit-like structure underneath the chancel floor. Thus the geometry of the Rose theatre drawings helps to tie the site of the church to Mary Sidney, whose husband owned the site. She was the mother of the 'incomparable pair', the third and fourth Earls of Pembroke, the dedicatees of the First Folio of Shakespeare's plays. We should also remember that *Burke's Peerage* describes the third Earl as 'The Grandmaster of Freemasonry'.

The measures discovered within the Rose drawings and the application of those measures to the site of St. Michael's can be seen in illustration 43. An examination of the two measures of 24 cubits suggests further possibilities. They highlight the place where Baldwin later placed the 'vault' for the double grave. I think he knew this place was central to the Elizabethan theatre legacy. He saw himself as its latest custodian and was hoping to pass that duty on. The brotherhood of the Freemasons had played a similar role earlier. The site itself had been singled out as special even before the reign of Elizabeth I. Inevitably Baldwin died and the man he hoped would follow in his footsteps, Henry Brudenell Somerset, also died. So the custodianship changed. Baldwin's death in effect buries significant facts about Tintern Parva's history. Fortunately, scholars from a variety of disciplines have provided a meaningful context for the investigator to work in and modern, non-invasive technology has enabled us to investigate St. Michael's in a new way.

Reviewing the different 'power groups' concerned with Tintern Parva and the results of the successive scans, I gradually came to the conclusion that the site could have been used down the centuries by different groups as a repository for artefacts. Did these include at one time Bacon's missing manuscripts? What has emerged is a 'hidden chapter' of loyal custodians who maintained a careful but discreet watch on the site. At times some relieved themselves of the responsibility. In the nineteenth century John Shapland Edmonds Stock, son of the Bristol Dr. Stock, carefully disentangled himself from his obligations. Early in the twentieth century the ninth Duke of Beaufort sold most of his Monmouthshire holdings.

John Loraine Baldwin was perhaps the last guardian or 'warden' to accept the responsibility and the duties that entailed. Sadly, he failed to secure the appointment of his successor. Since that time the activities of this 'hidden chapter' in the area have changed and aspects of Tintern's past history have been lost.

My interpretation of the radar surveys of September 2006 and April 2007 leaves me with the conviction that John Loraine Baldwin and his wife still lie buried in St. Michael's churchyard but possibly at a different level from where they were publicly laid to rest. That level lies underneath the present graveyard in the natural bedrock that I believe once housed the legendary Tewdric's cave. Cavities in that bedrock would provide a natural form of catacomb. The two ground-penetrating surveys close to the Watkins ledger carried out in 2004 and 2005 give an indication of a lower level of former activity. This may be registered at one point on the boundary wall by the insertion of a keystone and ashlar. Others may disagree.

The unchanging certainty of number is a constant handed down through the ages from one civilisation to another. The presence of the 72 measure in St. Michael's churchyard is an apt symbol for other truths that have lain hidden until now in and around Tintern Parva. Their revelation reminds us of the words of Jacob Cats:

> Though Truth lies here within the grave
> Yet what is hidden must emerge.

I believe that some of the Byrom drawings were being prepared by the de Bry family of printers for publication around the year 1623, the year the First Folio of Shakespeare's plays was published. However, one of the leading members of the firm, Johann Theodore de Bry, died that year. Inevitably this would cause a major disruption and the drawings were never published. His son-in-law, Matthaeus Merian, was responsible for producing one of the few engravings that we have of the Elizabethan playhouses.

It seemed to me that John Byrom had acquired some of the de Bry legacy of drawings in 1735 when he visited Bartholomew Close on 1 May. A diary entry states :

> I went to Sam's coffee house at one o'clock, called upon Mr. Charles Houghton by the way, found Dixon and Graham there, we went to Mr. . . . in Bartholomew Close, where he showed me his engine for cutting and working Egyptian pebbles, and the collection of nine figures and papers of Rose about the cabalistic alchemy etc. very extraordinary and many curiosities which I think to call some day to look at . . .

Byrom's interest in the Cabala had started some ten years earlier when he founded his Cabala Club. The 'papers of Rose' refer to Rosicrucian material in the Schweighardt book which had written on the front 'An Account of the Rosicruc. Fraternity … with the addition of several prints and miniature paintings by Mr. Rose'. Those included the two illustrations we looked at earlier in connection with Sir William Herbert's College. Rose was obviously a very convenient nom de plume for anyone wishing to write about Rosicrucian ideas. Such was Byrom's interest that he returned to Bartholomew Close and acquired the cabalistic papers. Although writing in shorthand, Byrom first omits the name of the man who owned the material. However, later he emerges as 'Mr Falkner' and that is a clue to the provenance of the papers. Falkner was the maiden name of Matthaeus Merian's mother, a member of the de Bry publishing dynasty. The Schweighardt book at some time was separated from the 516 drawings that comprise Byrom's collection. It became part of the Hans Sloane Collection and his library became the foundation of the British Library, where the book remains to this day. Sloane was, of course, a member of Byrom's Cabala Club.

Byrom's active interest in the Cabala helps to explain the presence in his collection of drawings connected with the Elizabethan playhouses. The cabalistic element in the Elizabethan theatre concept is evident and contributes to the geometrical sophistication of the design. For whatever reason it has not received recognition.

My research has led me to believe that leading aristocrats connected with the wireworks at Tintern, and landowners in the Tintern area such as the Earls of Pembroke and Worcester, Francis Bacon, and certain other patrons of the theatre companies, were initiated into the geometry and ideas inherent in the drawings by John Dee. Bacon's radical attitude to science made him Dee's natural successor. We see this clearly proclaimed in the Cats engraving *Lampada Trado*. The Rose depicted on Bacon's shoe shows him as an advocate of Rosicrucian ideals.

Alongside the shoe in the earliest edition of the engraving the letter 'C' can be seen on the blade of the shovel. It reminds us of its use as a code for Bacon's name. Removed from later editions of the engraving, the 'C' still remains repeatedly evident on the tomb in St. Michael's churchyard.

William Herbert, third Earl of Pembroke, was patron of St. Michael's at the time of Bacon's death. He and his brother, Philip, are the dedicatees of the First Folio of Shakespeare's plays in 1623. The original manuscripts from which the First Folio was constructed have never been found. The printer, William Jaggard, official printer to the City of London, joined forces with an established bookseller, Edward Blount, to publish the First Folio. Interestingly, William Jaggard dealt with Shakespeare's plays and also printed Bacon's *Essays* for his brother John to publish. William Jaggard died in November 1623, just one month before the First Folio appeared. His death may account in part for the loss of the original manuscripts of the venture. The same applies to Theodore de Bry, the senior member of his family's printing firm. He also died in 1623, when, as mentioned earlier, he was, I believe, planning to publish the Byrom Collection drawings concerned with the design concept of the Elizabethan playhouses. Such events can account not only for aborted enterprises but the loss of valuable materials.

The sudden death of the third Earl of Pembroke after dining at Fisher's Folly in London is yet another misfortune that distracts out attention from significant truths. The dinner took place on 9 April, 1630, the anniversary of Bacon's death in 1626. At the time of Bacon's disgrace in 1621, Herbert had intervened to support him. The two men were connected through Tintern, the wireworks, St. Michael's and shared hermetic interests. There had been every reason to investigate the enigmatic tomb in the churchyard.

In the process, many unexpected facts have been explored. They have been very enriching for me and will, I hope, enhance the history and beauty of this memorable part of our country for readers of this book.

"Cocteau's dexterity was quite remarkable, as was his gift for likeness."

Quote from leaflet: Notre Dame de France, London 2010

Section highlighted

39. Jean Cocteau mural, French Church, London

40. Jean Cocteau grave and mural, Milly-la-Forêt

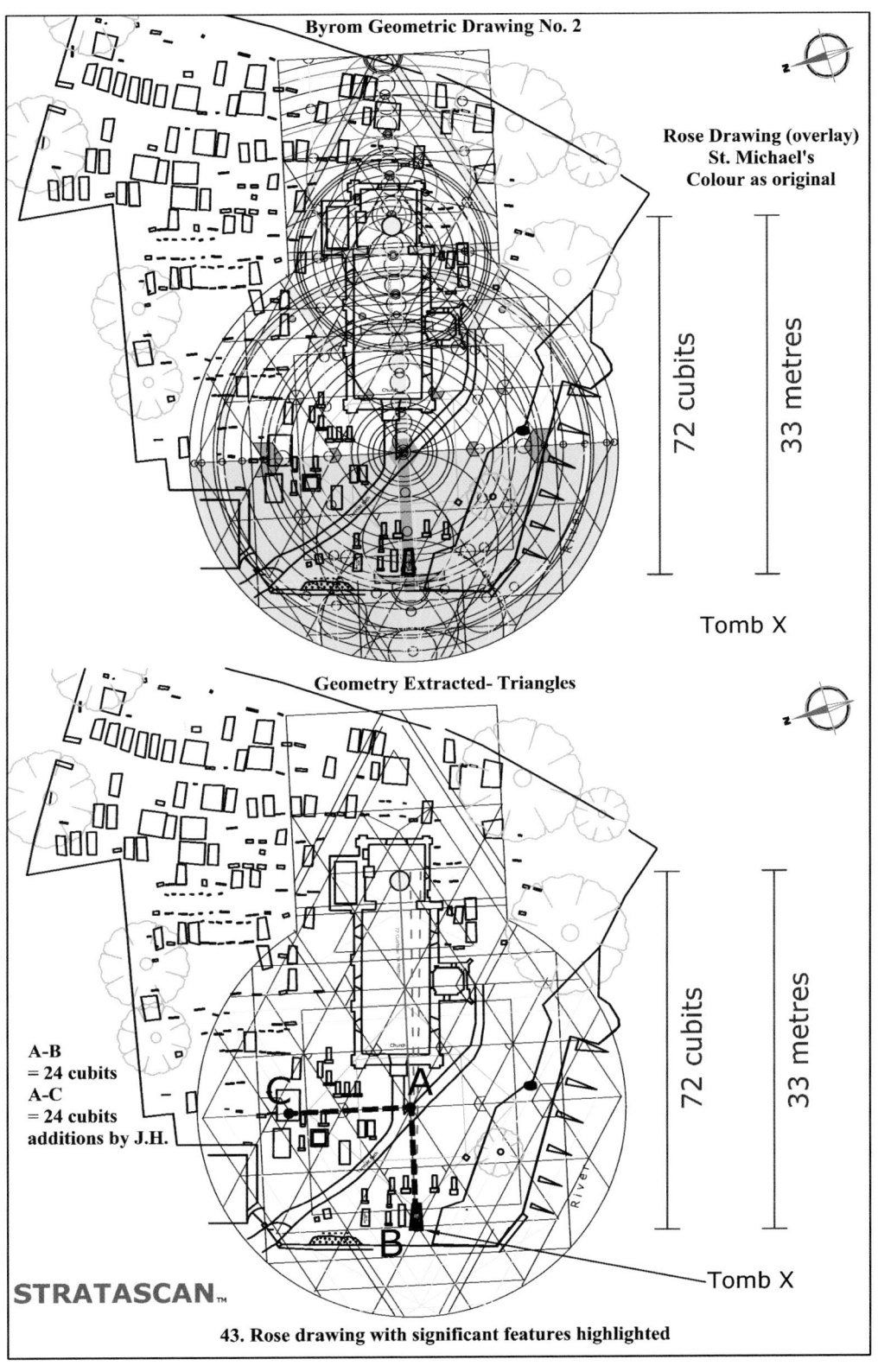

43. Rose drawing with significant features highlighted

44. *An Allegory*, full length

45. *An Allegory*, top section

46. *An Allegory*, middle section

47. *An Allegory*, bottom section

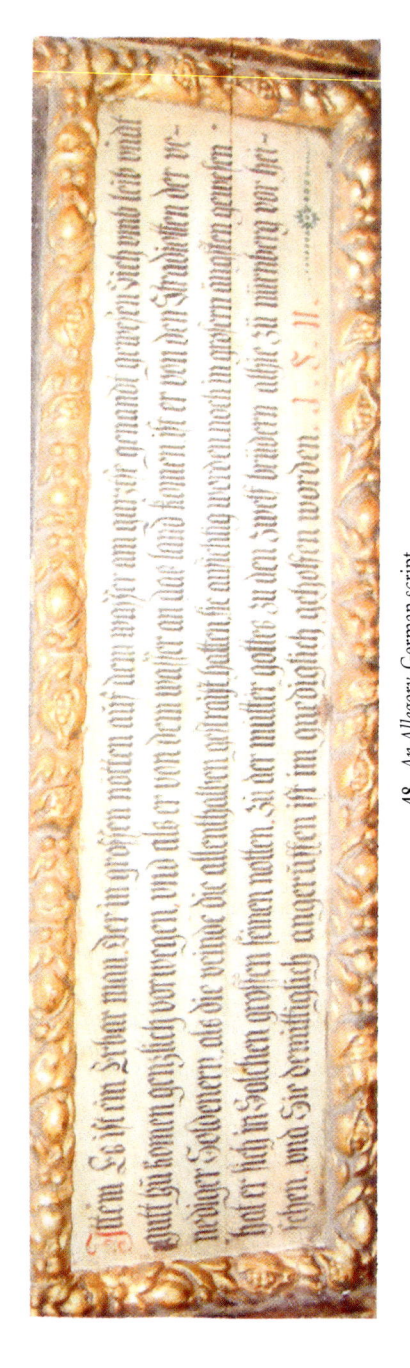

48. *An Allegory*, German script

CODA ONE

An Allegorical Painting

In 1997 I gave a lecture in London on the design concept of the Elizabethan theatres and the Byrom drawings. Some time later a member of the audience wrote to me about a painting in her family, bought at a London art auction in 2002. The painting was entitled *An Allegory* and she hoped I might be able to help her with the symbolism it contained. By that time I was fully engaged in researching the present book and looking into the received view of Francis Bacon among writers and historians. Certain features in the painting seemed to relate to some of what I had been reading, especially the newspaper reports of Dr. Owen's series of excavations along the river Wye at Chepstow.

I had also read an account of Bacon's life written by Alfred Dodd: *Francis Bacon's Personal Life Story*. In it he makes the claim that, according to one cipher, there were rumours circulating at the court of Queen Elizabeth I about the true birth of Francis Bacon. The rumours had started with his cousin, Robert Cecil, the son of Lord Burleigh, Secretary of State, to belittle Bacon whom he saw as a potential rival in his career.

> The story continues that while Lady Scales, a Lady-in-Waiting, was repeating to her companions Cecil's malevolent whispers that Francis was the Queen's bastard-son by Leicester, Elizabeth, overhearing the laughter from an adjoining room, dragged from the young Maid the reason for their merriment. By chance, Francis entered the room as the enraged Queen was violently beating the girl into insensibility. Attempting to intervene to save her, he was then told of the scurrilous chatter that was going round the Court, and in the passion of the moment, the truth of his parentage slipped from the Queen's lips. In the violence of her anger she screamed 'You are my own born son, but because you have taken sides against your mother to champion a graceless wench, I bar you for ever from the Succession.'[1]

Some students of Bacon maintain that this appalling discovery was the reason why Francis was included in the household of Sir Amias Paulet when he went as Ambassador to France in 1576. At the time he was still a youth of sixteen. Before he returned home he is known to have visited Rome and Venice.

The Hidden Chapter

I have always tried to maintain a neutral position towards the various conflicting claims made about Bacon's personal life. But I was forced to consider the connections that I thought might exist between the painting and certain facts that have emerged during the writing of this book. I felt justified in spending some time reflecting on what I considered to be one possible interpretation of *An Allegory*. Central to the picture is the figure of a youth in some distress appealing to heaven for help.

The painting is divided horizontally across the canvas into three sections. Each is self-contained, but each blends into the next. The top section is a representation of the Nativity; the middle section depicts a boat with its crew in some distress at sea; the bottom section shows us a scene on land with quasi-apocalyptic associations.

The German text enclosed within the frame is written in traditional Gothic script. It also contains words not in current use. For a reliable translation I am indebted to the German Department of Manchester University. The translation reads as follows:

> Well, then, there was an honourable man in great difficulties and distress on the water known as [Lake] Garda. He was afraid he would lose both his life and worldly goods. And when he reached the land from the water, he was rendered powerless by the stradiots from the Venetian mercenaries who had been searching for enemies everywhere. So being in even greater terror, he in his great distress with great humility called to the mother of God and to the twelve brothers here in Nuremberg and mercifully was helped.

The German text was fortunately specific about two places with its references to 'Garda' and 'twelve brothers here in Nuremberg'. This helped me to get an initial understanding of the overall message of the painting.

Nuremberg was the home of Wenzel Jamnitzer, the goldsmith we looked at briefly in Chapter Six. A copy of his book on geometrical figures had accompanied the brass plates when they were transferred to the Science Museum in London. The book was published in 1568, the same year that Elizabeth I granted a charter for the wireworks at Tintern. Jamnitzer's technical expertise was precisely the skill brought from Nuremberg by the German engineers imported to make the wireworks a success. Interestingly, the illustration in the front displayed a cross mounted on a base that was reminiscent of the crosses on the 'Baldwin' double grave. Furthermore, the reference in the inscription beneath the painting to 'the twelve brothers' reminded me of a famous painting by Dürer, *The Adoration of The Trinity*. That painting, too, had once stood on the altar of a Nuremberg almshouse built for elderly guildsmen, another 'twelve brothers' house'. It depicts the Holy Roman Emperor wearing the 'crown of Charlemagne' among the earthly potentates worshipping the Holy

An Allegorical Painting

Trinity. All these echoes encouraged me to look at the allegorical painting more carefully.

The topmost section is clearly intended as a Nativity scene. In it the Virgin Mary has two pillows on which to rest her head. They are evenly and deliberately divided into a pattern of nine squares marked out in green. However, what struck me most forcibly in this section was the depiction of Joseph seated before the bottom of the bed. He is shown working with a skein of wool or cotton on a rectangular frame that appears to be a primitive winding device. It is not a conventional spinning wheel. But then, the man is not the conventional Joseph, whom one normally thinks of, and sees depicted, as a carpenter. In St. Matthew's Gospel, Chapter 13, Verse 55 the question is asked about Jesus, 'Is not this the carpenter's son? Is not his mother called Mary?' This unexpected representation of Joseph is intended to raise questions in our minds. Why show a carpenter winding thread? If we then look at the figure of the Virgin Mary, she is sitting up in bed, leaning forward. Has she been disturbed by some cry? If so, it does not come from the infant Christ, who lies shining with sanctity by her side. She appears to be listening to the cries of the youth in the middle section of the painting, just below her bed.

Another important symbol we need to address is the boat itself, for it is the most revealing. Placed in the centre of the painting, it is drawn in such a simplified manner as to make us doubt its seaworthiness. The forecastle simply provides a platform for the youth to stand on. There is no wheel or tiller to steer this ship. Its fittings have been reduced to a minimum: a square sail, a mast, and a few oars. It is meant simply to represent the *idea* of a boat. At the same time, however, its shape clearly resembles something else, something hinted at immediately above it in the allegory – a weaver's shuttle. As far back as the thirteenth century, in the *Zeno Narrative* the author writes, 'The fishermen's boats are made like a weaver's shuttle.'[2] A traditional weaver's shuttle was an oblong weaving implement curving inwards to a point at each end, on which the weft thread was shot across between the warp threads. In the painting, Joseph sits with his winding frame directly above the boat. The proximity of the two images is deliberate. What is the significance of a shuttle in this allegory?

One Baconian author, Edward Johnson, claims that Bacon inserted 'a sixth line word cipher' in the First Folio of Shakespeare's plays and that the key word is 'shuttle' associated with the word 'tat'. He states that 'shuttle' occurs only once in the plays and defines a shuttle as

> an oval *boat shaped* piece containing a reel or bobbin of thread shot to and fro in a loom. To tat means to weave on a loom and this is the principle of the word cipher as we have to go backwards and forwards to get certain

words which are to be joined together like threads in a loom to give sentences.[3] [Emphasis added]

Dodd and Johnson were friends. Johnson helped Dodd with the proofs of his life of Bacon, and Dodd dedicated the book to him.

Although Johnson does not mention in which play the word is used, 'shuttle' does occur in *The Merry Wives of Windsor*. In Act V, Scene I, Falstaff proclaims:

> for in the shape of man, Master Brook, I fear not Goliath with a weaver's beam, because I know also life is a shuttle.

Textual editors tell us that here Falstaff has combined two separate quotations from the Bible. The first comes from Samuel Book 1, Chapter 17, Verse 7:

> The shaft of his [Goliath's] spear was like a weaver's beam.

The second quotation is from The Book of Job, Chapter 7, verse 6:

> My days are swifter than a weaver's shuttle.

The two biblical references are combined deliberately to allow Falstaff to show off his knowledge of the Bible. *The Merry Wives of Windsor* was first published in 1602.

The context of these references is worth looking at. The first passage from Samuel Book 1, Chapter 17 is:

> And the staff of his spear was like a weaver's beam; and his spear's head weighed six hundred shekels of iron: and one bearing a shield went before him.

After this intimidating report of Goliath, at Verse 38, the prophet states:

> Saul armed David with his armour and he put an helmet of brass upon his head.

When David has slain Goliath, the chapter ends with Saul asking in astonishment:

> Whose son art thou, thou young man? And David answered I am the son of thy servant Jesse the Bethlehemite.

The second passage from the Book of Job, Chapter 7, deserves quoting at some length. Verses 6-12 read as follows:

> My days are swifter than a weaver's shuttle,
> And are spent without hope.
> O remember that my life is wind:
> Mine eye shall no more see good.
> The eye of him that hath seen me shall see me no more:

> Thine eyes are upon me, and I am not.
> As the cloud is consumed and vanisheth away:
> So he that goeth down to the grave shall come up no more.
> He shall return no more to his house,
> Neither shall his place know him any more.
> Therefore I will not refrain my mouth;
> I will speak in the anguish of my spirit;
> I will complain in the bitterness of my soul.
> Am I a sea, or a whale
> That thou settest a watch over me?

Saul's astonished question to David, 'Whose son art thou?' and Job's cry of despair to God, 'Thine eyes are upon me and I am not' have a relevance to the inner dilemma of a Francis Bacon who was, according to several scholars, born of an absolute monarch and rejected by her. Similarly, both the references misused by Falstaff can be seen as an oblique reference to Bacon's condition portrayed visually in the allegory of the painting.

'Life', says Falstaff, 'is a shuttle.' In the Nativity scene of the *Allegory* painting Joseph appears to be engaged in an early form of spinning by hand with the thread winding onto a square-framed wheel. This image is suggestive of a mixture of Fortune and Fate. In Greek and Roman mythology, 'Fortuna' was the goddess of *good* luck, but was represented with different attributes: with a ball she symbolised the uncertainties of Fortune. Joseph in the painting is depicted holding a ball of thread in his left hand. 'Fate' for both Greek and Roman was represented by three goddesses, each with her allotted role. 'Clotho' was represented with a spindle of thread – the thread of each mortal's life; 'Lachesis' was the goddess who assigned man his fate; 'Atropos' represented the fate that could not be avoided. Here the painter appears to combine something of both 'Fortuna' and 'Clotho' into the single male figure of Joseph. A carpenter by tradition, he is shown engaged in a totally unfamiliar activity – spinning – and symbolically spinning the destiny of the central figure of the allegory. What does the rest of the painting tell us of that destiny?

When I looked at the bottom section, I noticed that the colours of the horses echoed the colours of the four horses of the Apocalypse, white, red, black and dun (Revelation, Chapter 6, Verses 2–8). The horsemen appeared to be riding away from the woman dressed in black, kneeling in supplication on the left. In addition, the four riders were wearing a distinctive type of hat, although the horseman dressed in green wears a different one from the others, and this sets him slightly apart from the rest. Moreover, this difference is emphasised by the manner in which the riders hold their pennants. Unlike the others, the man in green carries his flag over his shoulder.

It is noticeable, too, that the colours of his flag repeat the colours of Joseph's garments. In the same way, the green of his clothes is repeated in the green of the tunic of the youth at the helm of the boat with arms outstretched. This use of colour enables the artist to bind figures in the different scenes together. That this is deliberate can be seen by the repetition of green in the stole or scarf draped at the foot of the bed in the Nativity scene. The scarf itself is superfluous except as a unifying feature in the overall colour scheme. It links the youth on the ship and the rider to the mother figure, represented by the Virgin Mary. Likewise, the colours of the flag he carries link the same rider to the father figure, Joseph.

Green is the colour associated with rebirth and regeneration. The figures of the Green Men, gobbling and disgorging oak and vine leaves carved on Chartres Cathedral or Rosslyn Chapel are examples of this symbolism. Moreover, green is the colour traditionally associated with the House of Tudor. It was the colour of the livery worn by their household staff. It is no accident that the green in the Nativity Scene of *An Allegory* is found in the stole in which the infant Christ is destined to be wrapped. The implied use of the stole emphasises the importance of green throughout the painting. It leads the spectator to focus on the youth standing on the forecastle of the square-rigged ship.

He has a dominant position in the eye of the storm. His arms are stretched towards the heavens, which in the painting blend into the Nativity scene, the blue floor of which suggests the sky above the clouds. Although the youth wears a green tunic, his pink hat matches the colour of the garments of the figure whose arms are outstretched on the right. Colour links the two together, but this time more slightly by the suggestion of pink in the hat. There is a much more noticeable link between the figure in pink and the cover on the bed of the Virgin Mary above.

I turned next to the third figure on the boat, a woman wearing a cream or white bonnet. She is in a cowed position in the boat, either kneeling or sitting, and protecting her head from what is going on around her.

The final section takes the allegory forward in time. The scene is a shoreline where there are no signs of the preceding storm. The female here is dressed in mourning, and the horsemen are riding at a stately pace. Although the colours of their steeds recall the horses in the apocalyptic vision of St. John the Divine, these riders are not bringing death and destruction to the world. They are riding off to the right, into the East with its traditional associations of dawn and a new beginning. But the woman is a widow, and her heels in the hem of her garment obscure part of a coat of arms.

This is a strange detail but a deliberate one. Like so much else in the picture it raises a host of questions. Whose coat of arms is it? Is it real or symbolic? Why is part of it hidden? Why is it there at all? Let us start by considering its position. It is placed in the bottom left-hand corner, behind the back of the woman. That must mean something. We must assume they are the arms of the man caught up in the storm. They could therefore have been displayed fully, in accordance with custom, on the front of the ship's forecastle and thus drawn attention to the dignity of the endangered youth. But the arms have been almost pushed to one side.

If we see the right side of the painting as leading to the East, then the left leads us to the West, the setting sun, the dying day. Fittingly this is where the woman in widow's weeds kneels. With her back towards the coat of arms and part of the shield obscured, the gravity of the heraldry is diminished. The real importance lies in the direction she faces – towards the East with the birth of a new day which the men ride out to greet. Perhaps the artist is saying that the past is less important than the future, that pedigree however impressive, is not as important as a man's own achievement here and now.

What then was the meaning behind the allegory? Could it possibly be intended as a hidden commemoration of Francis Bacon? The painter I think most likely to be responsible for *An Allegory*, Joachim von Sandrart, was in England in 1627, the year after Bacon's 'death'. Queen Elizabeth had been dead some fourteen years. Artists were often employed as agents by their aristocratic patrons and in that role inevitably became their confidants. Sandrart's patron was the rich and influential Earl of Arundel. It is possible that he heard either from Arundel himself or someone in his circle rumours about the supposed royal birth of Bacon. Could Sandrart be using the allegorical form to retell that story?

Readers can see for themselves how the colour scheme links related personalities in the picture. The colours are a key. I think the man in green represents Francis Bacon and all the green features in the painting are associated with him. If we accept that and look at the bottom section first, then the man in green riding off to the East with the flag at rest over his shoulder is also Bacon, distinguished by a different shaped hat. He is the leader of the group. He is the person directing what is happening; just as he is the main person in the storm at sea, the person at the centre of the storm.

The widow-like figure in black would then be his wife, Alice Barnham. Alice became a 'widow' in 1626 although Bacon did not 'die' but disappeared into obscurity to start a new life. Eleven days after Bacon's 'death', Alice remarried, this time a member of her household, a gentleman usher, Sir John Underhill. She is depicted in the bottom section of the painting, seeing Bacon ride off. She must have been aware of what Bacon had planned, for she remarried with extraordinary haste. She and Bacon had no children. Bacon departs accompanied by his three closest supporters. The horseman in the foreground is, I believe, William Herbert, the fourth Earl of Worcester, at that time living at Raglan Castle, now elderly but still loyal to Bacon until his own death in 1628. The finest rider and jouster of his day, Worcester could here be riding into the lists once more with his lance-like pennant. The green of the flag allies him with Bacon. The red markings on the horse's bridle stand out against the white flank and the two colours together suggest the red cross of the Templars. Worcester was a loyal Catholic and had the Catholic's instinctive support for the original Templar ideals of chivalry, compassion and protection of the faithful. Red and white were colours associated with the Earls of Worcester. In adding a handsome forecourt to Raglan Castle the fourth Earl planned two new entrances: the White Gate and the Red Gate. (His castle at Chepstow was the site of Dr. Owen's investigations.)

In the allegorical painting, the rider dressed in white, reminiscent of a surplice and suggestive of spiritual purity, may well be Bacon's personal chaplain, William Rawley. The third rider is possibly Thomas Meautys, his private secretary and the eventual owner of Bacon's estate at Gorhambury. Rawley and Meautys were two of Bacon's most faithful friends and had continued to serve him after his fall from grace.

With the storm scene we come to the time when Bacon, a youth of sixteen, was packed off to France as a member of the household of Sir Amias Paulet, the Queen's new Ambassador to the King of France. The tempest can be seen to depict the fate of a youth fending for himself amidst the storms of life. On board the square-rigged ship there are three figures. The man in green on the forecastle is again Francis Bacon, but this time as a youth. The figure in pink standing with arms raised looks like a maternal figure. The clothes match the colour of the Virgin's bed cover in the scene above. Is this a hint that the prayers will be heard while the bonneted woman in the boat cringes in fear? Certainly, in the topmost section, the Virgin Mary sits up in bed as if stirred by the cries below.

If the reader feels overwhelmed by the wealth of meaning here, we should remember that we are in fact looking at three paintings, not one – a triptych vertically arranged, instead of side by side, but still inter-related. This is my own personal interpretation of the painting, based on the subject matter alone, but, I feel, a valid one.

What Dodd and Johnson say in words, *An Allegory* states visually. Moreover, when I finally read Johnson's demonstration of the sixth line word cipher, it was like reading a series of messages that echoed uncannily certain aspects of the story I have told in this book.

The German National Museum in Nuremberg possesses another version of the painting entitled *Votive Picture of Stephen I. Praun*. The artist is unknown but the problems of attribution are addressed in the *Catalogue of the 16th Century Paintings in the GNM* (1997). The reader will find a different account of the painting in that catalogue. At one time the Praun family in Nuremberg did possess a copy of the *Votive Picture*, but that disappeared some time after 1878. The version I know as *An Allegory* does differ in certain details from the one in the German National Museum and was part of the estate of a Spanish painter, Miguel Canals. For example, in the German version the hair of the white-hatted horseman has ringlets that are absent from *An Allegory*. Canals was based in Barcelona at the time of his death in 2001. Strenuous efforts with the help of Spanish cultural authorities to learn any more about its provenance have, alas, proved fruitless. Which of the two paintings came first, I cannot say, but the two paintings exist and a more technical examination by art historians could provide the answer.

Postscript

A story persists about a marriage between Elizabeth I and Robert Dudley, Earl of Leicester.[4]

> When Queen Victoria was staying at Wilton House, the Earl of Pembroke told her that in the muniment room was a document which formed written evidence that in 1560 Elizabeth I married the Earl of Leicester. The marriage was performed in secret under an oath of absolute secrecy. At the time of that marriage the Queen was pregnant by Lord Leicester. The French and Spanish Ambassadors reported this and the death of Amy Robsart to their courts. They also told the Queen that if this was confirmed by her marriage to Leicester, France and Spain would jointly invade England, to remove the Protestant Queen and replace her by a Catholic monarch.
>
> Queen Victoria demanded that this document should be produced, and, after she had examined it, she put it on the fire, saying 'one must not interfere with history'.
>
> This information was given to me by the 15th Earl of Pembroke, the grandfather of the present Earl.
>
> Andrew Lyell.

CODA TWO

The Funerals of Lady Russell and J.L. Baldwin

Lady Francis Russell

The complete account – extracted from microfiche.

The *Chepstow Weekly Advertiser*, Saturday, 11 February 1888:

February 2nd, at 19, Marine Parade, Dover, Kent
Elizabeth, Lady Francis Russell, wife of John Loraine Baldwin.

Saturday, 18 February 1888:

The late Lady Francis Russell.

The funeral obsequies of the above lamented lady wife of Mr. J. Loraine Baldwin, the custodian of Tintern Abbey, whose death at Dover, on the 2nd inst, was briefly recorded last week, took place on Thursday, the 9th, at the parish church of Tintern Parva, amidst every manifestation of respect and esteem on the part of all classes in the district; whilst as regarded the inhabitants of the villages of Chapel Hill, in which parish her ladyship had resided for many years, and Tintern, the expressions of regret at the loss of a tried friend and kindly benefactress were genuine and heartfelt. The deceased lady was the only surviving daughter of the late Rev. Sir Algernon Peyton, and sister of the present baronet, who is himself seriously ill. She married, first, Captain Lord Francis Russell, R.N., son of John 6th Duke of Bedford, and was left a widow in 1869. She married, secondly, in 1873, Mr John Loraine Baldwin, and resided certain portions of each year with him at his charming bijou residence at St Ann's, Chapel Hill, in which neighbourhood, by her numerous good works, and kind and gracious sympathy with all around her, she was greatly loved and esteemed. The body, which was enclosed in a shell in a massive brass mounted coffin of best polished oak, arrived at Chepstow from Dover by the 2.47 pm train, accompanied by two or three immediate relatives, with their attendants, and was there transferred to a hearse, provided by Mrs Garratt, of the Beaufort Arms Hotel, for conveyance by road to Tintern, whither it was attended by her husband Mr J. L. Baldwin, General Peyton (brother), General Wynn, and some members of the household. Upon arriving at St Ann's the cortege was met by the workmen in the employ of Mr Baldwin and the domestics of the establishment, and amongst the large number of gentry and others who were present with carriages or otherwise to testify their esteem for the deceased were noticed:

Henry Clay Esq, Piercefield Park;
Mrs. Lewis, St Pierre;
Rev. Fielding Palmer, Eastcliff;
Rev. W. H. Whiteley, St Lawrence;
H. Lowe Esq., Shirenewton Hall;
W.E.C. Curre, Esq., Itton Court;
A. Gallenga, Esq., and Mrs. Gallenga, The Falls, Llandogo;
Rev. ——————— Rees, Llandogo;
Dr. A.G. Lawrence, The Cedars, Chepstow;
C.W. Loftus Digby, Esq. Chepstow;
W. Verrinder, Esq., Troy House, Monmouth;
J.R. Griffiths Esq., Chapel Hill;
Mr. J. Woolley, Chapel Hill;
Mr. T Howell, Tintern; and others,

whilst at the gates of the churchyard there was a large assembly of residents of Chapel Hill and Tintern and the vicinity. The service, which was simply rendered, was performed by the Rev. W.E. Rosedale, vicar of Tintern and at its conclusion at the church the 'Dead March' (in Saul) was played by Mrs Rosedale. Wreaths, crosses, and other floral tributes, of most magnificent and the choicest of flowers were in such profusion from friends far and near that not only the coffin but the grave, a large square one bricked and cemented, were covered completely, as also was the grass for some distance surrounding it. Amongst the names of some we were enabled to gather were:

1. Lady Forrester,
2. Lady De Clifford,
3. General Peyton,
4. General Wynn,
5. The Dames of the Dover Habitation of the Primrose League, of which the deceased was Dame President, a beautiful wreath of Primroses

6. The Knights of the Dover Habitation (a wreath of primroses and violets),
7. Mrs. Lewis, St Pierre,
8. Mr. Clay, Piercefield,
9. Dr. and Mrs. Lawrence, Chepstow,
10. Mr. Verrinder, Monmouth,
11. Mr. and Mrs. Rosedale,
12. Mr. and Mrs. Digby,
13. Mr. and Mrs. Gallenga,
14. Mr. J. Woolley,
15. Mr. T. Davis, Glyn,

and a very large number of others from personal friends in addition to those from employees and other residents and cottagers of the two parishes by whom the deceased was so much loved and respected. The arrangements of the funeral were entrusted to Mr. Flashman, undertaker of Dover, and were carried out in a satisfactory manner.

As stated above, the deceased lady was Dame President of the Dover Habitation of the Primrose League and in making reference to the melancholy event, the Dover Telegraph of Wednesday, in last week contained an epitaph and the following lines :-

Life claims no greater fealty from the heart –
No simpler duty from the human mind –
Than that which prompts us each to our part
To make the World seem fairer to mankind.
Our own Primroses bright such lessons bring,
That bloom where the snow-flake lies;
Telling sweet stories of the coming Spring,
And how before the sunshine sorrow flies
In words that glow like stars down-dropt from far off skies.

Her life gave out its light as fragrance goes
From blush warm roses upwards towards the sky,
That fringe with odourous heart-love human woes,
Till having spent their fragrant force – they die.
The angry blast may tell its wintry tale,
And strive in wrath life's wrongs to sweep away;
But kindlier comes the language of the vale.
That breathes of hope and brings a brighter day,
Victor by love and deeds in life's tournay.

John Loraine Baldwin

The complete account – extracted from microfiche.

The *Chepstow Weekly Advertiser* Saturday, 5 December 1896:

Funeral of Mr. J.L. Baldwin of Tintern

The funeral obsequies of the late Mr. John Loraine Baldwin of St Ann's Tintern and 19, Marine Parade Dover, whose death we briefly announced in our last issue, took place at Tintern Parva Churchyard on Tuesday afternoon last, when not withstanding the inclemency of the weather a large number of relatives, friends and acquaintances assembled to pay their last token of respect to the deceased gentleman. Rain commenced just previously to the cortege starting from the house to the church, and fell heavily during the whole of the ceremony. The procession was headed by local police, then followed the hearse containing the coffin, which was literally hidden from view by the magnificent wreaths lying around it, and immediately behind the hearse walked the deceased's valet, who had during a lengthy servitude become greatly attached to his master. In the rear came a long line of mourning coaches, then members of the Trellech Llandogo and Tintern Friendly Societies, with which the deceased had associated himself from time to time, and following these additional empty carriages sent by sorrowing friends. In the various coaches were the following ladies and gentleman:

1st Coach	Miss A. Harcourt, Miss Daniell, General F. Peyton, and Mr. C.F. Millet, (Westminster).
2nd Coach	Mr. and Mrs. C.E. Lewis, Mr. Russell J. Kerr, and Mr. R. Palmer Jenkins.
3rd Coach	Mr. A.F.M. Spalding, Mr. Charles Carlos Clarke, Capt. Hamilton and Mr. Cowper Coles.
4th Coach	Col. J. Davis (Monmouth), Dr. Graham Kay, Dr. A.G. Lawrence, Mr. F. Bircham.
5th Coach	Mrs. J.R. Griffiths and Dr. Gwynne Lawrence.
6th Coach	Mr. H.L.P. Lowe.
7th Coach	The Servants of St. Ann's.
8th Coach	Rev. J.H. and Mrs. Whiteley.
9th Coach	Empty – from Mrs. Gallenga. The Falls, Llandogo.

The chief mourners were General Peyton (brother-in-law), Miss Daniell (niece), Miss Harcourt (cousin) and Mr C.F. Millett (cousin). Amongst

those who were present at the graveside were the Marquis of Worcester, Lord Edward Somerset, the Earl of Cork and Orrery, Col. Edward Curre, Mr. Henry Clay, Mr. H. Hastings Clay, Miss Clay, Rev. Watkin Davies, Messers G.C. Francis, J.W. Stanton, C.W.L. Digby, Arthur Price and others. The officiating clergy were the Revs. H.B. Hennell (Vicar of Tintern),
N. Shafto Barthropp R.D. (Itton Rectory)
L.H. Rees (Llandogo)
E.J. Hensley (Vicar of Chepstow)
W.E. Rosedale (Willenhall, Staffordshire)
Armstrong Willis (Monmouth)
J. Tilley (St. Arvan's)
and J. Stansfield (Whitebrook).

On entering the church, which had been prettily decorated with white chrysanthemums and evergreens, and was soon crowded in every part, the opening sentences were read by the Rev. H.B. Hennell, the 90th Psalm chanted, and the lesson for the occasion (1 Corinth. XV.20) read by the Rev. Armstrong Willis, after which Hymn 499 was sung by the surpliced choir, assisted by Mr. E. Palmer on the cornet and Miss Finch on the organ. On arrival at the graveside the concluding portion of the burial service was impressively read by the Rev. W.E. Rosedale, late of Tintern who had been on intimate terms with the deceased. The other hymn, ('Peace Perfect Peace') was to have been given over the grave, but the rain was by this time descending in such torrents that it had to be abandoned. The brick vault built for the reception of the remains was tastily lined with white chrysanthamums, moss and evergreens. The site of the grave was adjacent to that of the deceased gentleman's late consort, the Lady Francis Russell, who died 8 years ago; her tomb bears the following inscription:

> 'In loving memory of Lady Francis Russell, wife of J. Loraine Baldwin, 19 Marine Parade, Dover, in her 67th year on the 2nd February, 1888'

The remains were enclosed in two shells, the outer coffin being of dark polished oak with handsome brass mounts, the breastplate bearing the following inscription:

> 'John Loraine Baldwin, born 1 June 1809 died November 25th 1896 in his 88th year.'

The wreaths, some of which were magnificent, were sent from the following:

1. 'In memory, from his sincere and attached old friend George.' (H.R.H. Duke of Cambridge).

2. 'Londesborough and Edith Londesborough, in memory of many years.' (Earl and Countess Londesborough).
3. An I Zingari wreath 'For my dear old friend, S. Ponsonby Fane.' (The Hon Sir Spencer Ponsonby Fane).
4. A white wreath with I Zingari belt, 'In affectionate remembrance of a fine old English Gentleman, from his sorrowing friend, Augustus F.M. Spalding.'
5. 'In affectionate remembrance of many years from the Duke and Duchess of Beaufort and Marquis of Worcester.'
6. Lord and Lady E. Somerset 'In affectionate Remembrance.'
7. 'In Loving Memory of my oldest friend, B. Waterford' (Marchioness of Waterford).

Baldwin flowers cont.
Miss Daniell
Mrs. and Miss Harcourt
General and Mrs. Peyton
Sir Algernon and Lady Peyton
Nurse and Employees in and out of doors
The former servants of the family
Lady Duckworth
Countess Grosvenor
The Countess of Guildford
The Honourable Mrs. Yorke
Earl of Cork and Orrery
Baron and Baroness Deichmann
Lord and Lady Llangattock (The Hendre and the Hon Miss Rolls)
The Hon. Mr. and Mrs. Laurence Brodrick
The Hon. Mr. and Mrs. Chandos Leigh and Miss Violet Leigh
The Hon. C. and K. Somerset
Colonel Bayley
Colonel and Mrs. Howard Kingscote.
Major and Mrs. Ligonier Balfour
Captain C. Champney Powell
Captain Hamilton
Captain Lambert
Captain and Lady Cecelia Webbe
Captain and Mrs. Walter Marling
Mrs. Napier Sturt and Miss Violet Astley Sparke
Dean of Hereford
Rev. H.B. Hennell
Rev. and Mrs. Fielding Palmer

Rev. and Mrs. L.A. Rees
Rev. J. H. and Mrs. Whiteley
The Misses Bevan
Mrs. and Miss Millett
Mr. C.F. Millett
Dr. Sutton
Dr. England
Dr. A.G. Lawrence and Family
Dr. Graham Kay
Mr. and Mrs. John Browning
Mr. and Mrs. Layton Lowndes
Mr. and Mrs. G. Seys
Mrs. Henry Brenchley
Mrs. Emily Wombwell
Miss Ramsbottom
Mrs. J.R. Griffiths
Mrs. Mark Wood
Mrs. E. Longworth Lister
Mr. and Mrs. Charles Carlos Clarke
Mr. and Mrs. Hastings Clay
Mr. and Mrs. J.W. Stanton
Mr. and Mrs. Palmer Jenkins
Mr. and Mrs. F.T. Bircham and Miss Bircham
Mr. Henry and Miss Clay
Mr. H.L.P. Lowe
Mr. J. Woolley
Mr. and Mrs. H. Hurd
Mr. J. and the Misses Pillinger
Mr. and Mrs. C. Hoggett
Mrs. W.E. Clark and family
Mrs. F. Garrett and family
The Cricket Club Chepstow
The Cottagers and Inhabitants of Tintern and Chapel Hill.

The funeral arrangements were admirably carried out by Messrs. Flashman and Co. of Dover (undertakers to Her Majesty), under the personal superintendence of Mr. J. Relf; the coffin and shell were supplied by Mr. J. Johnson, Wyecliffe House Chepstow; and the open car and four mourning coaches were from the Messrs. Tovey Bros., Newport, the remaining being supplied by the Beaufort Hotel Company, Chepstow.

Biographical Sketch

The late Mr. John Loraine Baldwin was the only son of the late Lieut. Colonel John Baldwin, of Elton and Dover and was born near Halifax, Yorkshire, on June 1st 1809, and was therefore in his 88th year at the time of his death, previously to which he had undergone a long period of illness at St. Ann's, having been gradually breaking up during his last six months residence at Tintern. He was educated at Westminster and Christ Church Oxford and in 1873 at St. Paul's, Kinghtsbridge, entered the bonds of matrimony with the widow of the late Lord Francis Russell, who was a sister to the late Sir Thomas Peyton, Bart., and whom the deceased gentleman outlived by 8 years. For the last 23 years he was warden at Tintern Abbey.

Mr. Baldwin was in his younger days a well-known figure in Society, and was an acknowledged authority in regard to Club matters. He will be specially remembered for his connection with the founding of the I Zingari Club. In July, 1845, Mr. J.L. Baldwin gave a supper at the Blenheim Hotel to the Hon Frederick Ponsonby afterwards the Earl of Bessborough, General Sir Henry De Bathe, the Hon. Sir Spencer Ponsonby Fane (better known by his old name of Mr. Spencer Ponsonby) and others active in the cricket and theatrical doings of the Canterbury Week, when the idea suddenly occurred to the party to found a Cricket Club for the promotion of the game, and they then and there dubbed themselves I Zingari – the Gypsies – to show that they were to have neither Club-House nor Ground, and Mr. Baldwin, with the assistance of friends, drew up the rules and regulations. Mr W.P. Bolland was appointed perpetual president, and Mr. Baldwin the annual vice-president, a post he held up to the time of his death while the Hon. R. Grimston was the original treasurer. The rules were of a humorous, quasi-businesslike character and the mode of election of members was of an appropriate but distinctly original nature. The candidate was to be placed at a wicket, with or without a bat, as the captain might decide, and be bowled at by the A.V.P. or by any one member of the I.Z. so deputed by the A.V.P. one straight ball to exclude. The number of balls given not to exceed the number of members comprising I.Z. The stern rule of the Club was to the effect that no member should upon any occasion play as an opponent of I.Z. Among the caricatures which are archives of the Club is one showing Mr. J.L. Baldwin at short slip. The club badge of black, red and gold (those of United Germany by the way) which might also be worn by the wives, daughters and sisters of I.Z. bore the following inscription:

> 'All the men and women players keep your promise, keep your temper, keep your wicket up.'

The first match played by the Club was at Newport Pagnall, on August 25th and 26th 1845, when the papers described them as a new and rising club. They were faced by a strong team and did well in the first Innings, scoring 113 to their opponents' 199, but in the 2nd Innings the state of the Score was reversed, Newport Pagnall putting together 139 runs, while I.Z. could only make 96, and thus lost the match by 39 runs. Mr Tom Taylor, then a young barrister and afterwards Editor of Punch, was appointed Liberal Legal Advisor of the Club, which office is now held by Sir J. Chitty and Sir A.L. Smith – 2 judges as famous in Athletics as in the legal world.

Amongst the latter-day members are the names of the Prince of Wales, Duke of Cobourg, Prince Christian and his two sons, Prince Christian Vidor and Prince Albert of Schleswig-Holstein. The present secretary of the club is stated to be A. Secret. In June of last year I.Z. celebrated its Jubilee in a fitting manner at Lords when Mr. Baldwin presented to each member of the Jubilee team a copy of the records of their rigidly amateur society.

No one who was present at the Canterbury Cricket Week 20 or 30 years since is likely to have forgotten the very prominent part taken by Mr. John Baldwin in the matches by day and theatricals by night, which are always looked forward to with eager expectation, when the London season has just drawn to a close. He was the senior member of the 'Old Stagers' when he breathed his last, and on all matters affecting Club laws and Club articles of association at the West End he was an acknowledged, if not paramount, authority.

As an authority in framing and expounding the laws of short whist, écarté, bezique, and other card games Mr Baldwin was in this country unexcelled and among his intimates was known by the title 'King of Clubs'. Some years ago he wrote and published 'The Laws of Short Whist'.

Another famous society in the formation of which the deceased gentleman played an important part is the Senior Driving or Four-in-Hand Club, progenitor of the Junior or Coaching Club, of both of which the Duke of Beaufort we believe, President. Mr. Baldwin was elected Honorary Secretary to the Four-in-Hand on its formation in 1856. Two years later he started the Musical Club, which had amongst its members many persons of authority in such matters. This club was by some wits at once dubbed the 'Pig and Whistle' and Mr. Baldwin possessed amongst his treasures a sculptured pig with a silver whistle suspended from its neck presented to him by a satirical lady.

In the reorganization of the new Turf Club in Piccadilly out of the disintegrated materials of the old Arlington Club, Mr. John Baldwin played a very prominent part.

There is, therefore, little occasion for surprise that he was honoured by

The Funerals of Lady Russell and J.L. Baldwin

the friendship of the Prince of Wales and the Duke of Cambridge, or that on the official visits of the latter as Commander in Chief to Dover, – the permanent home of Mr. Baldwin – his Royal Highness never failed to make a complimentary call upon his old acquaintance. At Badminton Mr. Baldwin was ever a welcome guest. Like the late Captain Batchelor, no habituée of Clubland was at one time more widely known and more popular than Mr. John Loraine Baldwin. And among those who, although not members of that Club, are well entitled to call themselves 'Old Stagers' sincere regret will be expressed that, at a ripe old age, their former friend and merry companion has at last paid the debt of nature.

Mr. Baldwin's private life at St. Ann's was marked by a geniality and benevolence of nature that is as rare as it is welcome, and few if any who asked but were responded to in a generous spirit by the deceased. By his demise the poorer inhabitants of Tintern have lost a sincere friend, and the whole neighbourhood a respected resident.

CODA THREE

Some Reflections

WHEN THE FOUNDATION stone of the new Silurian Masonic Lodge was laid in Newport on 29 August 1855, the Lodge members proceeded ceremonially through the streets to St. Paul's church and afterwards to the Town Hall. The proceedings began in the open air before a large crowd with these words:

> Men, women and children here assembled today to behold this ceremony, – Know all of you that we be lawful Masons, true to the laws of our Country and established of old with peace and honour in most countries, to do good to our Brethren, to build great Buildings and to Fear God Who is the great Architect of all things. We have among us, concealed from the eyes of all men, secrets which may not be revealed, and which no man has discovered, but these secrets are lawful and honourable to know by Masons who only have the keeping of them to the end of time.[1]

Many of those listening on that occasion would not have been Freemasons, and one wonders whether some might not have felt intimidated by the main thrust of that statement. Freemasonry claims that it is not a secret society. But clearly, at that time, it was a society with secrets. And those secrets were solely for those within the brotherhood. I, therefore, would not have been eligible to know what those secrets could be on that day in August 1855.

The occasion was just a few weeks after the entry 'Noah's Ark' in Jenny Audland's diary for 12 March 1855. As recorded in Chapter Seven, Noah, according to Masonic legend, discovered 'the stone of foundation' and placed it in the Ark as an altar. My interpretation of Jenny's enigmatic brevity is that she is recording a meeting at Nurtons on that day for members of this exclusive brotherhood. (Jenny was the wife of John Audland, a general practitioner in Tintern.) By 1855 plans were already under way to build a new Masonic Hall in Newport:

> The plans [for the new lodge] were submitted in February, £870 had been collected by March, and by June the P.G.M. [Provincial Grand Master, Charles John Kemys-Tynte] had agreed to attend the Dedication ceremony of the stone laying.[2]

There may have been good reasons for the March meeting to be held at Nurtons. The Silurian Lodge replaced an earlier lodge in Newport called The Royal Cambrian Lodge. This lodge had been licensed by an 'Atholl warrant' in 1809, so called after the Duke of Atholl. Jenny Audland was a kinswoman of the Duke through her father's second marriage. Furthermore family members with connections to the Atholl line were at this time living at Nurtons. Reason enough for the house to be used for such a meeting. Jenny would be fully aware of these dynastic connections and their Masonic associations. The two words 'Noah's Ark' evidently contained a world of meaning to her and needed no elaboration.

Sir Christopher Audland, a descendant of Jenny, has edited her diary and journals to write a biography of her, published in 2008. In it he comments:

> on 12 March there is a strange and completely unexplained phrase: 'Noah's Ark'. Perhaps its meaning will one day become clear.[3]

During my research I had, of necessity, already become familiar with the *Freemasons' Guide and Compendium* and the legends it contains about Noah, his family and the Ark. The entry had helped me in identifying Schweighardt's illustration of a hermetic college as Nurtons. Jenny's husband, Dr. John Audland, was the local GP at the time of Christopher Heath's death. He was also Medical Officer for the districts of Tintern, Chepstow, Trellech and Monmouth. Interestingly, John Edmonds Stock, who had until very recently been owner of Nurtons, had also been a doctor, practising in Bristol. We know how keen senior medical staff at Bristol Infirmary were to encourage colleagues to join Freemasonry. Was John Audland a member? If so, there is a possibility that by 1855 Jenny had been long enough in Tintern to be part of the connection between Nurtons and Freemasonry. Hence the brevity of her entry 'Noah's Ark'.

Number Symbolism

The First Number: '0'

Number symbolism is important to members of the Brotherhood as it was to other, earlier groups or societies who have close affiliations with them, such as the Knights Templar. It is a useful method for encoding information. Numbers transcend language barriers and have an international currency that enables connections to be made by one individual or group and recognised by another. I had come to understand this from working with the mathematics of the Byrom geometric drawings.

There are 33 degrees in the hierarchical structure of American Freemasonry, the 33rd having a particular significance. In writing about

The Hidden Chapter

'the symbolic mathematics of the ancient doctrine', David Wood states, 'One must ignore zero and the decimal point' and goes on to say about zero:

> Apparently of no value, but significantly it is the first number and thereby is the origin ... from which issues knowledge. As such it equates with Noe of Noah and the ark, argha or the womb.[4]

When I read this I thought of the page numbering in the *Freemasons' Guide and Compendium*. The chapter that deals with Noah and the Ark begins on page 303. According to Wood, 303 can equate symbolically with 33.

'72', '303' and '3'

I may not have paid any attention to this if a fellow author, who knew of my current research at St. Michael's Church and Tintern Parva, had not got in touch with me and suggested that I should look at Dan Brown's novel *The Da Vinci Code* and particularly Chapter 72.

This was in 2003. I had not read the book, but the number 72 has had a certain fascination for me ever since I first discovered it as a unit of measure regularly used in the Byrom collection of geometric drawings. I had written about its use and significance in several different disciplines in *Kingdom for a Stage*. So it was with some curiosity that I turned to Chapter 72 in the novel. A short chapter of three pages, in the edition I had it occupied pages 302 to 304 and concerns the deciphering of a short poem. On page 303 I read the words 'A headstone praised by Templars is the key'. This was soon followed by the chief sleuth talking about a headstone being used as a marker 'of some sort'.[5] I must not digress into the plot of the novel, I quote merely to give the context. But it was strange to see references to the Templars, a headstone and a grave marker all on page 303 of Chapter 72. My friend had been sufficiently surprised to draw my attention to it and I must confess I was myself somewhat intrigued by the coincidence. It was as if this character was talking about my own research which was still in preparation.

I became more intrigued when I checked the printer of the book. It was the same firm that had earlier printed my biography of John Byrom, *The Queen's Chameleon* in 1994. I had not forgotten a peculiar incident connected with the printing of that book. I had completed the final checking of the galley proofs and returned them direct to the publisher. Fortunately I had retained a complete photocopy of the galleys with all the corrections I had made for permanent record and reference.

The book then appeared in print. To my dismay a critical omission (obvious to any reader) was evident – and it was an omission not present in the galley proofs I had corrected. My photocopy showed that. Writing about the Jacobite uprising of 1745 and the entry of Prince Charles Edward Stuart into Manchester, I had been careful to specify that the Prince, accompanied by the Dukes of Atholl and Perth, entered on 28 September at '3 o'clock'. In the galley proof the 3 was there. In the published book it was not.

Clearly without the '3' the entry made little sense. At the time I felt this was not carelessness because the omission was not a question of a compositor *forgetting* that the number had been left out, but of someone *deliberately taking out something already correctly in place*. The '3' had been removed. For this reason I found it difficult to accept my editor's explanation that it was a 'printer's slip'. Yet why should anyone wish to tamper with my narrative in this way?[6]

The actual time of the Prince's entry was, I am sure, full of significance. Three o'clock in the afternoon carries solemn resonances of the 'third hour' of the crucifixion of Christ. It was a solemn moment, too, when the Stuart claimant to the throne entered Manchester accompanied by two senior members of the Scottish aristocracy. When he had first landed in Scotland, the Duke of Atholl had proclaimed the 'Young Pretender' rightful sovereign of these islands.

I might have dismissed the irritation caused by the missing 3 except for something that happened in 2001. This time another colleague sent me a copy of a book entitled *The Arcadian Cipher* by Peter Blake and Paul S. Blezard. This time it was the other number – the ubiquitous 72 – that made me sit up. The authors paid tribute to the importance of John Byrom's collection of geometric drawings and their discovery and what they said appeared as a single, substantial entry on page 72. Another coincidence no doubt and one that made me smile until I checked the printer of the book. It was the firm that had printed *The Queen's Chameleon* and *The Da Vinci Code*. The coincidences were beginning to pile up as in a novel by Thomas Hardy. Fanciful though it seemed, it was as if someone was playing a game with me.

The series of little oddities I have just described belongs to a different order from anything I thought might arise from my books. Normally one can expect letters or cards with comments and queries from interested readers. Indeed these are often a welcome feedback after the solitary months preparing the final manuscript. Such correspondence can lead to mutually profitable exchanges. *The Byrom Collection* was no exception and led to some stimulating letters from across the world. This was both rewarding and flattering until, one day, I received from my publisher, via my agent, something very bizarre.

The Hidden Chapter

Curious Correspondence

A batch of letters arrived, written in the form of verses so allusive and enigmatic they required considerable time and skill to decode. The process was not helped by the fact that the author chose to adopt a number of roles, with different pseudonyms to mask his identity. (I soon concluded they were written by a man.)

The first batch appeared shortly after the publication of *The Byrom Collection*. Others followed and then there was a gap. I replied briefly but courteously each time, persuaded that they were the work of an enthusiast with whom I had neither the time nor the inclination to get involved.

There followed a gap of five years, and then, in 1997, after the official opening of the reconstructed Globe in London by the Queen, I received the largest batch. The package came the same route from my publisher to my agent and on to me. I noticed the poems were carefully arranged. The same short verse was placed at the beginning and end, rather like bookends, enclosing a sequence of twenty poems. The opening and concluding verse states:

> Some things come and some things stay,
> & others must always pass
> These words were spoke by an Astrolabe, sung by a
> tongue of Brass.
> Those mighty seventy Scholars high in the tower of Babel,
> they had things firm, they knew each term, of a chorus
> Astrolable.

As before, the lines were signed with an obvious nom de plume and beneath that were two large illustrations of astrolabes.

I was intrigued by the reference to the 'mighty seventy Scholars' in the tower of Babel. Who might they be? But I was even more intrigued by the identity of the mysterious versifier. The poems centred around my interpretation of some of the geometric drawings which I claimed were concerned with the Elizabethan playhouses, and the way I had dealt with the problems that brought. Again the poems were heavily encoded and cleverly put together as a sequence. Unravelling their content was very exacting and time consuming. Indeed often the most subtle allusions only became clear years later. The constant need to reappraise some verses in the light of later events never ceased to amaze me.

It was this that convinced me that the writer was so close to the centre of power at the time that he felt unable to reveal his true identity but, understanding the dilemmas I had been faced with in my work, wished to offer explanations and advice.

I have learned so much more about the provenance and nature of the geometric drawings since *The Byrom Collection* was published that I felt compelled to consider some of the knowledge and advice displayed in those verses despite the secretive way in which they were conveyed. I have always preferred my research knowledge to be in the public domain for all to share and enjoy. Yet I sensed that for some reason or other in this instance that was not timely.

The hidden chapter was playing its part and 'Janus' (one of my correspondent's noms de plume) was ready to pronounce that in his opinion 'A Truth Lies standing' (*sic*). By then the newly opened Globe was proving to be commercially successful.

My earnest correspondent remained hidden behind the veil of pseudonyms and I have spent many sleepless nights blessing the silent rhetoric of his anonymity, but I salute his courage.

Encounter With an Airbrush

The search for the truths associated with the concepts behind the geometric drawings has continued. Number symbolism is part of that truth.

We must return for a moment to the site of the tomb of interest, 'tomb X', at St. Michael's in Tintern. The distance of 72 cubits (33 metres) between the tomb and a designated spot in the chancel is evidence of this. In Chapter Thirteen we saw how Jacob Cats's engraving of a churchyard (*Lampada Trado*) can be identified with St. Michael's, John Dee and Francis Bacon and how the writer Manly P. Hall linked the Cats engraving of a chancel (*Verita*) with Francis Bacon and the date of his 'death'. In examining the *Lampada Trado* engraving from *Orders of Universal Reformation* and comparing it with the illustration of the engraving I obtained from Glasgow University, the reader will note that the building clearly visible in the Glasgow copy is not to be seen in Manly Hall's copy, thus erasing a recognisable feature that can be identified with a specific place, in my opinion Tintern.

Manly Hall was a 33 Degree Mason, member of the American Scottish Rite Freemasonry Movement and an admirer of Francis Bacon's legacy. Who was responsible for removing such an important detail from the copy of the engraving he used?

A decision had to be made to airbrush the building out of the illustration. In this instance 'the truth' had been visually changed and the site depicted became unidentifiable. Why was it considered necessary or desirable to do such a thing in an American Philosophical treatise? The answer must lie with who or what is contained within the church

> *The* Hidden Chapter
>
> ORDERS OF UNIVERSAL REFORMATION 65
>
> the world endured, should the lamp of tradition, the light of truth be darkened or extinguished.*
>
> Bearing the problem of the *Traditio Lampadis, etc.* in mind, we turn to *Alle de Wercken,* by Jacob Cats, published
>
>
>
> —From *The Works of Jacob Cats* (Amsterdam, 1655)
> LAMPADO TRADO
>
> in Amsterdam, 1655. Jacob Cats, lovingly spoken of as "Father Cats," was a Dutch poet and humorist who wrote many emblem books, and was a gentleman farmer. While
>
> *See *Francis Bacon, and his Secret Society.*

49. Jacob Cats: *Lampada Trado*, 1655, Dee and Bacon, from Manly P. Hall's *Orders Of Universal Reformation*

boundaries. From an accurate version of the engraving, I had identified the possible site in Wales. What, apart from human remains, could be deemed so significant as to warrant such subterfuge?[7] Manly Hall died in 1990 so I was unable to obtain an answer from the author himself.

Tewdric's Grave Revisited

I firmly believe that the cave to which Tewdric retired 'among the rocks of Tintern' is to be found around the site of St. Michael's Church. His actual burial place is a few miles away in the chancel of Mathern Church.

The grave has been investigated twice, once in 1608 by Bishop Francis Godwin of Llandaff. A plaque in the church commemorates that occasion. The second time was in 1881 and the work was carried out by the rector, Rev. Watkin Davies and others including the Rev. Robert Vaughan Hughes, former patron of St. Michael's, Tintern Parva. The investigation took place under the supervision of the Llandaff diocesan architect, John Prichard. A number of alterations were being made to the church at the time, but I have seen no explanation as to why the grave was opened up again.

Bishop Godwin was a contemporary of Francis Bacon and shared some of his ideals. What persuaded him to open up Tewdric's resting place and repair it in the first place? Was it the spirit of intellectual enquiry that Bacon advocated? Godwin is a surprising figure for his time. His interest in history may fit with his episcopal status, but the book he wrote entitled *The Man in the Moone*, published in 1638 five years after his death, places him in a different category. A tale of a Spaniard carried to the moon by large swan-like birds, it is in effect the first science fiction adventure in the English language but with a Utopian vision. Godwin was a man of wide and deep learning. His interest and skill in mathematics reminds one of Dee, and the editor of a recent edition of the book suggests that the idea of using birds to achieve flight might have come from Bacon's *Sylva Sylvarum*, a collection of writings on a variety of topics, published in 1627.[8]

33 Degree Scottish Rite Freemasons

372 years have passed since then. Rapid advances in science and technology make it possible now to put a man on the moon. Bishop Godwin's fiction has become fact, and that is a humbling realisation.

Astronauts such as Neil Armstrong and Buzz Aldrin have risked life and limb to reach the Moon. So, too, did the late Leroy Gordon Cooper. His achievements and discoveries led Timothy Good to dedicate his book *Need to Know* (2006) to him. I was more than a little intrigued when I learned that Buzz Aldrin and the late Colonel Leroy Gordon Cooper were both 33 Degree Scottish Rite Freemasons. Others involved in the exploration of space were also 33 Degree Scottish Rite Freemasons. However, Masons or not, all involved have displayed courage beyond our comprehension.

Members of the Ancient and Accepted Scottish Rite of Freemasonry, Southern Jurisdiction, USA will be familiar with Albert Pike's collection of lectures on each of the 32 Degrees entitled *Morals and Dogma*. The Supreme Council of the Thirty-third Degree is the overall authoritative body of the organisation. The 18th Degree is called the 'Knight Rose Croix'. According to Pike, it is

> devoted to and symbolises the final triumph of truth over falsehood, of liberty over slavery, of light over darkness, of life over death, and of good over evil.

The values embodied in such an organisation are totally commendable. The published works of Manly P. Hall promote in principle the same teachings. This makes one all the more curious as to how he came to use an 'edited' version of the Cats engraving in the America publication *Orders of Universal Reformation*. Perhaps it is relevant that Manly P. Hall was another 33 Degree Mason of the same organisation.

The structure of the different groups and lodges in Freemasonry varies considerably and certainly there are different emphases between American and United Kingdom lodges. However in both countries there is a uniform aim and sense of fulfilment throughout Freemasonry in supporting charities and promoting good works. Yet it is still regarded by many today as 'a society with secrets'. Public pronouncements like the one made in Newport 155 years ago are largely responsible for this. However my own experience is somewhat different.

Throughout twenty years and more of research, I have been engaged in healthy discussions with the Rev. Neville Barker Cryer. A senior Freemason, he has been unfailingly courteous and helpful, as can be seen in this book. If there are secrets that he is not permitted to divulge, I have not been aware of them during our stimulating exchanges.

With time fashions change and I doubt if a statement like the proclamation at Newport would be made in quite the same way today.

The research recounted in this book is part of a programme of 'unfolding' that I began many years ago. The work has been carried out as simply as possible, a step at a time, although the discoveries have proved complex, and I have had to learn to be prepared for the unexpected. I have not been attached to any particular group of interests. I truly believe that Tintern and Tintern Parva is an area rich in a history and knowledge that we have 'lost'. As John Byrom said, 'martyrs are not still' and some of this knowledge is now re-emerging with new glimpses of the 'hidden chapter'.

Thomas of Bononia

This book is dedicated to Thomas of Bononia, Physician to Charles VIII, King of France 1483–1498, the godson of Prince Edward, only son of King Henry VI of England. I chose Thomas of Bononia because he reminds us that an historical figure lost in enigmatic obscurity can emerge to point a way to unexpected connections. At least that is what he has done for me.

King Charles VIII is said to have died suddenly after playing a game of tennis and knocking his head on a lintel in 1498.

Almost seventy years later another tennis game took place that is described in an illustration by Mr. Rose in the Schweighardt Scrapbook, entitled *The Whole Workes Emblem*.[9] This is an original drawing of a coat of arms set within verses which depict a royal couple with two offspring. The verses contain references to 'ye brotherhood' and the 'first chapter'. The writer of them appears to be using the historical Thomas of Bononia (or Bologna) as a pseudonym to draw parallels between the two games of tennis.

>...
> he is extolled, where being spyed at Game
> of Tennis with faire Venus, he for shame
> Doth Blush & foame with Aphroditik art
> The Heavenly Urne to joy ye Dumpish ♥
>...
> This Thomas of Bononia does write
> To noble Bernard as no common slight.

A detailed account of this incident is given in a letter written by the Scottish Ambassador to the court of Elizabeth I to Sir Thomas Throckmorton on 31 March 1565:

> ... lately the duke's grace and my lord of L[eicester] were playing at tennes, the Quene beholding of them, and my lord Rob[ert] being verie hotte and swetinge, took the Quene's napkin owte of her hande and wyped hys face, which the Duke seing, saide that he was to sawcie and swhore he wolde laye his racket upon his face. Here upon rose a great troble and the Quene offended sore with the Duke ...

Only two months earlier the Duke in question, Norfolk, and the Earl of Leicester had been admitted to the Order of St. Michael in an imposing ceremony in the chapel at Westminster Palace, an honour conferred on them by the King of France. The Order of St. Michael, France's oldest order of chivalry, was established by Louis XI, father of Charles VIII.

'Mr. Rose', the compiler and collator of the Schweighardt Scrapbook, is, I think, Sir Thomas Herbert of Tintern. His knowledge and experience of the aristocracy fit him well for that role.

Notes

Chapter One

1. Acts of the Privy Council of England 22 November 1613.
2. Edward D. Johnson, *Bacon–Shakespeare Coincidences* (The Bacon Society 1950), p. 43.
3. Jean Overton Fuller, *Sir Francis Bacon* (George Mann, Maidstone, 1994), p. 345.
4. Theophilus Schweighardt, *Speculum Rhodo-Stauroticum* (Frankfurt, 1618).
5. G. Munro Smith, *A History of Bristol Royal Infirmary* (J.W. Arrowsmith, 1917).

Chapter Two

1. 1553 Letters patent granted by Edward VI to Earl of Pembroke.
2. Bradney in Vol. 2, Part 2 of his *History of Monmouthshire* includes a sketch of St. Michael's shortly before the rebuilding in 1846. It shows that until then the entrance to the nave was from the south porch. A door into the chancel now blocked up can also be seen. The Tudor roses in the porch ceiling indicate the time of this addition to a building that was almost half its present size.
3. Bradney, op. cit., Vol. 3, Part 1, pp. 2, 5 and 6.
4. *Victoria History of The County of Hertfordshire*, Vol. 3, p. 110.
5. Ibid., p. 153.
6. Ibid., p. 110.

Chapter Three

1. E.T. Davies, *The History of the Parish of Mathern* (Mathern PCC, 1990), p. 31.
2. Ibid., pp. 30–1.
3. Fred J. Hando, *Out and About in Monmouthshire* (R.H. Johns, Newport), p. 32.
4. J.M. Wallace-Hadrill, *The Long-haired Kings* (Toronto University Press, 1962), p. 174, n. 2.
5. Robert Rickards, *Church and Priory of St. Mary, Usk* (Bemrose and Sons Ltd., 1904), p. 15.
6. M. Green and R. Howell (eds), *The Gwent County History*, Vol. I (University of Wales Press, Cardiff, 2004), pp. 254–6.
7. J.M. Wallace-Hadrill, op. cit., p. 162.

Chapter Four

1. *Encyclopedia Britannica 2002*, Pippin III.
2. Laurence Gardner, *Bloodline of the Holy Grail* (Element, 1996), p. 134.
3. Alison Weir, *Eleanor of Aquitaine* (Pimlico, 2000), p. 138.
4. *Westminster Abbey Official Guide*, 1977 edition, p. 40.

Chapter Five

1. Lordships of Usk 1550 letters patent by Edward VI.
2. Laurence Gardner, op. cit., p. 246.

Chapter Six

1. H.W. Paar and D.G. Tucker, The Technology of Wire-Making at Tintern, Gwent 1566–c1880 *(Historical Metallurgy* 11:1, 1977), p. 16.
2. Ibid., p. 10.
3. William Rees, *Industry Before The Industrial Revolution, Vol. II* (University of Wales, 1968), p. 608.
4. Ibid., p. 614.
5. M.B. Donald, *Elizabethan Monopolies, The History of the Company of Mineral & Battery Works 1568–1604* (Oliver & Boyd, 1961), p. 127.
6. William Rees, op. cit., p. 638.
7. Ibid., p. 639.
8. S.D. Coates, *The Water Powered Industries of the The Lower Wye Valley* (Monmouth Borough Museums Service, 1992).

Chapter Seven

1. J. Overton Fuller, op. cit., p. 346.
2. 1) British Library, London, in the Schweighardt volume; 2) Science Museum Library, London; 3) Maritime Museum, Washington, USA.
3. Frances Yates, *The Rosicrucian Enlightenment* (Ark, 1986), p. 94.
4. Bernard E. Jones, *Freemasons' Guide and Compendium* (Harrap, 1950), p. 317.

Chapter Eight

1. John Kopec, *The Sabines at Riverbank* (Acoustical Society of America, New York, 1997), pp. 4–6.
2. Lisa Jardine and Alan Stewart, *Hostage to Fortune: The Troubled Life of Francis Bacon* (Victor Gollancz, 1998), p. 467.
3. Ibid., p. 468.
4. Ibid., p. 477.
5. Ibid., pp. 477–8.
6. *Dictionary of National Biography*, p. 184 (Oxford 1917 edition).
7. A. Chambers Bunten, *The Life of Alice Barnham* (Oliphant, 1928).

8. J. Overton Fuller, op. cit., p. 261.
9. T.W. King and F.R. Raines *Lancashire Funeral Certificates* (Chetham Society, Manchester, 1869), pp. 69–70.
10. Alfred Dodd, *Francis Bacon's Personal Life Story Vol. II* (Century Hutchinson, 1986), p. 542.
11. *Dictionary of National Biography* (Oxford 1917 edition).
12. Sir Thomas Herbert, *Herbertorium Prosapia*, MS, c. 1651, Cardiff Central Library, p. 92.
13. Lisa Jardine and Alan Stewart, op. cit., p. 321. The original letter is in the British Library: Lansdowne MS 91, fo 183.

Chapter Nine

1. Transcribed by Rev. Professor Kenneth Newport, Pro Vice-Chancellor, Liverpool Hope University, 2008.
2. The name Edmonds or Edmunds varies down the centuries, while clearly referring to the same family. It has been standardised to Edmonds, as it appears in a legal MS dated 19 May 1808 in the possession of Elsa and Adrian Wood.

Chapter Ten

No notes

Chapter Eleven

1. Stratascan Geophysical Survey Report, *The Church of St. Michael and All Angels* (J1859, March 2004), p. 6.
2. Ibid., p. 23.
3. Cambrian Archaeological Projects, *St. Michael and All Angels Church, Tintern Parva Archaeological Evaluation Report No 359* (Feb. 2005), p. 9.
4. Ibid., p. 20.
5. Ibid., p. 20.
6. Ibid., p. 20.
7. Miranda Green and Ray Howell, *Celtic Wales* (University of Wales Press 2000), p. 55.
8. Anonymous, *The History and Legends of Old Castles and Abbeys* (John Dicks, 1875), p. 505.

Chapter Twelve

1. Frank C. Higgins, *Ancient Freemasonry* (Pyramid Books, New York, 1923) pp. 65–7.
2. N.B. Cryer, *Masonic Halls of South Wales* (Lewis Masonic, 1990), p. 23 and *Masonic Halls of North Wales* (Lewis Masonic 1990), p. 34.
3. Stratascan Geophysical Survey Report, *The Church of St. Michael and All Angels* (J2040, August 2005), pp. 12–15.

The Hidden Chapter

Chapter Thirteen

1. Stratascan Geophysical Survey Report, *The Church of St. Michael and All Angels* (J 1993, March 2005).
2. Manly P. Hall, *Orders of Universal Reformation* (Philosophical Research Society, Los Angeles, 1949), p. 66.
3. Poems translated by N. Barker Cryer from the original Dutch by Jacob Cats in *Alle de Wercken* (J.J. Schipper, Amsterdam, 1655), pp. 170 and 141.
4. Manly P. Hall, op. cit., p. 57.
5. *Merchant of Venice*, Act II, Sc. ii, line 86.

Chapter Fourteen

1. R.L. Arrowsmith, B.J.W. Hill and A.S.R. Winlaw, *I Zingari* (JJG Publishing, 2006), passim.
2. *Aubrey's Brief Lives* (Penguin Classics, 1987), p. 118.
3. Ibid., p. 125.
4. For this information I am indebted to David Edwards, Warden at St. Mary's Church, Doddington, Cambs.
5. Arrowsmith et al., op. cit., p. 3.

Chapter Fifteen

1. Stratascan Geophysical Survey Report, *The Church of St. Michael and All Angels* (J2222, November 2006), p. 9.
2. Stratascan, op. cit. (J2222, May 2007), p. 9.
'The original radar survey used a velocity of 0.09m/n.sec which is typical of the soils and moisture levels found on the site. However, the intrusive investigation [of the three trenches] allowed the radar velocity to be calculated at 0.05m/n.sec – much slower than expected. Subsequent research indicates that the high level of iron waste in the soil from the Roman period will markedly change the dielectric properties, substantiating the slower velocity of 0.05 m/n.sec. It is assumed that similar soils are present within the double Russell Baldwin grave resulting in the shallow calculated depth of 0.9m for the anomalies found.' (Peter Barker, 19 March 2010.)

Chapter Sixteen

1. Catherine S. Gaines, *Francis Davis Millet and Millet Family* (Smithsonian Archive of American Art, 2003), p. 5.

Chapter Seventeen

1. Sir Lambton Loraine, *Pedigree and Memoirs of the Family of Loraine of Kirkharle* (J.B. Nichols and Sons, 1902), p. 179.

2. Gordon Waterfield, *Professional Diplomat: Sir Percy Loraine of Kirkharle, Bt.* (John Murray, 1973), p. 6.
3. Ibid., p. 30.
4. Patrice Chaplin, *City of Secrets* (Robinson, 2007), pp. 34–6.
5. Gordon Waterfield, op. cit., p. 294.
6. Piers Dixon, *Double Diploma* (Hutchinson, 1968), p. 228.

Chapter Eighteen

1. Jean Cocteau, *Past Tense, Diaries Volume One* (Hamish Hamilton, 1987), p. 33.

Chapter Nineteen

1. Bradney, op. cit., Vol. 2, part 2, p. 147.
2. *Dictionary of National Biography.*
3. Bertrand Russell, *Autobiography of Bertrand Russell* (George Allen & Unwin, 1967), Vol. 1, p. 15.
4. Peyton family pedigree.
5. J. Wimpenny (ed.), *Trellech 2000* (Bioline, Cardiff, 2000), pp. 294–5.
6. N.B. Cryer, *Masonic Halls of South Wales* (Lewis Masonic, 1990), p. 97.
7. Bradney, op. cit., Vol. 2, part 2, p. 148.
8. Wimpenny, op. cit., p. 293.
9. J.W. Kopec, op. cit., p. 179.
10. J.W. Kopec, op. cit., p. 181.

Coda One

1. Alfred Dodd, op. cit., Vol. I, pp. 80–1.
2. Andrew Sinclair, *The Sword and the Grail* (Century, 1993), p. 200.
3. Edward Johnson, *Francis Bacon's Maze* (Francis Bacon Research Society, 1961), p. 3.
4. This story, dated 2001, is included in an issue of the *Newsletter of the Shakespeare Authorship Information Centre* (Director Francis Carr) sent to me in 2002 after the publication of *Kingdom for a Stage.*

Coda Two

No notes

Coda Three

1. N.B. Cryer, *Masonic Halls of South Wales* (Lewis Masonic, 1990) p. 121.
2. Ibid., p. 124.
3. Sir Christopher Audland, *Jenny* (Folio, Lancaster University, 2008), p. 182.
4. David Wood, *Genisis* (The Baton Press, 1985), pp. 208–9.

5. Dan Brown, *The Da Vinci Code* (Bantam Press, 2008), p. 303.
6. Joy Hancox, *The Queen's Chameleon* (Jonathan Cape, 1994) p. 184.
7. Manly P. Hall, *Orders of Universal Reformation* (The Philosophical Research Society, Los Angeles, 1976 edition, p. 65.
8. Francis Godwin, *The Man in the Moone*, edited by William Poole (Broadview Editions, Ontario, 2009), p. 17.
9. An illustration and an account of the drawing can be found in *Kingdom for a Stage*, pp. 181–6.

Bibliography

Place of publication is London unless otherwise stated

Ackroyd, Peter, *Poe, A Life Cut Short* (Chatto & Windus, 2008)
Anonymous, *The History and Legends of Old Castles and Abbeys* (John Dicks, 1875)
Arrowsmith, R.L., Hill, B.J.W., and Winlaw, A.S.R., *I Zingari* (JJG Publishing, 2006)
Attar, K.E., *Sir Edwin Durning-Lawrence: A Baconian & his Books* (The Bibliographical Society 7th Series, Vol. 5, No. 3, Sept. 2004)
Aubrey, John, *Brief Lives*, ed. O.L. Dick (Penguin, 1987)
Audland, Sir Christopher, *Jenny* (Folio, Lancaster University, 2008)
Bacon, Francis, *The Advancement of Learning* (Dent, Everyman Library, 1954)
—— *Essays* (Oxford University Press, 1999)
Baigent, M., Leigh, R. and Lincoln, H., *The Holy Blood and The Holy Grail* (Corgi, 1983)
—— *The Messianic Legacy* (Corgi, 1987)
The Bible
Bokenham, T.D., *Bacon, Shakespeare & the Rosicrucians* (privately printed, 1994)
Bosanquet Papers (Cwmbran Record Office)
Bowen, Catherine Drinker, *Francis Bacon, The Temper of the Man* (Hamish Hamilton, 1963)
Bradney, Sir Joseph, *A History of Monmouthshire*, 4 volumes (1904–33)
Brown, Dan, *The Da Vinci Code* (Bantam Press, 2008)
Brown, Frederick, *An Impersonation of Angels* (Longmans, 1969)
Bunten, A. Chambers, *The Life of Alice Barnham* (Oliphant Ltd., 1928)
Byrom, John, *The Private Journal and Literary Remains* (Chetham Society, Manchester, 1854)
Calendar of State Papers Domestic, 1611
Caraman, Philip, S.J., *The Hunted Priest* (Fontana, 1964)
Cats, Jacob, *Alle der Werken* (Amsterdam 1655 and 1658)
Censuses of England and Wales 1841–1991

Chaplin, Patrice, *Albany Park* (Sceptre, 1987)
—— *Another City* (The Atlantic Monthly Press, New York, 1988)
—— *Happy Hour* (Pan Books, 1999)
—— *City of Secrets* (Robinson, 2007)
Clarke, Charles Cyril, *The Society of Merchant Venturers* (lecture delivered 1922, privately printed)
The Clergy Lists (published annually by Ecclesiastical Gazette Office, 19th century)
Coates, S.D., *The Water Powered Industries of the Lower Wye Valley* (Monmouth Borough Museums Service, 1992)
Cockburn, N.B., *The Bacon–Shakespeare Question* (privately printed, 1998)
Cocteau, Jean, *Past Tense, Diaries Volume One* (Hamish Hamilton, 1987)
—— *Past Tense, Diaries Volume Two* (Methuen, 1990)
The Complete Peerage (St. Catherine's Press, 1945)
Colville, Sir John, *Those Lambtons!* (Hodder & Stoughton, 1988)
Crockford's Clerical Directory (published annually)
Cryer, N.B., *The Arch and The Rainbow* (Lewis Masonic, 1996)
—— *Masonic Halls of England – The South* (Lewis Masonic, 1989)
—— *Masonic Halls of North Wales* (Lewis Masonic, 1990)
—— *Masonic Halls of South Wales* (Lewis Masonic, 1990)
Daily Express (February–March 1911)
Das Hausbuch der Mendelschen Zwolfbruderstiftung zu Nurnberg (Bruckmann, Munich, 1965)
Davies, Mrs. Andrew, *The History of the Parish of Carno* (Montgomery Collection Vol. 33)
Davies, Robert, *Thomas Herbert* (The Yorkshire Archaeological & Topographical Journal, Vol. I, 1870)
Dawkins, Peter, *Arcadia* (The Francis Bacon Research Trust, 1988)
—— *Dedication to the Light* (The Francis Bacon Research Trust, 1984)
—— *The Shakespeare Enigma* (Polair Publishing, 2004)
de Camp, L. Sprague, *The Ancient Engineers* (Souvenir Press, 1963)
Dictionary of National Biography (Oxford, 1917 and 2004)
Dictionary of Welsh Biography Down to 1940
Dixon, Piers, *Double Diploma* (Hutchinson, 1968)
Dodd, Alfred, *Francis Bacon's Personal Life Story* (Vol. I, Kessinger Pub. Co., Montana, n.d. and Vol. II, Century Hutchinson, 1986)
Donald, M.B., *Elizabethan Monopolies, The History of the Company of Mineral & Battery Works, 1568–1604* (Oliver & Boyd, 1961)
Durant, Horatia, *Raglan Castle* (The Starling Press, Newport, 1980)
—— *The Somerset Sequence* (Newman Neame, 1951)
Encyclopedia Britannica (2002)

Fellows, Virginia M., *The Shakespeare Code* (Snow Mountain Press, USA, 2006)
Fenton, Edward (ed.), *The Diaries of John Dee* (Day Books, Charlebury, 1998)
The Genealogists' Magazine (Vol. 17, March 1935 to December 1937: published 1938)
Gaines, Catherine S., *Francis David Millet and the Millet Family* (Smithsonian Archive of American Art, 2003)
Gardner, Laurence, *Bloodline of the Holy Grail* (Element, 1996)
Geoffrey of Monmouth, *The History of the Kings of Britain* (trans. L. Thorpe) (Penguin Classics, 1986)
Godwin, Francis (ed.),William Poole, *The Man in the Moone* (Broadview Editions, Ontario, 2009)
Gorst-William, Jessica, *Elizabeth, The Winter Queen* (Abelard, 1977)
Green, Miranda and Howell, Ray, *Celtic Wales*, (University of Wales Press, Cardiff, 2000)
—— *The Gwent County History* (University of Wales Press, Cardiff, 2004)
Guy, John R. and Smith, Ewart B., *Ancient Gwent Churches* (Starling Press, 1979)
Hall, Manly, P., *Orders of Universal Reformation* (Philosophical Research Society, Los Angeles, 1949)
Hammond, Fred, *The Truth About the Search at Chepstow* (Bacon Society, *Baconiana*, February issue, 1932)
Hancox, Joy, *The Byrom Collection* (Jonathan Cape, 1992)
—— *The Queen's Chameleon* (Jonathan Cape, 1994)
—— *Kingdom for a Stage* (Sutton Publishing, 2001)
Herbert, George, ed. Gilfillan, *Poems* (J. Nichol, Edinburgh, 1853)
Herbert, Sir Thomas, *Memoirs of the Last Years of King Charles* (Neame, 1813)
—— *History of the Race of Herbert* (MS *Herbertorium Prosapia* c. 1651, Cardiff Central Library)
Higgins, Frank C., *Ancient Freemasonry* (Pyramid Books, New York, 1923)
Illustrated London News, March 1911
Jardine, Lisa and Stewart, Alan, *Hostage to Fortune: The Troubled Life of Francis Bacon* (Victor Gollancz, 1998)
Johnson, Edward, *Bacon–Shakespeare Coincidences* (The Bacon Society, 1950)
—— *Francis Bacon's Maze* (Francis Bacon Research Society, 1961)
Jones, Bernard E., *Freemasons' Guide and Compendium* (Harrap, 1950)
Jones, Judith, *Monmouthshire Wills* (South Wales Record Society, Cardiff, 1997)
Jordan, W.K., *The Threshold of Power* (Allen & Unwin, 1990)

Kenyon, John R., *Raglan Castle* (Revised edition, Cadw, 2003)

King, Sir Edwin and Luke, Sir Harry, *The Knights of St. John in the British Realm* (St. John's Gate, 1967)

King, T.W. and Raines, F.R., *Lancashire Funeral Certificates* (Chetham Society, Manchester, 1869)

Kissack, K.E., *Medieval Monmouth* (Monmouth Historical & Educational Trust, 1974)

Kopec, John, *The Sabines at Riverbank* (Acoustical Society of America, New York, 1997)

Lamy, Lucie, *Egyptian Mysteries* (Thames & Hudson, 1989)

Lee, Sir Sidney (ed.), *The Life of Edward, Lord Herbert of Cherbury* (1886)

Like A Tree Planted: Brockweir Moravian Church 1833–1933 (privately printed)

Lilien Otto, M., *J. Christofle Le Blon* (Anton Hiersemann, Stuttgart, 1985)

Loraine, Sir Lambton, *Pedigree and Memoirs of the Family of Loraine of Kirkharle* (J.B. Nichols and Sons, 1902)

Maier, Michael, ed. J. Godwin, *Atalanta Fugiens* (Phanes Press, MI USA, 1989)

Matthews Street Directory of Bristol

McCann, W.A., *Reports of Geophysical Surveys, Nov. 2000 & July 2001; Borehole Investigation July 2001 at St. Michael and All Angels, Tintern* (unpublished)

Michell, John, *The Dimensions of Paradise* (Harper & Row, San Francisco, 1986)

—— *The Temple of Jerusalem: A Revelation* (Gothic Image Publications, Glastonbury, 2000)

—— *Who Wrote Shakespeare?* (Thames & Hudson, 1996)

Minutes of the Infirmary Committee, Bristol (Original MS, Bristol Record Office)

Morton, Alan Q. and Wess, Jane, *Public and Private Science, The King George III Collection* (Oxford University Press and The Science Museum, 1993)

Munro Smith, G., *A History of Bristol Royal Infirmary* (J.W. Arrowsmith, 1917)

Nixon, J.A., *Bristol Royal Infirmary. The Association of Bristol Royal Infirmary with British Masonry* (T. & W. Goulding Ltd., Bristol, n.d.)

Nooks & Crannies of Old Monmouthshire. A Catalogue of Paintings by Mary Ellen Bagnall-Oakley, 1833–1904 (Monmouth Museum)

Oakeshott, R. Ewart, *The Sword in the Age of Chivalry* (Arms and Armour Press, 1964)

Overton Fuller, Jean, *Sir Francis Bacon* (George Mann, Maidstone, 1994)

Owen, Orville W., *Sir Francis Bacon's Cipher Story* (Kessinger Pub. Co.,

Montana, n. d.)

Paar, H.W. and Tucker, D.G., *The Technology of Wire-Making at Tintern, Gwent, 1566–c1880* (Historical Metallurgy, 11:1, 1977)

Puttnam, W.G., *Excavations at Caer Neddfa Carno* (Montgomery Collection, Vol. 60)

Rees, William, *Industry Before the Industrial Revolution* (The University of Wales, Cardiff, 2 vols, 1968)

Rex, Richard, *The Tudors* (Tempus Publishing Ltd., Stroud, 2002)

Rickards, Robert *Church and Priory of St. Mary, Usk* (Bemrose and Sons Ltd., 1904)

Robinson, David, M. (ed.), *The Cistercian Abbeys of Britain* (Batsford, 1998)

Rohl, John C.G., Warren, Martin and Hunt, David, *Purple Secret* (Bantam Press, 1998)

Russell, Bertrand, *Autobiography of Bertrand Russell* (George Allen & Unwin, 3 vols, 1967–9)

Russell, Judith (ed.), *Tintern's Story* (P.C.C., St. Michael's Church, Tintern, 1990)

Schweighardt, Theophilus, *Speculum Sophicum Rhodo-Stauroticum* (1618)

Selenus Gustavus, *Cryptomenytices et Cryptographiae*, Libri IX (1624)

Silvester, R.J., *The Llanwddyn Hospitium* (Montgomery Collection, Vol. 85, 1947)

Sinclair, Andrew, *The Sword and the Grail* (Century, 1993)

Stow, John, *Survey of London* (Dent, Everyman's Library, 1995)

Taylor, Thomas (trans.), *'Porphyry' Or the Cave of the Nymphs*, (Phanes Press, 1991)

Tintern Guide Book (Ministry of Buildings & Works, 1965)

Treue, Wilhelm *et al.* (eds.), *Das Hausbuch der Mendelschen Zwolfbruderstiftung zu Nurnberg* (Munich, Bruckmann, 1965)

Vaughan, Rowland, ed. E.B.Wood, *Most Approved & Long Experienced Waterworkes* (1610)

Victoria History of the County of Hertfordshire (St Catherine's Press, 1912–23)

Wallace-Hadrill, J.M., *The Long-Haired Kings* (Toronto University Press, 1962)

Ward, E. and Richard Blake, *The Royal Lodge of Bristol and its R.A. and K.T. Appendages* (Transactions of the Quatuor Coronati Lodge, 1960)

Waterfield, Gordon, *Professional Diplomat: Sir Percy Loraine of Kirkharle, Bt.* (John Murray, 1973)

Watson, George, *Militia and Sappers* (The Castle Regimental Museum, Monmouth, 1996)

Weir, Alison, *Eleanor of Aquitaine* (Pimlico, 2000)

Westminster Abbey Official Guide, 1977 edition
Wheatley, Dennis, *The Deception Planners* (Hutchinson, 1980)
Wimpenny, J. (ed.), *Trellech 2000* (Bioline, Cardiff, 2000)
Wood, David, *Genisis* (The Baton Press, 1985)
Yates, Frances, *The Occult Philosophy* (Routledge & Kegan Paul, 1983)
—— *The Rosicrucian Enlightenment* (Ark, 1986)
——*Theatre of the World* (Routledge & Kegan Paul, 1969)

Index

A
Acacia, 93, 165, 167
Alaric I, 35
Alban, Julian and Aaron, 150
Aldrin, Buzz, 283, 284
Allegory, An, 257–265
Amberley, Lord and Lady, 238–240, 243, 244, 246
Anderson, James, 40, 42
Andreae, Johann Valentin, 96
Andrews, Lancelot, 110
Anne, Countess of Worcester, 75
Arcadian Cipher, The, 279
Aristotle, 99
Ark of the Covenant, 92, 154
Armstrong, Neil, 283
Arthur, King, 35, 46, 270
Ashlar, 152, 154, 155, 237, 245, 253
Attorney General, 2, 101, 112
Audland, Dr. John, 276, 277
Audland, Jenny, 94, 276, 277
Audland, Christopher, Sir, 277, 291

B
Bacon, Lady Anne (Cooke), 75, 114, 115, 160, 180
Bacon, Montagu, 118, 120, 126
Bacon, Francis, Sir, 2, 97–105, 111, 283,
    Boyle, Robert, influence on, 96, 190
    Cats, Jacob (engravings)
        Lampada Trado, 165, 167, 169, 172, 174, 190, 255, 281
        Verita non puo star sepolta, 170, 174, 281
    Codes, 112, 120–122, 207
    Death, 8, 103, 111, 113, 116, 180, 202, 255
    Downfall and trial, 104
    Egerton family, 84, 108, 109, 210
    Elizabeth I, 257, 263
    Elizabeth, Lady Russell, 176, 181, 184, 191, 251
    Field Nathaniel, 109
    Field Richard, 110
    Field Theophilus, 99, 109, 110
    Gorhambury, 180
    Herberts, 87, 88
    Herbert's College, 137
    Legal career, 2, 101
    Maier, Michael, connection with, 57
    Marriage, 103, 107, 264
    Missing Mss., 139, 198, 253
    Mother's funeral, 160
    Name in numerology, 7
    Parentage/family, 8, 75, 175, 264
    Russell, Anne, 176, 239
    Shakespeare, 207, 208
    Titles, 101
    Vaughan family, 105–107, 118, 124
    Wireworks, 2, 71–78, 234
    Writings
        Advancement of Learning, 2, 89, 97, 120
        Essays, 100, 209, 255
        New Atlantis, 96, 99
        Novum Organum (Instauratio Magna), 99, 100
        Psalms (translation), 88
        Sylva Sylvarum, 283
Bacon, Nicholas, Sir, 71, 103, 107, 113, 118, 180, 233
Bacon, Robert, Sir, 181
Baldwin, John Loraine, 176–213, 216–219, 226, 229, 232–234, 237, 238, 244, 249–253, 258, 266–275
Barker, Peter, 143, 192, 193, 194, 195, 290
Barnham, Alice, 103, 107, 108, 263
Barnham, Dorothy, 106, 107
Baynards Castle, 113
Beaufort
    first Duke of, 126
    fourth Duke of, 124, 155
    seventh Duke of, 148
    eighth Duke of, 179, 200, 201, 234, 250, 274
    ninth Duke of, 198, 202, 207, 219, 234, 251, 253
Beaufort, Dukes of, 128, 176, 191, 202, 207, 244

Index

Beddoes, Dr Thomas, 128, 129
Benedictines, 35, 47, 53, 65, 66
Bernard of Clairvaux, 54
Bevan, David Augustus, 266, 227
Bevan, John Henry, 227, 229, 230, 231, 237, 272
Billingsley, Henry, 74, 88, 89, 247
Blockley, Kevin, 79, 143, 146
Blount, Edward, 255
Body snatchers, 15
Boleyn, Anne Marchioness of Pembroke, 20, 64, 69, 203, 234, 244
Bononia, Thomas of, 285
Bosanquet Papers, 82,
Boyle, Robert, 96, 97, 120, 185, 190, 191, 198
Bradney, Joseph, Sir, 9, 20, 25, 52, 80, 134, 211, 238, 240, 246
Bristol Castle, 52
Bristol Record Office, 16
Bristol Royal Infirmary, 14, 15, 136
Brockweir, 9, 12, 13, 19, 81, 148
Burke's Peerage, 154, 252
Byrom, John, 1
    Bacon, Montagu (friend), 118, 120
    Brass plates, 71, 72, 87, 126, 163, 185, 190
    Byrom Collection, The, 1, 89, 114, 163, 279, 280, 281
    Cabala, 224, 254
    Caroline of Anspach, 117, 123
    Codes, 120–122
    de Bry, 253–255
    Freemasonry, 118, 136
    Geometric drawings, 87, 90, 136, 277
    Elizabethan Playhouses, 1, 24, 162, 164, 174, 207, 225, 249, 250, 252–255
    Holy of Holies, 154
    Temple Church, London, 61
    Westminster Abbey, 40, 44, 61, 222, 224, 232
    Herbert's College, 86–89, 97
    Jacobites, 122–125, 155
    Leycester, Ralph, diary, 116, 117
    Queen's Chameleon, The, 116, 117, 121, 278, 279
    Science Museum catalogue, 163

C
Cabala, 118, 223, 224, 225, 254
Cabala Club, 118, 254
Caerleon, 38, 46, 145, 150
Caesar, Julius, Sir, 74, 78, 111–113
Cambrian Archaeological Services Ltd., 143, 145
Camden, William, 32, 33
Canterbury, 31, 48, 50, 110, 139, 143, 160, 200
Canterbury Cricket Week, 182, 273, 274
Cantilupe, Thomas, Bishop, 210
Cardiff Public Library, 77

Caroline of Anspach, 90, 117, 123
Carolingian, 42, 44, 53, 213
Catbrook, 73, 81
Catchmay, 74, 106
Catherine of Aragon, 20, 26, 69, 203
Cats, Jacob (engravings)
    Lampada Trado, 166–174, 190, 255, 281, 284
    Verita non puo star sepolta, 170–174, 281
Cecil, Robert, 101, 257
Cecil, William, 71
Cemmaes, 134, 135
Chapel Hill, 77, 175, 185, 186, 200, 266, 267, 272
Chaplin, Patrice, 223, 224
Charlemagne, 42, 44, 53, 55, 213, 223, 224, 258
Charles I, 25, 75, 76, 84, 85, 86, 96, 135, 155, 169, 180, 203
Chepstow (passim),
Chepstow Museum, 146
Chepstow Weekly Advertiser, 266–275
Childeric I, 38, 39, 44
Chinon, 45, 48, 49
Chlotar I, 37
Cistercians, 24, 65–67
City of Secrets, 223
Clarke, William, 23–30, 35, 47, 49, 64, 65, 247, 250
Cleddon, 237–246
Clifton, 13, 14, 129
Clovis, 33, 35, 39, 42, 44, 53
Cocteau, Jean, 220–224, 228, 231, 232
    Past Tense, 231
Codes, 7, 61, 103, 117, 120, 121, 122, 158, 160, 163, 207, 208, 251, 255
Common Prayer, Book of, 22
Cooke Elizabeth, 75, 114
Cooper, Leroy Gordon, 283, 284
Cork and Orrery, Earl of, 184, 185, 189, 198, 270, 271
Cowell, Major D., 9, 11, 154, 161, 192
Cranmer, Archbishop, 22
Crockford's Clerical Directory, 14, 15, 19
Cruttwell Family, 133
Cryer, Revd. Neville Barker, 153, 156, 236, 245, 284
Cryptomenysis Patefacta, 121
Cuffe, Henry, 100
Curre, John, 126
Cwmbran Record Office, 10, 11, 82

D
Da Vinci Code, The, 278, 279
d'Acres, Joan, 51, 52, 62, 68, 222, 234
Dagobert, 29, 53, 54
Darius, 225, 232
Darlington, Michael, 8
de Bar, 62, 213, 222, 223, 224

Index

de Bry, Theodore, 97, 250, 253, 254, 255
de Burgh, Elizabeth, 25, 64
de Clare, 47, 49, 52, 62, 222
de Montherimer, Sir Ralph, 52
de Valence, Aymer, 27, 51, 62, 65, 68
de Valence, Mary, 65
de Valence, William, 27, 49, 50, 51, 52, 66, 67, 247
de Wenlocke, Walter, 51, 52
Deception Planners, The, 230, 237
Dee, John, 1, 9, 24, 57, 72, 86, 87, 89, 96, 115, 165, 167, 169, 170, 172, 175, 176, 180, 247, 248, 255, 281, 283
    Monas Hieroglyphica, 85, 222, 248
Devise, 22–24, 71
Dissolution of the Monasteries, 28, 46, 65, 66, 75, 133, 134, 187, 242
Dixon, Pierson, Sir, 227–230
Dodd, Alfred, 257, 260, 264
Doe, Professor C. N., 139, 140, 194
Double Diploma, 228
Dudley, Guildford, 22
Dudley, John, Duke of Northumberland, 22, 71
Dudley, Mary, Duchess of Northumberland, 8, 24
Dudley, Robert, Earl of Leicester, 8, 24, 71, 72, 165, 247, 265
Dugdale, William, Sir, 53
Dunckerley, Thomas, 136
Dürer, 222, 258

E
Edward I, 27, 50, 51, 52, 57, 62, 65, 66, 67, 68, 210, 213, 222, 234
Edward II, 25, 27, 62, 64, 67, 68
Edward III, 51, 57, 64, 65, 68
Edward the Confessor, 40, 44, 50, 51, 55, 65, 68
Edward VI, 3, 20, 24, 25, 27, 28, 35, 37, 47, 64, 65, 69, 82, 85, 113, 142, 234
Edward VII, 135, 216, 226
Egerton, Alice, 106, 108, 109
Egerton, Magdalene, 106, 108
Egerton, Mary, 9, 106, 108
Egerton, Thomas, 9, 84, 108, 109, 210
Eleanor Duchess of Aquitaine, 44-46, 48, 49, 51, 53, 54, 67, 70, 188
Elizabeth I, 1, 2, 8, 17, 23, 24, 48, 69, 71, 85, 118, 165, 203, 234, 247, 252, 257, 258, 265, 285
Elizabeth, Queen of Bohemia, 169
Erskine, Thomas, Sir, 105, 106, 107
Euclid
    Elements of Geometrie, 24, 89, 247
Euroscan Subsurface Imaging Ltd., 9, 141

F
Fabyan, Colonel, 122, 251, 252
Falconer, John, 120, 121, 122
Field Nathaniel, 109
Field Richard, 110
Field Theophilus, 99, 109, 110
Fielding, Elizabeth, 126
First Folio 1623, 3, 7, 74, 87, 209, 252, 253, 255, 259
Fishers Folly, 113
FitzGilbert, Gilbert, 47
Flashman and Co., 188, 194, 195, 272
Florencia (see Herbert), 28, 78, 83, 85, 124, 134, 137
Fludd, Robert, 57, 232
Forest of Dean, 2, 8, 73
Friedman, William, 252
Fryer's Wharf, 147–149, 152
Fuller, Jean Overton, 8

G
Geoffrey of Monmouth, 46, 150, 295
George III, 87, 185, 192
George III Collection, 87
George, Duke of Cambridge, 185, 189, 192, 213, 270, 275
Girona, 223–225
Glastonbury, 25, 28, 46, 47
Glastonbury Abbey, 46
Globe Theatre, 3, 76, 164, 280, 281
Godwin, Bishop Francis, 32, 33, 283
Goldsmith, 71, 74, 258
Good, Timothy, 283
Goodrich, 49, 66, 67, 68, 233, 234, 247
Goose and Gridiron, 117
Gregory of Tours, 35, 37
Grey, Lady Jane, 22
Grimston, Harbottle, 180
Grimston, Robert, 179, 180, 181, 184
Gwyn, John, 75, 76

H
Hackett, Thomas, 75–77
Hall, Manly P., 165, 171, 281–284
    Orders of Universal Reformation, 281, 282, 284
Hanbury, Richard, 74, 77, 78
Harcourt, Elizabeth Alice Annie, 184, 189, 201, 204, 269, 271
Harvard University, 208
Hatfield, 23, 25–28, 65
Heath, Christopher, 9–14, 18, 19, 79, 80, 132, 133, 277
Henry II, 44-48, 50, 51, 54, 55, 224
Henry III, 27, 48–55, 59, 65–67, 247
Henry V, 55, 57, 59
Henry VIII, 3, 20, 24-30, 35, 51, 64, 66, 69, 75, 83, 134, 176, 202, 203, 207, 233, 234, 242
Herbert (Earls of Pembroke)

301

Index

William, first Earl of Pembroke, 3, 20, 22, 24, 25, 28, 47, 64, 69, 71, 72, 82, 234, 247
Henry, second Earl of Pembroke, 250
William, third Earl of Pembroke, 2, 3, 8, 9, 74, 87, 88, 94, 107, 111, 113, 154, 169, 255
Philip, fourth Earl of Pembroke, 3, 74, 255
Reginald, fifteenth Earl of Pembroke, 265
Herbert, Edward (Lord Herbert of Chirbury), 83, 115
Herbert, Florencia, 28, 78, 83, 85, 124, 134, 137
Herbert, George, 87, 88
Herbert, Henry, Sir, 87
Herbert, Mary, 9, 106, 115
Herbert, Richard, 77, 84, 85, 106
Herbert, Thomas, Sir, 9, 75–77, 84, 85, 106, 113, 114, 126, 180, 286
History of the race of Herbert, 84, 113
Herbert, Walter, 83
Herbert, William (of St. Julian's), 1, 3, 9, 24, 28, 77–79, 82, 83, 85, 88, 94, 106, 111, 115, 124, 134, 137, 156, 165, 234, 248, 254
Hermetic ideas, 57, 86, 87, 96, 113, 137, 165, 169, 223, 234, 248, 255, 277
Hickes, Michael, Sir, 114, 115
Hochstetter, Daniel, 72
Holy of Holies, 92, 154, 225
Hospice, 81, 151
Hughes, Revd. Robert Vaughan, 33, 34, 131, 133, 135–138, 246, 283
Humfrey, William, 77

J
Jacobite, 28, 122, 123, 124, 125, 126, 155, 279
Jaggard John, 255
Jaggard William, 255
James I, 2, 57, 82, 85, 93, 97, 100, 106, 107, 110, 111, 112, 170, 216, 247
James II, 122
Jamnitzer, Wenzel, 71, 258
John of Chinon, 45, 70
Johnson, Edward, 7, 259, 260, 264
Jones, Inigo, 94
Jonson, Ben, 94
Joseph of Arimathea, 46

K
Keeper of the Great Seal, 9, 101, 118, 167
Kemeys Commander, 134, 137
Kemeys Inferior, 134
Kemys-Tynte, Charles John, 276
Kensal Green, General Cemetery of All Souls, 191, 192
Keystone, 152–157, 191, 236, 237, 245, 253
Kingdom for a Stage, 8, 89, 278

Knights Hospitaller of St John, 27, 29, 30, 61, 133, 135
Knights of the Helmet, 108
Knights Templar, 27, 29, 51, 67, 134-136, 210, 277
Knights Templar (Masonic), 217, 218

L
La Trobe, John Antes, 17, 18
Leibnitz, 97
Leigh, Very Revd. James Wentworth (Dean of Hereford), 209
Letters Patent (1553), 20, 23–26, 28–30, 35, 47, 64, 65, 82, 94, 113, 247
Lewin's Mead Society, 129, 130
Leycester, Ralph, 116–118
Liber Landavensis, 31, 32
Litten, Julian, 193
Llandaff, 25, 32, 109, 110, 150, 243, 245, 246, 283
Llywelyn ap Owain, 64
Loraine, Eustace Broke, 218
Loraine, Lambton, Sir, 211, 213, 216–219, 223–229, 233, 234
Loraine, Percy, Sir, 211, 221, 223–228, 231, 232
Lord Chancellor, 84, 93, 101, 104, 105, 107, 108, 110, 170, 180, 210
Louis VI, 53, 54

M
Maier, Michael, 57
Mais, Rev. John, 11–19, 33, 130–134, 137, 141, 158, 175
Marsh, E.S., 12–14
Marshall, William, 47–50, 62, 66, 67, 247
Marston, John, 7
Martel, Charles, 42, 53, 224
Martin, Richard, Sir, 74
Master of the Revels, 87
Mathern, 32–34, 37, 109, 151, 246, 283
Matthew, Toby, 111
Meautys, Thomas, Sir, 8, 180, 264
Merian, Matthaeus, 254
Merovingian, 33, 35, 37–40, 42, 44, 45, 47, 49, 52–55, 79, 213, 224, 234
   buckles, 38, 49, 79
   Major Domus, 42
Merry Wives of Windsor, The, 260
Meurig, 31, 32, 151
Milhaud, Darius, 232
Millet, J. B., 208
Millett, Charles Frederick, 184, 189, 199–211, 216, 219, 226, 233, 234, 269, 272
Mines Royal, 72
Monmouthshire Militia, 240, 242, 243
Monopoly, 74, 76, 78

302

Index

Moravian, 12, 13, 18, 19
Morgan, David, 28, 123, 124, 126
Morgan, John, 28
Morgan, William, 28, 83, 134
Mortlake, 1, 86, 115
Mount St. Albans, 8, 114

N

Newton, Isaac, 190, 225, 226, 230, 237
Noah's Ark, 94, 276, 277, 278
Norman Conquest, 37
Notre Dame de France, Church of, 222, 223
Nuremberg, 71, 72, 73, 96, 258, 265
Nurtons, 5, 33, 34, 78, 81, 82, 94, 115, 126, 128, 130, 131, 133, 135, 136, 138, 145, 149, 159, 276, 277

O

Oath of Abjuration, 125
Oriflamme, 54
Owen, Dr. Orville, 122, 132, 198, 207–209, 219, 251, 252, 257, 264

P

Paulet, Amias, Sir, 112, 257, 264
Peyton, General, 186, 189, 267, 269
Peyton, Revd. Sir Algernon, 182, 183, 266
Peyton, Thomas, Sir, 183, 273
Pike Plot, 128
Pinniger, Broome, 12, 13
Pippin III, 42, 44
Pitman, James, Sir, 120
Poe, Edgar Allan, 239
Poitiers, 37
Pondesborne, 23–30
Primrose League, 187, 267, 268
Priory of Usk, 23, 35, 37, 68
Professional Diplomat, 223, 230, 231

R

Raglan Castle, 77, 239, 264
Ravenscroft, 239, 240, 244
Rees, Dr. William, 73
Rees, Revd. Philip, 192
Richard II, 55,64
Richard II, 65
Roberts, John Chapman, 240–246
Roman
    Caerleon, 38, 46, 145, 150
    effect of iron waste on soil, 290
    numeral, 7
    post-Roman Wales, 38, 79
    presence in Tintern and archaeology, 145–147, 154, 157, 161–163, 191, 247

Roman version of Tewdric, 31
Rose
    Mr. Rose, 254, 285, 286
    Rose Theatre, 248, 250
Rosicrucian, 93, 96, 254, 255
Royal Society, 96, 97, 120
Rudolf II, Holy Roman Emperor, 57, 71
Rudolf of Nuremberg, 72
Russell, Elizabeth Lady Francis, 175–177, 181–189, 191, 194, 195, 199, 204, 208, 233, 238, 239, 266, 268, 270
Russell, Lord Francis John, 177, 181, 238, 266, 273
Russell, Bertrand, 239, 240

S

Salley, Miles, 32, 33
Sandrart, Joachim von, 263
Scales, Lady, 257
Schweighardt, 8, 89, 90, 93, 96, 254, 277, 285, 286
Science Museum, 1, 7, 71, 79, 87, 163, 250, 258
Seal of Solomon, 248
Seventy Two [72], 164, 165, 174, 249, 252, 253, 278, 279, 281
Shaw, Dr Peter, 120
Sherwood, Robert, 252
Siddal, Thomas, 123, 126, 128
Sidney, Henry, Sir, 48, 71
Sidney, Mary, 250, 252
Sidney, Philip, Sir, 2, 122, 250
Silurians, 150
Simpson, J, 147–149, 152
Smith, Richard, 130
Solicitor General, 2, 101
Solomon, 35, 66, 67, 153, 154, 225, 245, 248
Somerset, Edward, Lord, 189, 198, 201–203, 207, 216, 233, 251, 270
Somerset, Henry, second Earl of Worcester, 203, 207
Somerset, Henry, Marquis of Worcester, 198, 202
South porch, 24, 141, 142, 162, 163, 236
Southwark, 75, 76, 125
Spies, 1, 121
St. Augustine, 31
St. Benedict, 57, 65, 66
St. Denis, 53, 54, 55, 66, 67, 69, 72
St. Dennis, 53
St. John the Baptist, 26–29, 65
St. Julian's, 3, 7, 24, 28, 83, 86, 87, 88, 94, 111, 114, 115, 124, 134, 137, 150, 165, 234, 247
St. Katharine, 28
St. Mary Redcliffe, 15, 17, 19, 130
St. Michael, Church of (passim)
St. Oudoceus, 32
St. Radegund, 37, 39, 45, 47, 49, 69, 70, 79, 187, 188, 222, 234

Index

Stanley, Ferdinando, 108, 109, 210
Stock, John Edmonds, 126, 128–131, 253, 277
Stock, John Shapland Edmonds, 131, 253
Stratascan Ltd., 142, 143, 157, 162, 163, 164, 191–194, 195, 197, 248, 249
Suger, Abbot, 53, 54
Sun Club, 118
Swan Lodge, 118

T
Tabernacle, 90, 92, 93
Taylor, George, 242
Taylor, Ian, 252
Tempest, The, 248
Templar, 18, 48, 62, 67, 133, 210, 264
Temple, 48, 49, 61, 62, 66, 67, 88, 92, 121, 153, 154, 225, 245, 248
Temple Church, Bristol 17, 18
Temple Church London, 48, 49, 61, 62, 67
Tewdric, 31, 32, 33, 34, 35, 37, 38, 39, 42, 47, 69, 70, 79, 147, 150, 151, 234, 246, 248, 253, 283
Theodoric(us), 32, 33, 35, 37, 39
Tintern Abbey, 47, 48, 49, 53, 66, 67, 69, 75, 78, 145, 149, 151, 176, 181, 185, 201, 202, 203, 207, 210, 229, 233, 266, 273
Tintern Parva (passim)
Tintern Parva Estate, 9, 25, 52, 64, 68, 69, 75, 77, 78, 81–86, 106,113, 124, 126, 128, 130, 132, 134, 137, 151, 180, 210, 234
Tireman, Catherine, 131, 132
Titanic, 208, 209, 219
Tomb of Interest, 5, 7, 9, 10, 11, 12, 14, 19, 79, 81, 94, 103, 111, 132, 138, 139, 142, 143, 146, 149, 157, 162, 164, 167, 172, 174, 217, 249, 252, 281
Tree of Life, 222
Trellech, 8, 73, 74, 81, 128, 149, 151, 188, 237, 238, 242, 277
Trostrey, 23, 38, 79
Troy House, 128, 239, 267
Tyler, 156, 236

U
Unitarian, 129
United Grand Lodge, 118, 217, 236
Usk, 8, 23, 35, 37, 38, 45, 47, 49, 62, 64, 69, 74, 79, 134, 188, 222, 233, 234

V
Valence (see under de Valence)

Vaughan, John, Sir, 105–107
Vaughan, William, 106–107
Villiers, George, 104

W
Wallace-Hadrill, J. M., 35, 38, 44
Walsingham, Francis, Sir, 1, 86
Waterfield, Gordon, 223, 230, 231
Watkins, Ann, 156–159, 161, 175, 194
Watkins, Emma, 159
Watkins, William, 123, 154–156, 159
Wesley, Charles, 117
Wesley, John, 117
West, Lewis, 12, 13, 14, 19
Westminster Abbey, 40, 44, 47, 50, 51, 53, 54, 57, 65, 143, 210, 232, 249
  chest, 55, 59
  guide book, 55
Wheatley, Dennis, 230, 231, 237
White, Bill, 193
Whitehead/Whytehead, 88, 89
Widener, Harry Elkins, 209
William of Glastonbury, 25
William the Conqueror, 44, 50, 55, 213
Williams, Annabella, 243, 246
Wilton House, 22, 265
Wireworks, 71–78, 239
Wood, Anthony, 89
Wood, David, 278
Wood, Elsa and Adrian, 82, 237, 289
Woolven, David, 10, 11, 80, 175
Worcester, Earls of, 77, 111
  second Earl of, 69, 176, 203, 207, 234
  fourth Earl of, 264
  fifth Earl of, 75, 76, 136, 180, 239
Wycliff, John, 96
Wye River, 3, 12, 24, 31, 81, 92, 122, 143, 147, 148, 149, 150, 198, 207, 251, 257
Wye Valley Railway, 80
Wyelands, 33
Wynn, Watkin Williams, Sir, 124, 155

Y
Yates, Dame Francis, 86, 93
York House, 105, 107

Z
Zingari I, Cricket Club, 179, 181, 182, 184, 185, 200, 204, 209, 216, 217, 271, 273,